Žižek Responds!

Also Available from Bloomsbury:

Žižek on Race: Toward an Anti-Racist Future, Zahi Zalloua
Surplus-Enjoyment: A Guide for the Non-Perplexed, Slavoj Žižek
Hegel in a Wired Brain, Slavoj Žižek
Sex and the Failed Absolute, Slavoj Žižek
Disparities, Slavoj Žižek

Žižek Responds!

Edited by
DOMINIK FINKELDE AND
TODD McGOWAN

BLOOMSBURY ACADEMIC
LONDON • NEW YORK • OXFORD • NEW DELHI • SYDNEY

BLOOMSBURY ACADEMIC
Bloomsbury Publishing Plc
50 Bedford Square, London, WC1B 3DP, UK
1385 Broadway, New York, NY 10018, USA
29 Earlsfort Terrace, Dublin 2, Ireland

BLOOMSBURY, BLOOMSBURY ACADEMIC and the Diana logo are trademarks of Bloomsbury Publishing Plc

First published in Great Britain 2023

Copyright © Dominik Finkelde, Todd McGowan, and Contributors, 2023

Dominik Finkelde and Todd McGowan have asserted their right under the Copyright, Designs and Patents Act, 1988, to be identified as Editors of this work.

For legal purposes the Acknowledgments on p. xi constitute an extension of this copyright page.

Cover design: Ben Anslow
Cover image: Portrait of Slavoj Zizek, who is a Slovenian psychoanalytic philosopher, cultural critic and Hegelian Marxist, Istanbul, Turkey, December 3, 2009.
(© Sahan Nuhoglu / Shutterstock)

All rights reserved. No part of this publication may be reproduced or transmitted in any form or by any means, electronic or mechanical, including photocopying, recording, or any information storage or retrieval system, without prior permission in writing from the publishers.

Bloomsbury Publishing Plc does not have any control over, or responsibility for, any third-party websites referred to or in this book. All internet addresses given in this book were correct at the time of going to press. The author and publisher regret any inconvenience caused if addresses have changed or sites have ceased to exist, but can accept no responsibility for any such changes.

A catalogue record for this book is available from the British Library.

A catalog record for this book is available from the Library of Congress.

ISBN:	HB:	978-1-3503-2892-1
	PB:	978-1-3503-2893-8
	ePDF:	978-1-3503-2894-5
	eBook:	978-1-3503-2895-2

Typeset by RefineCatch Limited, Bungay, Suffolk

To find out more about our authors and books visit www.bloomsbury.com and sign up for our newsletters.

CONTENTS

Notes on the Contributors vii
Acknowledgments xi

Introduction *Dominik Finkelde and Todd McGowan* 1

PART ONE Ontology 25

1 Cake or Doughnut? Žižek and German Idealist Emergentisms *Adrian Johnston* 27
   Response to Johnston *Slavoj Žižek* 52
2 Truth as Bacchanalian Revel: Žižek and the Risks of Irony *Dominik Finkelde* 55
   Response to Finkelde *Slavoj Žižek* 67
3 Žižek and the Retroactivity of the Real *Graham Harman* 73
   Response to Harman *Slavoj Žižek* 85
4 Slavoj Žižek's Hegel *Robert B. Pippin* 89
   Response to Pippin *Slavoj Žižek* 112

PART TWO Ideology 117

5 Slavoj Žižek Is Not Violent Enough *Todd McGowan* 119
   Response to McGowan *Slavoj Žižek* 134
6 Žižek's Foundationless Building: Ideology Critique as an Existentialist Choice *Hilary Neroni* 139
   Response to Neroni *Slavoj Žižek* 157
7 The Subject Is Not Enough *Henrik Jøker Bjerre* 163
   Response to Bjerre *Slavoj Žižek* 179

8   Žižek and Derrida: Hospitality, Hostility, and the "Real" Neighbor *Zahi Zalloua* 183
    Response to Zalloua *Slavoj Žižek* 208

9   The Politics of Incompleteness: On Žižek's Theory of the Subject *Nadia Bou Ali* 215
    Response to Nadia Bou Ali *Slavoj Žižek* 226

PART THREE Psychoanalysis 235

10 Reading the Illegible: On Žižek's Interpretation of Lacan's "Kant with Sade" *Dany Nobus* 237
    Response to Nobus *Slavoj Žižek* 260

11 Raising a Mundane Object to the Dignity of the Thing: When Desire is Not the Desire of the Other *Mari Ruti* 265
    Response to Ruti *Slavoj Žižek* 281

12 Hoping Against Hope: Žižek, *Jouissance*, and the Impossible *Jennifer Friedlander* 287
    Response to Friedlander *Slavoj Žižek* 298

13 Žižek and the War in an Era of Generalized Foreclosure *Duane Rousselle* 301
    Response to Rousselle *Slavoj Žižek* 307

14 Harpo's Grin: Rethinking Lacan's Unthinkable "Thing" *Richard Boothby* 317
    Response to Boothby *Slavoj Žižek* 330

Index 333

NOTES ON THE CONTRIBUTORS

Henrik Jøker Bjerre is Associate Professor of Applied Philosophy at Aalborg University, Denmark. He has published on the philosophy of culture and on theories of subjectivity in Kant, Kierkegaard, Lacan, and others. His books include *Analyzing the Cultural Unconscious*, ed. with Hansen, Hyldgaard, Rosendal, and Rösing (Bloomsbury, 2020); *Handl!* with Brian Benjamin Hansen (Mindspace, 2017); *Analysér!* (Mindspace, 2015); *Den nyttige idiot ["The useful idiot"]*, with Carsten Bagge Laustsen (Samfundslitteratur, 2013); and *Kantian Deeds* (Continuum, 2010).

Richard Boothby is Professor of Philosophy at Loyola University Maryland. He has published on contemporary philosophy, especially with regard to psychoanalysis in the tradition of Freud and Lacan. His publications include *Freud as Philosopher: Metapsychology After Lacan* (Routledge, 2001) and *Is Nothing Sacred? The God Question from Freud to Lacan* (Northwestern University Press, forthcoming 2022).

Nadia Bou Ali is Associate Professor and Director of the Civilization Studies Program at the American University of Beirut (AUB). She has a DPhil from the University of Oxford. She is currently co-investigator (with Dr. Surti Singh) in the Andrew W. Mellon project *Extimacies: Critical Theory from the Global South*. She is the author of *Hall of Mirrors: Psychoanalysis and the Love of Arabic* (Edinburgh University Press 2020) and co-editor of *Lacan contra Foucault: Subjectivity, Sex and Politics* (Bloomsbury 2018), and *Extimacy: Encounters between Psychoanalysis and Philosophy* (forthcoming). She is currently working on two projects: a book entitled *Structure and Form: the Afterlives of Marx and Freud in Arabic* (forthcoming with Verso) and a book on anxiety and freedom. She has a private psychoanalytic practice in Beirut and she is a member of the Lacanian School for Psychoanalysis in the Bay Area, San Francisco.

Dominik Finkelde is Professor for Epistemology and Contemporary Philosophy at the Munich School of Philosophy. He has published on contemporary philosophy and German idealism, especially on Hegel, Kant, Frege, Wittgenstein, Žižek, and Badiou. Recent publications are: *Parallax: The Dialectics of Mind and World*, edited with Slavoj Žižek and Christoph Menke (Bloomsbury, 2021); *Idealism, Relativism, and Realism: New Essays* on *Objectivity Beyond the Analytic Continental Divide*, edited with Paul M. Livingston (De Gruyter, 2020); and *Excessive Subjectivity: Kant, Hegel, Lacan, and the Foundations of Ethics* (Columbia University Press, 2017).

Jennifer Friedlander is the Edgar E. and Elizabeth S. Pankey Professor of Media Studies at Pomona College. She is the author of *Feminine Look: Sexuation, Spectatorship, and Subversion* (SUNY, 2008); and *Real Deceptions: The Contemporary Reinvention of Realism* (Oxford University Press, 2017). She has published articles in *Discourse: Journal for Theoretical Studies in Media and Culture*; *CiNéMAS: Journal of Film Studies*; *Subjectivity*; *(Re)-turn: A Journal of Lacanian Studies*; *Journal for Psychoanalysis of Culture and Society*; *Subjectivity*; and *International Journal of Žižek Studies*, as well as in several edited volumes. She was the 2021 Fulbright-Freud Visiting Scholar at the Freud Museum Vienna.

Graham Harman is Distinguished Professor of Philosophy at the Southern California Institute of Architecture. He has published on the metaphysics of objects and developed an object-oriented ontology. He is a leading proponent of speculative realism and the series editor of *Speculative Realism* published by Edinburgh University Press. Recent books are *Architecture and Objects* (Minnesota, 2022) and *The Graham Harman Reader*, edited by Jon Cogburn and Niki Young (Zero, 2022).

Adrian Johnston is Distinguished Professor in and Chair of the Department of Philosophy at the University of New Mexico at Albuquerque. He has published extensively on dialectical materialism and German idealism. Recent publications are: *A New German Idealism: Hegel, Žižek, and Dialectical Materialism* (Columbia University Press, 2018) and *Prolegomena to Any Future Materialism, Volume Two: A Weak Nature Alone* (Northwestern University Press, 2019).

Todd McGowan teaches theory and film at the University of Vermont. He is the author of *Emancipation After Hegel: Achieving a Contradictory Revolution* (Columbia University Press 2019); *Only a Joke Can Save Us: A Theory of Comedy* (Northwestern University Press, 2017); *Capitalism and Desire: The Psychic Cost of Free Markets* (Columbia University Press, 2016), and other works. He is the editor of the Film Theory in Practice series at Bloomsbury and co-editor of the *Diaeresis* series at Northwestern University Press.

Hilary Neroni is Professor of Film and Television Studies at the University of Vermont. Her books and articles engage the nature of ideology as it is represented in film, television, and other media. Recent publications include: *Realist Film Theory and Bicycle Thieves* (Bloomsbury, 2022); *Feminist Film Theory and Cleo from 5 to 7* (Bloomsbury, 2016); *The Subject of Torture: Psychoanalysis and Biopolitics in Television and Film* (Columbia University

Press, 2015); and *The Violent Woman. Femininity, Narrative, and Violence in Contemporary American Cinema* (SUNY, 2005).

Dany Nobus is Professor of Psychoanalytic Psychology at Brunel University London, Founding Scholar of the British Psychoanalytic Council, and former Chair and Fellow of the Freud Museum London. He has published widely on the history, theory and practice of psychoanalysis, the intersections between psychoanalysis, philosophy and the arts, and the history of ideas, with special reference to the Renaissance and Early Modern periods. Recent books include *Critique of Psychoanalytic Reason: Studies in Lacanian Theory and Practice* (Routledge, 2022) and *The Law of Desire: On Lacan's 'Kant with Sade'* (Palgrave, 2017). In 2017, he was the recipient of the Sarton Medal of the University of Ghent for his outstanding contributions to psychoanalytic historiography.

Robert B. Pippin is Evelyn Stefansson Nef Distinguished Service Professor of Social Thought and Philosophy at the University of Chicago. He has published extensively on Hegel but also on Kant, Nietzsche, Proust, Hannah Arendt as well as on the Hollywood Western. His recent publications are: *Hegel's Realm of Shadows: Logic as Metaphysics in Hegel's Science of Logic* (Chicago University Press, 2018); "The Dynamism of Reason in Kant and Hegel," in *Kant on Person and Agency*, edited by E. Watkins (Cambridge University Press, 2017); and "Hegel on Logic as Metaphysics", in: *The Oxford Handbook to Hegel*, edited by D. Moyar (Oxford University Press, 2017).

Duane Rousselle is a Visiting Associate Professor of Sociology at University College of Dublin and Visiting Professor of Sociology at Nazarbayev University. His forthcoming book, currently in review, is titled *Singularities: Psychoanalytic Sociology for a Strange Time*. His other recent books include: *Real Love: Essays in Psychoanalysis, Religion, Society* (Atropos, 2021); *Gender, Sexuality, and Subjectivity: A Lacanian Perspective on Identity, Language, and Queer Theory* (Routledge, 2020); *Jacques Lacan and American Sociology: Be Wary of the Image* (Palgrave, 2019); *Lacanian Realism: Political and Clinical Psychoanalysis* (Bloomsbury, 2018); and *Post-Anarchism: A Reader* (Pluto Press, 2012).

Mari Ruti is Distinguished Professor of Critical Theory and of Gender and Sexuality Studies at the University of Toronto. She is the author of thirteen books, most relevantly *The Singularity of Being: Lacan and the Immortal Within* (Fordham University Press, 2012); *Between Levinas and Lacan: Self, Other, Ethics* (Bloomsbury, 2015); and *Distillations: Theory, Ethics, Affect* (Bloomsbury, 2018).

Zahi Zalloua is Cushing Eells Professor of Philosophy and Literature at Whitman College and editor of *The Comparatist*. He has published on literary theory, experimental fiction and on authors such as Montaigne, Diderot, Stendhal, Sartre, Levinas, Robbe-Grillet and others. His recent publications include *Continental Philosophy and the Palestinian Question: Beyond the Jew and the Greek* (Bloomsbury 2017) and *Žižek on Race: Toward an Anti-Racist Future* (Bloomsbury 2018).

Slavoj Žižek is Professor at the European Graduate School in Switzerland and International Director of the Birkbeck Institute for the Humanities, Birkbeck College, University of London. He has authored numerous books, including *Less Than Nothing: Hegel and the Shadow of Dialectical Materialism* (Verso, 2012) and *Absolute Recoil: Toward a New Foundation of Dialectical Materialism* (Verso, 2014).

ACKNOWLEDGMENTS

The editors would like to give thanks for permission to reprint the following texts:

Chapter 4 is a reprint of Robert Pippin's "Slavoj Žižek's Hegel" published in Robert Pippin, *Interanimations: Receiving Modern German Philosophy* (Chicago: Chicago University Press, 2015), 91–116. It is republished here with the kind permission of University of Chicago Press.

Chapter 13 is based on a previous article written by Duane Rousselle published under the title "Psychoanalysis in Exile: Rambling without a World" on the website of the *European Journal of Psychoanalysis* (March 15, 2022). It is republished here with the kind permission of the *European Journal of Psychoanalysis*.

Introduction

Dominik Finkelde and Todd McGowan

Pavlovian Reactions Aren't Just for Dogs

For years now, judgments about the Slovenian philosopher Slavoj Žižek have been, like Žižek himself, extreme. Critics have accused him of charlatanism, on the one hand, while others have lauded his genius, especially as a public intellectual, on the other. This makes it difficult to discover an apt critical appraisal of his contribution to thought. Moreover, some of his readers consider the results of Žižek's speculative thinking excessively complicated; for others, the chains of his arguments are all too marked by ratiocinations and, as such, lack the stringency of deductive argumentation and reasonable inference. This judgment applies especially to devotees of analytic philosophy. They often see Žižek as the embodiment of the "dark side of the force" of continental philosophy which has been condemned at least since Rudolf Carnap's famous disapproval of Martin Heidegger's philosophical style of writing. According to this line of thought, Žižek may articulate propositions that strike intellectual sparks, but since their origin is caused by false surface grammars or unclear thoughts, "the true" or "the false," to quote Gottlob Frege, cannot be reached. For such critics, philosophy of this kind remains senseless.

But behind the aforementioned extremes of veneration and disdain, there is a *third Žižek*. This is the philosopher who, like no other of his generation, has stimulated philosophical debates that radiate far beyond philosophy's borders into all disciplines of the humanities. He has done so both through his radical materialist reinterpretation of concepts of German Idealism, especially Hegel's legacy, and through his combination of Marxist ideology critique with the philosophy of psychoanalysis as developed by Freud and Lacan. With this theoretical background, he has produced more than fifty books focused on classical questions of ontology, epistemology, the philosophy of subjectivity, and cultural theory.

In his works the reader does not encounter a methodical blueprint of a philosophical system. Instead, one encounters texts that, in ever new readings of classical authors from Kant, Hegel, and Marx to Derrida and Dennett, rotate around an ultimately inert, unassimilable core, as if it were a piece of the Lacanian real that cannot be intercepted. It is around this core that Žižek's thought revolves in constantly regenerating and sometimes contradicting theoretical impulses. From Lacanian and Hegelian perspectives and with a view to phenomena of popular culture, the classical questions of truth, meaning, subject, and object are thereby discussed from constantly new perspectives often rejecting traditional disciplinary boundaries.

Now, if one had to summarize Žižek's philosophy in one sentence, or "to put it in a nutshell," it would certainly not be wrong to claim that his texts are something like introductions to developing or even training an anamorphic view of reality. As is well known, the concept of anamorphosis goes back to the visual arts of the sixteenth and seventeenth centuries, in which perspective-distorted motifs, e.g., in a cathedral's vault, only become decipherable when viewed from a specific vantage point. In the same way that the anamorphic illusion of an object's being can only be detected by leaving the aforementioned vantage point, Žižek's texts often prove to be marked by a similar movement. It seems as if he is concerned with a radical reversal of the respective doxa, the respective established structure of meaning, by—symbolically speaking—abandoning the central (but clandestinely distorted) perspective on "reality" that guarantees us a supposedly "natural" view upholding the coherence of facts in politics, science, philosophy, art, etc. He often introduces this with the words "but what if ...", whereupon, almost as a rule, his reinterpretation of philosophical problems begins that radically distances itself from classical readings of his philosophical dialogue partners.

This "but what if ..." accompanies his works like a leitmotif, like a guiding formula. What Žižek thereby reveals in the reversal of the respective doxa is not a view of an "other" reality, of a world of "this is how it really is." Rather, his reversals provoke irritations that make the most self-evident suddenly tremble for a moment, being grasped as if from the backstage of reality, in theatrical terms: the so-called "Off," the off-stage of reality. This concerns both philosophical as well as political interpretations; for example, when—in accordance with this "but what if ..." he defends Martin Heidegger's radical engagement with the Nazi movement, questions Habermasian discourse ethics as the ultimate model of justice and society, criticizes Greta Thunberg (a child!) for not being radical enough, or interprets the secret and excessive messages of the market economy using the example of Kinder's surprise egg. Žižek is not concerned with an attention-begging reflex of provocation based on the desire to set himself apart from the masses of intellectual elites. Rather, he represents a way of thinking that aims at bringing the phantasmagorias with which we feed our realities (and thus also our ontologies) out of their statics again and again by re-marking or by pointing out their—in the vocabulary of psychoanalysis—repressed truths. This is why one often senses a kind of childishness in Žižek's writing style, a childlike yearning to clear the table by knocking over the Lego castle and to "start from scratch." He wants to rediscover everything anew and to interpret the history of philosophy once again from a perspective tinted by the vocabulary of Lacan, Hegel, and Marx. This could be seen as neurotic compulsive or, on the contrary, as the very gesture of what philosophy is about.

For Gilbert K. Chesterton, repetition was characteristic of a child's vitality. It can hear the same stories over and over again, play the same games, and enjoy them as it did the first time. This is the impression one sometimes gets from Žižek. His desire to "start from scratch" seems to be an essential impulse of his writing and thinking style. This has not infrequently earned him the reproach of all too often retelling himself and his audience—ad nauseam even—similar stories. What the accusation, justified as it may be, may neglect nevertheless is that it is rarely a case of repeating the same thing. Rather, we encounter repetitions that create something new in the Kierkegaardian sense, because they are always in new arrangements.

On Critics and Disciples

There are numerous monographs that introduce readers to Slavoj Žižek's philosophy or analyze specific themes, as well as several edited volumes that have contributed to a critical evaluation of his thought. Among the introductions are Rex Butler's *Slavoj Žižek: Live Theory*,[1] Dominik Finkelde's *Slavoj Žižek zwischen Hegel und Lacan*,[2] Sarah Key's *Žižek: A Critical Introduction*,[3] Tom Myers' *Slavoj Žižek*,[4] and Ian Parker's *Slavoj Žižek: A Critical Introduction*,[5] to name but a few. Among edited volumes that critically engage with Žižek's work, the following are particularly noteworthy: *The Truth of Žižek* (eds. Paul Bowman and Richard Stamp),[6] *Did Somebody Say Ideology?* (eds. Fabio Vighi and Heiko Feldner),[7] *Traversing the Fantasy: Critical Responses to Slavoj Žižek* (eds. Geoff Boucher, Jason Glynos, and Matthew Sharpe),[8] and *Repeating Žižek* (ed. Agon Hamza).[9] Three of the aforementioned volumes are more than fifteen years old and thus do not comment on Žižek's publications of recent years. But the present volume also differs formally from those mentioned: specifically, it gives Žižek more space to respond vis-à-vis with individual inquiries about his philosophy. Beyond that, however, by enhancing a deliberately constructive dialogue with him, it achieves something that these earlier works often do not. In this respect, the volume is less interested in rejecting Žižek's philosophy or of evoking conflicts with him but deepening the insights his many publications offer. To underline this is necessary because anthologies on Žižek often pursue something else: they aim to criticize Žižek and minimize the theoretical depth of his philosophy, which is sometimes provoked by Žižek's own way of engaging with other philosophers. This is especially the case with the aforementioned volume *The Truth of Žižek*. Despite some valuable individual contributions, it includes many essays in which the sole goal seems to be maligning Žižek not just as a thinker but even as a person. The form of attack in many of the articles leads to such severe distortions of Žižek's positions that it becomes unrecognizable. Unfortunately, these responses typically do not attend to the precision of Žižek's arguments.[10] This is evident, among other things, with reference to Žižek's theory of the act, which is wildly distorted in articles by Mark Devenney and Oliver Marchart. The same holds true for some of the articles in the otherwise commendable anthology *Traversing the Fantasy: Critical Responses to Slavoj Žižek*. It is devoted to Žižek's work in six sections (psychoanalysis, culture, ideology, politics, ethics, and philosophy), but with so many inquiries that one can ask, in Rex Butler's words, "What is it that they [Žižek's critics] really want? Is there anything that could finally satisfy them?"[11] Fabio Vighi's and Heiko Feldner's 2007 anthology *Did Somebody Say Ideology?* is devoted specifically to Žižek's theory of ideology and isn't concerned with other topics. Finally, the volume *Repeating Žižek* by Agon Hamza must be mentioned. As the title of the volume suggests, the focus is primarily on repeating or rethinking Žižek's readings rather than on a specific examination of his philosophy. Accordingly, the focus is on authors such as Hegel, Plato, Marx, Freud, Derrida, and Lacan, who are reevaluated with reference to Žižek's publications on them. The aim of the current volume is not to focus on violent polemics that Žižek will then respond to with equal violence. Its goal is, instead, to show criticisms that most often take as their point of departure internal contradictions within Žižek's project to underline their philosophical value or even necessity. The volume thus has less heat than a volume such as *The Truth of Žižek*, but it also has, we hope, considerably more light.

Next to the mentioned polemics surrounding Žižek's work, another observation can be made which somehow stands in contrast to Žižek's popularity. He tends not to produce theoretical disciples, which may be related to the idiosyncratic nature of his theorizing. Although Žižek has numerous philosophical comrades and fellow travelers, he does not create, as mentioned above, a coherent doctrine to which a group of followers might simply adhere, unlike theoretical forerunners such as Michel Foucault and Jacques Derrida. Even though these earlier theorists are long dead and buried, there remain many more Foucauldians and Derrideans in the world than Žižekians, thanks to the latter's irreducibility to a reproduceable doctrine. It is impossible to be a doctrinal follower of Žižek since he himself is never doctrinal in relation to his own thought. Even Žižek is not straightforwardly Žižekian, so how could anyone else be? If Žižek's opponents attack him in hyperbolic polemics, his allies for the most part leave the productive development of his concepts unthought and unspoken.

As a result of this situation, there are relatively few detailed and sustained engagements with the most important claims of Žižek's philosophy, few attempts to push him where an idea requires more development, few efforts to criticize him where he seems to fall into contradiction, or few endeavors to take an important thought into a realm that he doesn't explore. Despite the fact that one could reasonably contend that he is the best-known living philosopher, there is much less critical interaction with his thought than one would expect of such a figure. Žižek provokes and stimulates thinking across the theoretical spectrum, but his works are not typically the subject of extensive exploration. This is a situation that the present collection hopes to rectify.

This volume includes a variety of responses to Žižek's work. Some contributions come from allies seeking to further certain of his ideas into regions that he hasn't explored. Others look at questions that his theorizing raises and hope to address those questions or persuade Žižek himself to do so. Still others seek to point out and resolve contradictions that arise in the course of his thinking, while certain respondents try to clarify Žižek's relationship to his philosophical antecedents. Finally, a few of Žižek's theoretical opponents are included as well, and they seek to challenge some of his best-known and cherished claims.

The collection opens up a variety of avenues into Žižek's thought. Not only will it highlight extended engagement with Žižek's own philosophy and the texts that constitute it. It also includes Žižek's responses to this engagement—a kind of critical dialogue that rarely occurs surrounding his theoretical contributions. Žižek himself has written a response to each critical essay, so that the book has the structure of a series of dialogues between Žižek and his interlocutors.[12] Since not every reader of the chapters of this volume may be familiar with his life and work, the following sections provide a brief introduction to both.

The Unemployed Theorist

Slavoj Žižek burst onto the global theoretical scene with his first book in English, *The Sublime Object of Ideology*, in 1989. This book stood out starkly from the spirit of the age because rather than taking up a critical view of central figures in the tradition of Western philosophy, Žižek openly embraced them for their radicality. While thinkers such as Theodor Adorno, Michel Foucault, Gilles Deleuze, and Jacques Derrida often tried to undermine or dismantle the dominance of Western philosophy from René Descartes to Hegel, *The Sublime Object of Ideology* and the many books that followed in its wake took Descartes, Kant, and Hegel seriously as theorists with something to contribute to the contemporary situation. These thinkers were not, for Žižek, targets for deconstruction or historicist contextualization but vital theorists who could shed light on the dead ends of current thinking. Rather than seeing them as old masters that we needed to move beyond, Žižek grasped them as figures of an undiscovered radicality, a radicality that challenged not just that of Marx but also that of new leftist movements.

Žižek was born in 1949 in Ljubljana, Slovenia, and grew up in communist Yugoslavia under Tito. As a young thinker in Yugoslavia, he was influenced by Martin Heidegger and Jacques Derrida, an influence that allowed him to draw away from the Marxist party line. He wrote his first book in Slovene called *The Pain of Difference* when he was twenty-two, and it reflected the thought of these thinkers.[13] He wrote his doctoral dissertation on Heidegger, but in the mid-1970s, Žižek turned to the thought of Lacan, which was a decisive move in his intellectual trajectory. Žižek's embrace of French thought cost him the opportunity of landing a job in Yugoslavia. From 1973 to 1977 he was an unemployed Ph.D. He was thought not to be Marxist enough to be counted on as professor. The communist authorities did not want Žižek corrupting the Yugoslavian young. Finally, even though he was a philosopher, he got a job as a researcher at the Institute for Social Sciences at the University of Ljubljana in 1979. He was thought too dangerous to be allowed to be a professor, but here he would have no access to students. This allowed him great freedom to work and think. He often says that this punishment had the effect of freeing him and allowing him to develop as a global philosopher. Had he been allowed to teach, he would have remained, he wagers, just a mid-level professor in Slovenia.

In the early 1980s, Žižek went to Paris to obtain a second Ph.D. in psychoanalysis. There he studied with and was analyzed by Jacques Lacan's son-in-law and chief intellectual executor Jacques-Alain Miller. He claims to have lied completely to Miller during the analysis, to have invented symptoms and falsified dreams. He also claims to hate the practice of self-analysis, preferring theorizing to probing his own symptoms or neurosis. Žižek published books in Slovenia, France, and Germany during this time, but it was *The Sublime Object of Ideology* that instantly changed the landscape of cultural theory in the Anglophone world. Very quickly, Hegel and Lacan became significant points of reference within the theoretical universe, thanks to Žižek's contribution.

Since 1989, Žižek has averaged a little more than one book per year in English. He also lectures often worldwide and has perhaps become the most-recognized living philosopher since the death of Derrida in 2004. In 1990, he ran for the presidency of the new republic of Slovenia and finished fifth. Though he dropped out of personal involvement in politics, he remains an engaged political thinker. He makes public pronouncements on significant political events and often speaks to political movements like Occupy Wall Street in 2012. His various political interventions appear on various leftist websites and news sources.[14]

Žižek brings together philosophy and popular culture, a combination that accounts in large part for his influence. His second book in English, *Looking Awry: An Introduction to Jacques Lacan through Popular Culture*

(1991), turned to film and especially Alfred Hitchcock in order to explain Lacan's most difficult ideas. His most important works are *Tarrying with the Negative: Kant, Hegel, and the Critique of Ideology* (1993), *The Ticklish Subject* (1999), *The Parallax View* (2006), and *Less than Nothing: Hegel and Dialectical Materialism* (2012), a 1,000-page magnum opus on Hegel and his intersection with Lacan.

Žižek's celebrity doesn't just stem from his ability to weave together philosophy and popular culture, it also results from his mode of writing and his use of humor. All of Žižek's books include jokes to illustrate his ideas. His arguments zigzag from point to point without making clear exactly where they are headed until one finds oneself at an end point that actually brings everything together. This style maddens many critics, but it also creates an exciting pace that appeals to readers. When confronted with a Žižek book, one must piece together the argument after the fact, recognize how he communicates the idea through the elliptical style.

The celebrity of Žižek led to the making of a documentary film about him entitled simply *Žižek!* (2005). He himself has made two documentaries about cinema and about ideology, both directed by Sophie Fiennes, called respectively *Pervert's Guide to Cinema* (2006) and *Pervert's Guide to Ideology* (2012). He appears on numerous podcasts and in countless YouTube interviews. His lectures are often attended by thousands of people.

A Threefold Cord: Lacan, Hegel, Marx

As a thinker, Žižek tries to bring together three different lines of thought: Lacan, Hegel, and Marx. Trying to discover a psychoanalytic politics is probably the key dimension of his project, but he never wants to lose the critical edge that psychoanalysis provides when emphasizing a political project. Lacan provides Žižek with a way of thinking about the structure of subjectivity and society—and the relationship between subjectivity and society. Unlike other thinkers of his time, Žižek is a vigorous defender of the idea of subjectivity. He rejects the deconstruction of the subject and argues that the subject is also the point of departure for Lacan.

Žižek returned Lacan to prominence in cultural theory. Often, theorists, especially American theorists, simply lumped Lacan together with Foucault, Derrida, and Deleuze as a representative of poststructuralism (a term not employed by any of these thinkers themselves). But Žižek shows how Lacan differs dramatically from these other French theorists primarily through his insistence on retaining the subject as a point of departure. Separating Lacan from this imaginary entity known as "poststructuralism" was one of Žižek's major accomplishments. He does this by emphasizing Lacan's category of the real at the expense of the symbolic order and the imaginary, his other two categories. The real, for Žižek, is the source of enjoyment or *jouissance*. Enjoyment determines how subjects act. Žižek sees that every symbolic structure stumbles on a real, but this is a real internal to the symbolic, not a reality that exists outside of it. There is no beyond or outside, and it is only by abandoning our thought of the beyond that we can arrive at the real. The real is just the distortion within the symbolic structure and thus akin to the dream work in Freud's thought. The real of the dream is neither the manifest not the latent content. It is the distortion of the latent content into the manifest content that occurs when the subject dreams. This distortion becomes visible, Žižek believes, in works of art, in jokes, or in displays of excess. This is why Žižek focuses so intently on the interpretation of artworks, the telling of jokes, and the performance of excess.

Hegel provides Žižek with a way of thinking that turns back on itself. Hegel's dialectical thought demands the inclusion of the subject's own position in its conclusion. It always includes itself in what it finds. Hegel's philosophy of tarrying with the negative not only informs Žižek's own thinking, but it also provides him with the title for his fifth book in English. Hegel is the thinker of contradiction, seeing that contradiction exists not just in our thinking but in being itself. Contradiction animates being and makes thought possible. Hegel's notion of absolute knowing is not a complete solution to contradiction but a recognition that we will never overcome contradiction. Žižek tries to incorporate this recognition into his idea of political struggle. The absolute is not the point at which every part has its place but where the whole is divided with itself, where a hole becomes visible within the whole. Freedom, for Žižek, isn't the achievement of harmony but the integration of the disturbance of harmony into our political project.

In his analyses, Žižek follows Hegel by showing the dialectical nature of our social reality. He emphasizes how seeming opponents are actually linked together unknowingly in the same position. One of his favorite examples of this is the connection between radical Zionists and fervent anti-Semites. Both follow the same logic of wanting to isolate the Jews. Even Reinhard Heydrich, who decided on the so-called *Endlösung* (Final Solution, i.e., the Genocide of Jews during World War II), was first a Zionist. Today, we have the figure of the Zionist anti-Semite who concretizes this dialectical link. This figure, often incarnated in Christian fundamentalists, vehemently supports the state of Israel as a bulwark against Islam while at the same time lamenting the number of Jews in Europe. As this example makes clear, Žižek sees how anti-Semitism is not simply a straightforward phenomenon but one that must be interpreted through its contradictory structure. This is at the heart of his dialectical analysis.[15] Although Žižek is probably more known as a proponent of Lacanian psychoanalysis, it is Hegel who serves as the pivot point for his thought. His persistent call for a Hegelian critique of Marx represents his most significant political intervention. In an interview in 2003 entitled "Liberation Hurts," he claims:

> What really interests me is philosophy, and for me, psychoanalysis is ultimately a tool to reactualize, to render actual for today's time, the

legacy of German idealism. And here, with all of my Marxist flirtings I'm pretty arrogant. I think you cannot understand Marx's *Capital*, its critique of the political economy, without detailed knowledge of Hegelian categories. But ultimately if I am to choose just one thinker, it's Hegel. He's the one for me. And here I'm totally and unabashedly naïve. He may be a white, dead, man or whatever the wrong positions are today, but that's where I stand.[16]

Žižek's affection for and devotion to Hegel stems from the latter's ability to grasp the centrality of self-negating negativity. This negativity that constantly undermines itself is the subject, and its activity is what Freud later theorized as the death drive, which is perhaps the central category in Žižek's thought. In Freud, the category of death drive is not simply the concept of a loss of biological life forces. Death drive denotes the immortal dimension of a super- and anti-biological, partly symbolic force. Beyond the mere vegetative existence of human beings, it belongs to the basic structure of reality like a metaphysical quantity. In Žižek's words: "[H]uman life is never just life: humans [. . .] are possessed by a strange drive to enjoy life in excess."[17] This excess not only drives the subject. It also drives Žižek himself.

The Jester's Epistemic Stance

Žižek reformulates the concept of the death drive in a way different from both Freud and Lacan, even if Žižek himself associates his conception with Lacan's. For Žižek, death drive is an insistence of repetition that impels the subject to encircle its lost object without ever obtaining it. It leads to a series of failures on the part of the subject, but these failures are the path through which the death drive produces satisfaction. Contrary to the implication of the term itself, Žižek sees death drive as the eternal core of subjectivity, what insists beyond death. The subject finds satisfaction or *jouissance* in failure rather than success as a result of the death drive.[18] The existence and persistence of the death drive implies that we don't pursue happiness but happiness with regard to the unhappiness of ever missing it. There is no good, no object—in the pursuit of "the good life"—on behalf of which we act, as philosophers from Aristotle onward have mistakenly believed. Instead of seeking the good, we endeavor to repeat. In Samuel Beckett's famous words: "Try again, fail again, fail better." Creativity manifests itself in the act of repetition that enjoys the postponement of the solution, of fulfillment.

We don't recognize the functioning of the death drive in our psyche because we always experience it through the lens of fantasy. Fantasy provides a narrative structure through which the subject can avoid confronting the necessity of loss or castration. Death drive becomes narrativized through a fantasy scenario that enables subjects to avoid confronting their unconscious investment in failure. Fantasies are an "*ex*timate" (not an "*in*timate") socially constructed phenomenon. As such they form the borderline between subject/individual and object/community as the individual acts through them in the same way as the mind perceives, according to Kant, through schemata of category regulation. Fantasies are extremely ambivalent, as they always embody the way in which we as subjects are answers to questions emitted directly or indirectly by what Lacan calls the big Other, the symbolic order. They shape the individual as well as the collective access to reality where facts cannot be distilled from values and fantasies about values. The community then welcomes the adult in its collective enjoyment of a more or less pure space of reasons of what it means to be a member in a nation-state sanctuary of collective enjoyment of various historic-political and social-political factors. For Žižek it is important to understand how exactly structures of enjoyment through collaborative and supported fantasies concretely unify subjects and communities. Especially the political function of the canalization of pleasure that fantasies achieve proves for him to be decisive.

With regard to the mentioned avoidance of unconscious investment in failure, fantasy doesn't eliminate loss but places loss within a narrative that enables us to believe that it is possible to overcome it. In this sense, fantasy has an ideological function both for the individual as well as for the community of fantasizers. It supplements the stated or public ideology and coexists with it. Fantasy, according to Žižek, is the underside of ideology.

Perhaps Žižek's most important contribution to contemporary theory is the reintroduction of the critique of ideology to the theoretical agenda. After Louis Althusser made the critique of ideological interpellation central to social analysis, ideology critique soon came under fire from other leftists.[19] Thinkers like Michel Foucault and Jacques Derrida discredited the critique of ideology by showing how this critique relied on shaky epistemological foundations. That is, critics of ideology assumed that they themselves could see through the ideological deception that fooled everyone else. But for someone like Foucault, it is precisely this sort of expert knowledge that functions as the vehicle for power. Thus, critics of ideology were actually serving the power apparatus just when they thought that they were seeing through the ideological deception.

Žižek transforms the critique of ideology by taking it away from the terrain of knowledge and thereby sidestepping Foucault's criticism. For Žižek, ideology functions not through giving us false knowledge or manipulating our consciousness but through its deployment of our enjoyment or *jouissance*. We are in ideology not because we don't know the truth but because we enjoy in a way that upholds social authority or what Lacan calls the big Other. In the *Sublime Object of Ideology*, Žižek offers his most important statement about ideology. He says, "The function of ideology is not to offer us a point of escape from our reality but to offer us the social reality itself as some escape from some traumatic, real kernel."[20] Ideology is respite from the trauma of the real, which is the trauma of a primary deadlock or of an impossibility of achieving any harmony. Most often, ideology works by leading us to what appear as transgressions. According to Žižek, it is the shared transgression, not collective obedience, that really ensconces us within ideology.[21]

Almost no one simply obeys and avows that they are obeying today. What causes subjects to subject themselves to social authority is not a public ideology itself but the underside of that ideology or the ideological fantasy. This fantasy violates the rules that govern the public ideology, but it does so in a way that supports it rather than undermining it. Especially in political crises this becomes clear, i.e., when the public normative law is allegedly close to failure. Then an obscene underside of the law "kicks in" and unites the community via a shared transgression of the failing law. Žižek states: "the public law is compelled to search for support in an illegal enjoyment."[22] So now it is illegal enjoyment—not formal reason—that guarantees the social contract.

Žižek's focus on the obscene fantasmatic underside of ideology is the key to his critique of ideology.[23] He looks at popular culture in order to unearth the fantasies that sustain the contemporary order because he believes that the only possibility for undermining ideology lies in breaking the power of these fantasies. One of the most powerful fantasies today, according to Žižek, is Western Buddhism. Western Buddhism gives the subject the belief that capitalist relations of production are unreal and that all of the activity of capitalist life is really nothing at all. But this belief doesn't destroy the subject's capacity for acting like a capitalist subject. In fact, Western Buddhism makes this activity possible by providing an inner distance from the horrors of the capitalist system for the subject. One can act ruthlessly as a capitalist if one believes that none of one's ruthless actions really matter.

This emphasis on the underside of ideology leads Žižek to value what he calls over-conformity to the public ideology. Instead of transgressing public ideology while adhering to its obscene underside, Žižek argues that the political act involves the opposite—adhering to the letter of the law rejecting the obscene underside. The task of the critical intellectual is not one of constant resistance but instead one of seeing how civilization itself is already premised on a radical act. The orthodox is already transgressive and excessive, but we must make this excess visible.

The problem is that subjects deny the existence of the excess within the social order. We believe that life itself is the ultimate value and that survival is worthwhile for its own sake. But it is only our excessive attachment to our way of life that makes life worth living. This is evident in the case of love, which disturbs the normal functioning of life and at the same time gives us a reason to live. Love is always excessive and demands the renunciation of the little pleasures that keep us ensconced in normality. In love, we touch the other in the real and not just our fantasy version of the other.

Žižek's constant provocations attempt to encourage love in this sense of the term. It would be a revolutionary love because it would confront the traumatic real and see this confrontation as the source of the subject's satisfaction. This confrontation is always violent, and Žižek sometimes seems like an apostle of violence. But the violence that he praises is not necessarily physical violence inflicted on others. It does not have to be since every single general strike can soon be called by the government it tries to topple violent enough to be ended with the national guard.

Real Communism

When *The Sublime Object of Ideology* appeared in 1989, Žižek was an advocate for democracy. He even went so far as to cite approvingly Churchill's famous quip about democracy being the worst political system except all the others. His vision of democracy saw it in a radical form distinct from capitalism, but he was nonetheless a believer in the democratic ideal.[24] In the 1990s and early 2000s, he moved away from his attachment to democracy and began to see communism as the only possible alternative to capitalism. Democracy became, in Žižek's eyes, irrevocably attached to the capitalist system.

Marx provides the basis of Žižek's political agenda. Above all, Žižek remains a politically committed thinker in a Marxist vein, despite the fact that he wasn't Marxist enough to be employed as a professor in the old Yugoslavia. He takes the side of communism and unapologetically employs this signifier, even if he redefines it in his own way. He attacks other leftist modes of thought for their failure to be radical enough and for their investment in the capitalist system. His targets include liberalism, multiculturalism, deconstruction, and identity politics. His political thought is vehemently anticapitalist.

But Žižek's communism is not that of Marx, in which all limits are eviscerated and production can proceed untrammeled. He criticizes this image of the communist future that Marx proposes as just a capitalist fantasy. Communism for Žižek is just the name for a society in which the encounter with the real would be privileged over the attachment to the societal underside. It would be a society that valued the commons above private interest. Žižek believes in revolution but not in what the revolution would attain. This has led to a great deal of criticism of Žižek for remaining constantly in a critical attitude and never advocating any positive politics.

Even when he spoke to Occupy Wall Street, Žižek warned about the errors that the movement might make rather than offering his vision of where it should go. In this sense, Žižek seems at times like a prophet of permanent revolution, but he also attacks this idea. He doesn't want resistance for its own sake but a society in which the negative has priority. But there is no sense in his thought of what this society might look like. And this obviously has frustrating consequences for his readers worldwide. He purposely leaves the image of the future blank because he believes that it must be produced from material political action and not from theoretical speculation. In this way, he is a materialist thinker, just as he claims.²⁵

Beginning in 2000 with *The Fragile Absolute, or, Why the Christian Legacy Is Worth Fighting For*, Christianity becomes a significant point of reference for Žižek. Though he calls himself a fighting atheist, Žižek finds in Christianity a foundational idea for his philosophical and political project. He appreciates Christianity in exactly the way that Hegel did. Christianity is the first religion to conceive of God's self-division and emergence from the beyond (which is where other religions place God) into the finite world. The birth of Christ is thus also for Žižek the death of God as a transcendent figure. God comes down to earth with Christ and escapes from eternity into time. As Hegel puts it in the third volume of the *Philosophy of Religion*, "The identity of the divine and the human means that God is at home with himself in humanity, in the finite, and in [its] death this finitude is itself a determination of God."²⁶ Thus, the ultimate figure of authority, the ultimate Other, is nothing but a weak human being. This is the lesson of Christianity. It is both a philosophical and a political lesson.

But in order to understand the lesson of Christianity, one must look at it in a new way. Christianity is not a narrative of the fall and a subsequent salvation but a retrospective rereading of the fall. Rather than a fall from a perfect state, the fall is the original creative act. We fail to see the fall as liberation and instead view it as an enslavement in sin. Our mistake consists in looking on sin as sin or on evil as evil. Thus, we don't need redemption from the fall but the insight that the fall is the condition of true ethical deeds. This may also explain why Žižek, like his interlocutor Alain Badiou, rejects the idea of "radical evil" in the realm of politics with the Holocaust, for example, often put at center stage. And it is from here that his skeptical opposition to Habermas's discourse-ethical philosophy and its multiple sub-schools can be understood. These schools fail to recognize the extent to which even under ethical surveillance the measurement of good and evil always occurs in the name of a measure that cannot calculate its own excess, its inherent lack of measure. In other words, a discourse that depends on its distance to what is "radical evil" does not recognize how the proclaimed distance can have the shape of this same radical evil in an inverted form. To locate "radical evil" in the Holocaust, for example, would thus be just as naive as to build an ethics on the "wholly other" as presented by Emmanuel Levinas.

This debate cannot be detached from the modern multiplicity of all kinds of belief-systems. Belief is a central problem in the contemporary world for Žižek. Most intellectuals and cultured people claim not to believe or hold to a very liberal idea of belief. And yet belief functions nonetheless as our dirty little secret. We distance ourselves from belief because we believe so strongly, for example in values of Western democracy originated through, among others, liberal economy. We believe not directly but through the Other, what Žižek calls a subject supposed to believe. He is alive through all kinds of institutions who administer our desires and fantasies and maintain the belief of everyday life as some kind of natural fact. And this is a good and a necessary thing. But it is also a belief-maintained in practices and deeds similar to religious practices and their deeds. In this sense one can say that the fascination with the fundamentalist terrorist is a disavowal of our own belief and a disavowal of our hidden investment in the Other who really believes in and through us. We believe that the fundamentalist really believes, while we, as liberals, can take a distance from our beliefs. But we too cling to our belief system without recognizing the religious-like investment in our lifeform. By pointing out this belief through the Other, Žižek hopes to pave the way to a different form of belief, a belief in a fallen or a castrated God. This is the basis for Žižek's version of communism.

Universally Antagonistic

Communism is Žižek's name for a politics of the universal. For Žižek, universality is not the whole or an all that might be imposed on each particular. This is how theorists commonly conceptualize universality in order to criticize it as imperial or a mode of domination. Žižek sees universality otherwise. It is an antagonism that cannot be resolved and, therefore, explains why particulars ever come into existence. There are particular things because there is a universal antagonism, a failure at the core of universality.

We can think of a specific form of universality, like universal equality. We can never realize universal equality, but particular forms of equality emerges through the failure of the universal to constitute itself. There is particular equality because universal equality has an antagonistic structure. Žižek states, "a universality which is not just the common denominator of its particular forms but the name of a tension/antagonism/gap, of the impossibility of becoming what it is, to actualize its potentials, and its particular forms are the (ultimately failed) attempts to resolve its constitutive deadlock."[27] Since universality is an antagonism, it necessarily gives rise to particular struggles to surmount the antagonism. But no particular ever achieves this. Particularity is always a form of failed universality.

The antagonism that defines social relations is what holds the conflicting parts of society together. This is how Žižek thinks of sexual difference or class difference. There is no common ground that then divides into two. Instead, the different sexes or classes emerge through the social antagonism itself. The emancipatory project, as Žižek sees it, consists in naming and insisting on this antagonism. By holding fast to the existence of the antagonism, we engage in the struggle against oppression. There is no future society beyond antagonism because the antagonism constitutes the social order. Thus, Žižek, despite invoking utopia from time to time, is radically anti-utopian. There is no utopian society that could exist without antagonism.

Žižek is doing the only political act possible—insisting on the antagonism rather than trying to obscure it.[28]

The conservative position, in contrast, is predicated on not seeing the antagonism. From this perspective, there is a whole, but there are agitators who disrupt the whole at its edges. The conservative preserves the image of the whole through the fetishistic disavowal of the antagonism. In this way, conservatism misses the constitutive function of the antagonism and avoids confronting its necessity. For this position, there is a shared social space that then subsequently divides into two, those who are in and those who are out. All are part of this shared social space, except for those who threaten it from the outside.

According to Žižek, the fundamental rift in space marks the impossibility of any harmonious social structure. All that the two sexes and classes have in common is what they don't have—the antagonism. Žižek states, "there is no shared common space between the two sexes or classes—what they share, what holds the social space or the space of sexuality together, is ultimately antagonism itself."[29] Every particular identity shares its relation to antagonism. No matter what form the identity takes, it must confront the inevitability of antagonism. Thus, every identity must confront another identity that destabilizes it.

The sexes or classes are not simply different but dialectically at odds with each other, in an antagonistic relation. The move from difference to dialectic that Žižek makes enables him to explain how conflict between differences arises. They exist in an antagonistic relation, not in an oppositional relation. Two positions are not externally opposed to each other but two different particular manifestations of the same universal antagonism. Dialectical antagonism becomes obfuscated when discussed in terms of differences or opposites.

The dialectical conception of contradiction has nothing to do with the struggle between opposites, which is how Mao wrongly defines contradiction, according to Žižek.[30] The topology of the Moebius strip, which Lacan highlights, shows how a dialectical contradiction works. The Moebius strip has only one side, even though it has a front and back. One follows one side of the strip and then ends up on the other. It functions as a topographical model not just for Lacan's conception of the real but also for Hegel's absolute. Taking a position up absolutely puts one into the opposite position because the space that the position must traverse is itself inherently antagonistic.

The consistency of the external objective world depends on the suturing act of subjectivity. We must add a supplement to create a sense of reality. This supplement is what Lacan calls the *objet a*. It is the object that curves space, that produces the movement from one side to the other on the Moebius strip. The *objet a* is the piece of subjectivity added to the objective world to create the sense of reality. A world without the *objet a* would seem lifeless and could never arouse our interest.

This singular point is an excremental point, a point foreign to the objective world introduced into it. The group that doesn't belong among the objective classifications is necessary for these objective classifications. The social order depends on this category, as does the objective social analysis. The singular excremental point is the universal. As the object that doesn't fit, it embodies the antagonism. Everywhere else in the social order, the antagonism becomes obscure. But in the singularity of the excremental point, the antagonism is clear, which is why Žižek is drawn to it and sees in this point the project of emancipation.

Insisting on the universality of the excremental point is the Christian project. The point of Christianity is to take up all who are excluded, to contain the universality of those who don't fit. Even though Christianity often deviates from this core principle, its basic project is a universalist one that takes the side of the excluded. It sees all humanity embodied in the figure of the excremental point.

The excremental point is a symptom within the social order. A symptom marks the moment at which a system produces an effect that undermines it. And yet, the symptom is also the path through a system structures its enjoyment. What Hegel calls the rabble—those who aren't productive—is a symptom of capitalism. It embodies the failure of capitalism to function smoothly. The normal functioning of capitalism produces this excess that has no place within the system—the rabble. The symptom is the point of universality from which any emancipation must arise.

Our desire doesn't strive to find an identity. It seeks out an *objet a* that goes beyond every identity and thwarts every identity. Identity attempts to bring the *objet a* into a symbolic category, but this is not satisfying because what we desire is what cannot be contained in any such category. The invention of new categories still leaves us desiring what resists all categorization. It is antagonism that is universal, and it exists even within each sexual identity, not just between them. Lacan believes that there is no sexual relationship not because there is a problem between men and woman but because there is an internal antagonism in each sexual identity. No one can simply be a man or be a woman but is instead riddled within antagonisms internally. This is why there is no utopia where we can all just freely assert our sexuality. The assertion of our sexuality is always antagonistic and disturbed, even just on its own terms, outside of the repressive forces of the social order. We wrongly assume that our inner identity is free of antagonism and that is actually belongs to us. Our inner identity is actually not under our control.

In light of his understanding of the constitutive role that antagonism plays in the social order, Žižek rereads Plato's Allegory of the Cave. The point is not to escape and see in the light of day, as Plato would have it, but to recognize the contradictions within the shadows. There is no space outside the cave, but a possibility for freedom exists within the cave because the shadows are not self-consistent. The only way to break out of our enslavement in the cave—our enslavement within capitalism—and to recognize the antagonism is through the devotion to a cause. A cause disturbs our symbolic identity and uproots us from the givens of our symbolic situation. This is why it is freeing.

What we can't see while we are enchained in the cave is our own inscription within the image that we see. What we see appears to be objective to us. But one of the great achievements of Alfred Hitchcock, for instance, is to show the subjective moment of the objective world, as in the God's eye shot from *The Birds* (1963). Here, what initially looks like a simple objective shot of Bodega Bay becomes visible as a shot from the perspective of the attacking birds—the objective becomes evident as always already subjective. Or in other words: within every perspective on "what is the case" the potentiality of another view, redefining states of affairs, is a priori inscribed. Facts resist, as such, objective descriptions, since they reveal themselves as being not identical with themselves. This epistemic thesis has practical and normative consequences, since it guarantees the condition of the possibility for freedom. It enables us to take the position of the universal antagonism: we see that there is no objective view of society, that we must take up the perspective of what doesn't fit. Ideology obscures the antagonism by covering over this opening, making the symbolic structure seem as if it doesn't have any rupture.

But subjectivity cannot stay removed from antagonism. A fundamental perspectivism is part of the objective's world inner-antagonistic core. Antagonism means that I cannot just be another object in the field of objects. I appear in the field of perception as a distortion. The subjective distortion is immanent in the objective structure. I don't recognize myself in a mirror but in decentered otherness. I am the distortion in the image, not the image of myself. This distortion is the site of the universal.

The essays that follow attempt to confront the radical universality of Žižek's thought, to engage him at his most demanding point. They address his theorizing at the times where the writers detect some tension, some moment where Žižek is at odds with himself, which has the effect of generating responses from Žižek that illuminate his positions in ways that he has not hitherto done. By looking beyond Žižek's provocations, the contributors seek to provoke Žižek himself into further elaborations and conclusions. The provoker has been provoked.

The Chapters

Adrian Johnston's text "Cake or Doughnut? Žižek and German Idealist Emergentisms" examines Žižek's ambivalent attitude toward Schelling and Hegel as the two most important and yet mutually exclusive idealist sources of his materialist ontology. It simply proves to be problematic when Žižek relates his speculations on quantum physics to Schelling's philosophy of nature and maintains to still remain a Hegelian. In doing so, he necessarily adopts the modal concept of potentiality as metaphysic's fundamental concept, whereas Hegel primarily reveals, respectively, the concept of contingency in relation to reality as the fundamental modal category of his metaphysics. Žižek thus runs the risk with Schelling of adhering to a theory of emergence within the framework of a Spinozist substance monism (the cake-model of reality with different layers), which, reductionistically interpreted, no longer allows him—with Hegel—to interpret the subject as a gap in the basic structure of reality (the doughnut-model of reality). So how can, Johnston asks, Žižek be both a Schellingian and a Hegelian at the same time?

Dominik Finkelde describes in "Truth as Bacchanalian Revel: Žižek and the Risks of Irony" how Žižek's philosophy is not only marked by the refusal of a systematic approach that characterizes many of his works, but by the celebration of a way of thinking as well that, in ever new associations and leaps of thought, apparently sometimes deliberately seeks to deprive its readers of the secure hold of valid arguments. In this way he has invented his own and ultimately unique genre—as can be seen as well in anti-systematic works from philosophers like Nietzsche to Wittgenstein: a thinking that has elevated the transgression of boundaries (including those of philosophical disciplines) to its program. But a serious problem, which is at the heart of this essay, remains: whether Žižek's philosophy has not unconsciously subscribed itself to irony as a philosophical stance. Irony has been criticized famously in the late nineteenth and early twentieth century by Søren Kierkegaard and Carl Schmitt among others. But before that it was especially Hegel who in his Berlin years criticized the romantic adoption of irony as a confused philosophical stance. But isn't there an elective affinity between Žižek's dialectics and the ironic stance rejected by Hegel?

Graham Harman's "Žižek and the Retroactivity of the Real" takes the opposite approach to Johnston and reproaches Žižek of the Kantian legacy his philosophy is intertwined with. The chapter focuses especially on Žižek's *Less than Nothing*, i.e., his most ambitious attempt to deploy quantum theory in support of his generally Hegelo-Lacanian ontology. Harman's analysis is guided by his own Object-Oriented-Ontology and from this perspective concentrates on the following question: Is the result of Žižek's theory too idealist in spirit, or is it too dependent on the Copenhagen Interpretation of quantum theory? Harman follows these questions and guides the reader within the complexity of thinking ontology with modern physics.

Robert Pippin shows in his essay "Slavoj Žižek's Hegel" how the Slovene philosopher, despite his compelling interpretation of Hegel's philosophy, inserts a theory of radical and Marxist politics into Hegel that the idealist's ontology doesn't support. According to Pippin, this political bent, derived from the influence of Lacan and Marx on Žižek's thought, derails his apprehension of Hegel to no good end. Žižek fails to see that, for Hegel, we can rely on reason, despite what Lacan calls the inexistence of the big Other. As a result, there are possible reforms that we can institute within contemporary capitalist society that would be in keeping with the Hegelian project of enlightenment. Žižek's call to revolution steps over Hegel's own politics and misses the practical possibilities that he opens for us,— possibilities which are presented today, among others, by the Pittsburgh Hegelians, Robert Brandom and John McDowell.

Todd McGowan asks in "Slavoj Žižek Is Not Violent Enough" why many angry critics reproach him of being unable to proclaim politically concrete acts of violence, while his theory of violent deeds (called "theory of the act") is exactly what his philosophy constantly asks for. Another problem follows from here. Žižek makes no sustained attempt to integrate the self-destructive violence of this act into a conception of what an emancipatory governance could look like if some kind of "act" would have shaken up the states of political affairs. So Žižek has not yet integrated his conception of violence into a theory of rules. He imagines revolt in terms of striking against oneself in the manner of Tyler Durden (Brad Pitt) and *Fight Club* (David Fincher, 1999), but he doesn't extend this violence against the self into a conception of anti-capitalist governance.

Hilary Neroni comments in her chapter "Žižek's Foundationless Building: Ideology Critique as an Existentialist Choice" on how one of Žižek's most important contributions to contemporary thought remains his theory of ideology. Laid out throughout the first half of his oeuvre, he brings to the concept of ideology several groundbreaking innovations. Most importantly, shifting away from Althusser's argument that ideology itself hails one as a subject, he argues that ideology interpellates us away from subjectivity. According to his theory, when we are drawn away from subjectivity, we may see the contradiction within ideology but then disavow what we have seen. But can Žižek's idea of ideology also fully explain modern forms of fascism within authoritarian regimes (from Donald Trump in the United States to Viktor Orbán in Hungry) or does the enduring nature of—if not the mounting enthusiasm for—authoritarianism, suggest that we need to expand the theory of ideology beyond Žižek's insights to be able to better understand this trend?

Henrik Jøker Bjerre's essay "The Subject is Not Enough" presents a reading of the story about Zhuang Zi who dreamt that he was a butterfly and relates it to the avant-garde music group Laibach as critique of ideology. He thereby dismantles inherent contradictions of the playful play with ideology being (possibly) itself maintained by true fascistic ideals. Put differently: How do we know that Laibach are not fascists? The author's claim is that we know it in a way that could be compared to how Zhuang Zi knows that he is not a butterfly. Of importance is here the question of how the subject seems at once to be the condition of possibility of critique, and the condition of possibility of an ideology's smooth functioning itself. How may we distinguish between the subject that is "in ideology" precisely because of its critical or ironic distance to it, and the subject which is "outside" ideology, i.e., inside-looking-out. Žižek's philosophy appears not to give a clear answer to this problem but, in contrast, to perform in philosophy the gesture which Laibach personifies in music.

Zahi Zalloua analyzes Žižek's relationship to Derrida and Levinas in order to reframe the question of a European universalism under the imperative of "love they neighbor." This universalism is challenged by, among other things, the presence of various refugee crises and, as such, often splits into the extremes of "pure hostility" and "pure hospitality." As Zalloua points out, Žižek occupies a peculiar intermediate position in his comments on Derrida and Levinas. On the one hand, he cuts through the fantasy image of a "friendly neighbor" who can simply be integrated into an autoimmune Europe. On the other hand, he rejects the political aims of right-wing nationalist parties.

Nadia Bou Ali refers in her chapter "The Politics of Incompleteness: On Žižek's Theory of the Subject" to Judith Butler who accuses Žižek of an ahistorical Kantian formalism: of elevating sexual difference into a transhistorical a priori. Bou Ali takes this critique as a starting point to draw the political implications of the psychoanalytic notion of an incomplete subject. She doubts that the incompleteness of the subject can be the opening and the site for any emancipatory politics. For Bou Ali, incompleteness alone may just reproduce the anxiety of a contemporary subject. Something else than anxiety is needed, and her question is if Žižek's philosophy can offer this: a pathway of transformation from anxiety to certainty, to a new positive emancipatory project that formulates what has to be done.

Dany Nobus shows in "Reading the Illegible: On Žižek's Interpretation of Lacan's 'Kant with Sade'" how Žižek has maintained from his doctoral thesis until his most recent books on Hegel, ontology and political ideology, a constant critical focus on "Kant with Sade," one of Lacan's most challenging and most ignored *écrits*. Even though Žižek's participation in Jacques-Alain Miller's closed seminars on "Kant with Sade" during the early 1980s in Paris clearly inspired and directed his interpretation of the text, over the years he has also developed his own idiosyncratic reading of this allegedly illegible essay, whereby it has served the dual purpose of Lacanian bedrock for a critique of Kantian reason and intellectual cornerstone for the articulation of the fantasy as a political category. In the essay, Nobus traces, reconstructs, and critically analyzes Žižek's numerous interpretations of "Kant with Sade" as they appear throughout his works, stress-testing his arguments and conclusions against Lacan's own propositions, evaluating the coherence and consistency of Žižek's dialectical engagement with the text, and opening up some new perspectives on how (not) to read Lacan.

Mari Ruti explores in her essay "Raising a Mundane Object to the Dignity of the Thing. When Desire Is Not the Desire of the Other" Žižek's elaborations of Lacanian theory. The former draws a relatively categorical distinction between the normative subject—whose desire is invariably a reflection of the hegemonic desire of the Other—and the antinormative subject of the drive, who is capable of a rebellious ethical act of defying this desire. Žižek in fact claims that Lacan's ethical maxim regarding not yielding on one's desire is oxymoronic in the sense that desire by definition represents "a certain yielding, a kind of compromise formation." Ruti blurs Žižek's distinction between desire and the drive through a consideration of Lacan's dictum that sublimation—and therefore the ethics of psychoanalysis—is a matter of raising a mundane object to "the dignity of the Thing." That is, she illustrates the ethical potential of the kind of defiant desire that manages to capture traces of the *jouissance* of the real. If Žižek maintains that "desire and *jouissance* are inherently antagonistic," the author argues that the Lacanian ethical subject—a subject that is also a creative, galvanized subject—arises at the intersection of these concepts. Generally speaking, the paper's goal is to present a more affirmative reading of Lacan than is available in Žižekian theory.

Jennifer Friedlander takes Žižek's insistence on hopelessness as the point of departure for her essay, which illustrates what this philosophy has to offer contemporary politics. In "Hoping Against Hope: Žižek, *Jouissance*, and the Impossible," Friedlander shows how the embrace of hopelessness has the effect of opening up the impossible. The paradox inherent in Žižek's thought is that it is only through the recognition of hopelessness that we can transcend the limitations of the possible established through the capitalist order. As Friedlander indicates, this provides an instructive supplement to certain utopian tendencies within queer theory. Žižek's politics of hopelessness becomes the only avenue toward the genesis of hope today.

Duane Rousselle refers critically to Žižek's comments on the war in Ukraine in his chapter "Žižek and the War in an Era of Generalized Foreclosure," since he sees the Russian war on Ukraine as part of a general war. Žižek, though, does not take this general war into account. The latter manifests itself in an omnipresent growing inability of modern societies to bear internal contradiction and dissenting voices—from families to echo chambers to whole societies and empires. Modern societies thus appear doomed to fail. Their inability to deal with internal contradictions produces ever new singularities and ever new enemies of these singularities. Singularities approximate the other via a caricature and, in turn, become caricatures themselves.

Richard Boothby reminds the reader in his text "Harpo's Grin: Rethinking Lacan's Unthinkable 'Thing'" that no one has done more to reinvigorate the Lacanian legacy than Slavoj Žižek, and probably no one has contributed so much to our understanding of two cardinal Lacanian notions: the *objet a* and *das Ding*, the unknown Thing in the Other. But Žižek appears never to have articulated any linkage between the two. Boothby's essay asks why. The obvious answer is that Žižek merely follows Lacan himself, who seems to abandon *das Ding* almost immediately after introducing it in Seminar 7. But maybe the answer isn't so easy. That Lacan doesn't wholly reject his own concept is attested by a number of admittedly infrequent but obviously crucial references to *das Ding* in later seminars. One of the more charming, and more suggestive, is his rather off-hand remark in Seminar 16 that *objet a* "is what tickles *das Ding* from the inside." The chapter seeks to clarify how the *objet a* and the Thing can be seen to form an essential couplet, in which neither can ultimately be understood without reference to the other. If that wager is successful, it will leave us wondering why they appear to remain disjunct in Žižek's work. Is that disjunction merely an oversight, a lack of interest, or does it signal a deeper conceptual commitment of some sort? If the latter, what species of commitment might that be, and is it a commitment shared somehow by Lacan as well?

Notes

1. Rex Butler, *Slavoj Žižek: Live Theory* (London: Bloomsbury 2005).
2. Dominik Finkelde, *Slavoj Žižek zwischen Hegel und Lacan* (Vienna: Turia & Kant 2006).
3. Sarah Key, *Žižek: A Critical Introduction* (Cambridge: Polity Press 2003).
4. Tom Myers, *Slavoj Žižek* (London: Routledge 2003).
5. Ian Parker, *Slavoj Žižek: A Critical Introduction* (London: Pluto Press 2004).
6. *The Truth of Žižek*, eds. Paul Bowman and Richard Stamp (London: Continuum 2007)
7. *Did Somebody Say Ideology?* eds. Fabio Vighi and Heiko Feldner (Newcastle: Cambridge Scholars Publishing 2007).
8. *Traversing the Fantasy. Critical Responses to Slavoj Žižek*, eds. Geoff Boucher, Jason Glynos, and Matthew Sharpe (Burlington: Ashgate Publishing 2005).
9. *Repeating Žižek*, ed. Agon Hamza (Durham: Duke University Press 2015).
10. The vituperation hits a low point in Jeremy Gilbert's essay in the mentioned volume. Although he acknowledges that Žižek does at times produce "good work," his "bad work . . . notoriously deals in generalizations, logical inconsistencies, groundless assertions and aimless polemics is not somehow saved or justified by Žižek's irreducible genius: it is an embarrassment, which the academy and leftist intellectual community ought to be ashamed of having tolerated for so long." Jeremy Gilbert, "All the Right Questions, All the Wrong Answers," in *The Truth of Žižek*, 61. As Žižek points out in his response to the essays that make up this volume, critics feel licensed to launch insults in his direction that they would not use on any other theorist. Just substituting the name "Judith Butler" for "Žižek" in the above sentence proves this point.
11. Rex Butler, "Review on *The Truth of Žižek*," in *Philosophy in Review* 27, no. 6 (2007): 396–8, here: 397.
12. One model for the present book is Robert Brandom, ed., *Rorty and His Critics* (London: Wiley-Blackwell, 2000), although this volume aims at producing not just critical responses but also attempts to develop Žižek's ideas even further than he himself takes them.

13 Given the distance between Žižek's early work in Slovene and his mature work in English, he has made no effort to have this early work translated.

14 The provocative nature of Žižek's popular contributions have resulted in his quiet banishment from several publications, including the *New York Times* and the *Guardian*, outlets that used to publish his work regularly.

15 Žižek pursues this line of thought in *Did Somebody Say Totalitarianism?* There, he states, "the 'objective' ideologico-political content of the depoliticization of the Holocaust, of its elevation into the abyssal absolute Evil, is the political pact of aggressive Zionists and Western rightist anti-Semites at the expense of today's radical political possibilities." Slavoj Žižek, *Did Somebody Say Totalitarianism? Five Interventions in the (Mis)Use of a Notion* (London: Verso, 2001), 68.

16 Slavoj Žižek quoted in Eric Dean Rasmussen, "Liberation Hurts: An Interview with Slavoj Žižek," *Electronic Book Review* (July 1, 2004): http://www.electronicbookreview.com/thread/endconstruction/desublimation (accessed December 30, 2021).

17 Slavoj Žižek, *The Parallax View* (Cambridge, MA: MIT, 2006), 62.

18 One reason why Samuel Beckett functions as a central point of reference for Žižek is his emphasis on a repeated failure. The imperative to continue to fail and thus to fail better constitutes a central part of Žižek's politics.

19 See Louis Althusser, "Ideology and Ideological State Apparatuses." In *Lenin and Philosophy and Other Essays*, trans. Ben Brewster (New York: Monthly Review Press, 1971), 121–73.

20 Slavoj Žižek, *Sublime Object of Ideology* (London: Verso, 1989), 45.

21 As Žižek puts it, "The deepest identification which 'holds a community together' is not so much identification with the Law which regulates its 'normal' everyday circuit as, rather, identification with the specific form of transgression of the Law, of its suspension (in psychoanalytic terms, with the specific form of enjoyment)." Slavoj Žižek, "'In His Bold Gaze My Ruin Is Writ Large.'" In *Everything You Always Wanted to Know about Lacan (But Were Afraid to Ask Hitchcock)* (New York: Verso, 1992), 225.

22 Slavoj Žižek, *The Metastases of Enjoyment: Six Essays on Woman and Causality* (New York: Verso, 1994), 54.

23 The notion of the obscene underside of ideology as the decisive point within an ideological structure first appears in Žižek's work in Slavoj Žižek, *The Metastases of Enjoyment: Six Essays on Woman and Causality* (London: Verso, 1994) and then receives a fuller development in Slavoj Žižek, *The Plague of Fantasies* (London: Verso, 1997).

24 Žižek's early investment in democracy placed him in proximity with Ernesto Laclau and Chantal Mouffe, advocates of radical democracy. As his thought developed politically, this proximity lessened significantly.

25 Hegel's famous statement about the impotence of theory from the preface to the *Philosophy of Right* operates as a philosophical mantra for Žižek, which is why he cites it so often. There, Hegel claims, "A further word on the subject of issuing instructions on how the world ought to be: philosophy, at any rate, always comes too late to perform this function. As the thought of the world, it

appears only at a time when actuality has gone through its formative process and attained its completed state. This lesson of the concept is also necessarily apparent from history, namely that it is only when actuality has reached maturity that the ideal appears opposite the real and reconstructs this real world, which it has grasped in its substance, in the shape of an intellectual realm. When philosophy paints its grey in grey, a shape of life has grown old, and it cannot be rejuvenated, but only recognized, by the grey in grey of philosophy; the owl of Minerva begins its flight only with the onset of dusk." G.W.F. Hegel, *Elements of the Philosophy of Right*, trans. H. B. Nisbet, ed. Allen W. Wood (Cambridge: Cambridge University Press, 1991), 23. This emphasis on theory's belatedness leads Žižek to label Hegel, even more than Marx, a materialist thinker. Material history drives theoretical speculation, not vice versa, for Žižek.

26 G.W.F. Hegel, *Lectures on the Philosophy of Religion, Volume III: The Consummate Religion*, trans. R.F. Brown, P.C. Hodgson, and J.M. Stewart, ed. Peter C. Hodgson (Oxford: Clarendon Press, 2007), 220.

27 Slavoj Žižek, *Sex and the Failed Absolute* (London: Bloomsbury, 2020), 220.

28 Žižek's political project involves bringing antagonism to the fore and insisting on it, not attempting to overcome it. This is one feature that definitively separates him from Marxism, which identifies class antagonism in order to envision a revolution that would eliminate it.

29 Slavoj Žižek, *Sex and the Failed Absolute*, 224.

30 Žižek actually edited Mao's writing on contradiction. See Mao Zedong, *On Practice and Contradiction*, ed. Slavoj Žižek (London: Verso, 2017).

PART ONE
Ontology

CHAPTER ONE

Cake or Doughnut?
Žižek and German Idealist Emergentisms

Adrian Johnston

In the sixth and seventh chapters of my 2014 book *Adventures in Transcendental Materialism*, I initiated a debate with Slavoj Žižek focused on his dialectical materialist turns to quantum mechanics.[1] Following my initial criticisms of Žižek's speculative appeals to the physics of the extremely small, he put forward a number of responses to me.[2] In turn, I then defended and further justified my reservations and objections on several occasions (some of which became parts of my 2018 book *A New German Idealism*).[3]

This relatively recent debate between Žižek and me revolved around the issue of whether quantum physics or neurobiology is the best scientific partner for the philosophical project of forging an uncompromisingly materialist yet thoroughly anti-reductive theory of subjectivity. Previously, I have argued against Žižek's favoring of physics in the manner of a sympathetic immanent critique. More precisely, I have maintained that Žižek's privileging of quantum mechanics is in danger of being at odds with both the anti-reductive and the materialist commitments he and I share in common. Rooting the subject in the smallest building blocks of the physical universe threatens to validate long-established reductive explanatory strategies vis-à-vis human mindedness. Treating the zero-level of the physical universe as proto-subjective threatens to run contrary to materialism (dialectical or otherwise) by lending credence to spiritualist panpsychism. The risk is that Žižek might end up unintentionally with a both-are-worse combination of reductionism and spiritualism—and this despite his sincere anti-reductive and materialist inclinations.

In the past couple of years, further reflection on these matters has led me to the conviction that there is another dimension to this disagreement between Žižek and me yet to be addressed with adequate thoroughness. Behind the confrontation between Žižek's dialectical materialist rendition of quantum physics and my transcendental materialist rendition of human biology, a confrontation in which recent and contemporary science takes center stage, there lurks an older philosophical tension. Perhaps unsurprisingly, considering that Žižek and I both are especially passionate about the German idealists, this tension is most manifest between the metaphysical systems of F.W.J. Schelling and G.W.F. Hegel, particularly the philosophies of nature put forward by these two complexly entwined contemporaries.

My present intervention aims to revisit the back-and-forth between Žižek and me apropos interfacing empirical science with materialist philosophy in light of the divergences separating Schelling and Hegel. In both their overarching philosophical frameworks and their more specific *Naturphilosophien*, these two German idealists can and should be interpreted as emergentists *avant la lettre*. That is to say, they both see reality as stratified into multiple interlinked layers, with each layer having arisen from other layers preexisting it.

However, despite both arguably being emergentists, Schelling's and Hegel's emergentisms differ in certain crucial respects. First and foremost, in terms of the basic arrangement of emergent layers, Hegel presents a layer cake model, while Schelling offers a layer doughnut one. What do I mean by this? Hegel's *Realphilosophie* gets underway with the "mechanics" of *Naturphilosophie* (beginning with objectively real space and time), proceeding within the realm of nature through "physics" (including chemistry) and then onto "organics" (consisting of geology, botany, and zoology). Hegelian Philosophy of Nature culminates with the sentient animal organism as itself the transitional link to the next set of emergent layers, namely, the strata of *Geistesphilosophie* (grouped into the three broad headings of subjective, objective, and absolute mind/spirit [*Geist*]).

In short, Hegel puts forward a layer-cake model in which the bottom layer is spatio-temporal mechanics and the top layer is artistic-religious-philosophical *Geist* (with many layers in-between these two extremes). Although the highest layer allows for all the layers below it to be comprehended in their inherent intelligibility, there is no direct meeting up and merging together of top and bottom layers—and this despite Hegel's fondness for circle imagery. That is to say, various sublations (*Aufhebungen*) do not annul significant differences-in-kind between the mechanical and the spiritual.

Schelling's configuration of emergent layers, by contrast with Hegel's, is circular such that the lowest and the highest layers are made to converge—nay, are essentially the same single layer. One of the biggest bones of contention between Schelling and Hegel, starting with the latter's barbed remark about "the night in which all cows are black" in the preface to 1807's *Phenomenology of Spirit*,[4] is the former's enthusiastic embrace of Baruch Spinoza. The young Schelling, during the mid-1790s to the early 1800s period in which he is developing his interconnected *Naturphilosophie* and *Identiätsphilosophie*, indeed relies heavily upon Spinozism, particularly its distinction between *natura naturans* and *natura naturata*[5] (a reliance persisting well beyond the first stretch of his lengthy intellectual itinerary). Interestingly, Žižek, in 2020's *Hegel in a Wired Brain*, elevates Spinoza to enjoying an importance to Žižek's own thinking comparable to that enjoyed by Immanuel Kant and Hegel.[6]

That said, Schelling's emergentism begins with the fluid "ground" (*Grund*) of a primordial creative power (i.e., verb-like *natura naturans*) that then produces the fixed "existence" (*Existenz*) of stable entities (i.e., noun-like *natura naturata*). According to Schelling, human subjectivity, as the highest spiritual power, is nothing other than an irruption within the field of existence of the ground-zero substratum underlying and generating this field. In psychoanalytic terms, the subject is the return of repressed (Spinozistic) substance, the resurfacing of *natura naturans* within the domain of *natura naturata*. As such, reaching the highest Schellingian emergent layer amounts to reconnecting with the lowest one—hence a layer-doughnut model.

Tellingly, in nearly all of Žižek's discussions of quantum mechanics, he explicitly appeals to Schelling in particular (rather than Hegel, usually his preferred German idealist interlocutor). The middle-period Schelling of 1809's *Freiheitsschrift* is Žižek's favored reference in this vein. What Žižek values most is this 1809 essay's *Grund-Existenz* distinction. As I just implied, this distinction amounts to a renaming of the Spinozistic contrast between *natura naturans* and *natura naturata*. Moreover, the *Freiheitsschrift* clearly continues to uphold what I have characterized as the layer-doughnut model.[7]

Žižek's most recent major philosophical work, 2020's *Sex and the Failed Absolute*, involves him putting forward his Schellingian speculative interpretation of quantum physics (initially developed in 1996's *The Indivisible Remainder*) as the very foundation of his dialectical materialist theoretical framework. Given both this interpretation's reaffirmed importance for Žižek's philosophical apparatus as well as the previous disagreements between him and me regarding it, I feel it to be worthwhile on this occasion to reengage critically with Žižekian quantum metaphysics, especially as elaborated in *Sex and the Failed Absolute*. Such reengagement will afford me the opportunity both to deepen philosophically the debate between Žižek and me involving natural science as well as to bring to light the contemporary relevance of the Schelling–Hegel pair, particularly in terms of significant contrasts between their metaphysical edifices.

To be more precise, I herein will argue for the Hegelian layer-cake and against the Schellingian layer-doughnut emergentist models. In so doing, I will assert that Schelling's Spinoza-inspired approach to nature-as-ground both fails actually to explain the genesis of subjectivity as well as amounts to an implausible and not-at-all-materialist anthropomorphic panpsychism. Correspondingly, I will indicate that Žižek would do better to stick to his habitual Hegelian guns in philosophically appropriating natural scientific content. Doing so would enable him to articulate a dialectical *Naturphilosophie* consistent with his core materialist commitments. Žižek's long-standing choice of the "quantum physics with Schelling" combination is, I will contend, inconsistent with the dialectical materialism Žižek continues valiantly to advocate. Despite appearances to the contrary, Schelling is a *faux ami* of both materialism and naturalism. As I will show, when he speaks of "matter" (*Materie*) and "nature" (*Natur*), he actually is invoking God and Spirit, the intangible mind of a divine creator.

I will be focusing primarily on Žižek's 2020 book *Sex and the Failed Absolute*. I have chosen this focus for three reasons. First, *Sex and the Failed Absolute* is Žižek's most recent substantial theoretical work. Second, I already have dealt with the bulk of his preceding philosophical texts in my own prior publications. And, third, *Sex and the Failed Absolute* involves Žižek doubling-down specifically on his recourse to quantum physics as integral to his unique version of dialectical materialism.

Žižek's initial turn to quantum mechanics occurs in his 1996 book *The Indivisible Remainder*, in a chapter entitled "Quantum Physics with Lacan."[8] Perhaps this chapter should have been entitled "Quantum Physics with Lacan and Schelling," since the Schellingian philosophy being explored throughout this 1996 book is as important to its chapter on quantum matters as is Lacanian psychoanalysis. To be precise, the middle-period Schelling, from 1809's *Freiheitsschrift* to 1815's third and final draft of the unfinished *Weltalter* project, is Žižek's privileged partner (along with Jacques Lacan) in the context of his theoretical borrowings from quantum physics.

Many scholars consider the 1809 *Freiheitsschrift* as marking a break within Schelling's corpus, a rupture in his intellectual itinerary demarcating a divide between "early" and "middle" periods. I will not be debating here whether or not a radical discontinuity occurring in 1809 punctuates the unfolding of Schelling's thinking. For my limited present purposes, even if it does so, I would maintain that there nonetheless remain certain major lines of continuity between the pre-1809 and the 1809-and-after Schelling.

The first of these continuities is Schelling's commitment to select features of Spinozism as he construes it. His clarifications and qualifications apropos Spinozism in the *Freiheitsschrift* testify to how sharply he had been stung by Hegel's then-fresh 1807 dismissal of the Spinozistic "night in which all cows are black."[9] Hegel belatedly, in his Berlin *Lectures on the History of Philosophy*, registers an appreciation of these clarifications and qualifications insofar as he then recognizes the *Freiheitsschrift* as "deeply speculative in character."[10]

Yet, I would maintain that, whatever caveats Schelling tacks onto his relationship with Spinoza in 1809, he nonetheless retains certain essential features of Spinozism. More generally, Schelling's occasional distance-takings from Spinoza, his scattered criticisms of Spinoza's philosophy he voices periodically both before and after 1809, are far outweighed by his frequent embracing across the span of his philosophical journey of foundational tenets associated with this key predecessor and source of inspiration. Indeed, I would maintain that Schelling's 1795 declaration in a famous letter to Hegel that "I have ... become a Spinozist!"[11] continues to hold true long after 1795.

In terms of the Schelling of the *Freiheitsschrift*, he holds onto, most importantly, the Spinozistic "*natura naturans*" versus "*natura naturata*" distinction. This distinction is terminologically recast in the *Freiheitsschrift* as the contrast between "ground" (*Grund*) and "existence" (*Existenz*), with ground as producing, creating *natura naturans* and existence as produced, created *natura naturata*[12] (this recasting likewise is visible in Schelling's subsequent *Ages of the World*[13]). Hence, Žižek's enthusiastic explicit embrace of Schelling's ground-existence distinction[14] risks being tantamount to an implicit endorsement of Spinoza's pair of *natura naturans* and *natura naturata*.

A short while ago, I alluded to an ambiguity haunting Schelling's use of the word "matter" (*die Materie*) to designate the ontological and genetic ground-zero of the "sequence of stages" (*Stufenfolge*) constituting nature as a self-unfolding dynamic. This word typically connotes for non-Schellingians the sort of things subsumed under the Spinozistic heading of *natura naturata*. These things would be individuated, noun-like objects of determinate kinds, such as the particles, atoms, molecules, cells, etc. studied by different branches of the empirical, experimental sciences of nature—with Schelling clearly distinguishing between *Naturphilosophie* as "speculative physics" from natural science as "empirical physics." Although multiple commentators try to argue that Schelling's Philosophy of Nature remains deeply respectful of and influenced by modernity's experimental sciences of nature, his speculative physics functions as independent of and authoritative over empirical physics. Indeed, as Xavier Tilliette observes, "Of *Naturphilosophie* after 1800, the envelope only is scientific; the core is speculative and religious."[15] Regardless of when one dates this purported shift in the Schellingian Philosophy of Nature (whether before, during, or after 1800), I would argue that the reduction of the scientific to serving as the non-mystical shell of a mystical (i.e., speculative and religious) kernel is licensed from the very inception of Schelling's *Naturphilosophie* in the late 1790s thanks to the Spinozistic elements at its foundations. Similarly, Daniel Breazeale faults the hybrid Platonic–Spinozistic inclinations of the early Schelling for his epistemological recklessness specifically in the guise of a cavalier disregard for "empirical evidence."[16]

For Schelling before, during, and after 1809, "matter" *qua* the ultimate *unhintergehbar* basis of all existence both natural and subjective actually is nothing other than Spinoza's *natura naturans*. Schelling rightly dismisses (eighteenth-century French) interpretations of Spinoza as a materialist.[17] He likewise, in 1830's *Einleitung in die Philosophie*, rejects materialism as incompatible with his preferred dual-aspect monism hypothesizing a fundamental Identity underlying and cutting across the difference between the material and the spiritual.[18] In this same 1830 lecture series, he stipulates that the "original matter" (*ursprüngliche Materie*) lying at the basis of all things is not anything material in the ordinary, everyday sense, but, instead, "the matter of our matter" (*die Materie unserer Materie*), a "matter" more sublime and subtle than the banal tangible stuff of quotidian experience.[19]

Whereas empirical physics (i.e., the natural sciences) deals with *natura naturata*, Schellingian speculative physics (i.e., *Naturphilosophie* as the "Spinozism of physics"[20]) deals with *natura naturans*. And, as Schelling emphasizes, *natura naturans* as pure productivity, as the flowing activity of the creative power of φύσις, is different in kind from *natura naturans* as the secondary (by-)products of this productivity, the fixed results of the underlying restless pulse of vital generative *élan*. Schelling insists on this pure productivity being independent of all its products.[21] *Natura naturata* are mere coagulations or retardations of the ever-surging dynamism of *natura naturata*. While empirical physics is limited to pondering these coagulations/retardations, only speculative physics can contemplate *natura naturans* in its purity.[22] Hence, from a Schellingian perspective, the very first emergence, the origin (*Ursprung*) as original leap (*Ur-Sprung*), is not the rise of the chemical out of the physical or the organic out of the inorganic, but the birth of material entities *qua natura naturata* out of spiritual substance *qua natura naturans* (or, in terms of the doctrine of temporality developed in the *Weltalter* manuscripts, the birth of the reigning age of the present out of that of the repressed eternal past as a time before linear chronological time).

Similarly, in the 1815 third draft of *Ages of the World*, Schelling maintains that, "the inner being of matter is spiritual in a broader sense because forces, insofar as they are something incorporeal, are undeniably something spiritual"[23] (a contention already to be found nearly verbatim in the 1813 second draft of the *Weltalter*[24] as well as the notes for the 1811 first draft of it[25]). This Schellingian spiritualization of matter is an essential part of Schelling's *Naturphilosophie* from its inception in 1797.[26] Indeed, 1797's *Ideas for a Philosophy of Nature* describes how "matter, the first foundation of all experience, becomes the most insubstantial thing we know" (*die Materie, die erste Grundlage aller Erfahrung, wird das Wesenloseste, das wir kennen*).[27] The young Schelling latches onto those then-current developments in the sciences of nature (concerning electricity, galvanism, gravitation, magnetism, optics, and the like) seeming, from his perspective, to suggest that kinetic energies and forces, rather than static and inert bodies, constitute the zero-level foundation of nature and its *Stufenfolge*.[28] As for certain witnesses of the quantum revolution in physics approximately a century later, so too for Schelling starting with his early appreciations of the scientific *avant garde* of his time: Matter itself, as the rock-bottom base of the physical universe, undergoes dematerialization at the hands of specific scientific advances, with tangible bodies losing their fundamental ontological status and decomposing into yet more fundamental incorporeal forms, powers, and fluctuations.

Schelling, in his *Naturphilosophie*, portrays this as the material becoming spiritual *qua* immaterial. This dematerialization-as-spiritualization of matter is equivalent to Schelling's identification of the primordial *Ur*-dimension of all things as *natura naturans*. Additionally, he consistently throughout his early and middle periods emphasizes that *natura naturans* is subject-like, a sort of universal subjectivity, an organism or even mind writ astronomically large, animating the entirety of creation through its activity and generative powers. And, Schelling, in his late period, reaffirms all of this in an overtly theosophical key, maintaining in line with various religious narratives that the spiritual underlies and generates the material.[29] This later Schelling even goes so far as to claim that *Naturphilosophie* proves God's existence,[30] with foundational *natura naturans* as the one-and-only Absolute Ego generating out of itself both the objectivity of *natura naturata* and the subjectivity of the human conscious "I."[31] Incidentally, Žižek, pointedly *contra* the V.I. Lenin of 1908's *Materialism and Empirio-Criticism*,[32] celebrates the quantum version of the "disappearance of matter" already trumpeted by Schelling starting in the late 1790s.[33]

For Schelling, micro-scale human subjectivity, in its self-determination and self-consciousness, is a product (indeed, the highest product) of this productive agency as a macro-scale cosmic mega-subject (whether the latter be named Nature, God, Absolute *Ich*, etc.).[34] But, what is more, he directly identifies these two subjectivities with each other. There is an equivalence in his eyes between these macro- and micro-, infinite-cosmic and finite-human, subjects. To risk anachronism through recourse to psychoanalytic language, Schelling portrays the subjectivity of singular persons as the "return of the repressed," namely, the resurfacing within the existence (*Existenz*) of *natura naturata* of the underlying ground (*Grund*) of *natura naturans*[35] (with Sigmund Freud rightly appealing to Schelling in discussing the uncanniness of instances of the return of the repressed[36]). Schelling's *Philosophy of Art* describes miracles as the appearance in the finite-empirical-temporal world of the infinite-nonempirical-eternal Absolute.[37] Free human subjects are, for him, miracles in this exact sense. Relatedly, the Schellingian subject (or "soul" [*Seele*]) is not the ego *qua* atomic individuality or idiosyncratic personhood, since the former is the embodiment amidst finite determinations of the universality of absolute infinitude.[38]

The two extreme ends of Schelling's dynamic natural *Stufenfolge*, its Alpha as *natura naturans* and its Omega as transcendental subjectivity, are made by him to converge with and merge into one another.[39] Through this joining of base and pinnacle, Schellingian emergentism presents what I have been calling a layer-doughnut model. In 1801's *Presentation of My System of Philosophy*, Schelling maintains that, "*In no process can anything enter a body that is not already there* potentially."[40] One implication of this is that all (apparent) emergences, each and every arising power/potency, would be nothing more than instances of making explicit what is always-already implicit in the primal, foundational origin itself as the seed containing everything that subsequently will blossom out of it. In truth, nothing new or in excess of the origin arises in everything that proceeds forth from this beginning, with the end itself being a rejoining and resurfacing of this very beginning. Indeed, 1800's *System of Transcendental Idealism* associates philosophical systematicity with circularity.[41]

During the early 1800s, Schelling equates the emergent power/potency of the organic in general with this micro-scale resurgence, amongst the entities and events of *natura naturata*, of the living dynamism of *natura naturans*.[42] The individual organism is a spatio-temporal grain of sand refracting the universe as a whole, namely, the cosmic organism birthing all of creation. For Schelling, this infinite organism, organicism writ large, generates not only finite organic products, but even inorganic ones too. And, what holds here for (especially sentient) life in general holds too for sapient life in particular: Human subjects are Spinoza's God (i.e., Nature as *natura naturans*) becoming conscious of itself, returning and relating to itself with the clarity of self-consciousness.[43] Schelling directly equates the dynamic productivity of speculative physics (i.e., *Natur* as per *Naturphilosophie*) with the subjectivity of philosophy (as transcendental idealism).[44]

Schelling's layer doughnut also is on prominent display in his middle-period texts favored by Žižek. In the *Freiheitsschrift*, human beings, particularly in their freedom, are depicted as points of return for the darkness of *Grund* within the light of *Existenz*[45]—recalling that Schelling recasts *natura naturans* and *natura naturata* as Ground and Existence respectively in this 1809 text. The drafts of the unfinished *Weltalter* project echo this depiction.[46]

Žižek's elaborations of his dialectical materialist version of "quantum physics with Schelling" clearly involve embracing this Schellingian layer-doughnut model. From 1996 onward, Žižek periodically affirms the soundness of this model in which human subjectivity is the return of the repressed ontological ground-zero. In Žižek's updating of Schelling, this ontological ground-zero is identified as the domain of quantum indeterminacy prior to the collapse of the wave function. In the Schellingian vocabulary redeployed by Žižek, this collapse amounts to the transition from *Grund* to *Existence*, from shadowy proto-reality to the constituted being(s) of determinate reality.[47]

More recently, in both 2017's *Incontinence of the Void*[48] and 2020's *Sex and the Failed Absolute*, Žižek has taken to linking Hegel's logical "realm of shadows" (*Reich der Schatten, Schattenreich*)[49] with the proto-reality of quantum indeterminacy. *Sex and the Failed Absolute* features Žižek's most sustained discussions of this linkage. Therein, he proposes in this vein:

> If Hegel were to rewrite his system today, its three main parts would no longer have been: logic—nature—spirit, but: quantum real (pre-

ontological virtual space of quantum waves)—reality—spirit. One should note that the passage from each level to the next one is not simply some kind of "progress" but also involves a failure (loss, restraint): our ordinary reality emerges through the collapse of the wave function, i.e., through the erasure of virtual possibilities; reality gradually develops through life to the explosion of thought/spirit/subject—however, this explosion of spirit is also to a deadlock of animal life. Man is a failed animal, human consciousness is primordially the awareness of limitation and finitude.[50]

Of course, the early-twentieth-century overturning of the worldview of Newtonian physics radically alters the notions of space and time available to Hegel in his own era. Nonetheless, from what likely would have been Hegel's perspective had he lived to see this overturning, quantum mechanics remains within the domain of nature. This is because it still deals with spatio-temporal objects and processes despite its drastic departures from familiar mid-level, human-scale experiences and intuitions. Hence, Hegel would see Žižek's "quantum real" not as a replacement for *Logik*, but as a part of an appropriately revised *Naturphilosophie* (with Hegel himself already signaling the openness of his Philosophy of Nature to revisions in light of unforeseeable scientific developments,[51] such as the toppling of Newtonian physics in the opening years of the twentieth century).

In fact, Hegel characterizes Logic as a "realm of shadows" not so as to propose a Spinozistic–Schellingian ontology of a dark Ground-before-Existence, but, on the contrary, so as to warn against interpreting the field of the logical as constituting in and of itself a full-fledged ontology. As an Aristotelian hylomorphist rather than a Platonic metaphysical realist, Hegel asserts that the categories of *Logik* acquire actual ontological weight only if and when they are instantiated and realized within the myriad moments of *Realphilosophie* (i.e., *Naturphilosophie* and *Geistesphilosophie*, as per the second and third volumes respectively of the *Encyclopedia of the Philosophical Sciences*). On their own, the categories of Hegelian Logic merely determine what makes the Real intelligible. They delineate the conditions of possibility for the in-principle knowability of both objectivity and subjectivity as well as both *Natur und Geist*.

One implication of the preceding is that, for Hegel to accept Žižek's proposal of replacing the realm of the logical with that of the quantum in a new permutation of Hegel's encyclopedic System, quantum mechanics would have to be able to furnish out of itself the epistemological-transcendental explanatory framework provided by Hegel's own *Logik* in its intimate, indissoluble relationship with his *Realphilosophie*. Žižek has not (at least, not yet) explained how quantum physics might be able to take on playing this epistemological-transcendental role. Does his recent talk of moving "beyond the transcendental"[52] indicate an intention to refuse to articulate such an explanation? In substituting quantum physics for Logic, is Žižek also intentionally purging Hegelianism of the transcendentalist features and functions of *Logik*? If so, unanswered questions loom about the epistemology accompanying Žižek's materialism. This accompaniment is requisite on both Kantian and Hegelian grounds—with Kant and Hegel sharing in common a rejection as epistemologically indefensible of Fichte's and Schelling's recourses to intellectual intuition.

It must be acknowledged that Žižek is well aware of the tensions between himself and traditional Hegelian philosophy along the lines I just sketched. For instance, in *Sex and the Failed Absolute*, he states, "This pure pre-ontological real (and not logic, as Hegel thought) is the 'shadowy world' that precedes reality."[53] A couple of paragraphs later, Žižek avers that his own quantum ontology involves preferring Schelling over Hegel—specifically, the author of the 1809 *Freiheitsschrift*, with its distinction between Ground and Existence.[54] This Žižekian preference entails once again embracing Schelling's layer-doughnut model of ontological emergentism (with *Sex and the Failed Absolute* continuing to endorse this model[55]).

Immediately after affirming his favoring of Schelling in connection with quantum mechanics, Žižek addresses the apparent antagonisms between the Schellingian and Hegelian philosophies that both serve him as crucial sources of inspiration. He does so by reinterpreting the very opening of Hegel's *Science of Logic* so as to permit a rapprochement between Hegel and Schelling in relation to a dialectical materialist appropriation of quantum physics. On Žižek's interpretation, the first words of the *Science of Logic*'s main body—therein, "The Doctrine of Being" begins with the line "*Being, pure being*, without any further determination" (Sein, reines Sein,—ohne alle weitere Bestimmung)[56]—ought to be read as announcing that Hegelian Logic is based upon a "minimal idealization" of a "pre-ontological X."[57] Implicitly defanging the later Schelling's critique of Hegel's Logic,[58] Žižek recasts the logical starting point of the entire Hegelian System as a moment identical with the Schellingian transition from the indeterminate Real of unprethinkable Ground (*unvordenklicher Grund*) to the determinate Ideal of cognizable Existence.[59]

However, what numerous commentators on the *Science of Logic* have not noticed to date is that the opening line of "The Doctrine of Being" in the *Science of Logic* contains a subtle but direct reference to Schelling. The latter, in *Philosophy and Religion*, writes of "*pure absoluteness, without any further determination*" (reine Absolutheit, ohne alle weitere Bestimmung).[60] The identical wording between Schelling's 1804 *Philosophy and Religion* and Hegel's 1812–1816 *Science of Logic* is almost certainly no coincidence.

Associating the "pure absoluteness" of the early Schelling's *Identitätsphilosophie* (as well as the *natura naturans* of Schellingian *Naturphilosophie*) with indeterminate "pure being," the very opening of Hegelian *Logik* seeks to show, among other things, that where Schelling intends to begin systematic philosophizing cannot actually serve as a proper starting point. Any such mere, sheer indeterminacy (*ohne alle weitere*

Bestimmung) promptly succumbs to a dialectical-speculative implosion (as demonstrated by the opening triad of the logical moments of Being, Nothing and Becoming). Hence, the very initiation of Hegel's Logic harbors within itself an installment in the post-1807 critical feud between Hegel and Schelling. This complicates Žižek's maneuver, in *Sex and the Failed Absolute*, of utilizing Hegel's line about "*Being, pure being*, without any further determination" as a means of bridging the evident divide between the Schelling of the Ground-Existence distinction and Hegel.

Furthermore, the end of Hegel's mature Logic, with its transition from the logical to the Real (first as *Natur*),[61] reveals that the true beginning of full-fledged ontology is not the false start of any sort of pure indeterminacy, including in the guise of Schelling's Absolute Identity or Indifference *qua* the infinite, intellectually intuited Ground of *natura naturans* (incidentally, the later Schelling's attacks concerning the transition from the logical to the natural in Hegel's System are based on a misreading according to which the formal categories of Hegelian *Logik* are free-standing metaphysical realities preexisting in time what would be a subsequently arising extra-logical Real demoted to a lesser ontological status by comparison with the categorial forms of Logic in and of themselves[62]). Instead, the Hegelian ontology of the Real (as per *Realphilosophie* divided into *Naturphilosophie* and *Geistesphilosophie*) arises on the basis provided by objectively given spatio-temporal nature, first at the level of "mechanics" as falling under the explanatory jurisdiction of empirical physics (rather than the [pseudo-] explanatory jurisdiction of something like Schelling's "speculative physics"). That is to say, Hegel's ontological emergentism, unlike that of Schelling, begins with the light of the dialectically-speculatively thinkable existence of *natura naturata* as natural objectivities knowable thanks to (onto-)logical categories, rather than beginning with the darkness of the intellectually intuited unprethinkable Ground of *natura naturans* as spiritual subjectivity ineffable save for the confabulations (or *Schwärmerei*) of mythologies, religions, and theosophies.[63] A Hegelian Philosophy of Nature lets itself look forward to future scientific discoveries for further illumination of its subject matters. A Schellingian Philosophy of Nature ends up looking backward to various spiritualistic fictions receding far into humanity's past.

At this juncture, the differences between Hegel's and Schelling's emergentisms, between the former's layer-cake model and the latter's layer-doughnut one, become clear and crucial. As I explain elsewhere,[64] Hegelian *Naturphilosophie* is designed so as to thread the needle between the extremes of either an ontology of nothing but mindless matter (such as a reductionist or eliminativist worldview based on Newtonian mechanical physics) or one of matterless mind (such as variants of hylozoism, panpsychism, pantheism, vitalism, and the like). A general ontology of mindless matter refuses to explain the *Befreiungskampf* genesis of *Geist* out of *Natur*, explaining away the spiritual (i.e., sentience, sapience, mindedness, and like-mindedness) as epiphenomenal, fictive, hallucinatory, illusory, etc. For Hegel, this worldview one-sidedly absolutizes mechanics, physics, and/or inorganic chemistry, with their corresponding regional ontologies representative of specific levels (but specific levels only) of a many-layered natural and spiritual Real.

Correlatively but conversely, a general ontology of matterless mind, with equal but opposed one-sidedness, absolutizes organics and/or the spheres of the humanly spiritual (i.e., the domains and accompanying regional ontologies covered by Hegel's *Geistesphilosophie*). Such a general ontology also, like its opposed general ontology of mindless matter, refuses to explain the *Befreiungskampf* genesis of *Geist* out of *Natur*. This is because, for it, no emergence of life and/or mind actually occurs. Instead, they are purported to be immediately given from the get-go, supposedly present as underived, factical *Ur*-elements.

From Hegel's non-one-sided perspective, *Geist* is neither nowhere nor everywhere. It is a set of select strata that arise from pre/non-spiritual (i.e., natural) dimensions of being(s). Moreover, these mindless pre/non-subjective dimensions are knowable in themselves thanks to their inherent forms and sometimes come to be really known by the subjectivities that happen to have been eventually precipitated out of evolving nature. The Hegelian emergentist layer cake, as per his ontology *qua Realphilosophie* (an ontology whose epistemological possibility conditions are laid down by *Logik*), starts with the pre/non-spiritual objectivity of spatio-temporal *natura naturata* as accessible to empirical, experimental investigation by such disciplines as the natural sciences (i.e., Schelling's "empirical physics"). It ends with the spiritual subjectivity of humans and their social histories as comprehensible through philosophical versions of such disciplines as anthropology, phenomenology, psychology, law, ethics, politics, history, art, and religion. *Geist* neither never exists nor always exists. It comes to be, namely, it genuinely emerges.

Hegel would view Schelling's layer doughnut emergentism as pseudo-emergentism. This is due to the fact that the particular Spinozistic intuitions and inspirations relied upon by Schelling throughout the entirety of his long career commit him to a fundamental ontology of what ultimately would be matterless mind (i.e., spiritualized, de-materialized matter as the creative, productive agency of *natura naturans*). Matter *qua natura naturata* (i.e., determine physical entities and events situated in objectively real space and time) forms the ground-zero level in Hegel's emergentism, with the top layer of this cake (i.e., sapient human mindedness and like-mindedness) being placed at a distance from and not simply rejoining its base layer. For Schelling, on the other hand, a living, spiritual, subject-like *natura naturans* (as *Grund*) is simultaneously the Alpha and, through its irruptive return within the constituted fields of *natura naturata* (as *Existenz*), also the Omega of his doughnut, the point where two extremes unite in a single layer.[65] The "emergence" of Spirit out of Nature in Schellingian ontology is a pseudo-emergence insofar as it is not truly the genesis of the posterior out of the prior, the new out of the old, the higher out of the lower.

The Hegelian complaint against Schelling's ontologically hylozoist, panpsychist, pantheistic, and/or vitalist layer doughnut model would be that, as Lacan might put it, the rabbit Schelling pulls out of the hat is the one he put there in the first place.⁶⁶ Lacan usually employs this line about the rabbit and the hat to disparage modelings of psychoanalytic metapsychology on natural-scientific energetics (particularly physics with its constants and the conservation of energy). This disparagement also would be applicable to Schelling, especially considering Schelling's blending of energies, forces, and the like from the sciences of nature with Spinoza's *natura naturans* (a blending pioneered by J.G. Herder in his *God, Some Conversations*⁶⁷). Yet, on one occasion, Lacan depicts the "absolute knowing" (*das absolute Wissen*) of the concluding chapter of Hegel's *Phenomenology of Spirit* as itself a rabbit Hegel sneaks into his hat earlier in the *Phenomenology* through sleight of hand so as to pull it out at the grand finale.⁶⁸ Setting aside debates about how fair or not Lacan's jab at the *Phenomenology* is, Hegel's emergentist *Realphilosophie*, unlike enduring central features of Schelling's (pseudo-)emergentist metaphysics, does not smuggle the rabbit of *Geist* into the hat of *Natur* so as subsequently to feign having an explanation for the genesis of the spiritual out of the natural.

Schelling passes off a dubious anthropomorphization of nature as a satisfactory account of anthropogenesis. By contrast, Hegel's layer-cake emergentist model offers an arguably more satisfactory account of anthropogenesis while simultaneously refusing to anthropomorphize nature. When Hegel insists on characterizing *Natur* as alterity and externality vis-à-vis *Geist*,⁶⁹ one implication of this insistence is that pre-subjective nature must be regarded as radically non-subjective. That is to say, this is tantamount to a Hegelian repudiation of any sort of hylozoist, panpsychist, pantheistic, and/or vitalist *Naturphilosophie* (including Schelling's own permutations of his Philosophy of Nature—by 1811, in both the first version of the *Weltalter* as well as in a contemporaneous text polemically responding to a Jacobian charge of atheism, Schelling basically admits to being an idealistic pantheist⁷⁰). Of course, Spinoza himself forcefully forbids any anthropomorphizing of *Deus sive natura* as infinite substance.⁷¹ But, Schelling's linkage of his borrowings from Spinoza with his own layer-doughnut emergentism leads him to violate flagrantly the Spinozistic ban on anthropomorphizing. This violation is epitomized by, for instance, Schelling's animistic, panpsychist talk in the 1813 second draft of *The Ages of the World* of the history of the universe as that of "the development of an actual, living essence" (i.e., *Deus sive natura*) in which "the first or oldest of essences" is "primordially alive."⁷²

Another anti-Spinozism line from the preface to 1807's *Phenomenology of Spirit*, in addition to the one about "the night in which all cows are black," lies at the origins of the parting of ways between the former friends and collaborators Hegel and Schelling. This is the line according to which one must conceive "the True, not only as *Substance*, but equally as *Subject*" (*das Wahre nicht als* Substanz, *sondern ebensosehr als* Subjekt).[73] Schelling took it personally despite Hegel insisting that this, along with the cows remark, was a swipe aimed exclusively at Schelling's less talented followers rather than at Schelling himself.[74] Regardless of Hegel's own private intentions, Schelling was right to feel wounded. Hegel's thesis about substance-also-as-subject expresses a legitimate objection and alternative to Schelling's strong Spinozistic leanings.

The two little words "*sondern ebensosehr*" (but equally) in the *Phenomenology*'s "*nicht als* Substanz, *sondern ebensosehr als* Subjekt" signal a huge difference between Hegel and Schelling. Schelling's Spinozism and the layer-doughnut model tied to it amount to asserting that subject simply is substance, with both *Subjekt* and *Substanz* as one-and-the-same *natura naturans*. Against this Schellingian equation of the substantial and the subjective, Hegel's "*sondern ebensosehr*" indicates a non-identity between these two concept-terms. In other words, the "also" in the Hegelian substance-also-as-subject marks an ineliminable difference-in-kind between these two sides, with the emergent layer of the subject remaining irreducible to the layers of pre/non-subjective substance from which it arose (hence a layer cake instead of a layer doughnut). Subjectivity, itself a sublation (*als Aufhebung*) of substantiality, is a spirituality that really emerges from naturality, with the latter not already containing within itself the former.

Again and again, Schelling complains, throughout his writings, about modern philosophy remaining in the grip of stubbornly persistent dichotomizing tendencies.[75] He bemoans a preference, that of the "reflection" (*Reflexion*) of the understanding (*Verstand*), for thinking in terms of starkly black-and-white dualisms (a form of thinking allegedly transcended by reason [*Vernunft*] proper). Yet, ironically, Schelling's spiritualization of nature, with its "disappearance of matter" through the dissolution/decomposition of inert material bodies into dynamic energies, forces, etc., covertly relies upon precisely the sort of either-or dualism he so frequently decries. For Schelling, insofar as natural science reveals the basest dimensions of nature to be kinetic energies (for him, particularly those of electricity, galvanism, gravitation, light, and magnetism) rather than static entities (such as the elementary building blocks of atoms, corpuscles, elements, and the like), this means that nature is, at root, spiritual and subject-like (as active, fluid *natura naturans*) rather than material and object-like (as passive, fixed *natura naturata*).

But, this Schellingian inference trades upon a false dichotomy appearing in multiple terminological guises, including: *natura naturans* versus *natura naturata*; productivity versus product; spirit versus matter; mind versus body; and subject versus object. Just because the zero-level foundations of the physical universe, whether as the energies and forces of the natural sciences of Schelling's era or as the quantum phenomena (or even the ephemeral, vibrating strings of string theory) of current physics, do not resemble the mid-sized dry goods of human sensory-perceptual experience does not mean that they are therefore to be identified as subjects (*qua* the diametrical opposites of objects). Schelling's retention, inconsistent with his avowed anti-dualism, of a false dichotomy between the mental/spiritual and the bodily/material misleads him into a fundamental, general ontology of matterless mind (i.e., scientifically and philosophically dubious hylozoism, panpsychism, pantheism, and/or vitalism). For instance, this inconsistency is flagrantly on display in a single three-paragraph stretch of the 1813 version of *The Ages of the World*, with a paragraph complaining about dualistic thinking sandwiched in-between two paragraphs dematerializing matter by relying on a dualism according to which what is not bodily is spiritual.[76]

In a bad version of Hegel's positing a presupposition, a version akin to Lacan's rabbit and hat, Schelling pretends to posit the subjective as emerging out of the natural. But, Schelling's posit here presupposes the subjective as non-emergently always-already there within the natural from the outset. Schelling's pseudo-emergentist conjuring trick relies on deceptive spiritualist cheating. This should be somewhat troubling for Žižek, given his interlinked commitments to both Hegelianism and materialism.

With respect to Žižek, the cautionary case of Schelling's spiritualism ought to encourage him, especially in his engagements with matters quantum, to opt for a more Hegelian than Schellingian form of *Naturphilosophie*. At one point in *Sex and the Failed Absolute*, he indeed appears to do so:

> the big problem is not how we can pass from the classic universe to the universe of quantum waves, but exactly the opposite one—why and how the quantum universe itself immanently requires the collapse of the wave function, its "de-coherence" into the classic universe, i.e., why and how the collapse is inherent to the quantum universe. Instead of just standing in awe before the wonder of the quantum universe, we should turn around our perspective and perceive as the true wonder the rise of our "ordinary" spatio-temporal reality. It is not only that there is no classic reality which is not sustained by blurred quantum fluctuations; one should add that there is no quantum universe which is not always-already hooked onto a piece of classic reality. The problem of the collapse of the wave function through the act of measurement is that it has to be formulated in classic, not quantum, terms ... a measurement formulated in terms of classic reality is necessary for quantum mechanics itself to be consistent, it is an addition of the classic reality which "sutures" the quantum field.[77]

My assessment of this passage will be limited by my lack of expert knowledge of quantum physics. What I have to say about it concerns its implications for Žižek's philosophical position as it relates to German idealism. In particular, the above quotation calls for being read in relation to Schelling's and Hegel's divergent arrangements of modal categories.

To cut a long story short, Schelling and Hegel each privilege a different category of modality in terms of the fundaments of their metaphysical systems. Across the shifting landscape of his corpus, Schelling prioritizes possibility/potentiality as ultimate[78] (despite intermittent, and inconsistent, affirmations of the primacy of contingency and/as factical givenness during Schelling's middle and late periods[79]). This prioritization is reflected by Žižek's Schellingian recourses to the collapse of the wave function in quantum mechanics, in which the *Grund* of a teeming multitude of possible states contracts and distills itself into the single settled state of *Existenz* as actual reality. In this picture, possibility precedes and generates actuality.

Hegel is diametrically opposed to Schelling's (or anyone else's) privileging of possibility as the metaphysically most fundamental of the modal categories, a privileging already entrenched in German modern philosophy due to the influence of Leibnizian–Wolffian scholastic metaphysics. First and foremost, Hegel, in the last stretch of "The Doctrine of Essence" in his mature Logic, makes the actual (as *Wirklichkeit*), as also contingent, the primordial grounding modal category of his metaphysics. Both possibility and necessity are, for Hegel, to be treated as supervening upon the foundations laid by contingent actuality.[80]

Žižek rightly recognizes the priority enjoyed by the modality of contingency for Hegel. This enormously important Žižekian recognition runs contrary to the standard misreading of Hegel as a metaphysician of necessity, a philosopher for whom Absolute Spirit as a God-like mega-Mind teleologically orchestrates from above and in advance the fateful trajectory of all reality and history. Additionally, Žižek's restoration of *Zufälligkeit* to its central place in Hegel's thinking helps implicitly to challenge the criticisms from the later Schelling of the "positive philosophy" to the effect that Hegel surreptitiously presupposes without successfully positing the original contingent facticity of the Real (i.e., the "thatness" of there ever being something rather than nothing).[81] This late-Schellingian objection to Hegel's philosophy looks to be even more fully refuted once one appreciates that it is contingent actuality, not just contingency, that serves as the Hegelian Ur-modality. This means that Hegel gives the facticity of Schelling's positive-philosophical "thatness" a place within the very heart of *Logik*, in addition to it playing multiple roles within the *Realphilosophie*.

To return to the preceding block quotation from *Sex and the Failed Absolute*, Žižek now can be seen there to proffer a more Hegelian than Schellingian interpretation of the collapse of the wave function in quantum mechanics. At certain moments in this passage, it sounds as though Žižek is sticking to his Schelling-inspired interpretation in which the Ground of quantum possibilities comes first, secondarily giving rise to the Existence of classic actuality. However, by the close of this quotation, it is evident that, at least epistemologically if not also ontologically, Žižek reverses the Schellingian collapse sequence, with the *Grund* of pre-collapse possibilities having to be seen as shadowy outgrowths accompanying the *Existenz* of post-collapse *Wirklichkeit*. This reversal is that of Schelling's possibility-before-actuality into Hegel's actuality-before-possibility.

Hegel, with the greater epistemological conscientiousness he, unlike Schelling, inherits from Kant, at least would insist specifically on the intelligibility of the quantum Real being conditioned by classic reality. Žižek is being Hegelian rather than Schellingian when he insists upon this point ("a measurement formulated in terms of classic reality is necessary for quantum mechanics itself to be consistent, it is an addition of the classic reality which 'sutures' the quantum field"). Like everyone else, I can only guess at what Hegel might have made of quantum physics had he lived to witness it develop.

As for Žižek, I suspect that *Sex and the Failed Absolute* contains a sophisticated effort to approach quantum physics in a manner bringing together aspects of both Schelling's and Hegel's philosophies (a synthesis perhaps resembling Schelling's integration of the ontology of *Naturphilosophie* with the epistemology of transcendental idealism specifically in his 1800 *System of Transcendental Idealism*). More precisely, I am left with the hunch that Žižek wishes to couple a more Schellingian rendition of a quantum ontology with a more Hegelian epistemology (taking into account Hegel's doctrine of modal categories) qualifying and supporting this same ontology (with this effort at coupling deliberately bringing about a blurring of the lines of division between Schelling and Hegel). But, I might be wrong about this.

Much later in *Sex and the Failed Absolute*, Žižek remarks in an endnote that, "One should always bear in mind the scientific strength of so-called reductionism: Is science not at its strongest when it explains how a 'higher' quality emerges out of the 'lowest' ones?"[82] Žižek's use of the word "emerges" here calls for some disambiguation, particularly considering his recourse to the term "reductionism" in the same sentence. Apropos emergentism, it is typical to distinguish between multiple permutations of it in the form of differences of degree between "weak" and "strong" emergentisms. And these differences have everything to do with reductionism. Weak emergentisms admit the potential for (or even accomplishment of) reductive explanatory strategies exhaustively accounting for higher-level properties on the basis of lower-level ones. By contrast, strong emergentisms are vigorously anti-reductive, maintaining that higher emergent strata are irreducible to, even inexplicable in terms of, lower ones. Such higher emergent strata come to enjoy a certain amount of independence involving self-sufficient structural dynamics not to be found in the distinct structural dynamics of other strata below.

Žižek's just-quoted endnote comment makes it look as though the emergentism he is referring to and approves of is a weak variant compatible with scientific reductionism. Consistent with this, both Schelling himself, on my preceding reconstructions of his philosophical positions, and the Žižekian shotgun marriage of Schelling with quantum physics can be construed as licensing (or, in Žižek's case, at least risking to license) the reduction of the Existence of spiritual subject to the Ground of natural substance (whether this *Grund* be Spinoza's *natura naturans*, the forces of early-nineteenth-century physics and chemistry, or quantum mechanics). Given Žižek's growing insistence that his "quantum physics with Schelling" is central to his dialectical materialism, my critique is tantamount to saying that Žižek cannot hold onto everything he is trying to bring together, namely, Schelling, Hegel, dialectical materialism, and quantum physics. One to two of these things needs to be jettisoned for the sake of consistency. Most pointedly, the combination of Schelling and quantum physics bottoms out in one or another form of reductionism inconsistent with the rest of Žižek's philosophical agenda. With Schelling, one ultimately gets spiritualist reductionism (as anthropomorphism, hylozoism, panpsychism, pantheism, and/or vitalism). With quantum mechanics alone (i.e., minus the Schelling), one is in danger of endorsing physicalist reductionism. Only one of these options (i.e., physicalist reductionism) is materialist, and neither are dialectical.

Yet, numerous other facets of Žižek's thinking, facets bound up with his admirable endeavor to "re-actualize" for today the radically autonomous, *Cogito*-like subjectivity of classical German idealism, suggest that what he truly needs and wants is a strong-emergentist Hegelian layer-cake model whose anti-reductive strength goes so far as to posit the casually efficacious reality of so-called "top-down causation." The weak-emergentist Schellingian layer doughnut model, with its reductive Spinozistic spirit monism,[83] provides none of this. It delivers neither an authentic (dialectical) materialism nor a theory of denaturalized subjectivity as self-relating negativity. These are both desiderata of Žižek's philosophizing, things I too desire. Hence, I would encourage him to join me in ordering Hegel's cake instead of Schelling's doughnut, whether with or without a side of quantum physics.

Notes

1 Adrian Johnston, *Adventures in Transcendental Materialism: Dialogues with Contemporary Thinkers* (Edinburgh: Edinburgh University Press, 2014), 139–83.

2 Slavoj Žižek, *Absolute Recoil: Towards a New Foundation of Dialectical Materialism* (London: Verso, 2014), 221–6; Slavoj Žižek, *Disparities* (London: Bloomsbury, 2016), 38–53.

3 Adrian Johnston, "Interview about *Adventures in Transcendental Materialism: Dialogues with Contemporary Thinkers* with Graham Harman for Edinburgh University Press," Edinburgh University Press, April 2014. Available online: http://www.euppublishing.com (accessed August 17, 2021); Adrian Johnston, "Confession of a Weak Reductionist: Responses to Some Recent Criticisms of My Materialism." In *Neuroscience and Critique: Exploring the Limits of the Neurological Turn*, eds. Jan De Vos and Ed Pluth (New York: Routledge, 2015), 141–70; Adrian Johnston, *A New German Idealism: Hegel, Žižek, and Dialectical Materialism* (New York: Columbia University Press, 2018), 129–86.

4   G.W.F. Hegel, *Phenomenology of Spirit*, trans. A.V. Miller (Oxford: Oxford University Press, 1977), 9.
5   Baruch Spinoza, *Short Treatise on God, Man, and His Well-Being*. In Baruch Spinoza, *Spinoza: Complete Works*, ed. Michael L. Morgan, trans. Samuel Shirley (Indianapolis: Hackett, 2002), Chapter VIII (58), Chapter IX (58–59); Baruch Spinoza, *Ethics*. In Spinoza, *Spinoza: Complete Works*, Part I, Proposition 29, Scholium (234), Part I, Proposition 31 (234), Part I, Proposition 31, Proof (235); Baruch Spinoza, "The Letters: Letter 9: To the learned young man Simon de Vries, from B.d.S., February 1663 (?)." In Spinoza, *Spinoza: Complete Works*, 782.
6   Slavoj Žižek, *Hegel in a Wired Brain* (London: Bloomsbury, 2020), 2.
7   F.W.J. Schelling, *Philosophical Investigations into the Essence of Human Freedom*, trans. Jeff Love and Johannes Schmidt (Albany: State University of New York Press, 2006), 21–2, 29–33.
8   Slavoj Žižek, *The Indivisible Remainder: An Essay on Schelling and Related Matters* (London: Verso, 1996), 189–236.
9   Schelling, *Philosophical Investigations into the Essence of Human Freedom*, 12–13, 16–17.
10 G.W.F. Hegel, *Lectures on the History of Philosophy: Volume Three*, trans. E.S. Haldane and Frances H. Simson (New York: Humanities Press, 1955), 514.
11 F.W.J. Schelling, "Letter to Hegel: February 4, 1795." In G.W.F. Hegel, *Hegel: The Letters*, trans. Clark Butler and Christiane Seiler (Bloomington: Indiana University Press, 1984), 32.
12 Schelling, *Philosophical Investigations into the Essence of Human Freedom*, 29, 68–9.
13 F.W.J. Schelling, "Notes and Fragments to the First Book of *The Ages of the World: The Past*." In F.W.J. Schelling, *The Ages of the World, Book One: The Past (Original Version, 1811)*, trans. Joseph P. Lawrence (Albany: State University of New York Press, 2019), 205, 224, 234, 238–9; F.W.J. Schelling, *The Ages of the World: (Fragment) from the handwritten remains, Third Version (c. 1815)*, trans. Jason M. Wirth (Albany: State University of New York Press, 2000), 20–21, 56–60, 62, 88.
14 Žižek, *The Indivisible Remainder*, 20, 40; Slavoj Žižek, "The Abyss of Freedom." In Slavoj Žižek and F.W.J. Schelling, *The Abyss of Freedom/Ages of the World* (Ann Arbor: University of Michigan Press, 1997), 5–8; Slavoj Žižek, *The Plague of Fantasies* (London: Verso, 1997), 208; Slavoj Žižek, *The Ticklish Subject: The Absent Centre of Political Ontology* (London: Verso, 1999), 55, 87–8; Slavoj Žižek, *Organs without Bodies: On Deleuze and Consequences* (New York: Routledge, 2004), 75; Slavoj Žižek, "Hegel, Lacan, Deleuze: Three Strange Bedfellows." In Slavoj Žižek, *Interrogating the Real*, eds. Rex Butler and Scott Stephens (London: Continuum, 2005), 190–1; Slavoj Žižek, *Sex and the Failed Absolute* (London: Bloomsbury, 2020), 284.
15 Xavier Tilliette, *Schelling, une philosophie en devenir, 1: Le système vivant* (Paris: Vrin, 1992, second edition), 308.
16 Daniel Breazeale, "'Exhibiting the particular in the universal': Philosophical construction and intuition in Schelling's Philosophy of Identity (1801–1804)."

In *Interpreting Schelling: Critical Essays*, ed. Lara Ostaric (Cambridge: Cambridge University Press, 2014), 113.
17 F.W.J. Schelling, *Ueber das Wesen deutscher Wissenschaft*. In F.W.J. Schelling, *Ausgewählte Schriften: Band 4, 1807–1834*, ed. Manfred Frank (Frankfurt am Main: Suhrkamp, 1985), 17–18.
18 F.W.J. Schelling, *Einleitung in die Philosophie*, ed. Walter E. Ehrhardt (Stuttgart-Bad Cannstatt: Frommann-Holzboog, 1989), 2, 57.
19 Schelling, *Einleitung in die Philosophie*, 50.
20 F.W.J. Schelling, "Introduction to the Outline of a System of the Philosophy of Nature, or, On the Concept of Speculative Physics and the Internal Organization of a System of This Science." In F.W.J. Schelling, *First Outline of a System of the Philosophy of Nature*, trans. Keith R. Peterson (Albany: State University of New York Press, 2004), 194–5.
21 Schelling, *First Outline of a System of the Philosophy of Nature*, 76; Hans Heinz Holz, "Der Begriff der Natur in Schellings spekulativem System: Zum Einfluß von Leibniz auf Schelling." In *Natur und geschichtlicher Prozeß: Studien zur Naturphilosophie F.W.J. Schellings*, ed. Hans Jörg Sandkühler (Frankfurt am Main: Suhrkamp, 1984), 206; S.J. McGrath, *The Dark Ground of Spirit: Schelling and the Unconscious* (New York: Routledge, 2012), 85.
22 Schelling, "Introduction to the Outline of a System of the Philosophy of Nature, or, On the Concept of Speculative Physics and the Internal Organization of a System of This Science," 201–2, 217, 229; F.W.J. Schelling, *System der gesammten Philosophie und der Naturphilosophie insbesondere*. In F.W.J. Schelling, *Ausgewählte Schriften: Band 3, 1804–1806*, ed. Manfred Frank (Frankfurt am Main: Suhrkamp, 1985), 275.
23 Schelling, *The Ages of the World: Third Version (c. 1815)*, 61.
24 F.W.J. Schelling, *Ages of the World (second draft, 1813)*, trans. Judith Norman. In Slavoj Žižek and F.W.J. Schelling, *The Abyss of Freedom/Ages of the World* (Ann Arbor: University of Michigan Press, 1997), 148, 150–1, 157.
25 Schelling, "Notes and Fragments to the First Book of *The Ages of the World: The Past*," 230, 237.
26 F.W.J. Schelling, "Treatise Explicatory of the Idealism in the *Science of Knowledge*." In F.W.J. Schelling, *Idealism and the Endgame of Theory: Three Essays by F.W.J. Schelling*, trans. Thomas Pfau (Albany: State University of New York Press, 1994), 88; F.W.J. Schelling, *Philosophy of Revelation: The 1841–42 Berlin Lectures*. In F.W.J. Schelling, *Philosophy of Revelation (1841–42) and Related Texts*, trans. Klaus Ottmann (Thompson: Springer, 2020), 281; Reinhard Lauth, *Die Entstehung von Schellings Identitätsphilosophie in der Auseinandersetzung mit Fichtes Wissenschaftslehre* (Freiburg-München: Karl Alber, 1975), 194–5; Wolfram Hogrebe, *Prädikation und Genesis: Metaphysik als Fundamentalheuristik im Ausgang von Schellings »Die Weltalter«* (Frankfurt am Main: Suhrkamp, 1989), 33–4; Wolfgang Bonsiepen, *Die Begründung einer Naturphilosophie bei Kant, Schelling, Fries und Hegel* (Frankfurt am Main: Vittorio Klostermann, 1997), 281.
27 F.W.J. Schelling, *Ideas for a Philosophy of Nature*, trans. Errol E. Harris and Peter Heath (Cambridge: Cambridge University Press, 1988), 17.

28 F.W.J. Schelling, *System of Transcendental Idealism*, trans. Peter Heath (Charlottesville: University Press of Virginia, 1978), 6, 30; John H. Zammito, *The Gestation of German Biology: Philosophy and Physiology from Stahl to Schelling* (Chicago: University of Chicago Press, 2018), 305–6.

29 Schelling, *Einleitung in die Philosophie*, 111.

30 Ibid., 37.

31 Ibid., 55–6, 100, 110–11, 114.

32 V.I. Lenin, *Materialism and Empirio-Criticism* (Peking: Foreign Languages, 1972), 308–18.

33 Žižek, *The Indivisible Remainder*, 165, 230–1; Žižek, *Organs without Bodies*, 24–5; Slavoj Žižek, *The Parallax View* (Cambridge: MIT Press, 2006), 165, 239; Slavoj Žižek, *Less than Nothing: Hegel and the Shadow of Dialectical Materialism* (London: Verso, 2012), 807, 929; Žižek, *Absolute Recoil*, 5, 73; Adrian Johnston, *Žižek's Ontology: A Transcendental Materialist Theory of Subjectivity* (Evanston: Northwestern University Press, 2008), 200–3.

34 F.W.J. Schelling, *Ist eine Philosophie der Geschichte möglich?*. In F.W.J. Schelling, *Ausgewählte Schriften: Band 1, 1794–1800*, ed. Manfred Frank (Frankfurt am Main: Suhrkamp, 1985), 301; Schelling, *System of Transcendental Idealism*, 17; F.W.J. Schelling, *Presentation of My System of Philosophy*. In J.G. Fichte and F.W.J. Schelling, *The Philosophical Rupture between Fichte and Schelling: Selected Texts and Correspondence*, trans. and eds. Michael G. Vater and David W. Wood (Albany: State University of New York Press, 2012), 165, 201–3; F.W.J. Schelling, "On Construction in Philosophy," trans. Andrew A. Davis and Alexi I. Kukeljevic, *Epoché*, 12 (2008): 284; Schelling, *Ages of the World (second draft, 1813)*, 119, 136, 140; Schelling, *Einleitung in die Philosophie*, 42–3, 51, 53, 124; Schelling, *Philosophy of Revelation*, 81–2.

35 Schelling, "Notes and Fragments to the First Book of *The Ages of the World: The Past*," 172–5, 239; F.W.J. Schelling, *Ueber die Natur der Philosophie als Wissenschaft*. In Schelling, *Ausgewählte Schriften: Band 4, 1807–1834*, 389, 396–7, 402.

36 Sigmund Freud, "The Uncanny." In Sigmund Freud, *The Standard Edition of the Complete Psychological Works of Sigmund Freud*, 24 volumes, ed. and trans. James Strachey, in collaboration with Anna Freud, assisted by Alix Strachey and Alan Tyson (London: Hogarth Press and the Institute of Psycho-Analysis, 1953–1974), SE 17: 219–52.

37 F.W.J. Schelling, *The Philosophy of Art*, trans. Douglas W. Stott (Minneapolis: University of Minnesota Press, 1989), 69.

38 F.W.J. Schelling, *Bruno, or, On the Natural and the Divine Principle of Things*, trans. Michael G. Vater (Albany: State University of New York Press, 1984), 181–3; F.W.J. Schelling, "System of Philosophy in General and of the Philosophy of Nature in Particular." In Schelling, *Idealism and the Endgame of Theory*, 189; F.W.J. Schelling, *Über das Verhältnis der bildenden Künste zu der Natur*. In F.W.J. Schelling, *Ausgewählte Schriften: Band 2, 1801–1803*, ed. Manfred Frank (Frankfurt am Main: Suhrkamp, 1985), 602.

39 Schelling, *First Outline of a System of the Philosophy of Nature*, 192.

40 Schelling, *Presentation of My System of Philosophy*, 194.
41 Schelling, *System of Transcendental Idealism*, 232.
42 Schelling, *First Outline of a System of the Philosophy of Nature*, 157–8; Schelling, *Presentation of My System of Philosophy*, 200–1; Schelling, *Bruno*, 151; Schelling, *System der gesammten Philosophie und der Naturphilosophie insbesondere*, 244; Schelling, *Einleitung in die Philosophie*, 52–3.
43 F.W.J. Schelling, *Statement on the True Relationship of the Philosophy of Nature to the Revised Fichtean Doctrine: An Elucidation of the Former*, trans. Dale E. Snow (Albany: State University of New York Press, 2018), 86; Schelling, *The Ages of the World, Book One: The Past (Original Version, 1811)*, 63; Hogrebe, *Prädikation und Genesis*, 23–4, 51–5, 118; Markus Gabriel, "The Mythological Being of Reflection – An Essay on Hegel, Schelling, and the Contingency of Necessity." In Markus Gabriel and Slavoj Žižek, *Mythology, Madness and Laughter: Subjectivity in German Idealism* (London: Continuum, 2009), 84; Markus Gabriel, *Transcendental Ontology: Essays in German Idealism* (London: Continuum, 2011), 98.
44 F.W.J. Schelling, *Allgemeine Deduction des dynamischen Processes (Beschluss der im ersten Heft abgebrochenen Abhandlung)*. In *Zeitschrift für spekulative Physik: Ersten Bandes, zweites Heft, Zeitschrift für spekulative Physik*, ed. F.W.J. Schelling (Hildesheim: Georg Olms, 1969), 83–4, 86–7.
45 Schelling, *Philosophical Investigations into the Essence of Human Freedom*, 32–3, 73.
46 Schelling, *The Ages of the World, Book One: The Past (Original Version, 1811)*, 56–7, 73–4, 92, 154; Schelling, "Notes and Fragments to the First Book of *The Ages of the World: The Past*," 230, 241; Schelling, *The Ages of the World: Third Version (c. 1815)*, 56–7.
47 Žižek, *The Indivisible Remainder*, 220–8, 231; Žižek, *The Parallax View*, 165–73; Žižek, *Less than Nothing*, 918–21; Žižek, *Absolute Recoil*, 203; Johnston, *Žižek's Ontology*, 195–203.
48 Slavoj Žižek, *Incontinence of the Void: Economico-Philosophical Spandrels* (Cambridge: MIT Press, 2017), 36.
49 G.W.F. Hegel, *Science of Logic*, trans. A.V. Miller (London: George Allen & Unwin, 1969), 58–9.
50 Žižek, *Sex and the Failed Absolute*, 155.
51 G.W.F. Hegel, *The Encyclopedia Logic: Part I of the Encyclopedia of the Philosophical Sciences with the Zusätze*, trans. T.F. Geraets, W.A. Suchting, and H.S. Harris (Indianapolis: Hackett, 1991), §9 (33), §12 (37); G.W.F. Hegel, *Philosophy of Nature: Part Two of the Encyclopedia of the Philosophical Sciences*, trans. A.V. Miller (Oxford: Oxford University Press, 1970), §246 (6–8).
52 Žižek, *Absolute Recoil*, 16–17, 98, 109, 372–4; Žižek, *Incontinence of the Void*, 3; Žižek, *Sex and the Failed Absolute*, 60.
53 Žižek, *Sex and the Failed Absolute*, 283.
54 Ibid., 284.
55 Ibid., 283, 348.

56 Hegel, *Science of Logic*, 82.
57 Žižek, *Sex and the Failed Absolute*, 285.
58 F.W.J. Schelling, *On the History of Modern Philosophy*, trans. Andrew Bowie (Cambridge: Cambridge University Press, 1994), 134–63; F.W.J. Schelling, *Vorrede zu einer philosophischen Schrift des Herrn Victor Cousin*. In Schelling *Ausgewählte Schriften: Band 4, 1807–1834*, 628–9; F.W.J. Schelling, *The Grounding of the Positive Philosophy*, trans. Bruce Matthews (Albany: State University of New York Press, 2007), 128–31, 139, 148–51, 155, 169, 186, 204–5, 211.
59 Žižek, *Sex and the Failed Absolute*, 285–6.
60 F.W.J. Schelling, *Philosophie und Religion*. In Schelling, *Ausgewählte Schriften: Band 3, 1804–1806*, 39; F.W.J. Schelling, *Philosophy and Religion*, trans. Klaus Ottmann (Putnam: Springer, 2010), 18.
61 Hegel, *Science of Logic*, 843–4; Hegel, *The Encyclopedia Logic*, §244 (307); G.W.F. Hegel, *Lectures on Logic: Berlin, 1831*, trans. Clark Butler (Bloomington: Indiana University Press, 2008), §244 (232–3).
62 Schelling, *Einleitung in die Philosophie*, 62–5; Schelling, *On the History of Modern Philosophy*, 149, 153–5, 157–9; Schelling, *Philosophy of Revelation*, 78–80, 89, 91, 102; Schelling, *The Grounding of the Positive Philosophy*, 151, 186.
63 F.W.J. Schelling, "Stuttgart Seminars." In Schelling, *Idealism and the Endgame of Theory*, 199, 206–9, 213; Schelling, "Notes and Fragments to the First Book of *The Ages of the World: The Past*," 194, 196; F.W.J. Schelling, *Clara, or, On Nature's Connection to the Spirit World*, trans. Fiona Steinkamp (Albany: State University of New York Press, 2002), 12–13, 61; Schelling, *On the History of Modern Philosophy*, 66; F.W.J. Schelling, *Andere Deduktion der Principien der positiven Philosophie*. In F.W.J. Schelling, *Ausgewählte Schriften: Band 5, 1842–1852*, ed. Manfred Frank (Frankfurt am Main: Suhrkamp, 1985), 779–98; Schelling, *Philosophy of Revelation*, 124–5; Schelling, *The Grounding of the Positive Philosophy*, 183, 185–6, 198, 200–1, 203–4, 208; F.W.J. Schelling, *Historical-critical Introduction to the Philosophy of Mythology*, trans. Mason Richey and Markus Zisselberger (Albany: State University of New York Press, 2007), 7–8, 10–11, 17, 35–6, 38–9, 41, 45, 61, 66, 74–5, 78, 117, 129, 132, 137–8, 170; Walter Schulz, *Die Vollendung des deutschen Idealismus in der Spätphilosophie Schellings* (Stuttgart and Köln: Kohlhammer, 1955), 289.
64 Adrian Johnston, *Prolegomena to Any Future Materialism, Volume Two: A Weak Nature Alone* (Evanston: Northwestern University Press, 2019), 39–41.
65 Schelling, *Einleitung in die Philosophie*, 53, 134.
66 Jacques Lacan, *The Seminar of Jacques Lacan, Book II: The Ego in Freud's Theory and in the Technique of Psychoanalysis, 1954–1955*, ed. Jacques-Alain Miller, trans. Sylvana Tomaselli (New York: W.W. Norton and Company, 1988), 81, 107, 116, 184; Jacques Lacan, *The Seminar of Jacques Lacan, Book VII: The Ethics of Psychoanalysis, 1959–1960*, ed. Jacques-Alain Miller, trans. Dennis Porter (New York: W.W. Norton and Company, 1992), 284, 293; Jacques Lacan, *Le Séminaire de Jacques Lacan, Livre IX: L'identification*,

1961–1962, unpublished typescript, session of January 24, 1962; Jacques Lacan, "The Function and Field of Speech and Language in Psychoanalysis." In Jacques Lacan, *Écrits: The First Complete Edition in English*, trans. Bruce Fink (New York: W.W. Norton and Company, 2006), 247.

67 J.G. Herder, *God, Some Conversations*, trans. Frederick H. Burkhardt (Indianapolis: Bobbs-Merrill, 1940), 102–3, 105.

68 Jacques Lacan, *Le Séminaire de Jacques Lacan, Livre XVI: D'un Autre à l'autre, 1968–1969*, ed. Jacques-Alain Miller (Paris: Éditions du Seuil, 2006), 385.

69 Hegel, *Science of Logic*, 71, 118, 843–4; Hegel, *The Encyclopedia Logic*, §244 (307); Hegel, *Lectures on Logic*, §244 (232–3); Hegel, *Philosophy of Nature*, §247 (13–14), §248 (17); G.W.F. Hegel, *Philosophy of Mind: Part Three of the Encyclopedia of the Philosophical Sciences*, trans. A.V. Miller (Oxford: Oxford University Press, 1971), §389 (30–3).

70 Schelling, *The Ages of the World, Book One: The Past (Original Version, 1811)*, 108–9, 151; F.W.J. Schelling, *Denkmal der Schrift von den göttlichen Dingen ec. des Herrn Friedrich Heinrich Jacobi und der ihm in derselben gemachten Beschuldigung eines absichtlich tauschenden, Lüge redenden Atheismus*. In F.W.J. Schelling, *Friedrich Wilhelm Joseph von Schellings sämmtliche Werke, Band 8*, ed. K.F.A. Schelling (Stuttgart-Augsburg: Cotta, 1861), 25–6, 69.

71 Spinoza, *Ethics*, Part I, Proposition 15, Scholium (224–45), Part I, Appendix (240).

72 Schelling, *The Ages of the World, Book One: The Past (Original Version, 1811)*, 113.

73 Hegel, *Phenomenology of Spirit*, 10.

74 G.W.F. Hegel, "Hegel to Schelling: Bamberg, May 1, 1807." In Hegel, *Hegel: The Letters*, 80.

75 Schelling, *Ideas for a Philosophy of Nature*, 10–13, 40; Schelling, *System of Transcendental Idealism*, 32; Schelling, *Presentation of My System of Philosophy*, 145–6; Schelling, "Further Presentations from the System of Philosophy (1802) [Extract]." In Fichte and Schelling, *The Philosophical Rupture between Fichte and Schelling*, 207–10; Schelling, *Bruno*, 204, 209; F.W.J. Schelling, *On University Studies*, trans. E.S. Morgan (Athens: Ohio University Press, 1966), 67–9, 117; F.W.J. Schelling, "On the Relationship of the Philosophy of Nature to Philosophy in General." In *Between Kant and Hegel: Texts in the Development of Post-Kantian Idealism*, trans. George Di Giovanni and H.S. Harris (Indianapolis: Hackett, 2000), 373–4, 377; Schelling, *Philosophical Investigations into the Essence of Human Freedom*, 24, 68–9, 74; Schelling, *The Ages of the World, Book One: The Past (Original Version, 1811)*, 104; Schelling, *The Ages of the World: Third Version (c. 1815)*, 64.

76 Schelling, *Ages of the World (second draft, 1813)*, 150.

77 Žižek, *Sex and the Failed Absolute*, 280.

78 Schelling, *Bruno*, 179, 184, 187; Schelling, *The Ages of the World: Third Version (c. 1815)*, 48, 86–7; Schelling, *Philosophy of Revelation*, 125, 147; Schelling, *The Grounding of the Positive Philosophy*, 132–5, 141–2, 160–1.

79 Schelling, *Clara*, 27; Schelling, *Einleitung in die Philosophie*, 45; Schelling, *On the History of Modern Philosophy*, 147; Schelling, *The Grounding of the Positive Philosophy*, 128–31, 133–5, 139, 141–2, 160–1; Schelling, *Philosophy of Revelation*, 40–2; F.W.J. Schelling, *Abhandlung über die Quelle der ewigen Wahrheiten*. In Schelling, *Ausgewählte Schriften: Band 5, 1842–1852*, 594; Schelling, *Andere Deduktion der Principien der positiven Philosophie*, 792.

80 Johnston, *A New German Idealism*, 74–128.

81 Schelling, *On the History of Modern Philosophy*, 147; Schelling, *Philosophy of Revelation*, 41–2, 45; Schelling, *The Grounding of the Positive Philosophy*, 128–31, 133–5, 137, 139, 141–2, 151, 155, 160–1, 182–3, 186, 197–8, 204–5, 211.

82 Žižek, *Sex and the Failed Absolute*, 384.

83 Schelling, "Further Presentations from the System of Philosophy (1802) [Extract]," 225.

Response to Johnston

Slavoj Žižek

Let me begin by expressing my pleasant surprise at the high quality and depth of the critical texts in this volume—even when I don't agree with them, I admire the clarity of their argumentation and the way they draw the key distinctions. The length of my reply to a critical text in no way reflects my opinion of its quality. Due to space limitation, I do mostly just two things: clarify the points where I think I was misunderstood by my critic and draw a clear line of distinction between her/his and my position.

So let me begin with Johnston's text which continues our decades-long debate. I gladly accept his designation of our difference as the one between layer cake and doughnut. Yes, my model is that of a doughnut, a twisted space that resembles the structure of the Moebius band: if we progress to the end on one side, making a full circle, we find ourselves on the opposite side, at our starting point. The process of notional mediation, of making-discovering a rational structure beneath the contingency of immediate reality, can only be completed, brought to a conclusion (and Hegel's axiom is that to bring stability to a form of rationality it *has* to be brought to a conclusion), through a return to some figure of "brute immediacy" which actualizes (gives body to) the rational totality—*this* necessity of the return to immediacy is for Hegel the key feature of Reason that a mere Understanding cannot grasp. In Lacan's terms, every rational (symbolic) edifice has to be sustained by what Lacan called *le peu du réel*, a little piece of the contingent Real which acts as *la réponse du réel*, the "answer of the Real." Hegel was deeply aware of this paradox when he opposed ancient democracy to modern monarchy: it was precisely because the ancient Greeks did not have a figure of pure subjectivity (a king) at the summit of their state edifice that they needed to resort to "superstitious" practices—such as looking for signs in the flight-paths of birds or in the entrails of animals—to guide the polis in making crucial decisions. It was clear to Hegel that the modern world cannot dispense with this contingent Real and organize social life only through choices and decisions based on "objective" qualifications (the illusion of what Lacan later called the discourse of the University): there is always some aspect of ritual involved in being invested with a title, even if the conferring of the title follows automatically from certain "objective" criteria having been met. Another name for this final turn of the doughnut is "negation of negation," the return to immediacy, the cut that concludes the endless process of sublation/mediation. In clear contrast to this doughnut structure, the layer-cake model stands for simple gradual progress, layer upon layer . . .[1]

Moreover, I admit that in some sense I oscillate between Hegel and Schelling. While I fully endorse Hegel's critique of Schelling's early philosophy of identity, I find Hegel's reaction to Schelling's treatise on freedom (a brief note towards the end of his *History of Philosophy*) totally inadequate—Hegel simply misses the point there. So yes, Schelling is not reducible to Hegel; what he came up with in his *Freiheitsschrift* and *Weltalter* fragments is something breathtakingly new, in some sense a shock for himself, and he desperately tried to recuperate from this shock, to reinscribe it into the frame of traditional metaphysics, in his late philosophy of revelation. It is easy to find superficial continuities in Schelling's thought, but they are, I think, his attempts to downplay the radicality of his break. In short, concerning the choice between Hegel and Schelling, I do find myself in a kind of parallax situation: while both are indispensable, there is no common language; the one cannot be reduced to the other.

Where I disagree with Johnston is his basic interpretive premise according to which Schelling's distinction between *Grund* and *Existenz* (from his *Treatise on Freedom*) is just a renaming of Spinoza's distinction between *natura naturans* and *natura naturata*: Schelling

> begins with the fluid "ground" (*Grund*) of a primordial creative power (i.e., verb-like *natura naturans*) that then produces the fixed "existence" (*Existenz*) of stable entities (i.e., noun-like *natura naturata*). According to Schelling, human subjectivity, as the highest spiritual power, is nothing other than an irruption within the field of existence of the ground-zero substratum underlying and generating this field. In psychoanalytic terms, the subject is the return of repressed (Spinozistic) substance, the resurfacing of *natura naturans* within the domain of *natura naturata*. As such, reaching the highest Schellingian emergent layer amounts to reconnecting with the lowest one—hence a layer-doughnut model.

Johnston's critical point is that such a doughnut model "fails actually to explain the genesis of subjectivity": it either amounts to physicalist reductionism (discerning the basic structure of subjectivity already in the quantum reality) or to panpsychism (projecting into quantum reality the psychic structure of subjectivity). My view is that Johnston's layer-cake model implies a simple gradual evolutionary progress which ignores cuts and retroactivity that characterize a proper dialectical process. Let me explain this point.

What I find fascinating in Schelling's *Freiheitsschrift* and in quantum physics is that, in both cases, the elementary ontological couple (*Grund-Existenz*, wave oscillations and their collapse in a single reality) precisely cannot be reduced to the opposition between a dynamic production process and its fixation in determinate fixed entities. How/why does the collapse/fixation occur? My point is that there has to be a tension/gap already in the Ground or in the wave oscillations: there is no "pure" flux of production, a gap or obstacle must already be inscribed into it. More precisely, if human beings, in their freedom, are "points of return for the darkness of *Grund* within the light of *Existenz*," this means that the darkness of the Ground is not the primordial fact: this "darkness" already presupposes a Void it envelops, and it is this (primordially repressed) Void that "returns" in human freedom.

My name for this primordial tension is parallax. With regard to quantum physics, we should focus on how it turns around the common notion of that there is a self-identical thing beneath appearances, and that this thing appears differently to the objects with which it interacts (the ontological premise endorsed also by Harman): in quantum physics, particles do not just interact in the form of waves; particles also can be said to emerge at the points where different waves cut into each other. So, it is as if a thing is not the cause of how it appears in the interaction with other things, it is also something that emerges through the intersection of different appearances. Again, the parallax gap goes down to the bottom; it is irreducible.

Note

1 Recall the Stalinist logic of accusation: (1) You are a spy. (2) Even if you are not a spy, you are objectively serving the enemy by your indiscreet babble. (3) Even if you are not objectively serving the enemy, your spouse is doing this, so that makes you responsible. (4) Even if you did nothing and none in your family is serving the enemy, you witnessed counterrevolutionary speech at your workplace and you didn't report it, which makes you a collaborator of the enemy. (5) If none of this is true, the very fact that you put such an effort in appearing on our side indicates that your purity is the mask covering your betrayal. The last point is that of a Moebius band twist: no proof is needed since the very absence of a proof operates as a proof.

CHAPTER TWO

Truth as Bacchanalian Revel
Žižek and the Risks of Irony

Dominik Finkelde

Introduction

Many of Žižek's readers both make the experience of being quickly drawn into the fascination of his prose, but after reading several books enthusiastically, also of falling into a phase of exhaustion and disenchantment. The multitude of ideas and complex-theoretical insights crisscrossing philosophical disciplines can suddenly turn into a chaos of thoughts that can barely be classified and coherently sorted out. In some cases, the reader can even no longer cope with Žižek's oeuvre at all due to the lack of a systematic framework. And then, at the very latest, the question arises, for one or the other, whether the cognitive inundation is an intentional part of the author's rational. Doesn't Žižek's thinking resemble in many of his books the "bacchanalian revel in which no member is not drunk" mentioned by Hegel?[1] Not that Žižek, for all the complexity of his ideas and arguments about Marx, Hegel, and Lacan (to name just a few), does not repeatedly educate his readers with numerous insights that one would often not even hope to find in the works of other contemporary philosophers; for example, when he discusses the contradictions of a super-ego "injunction to enjoy" in contemporary capitalism,[2] puts forth the relation of Lacan's philosophy of split subjectivity with Hegel's concept of spirit in the structure of its retrospective becoming,[3] or when he explains the impact of enjoyment as a political factor.[4] Insights like these have an outstanding influence on Žižek's readers around the world because of their clarity. Nevertheless, their combination and re-combination in ever new books make readers also feel as if they were climbing an impossible Penrose staircase: ascending and descending within a strange loop that has no exit and a master leading the way that apparently has no answers to questions like "What can I know?", "What should I do?" and "What may I hope?"

Then again, and this is true as well, these two experiences do not exclude each other: on the one hand the intellectual force of clarity in detailed analyses of Lacan, via Marx to Hegel, and—on the other hand—a lack of unity of an oeuvre when it comes to the question of what constitutes the philosophical sum of Žižek's now more than fifty books. Do they form a totality, a system, a corpus? Or do we encounter atomistic, even occasionalist insights that deliberately refuse to be brought together in a synthesis— epistemological, cultural-philosophical, or ontological? Questions like these may be responsible for his ambivalent reputation within the academic world. Experts on Kant, Hegel, or Heidegger may ask whether Žižek actually *wants* to participate in an exegetical dialogue with them or whether he is not primarily interested in presenting—for example with reference to Hegel— his own *Žižegel*. And granted that this were the case, what status would, in this case, his thinking hold, according to scientific standards? Does it not already presuppose *Žižek-Studies* in a future to come, which interpret the words of the master and his understanding of what, provocatively said, the concept *Žižegel* for example stands for?

This ambivalence of clarity and (over-)complexity concerns Žižek's analyses as a public intellectual in current debates on economics and/or politics as well. Here, the search for systematicity is less the issue than the foundation of his political beliefs. Undoubtedly, his heart beats on the Left. But this Žižekian left can suddenly appear in right-wing places when he voices support, for example, for Donald Trump as president in 2016[5] or for Victor Orbán against the left-liberal elite of Europe in 2021.[6] Like no other living philosopher, he regularly manages to surprise his readers by assuming arguments that many liberals might have sensed in limbo as reasonable though not yet politically correct to be pronounced. This applies to his 2016 plea for Trump as president, just mentioned, as well as his friendly-critical debate with the LGBTQ critique and New Right spokesman Jordan Peterson.[7] Here Žižek often deliberately breaks with the worldview of those (left-wing) elites who belong to the core of his readership. And yet very few people resent him for this: perhaps because they know that tomorrow he will have already "betrayed" them (as well as himself) and so have "sublated" the belief he has appropriated today into a new belief of tomorrow. Today he is the exception to belief A, tomorrow he may be the exception to belief B, which cannot yet be guessed in the virtuality of reality—except by himself. This corresponds to his style of thinking, to change chains of argumentation and disciplines—from ontology to film theory—without interruption, as soon as a dialectical possibility of a new spark of thought arises.[8]

In Žižek's case it is not only the refusal of a systematic approach that characterizes many of his works, but the celebration of a way of thinking that, in ever new associations and leaps of thought, apparently sometimes deliberately seeks to deprive its readers of the secure hold of valid arguments In this way he has invented his own and ultimately unique genre—as can be seen as well in anti-systematic works from philosophers like Nietzsche to Wittgenstein: a thinking that has elevated the transgression of boundaries (including those of philosophical disciplines) to its program. It cannot simply be adopted or academicized by others. Similar to Nietzsche's *aphorisms*, Wittgenstein's *propositions*, or Benjamin's *Denkbilder* (images of thought), his thinking of dialectics autopoetically sets its own conditions of its reception. And is this not, counterintuitive as it may sound, one of his most central achievements for contemporary philosophy: the way his dialectical method sets new standards? Is not the radicality of *this* thinking more innovative than his readings of the works of Hegel, Lacan, Marx, and others? In any case, he has re-founded the dialectical method as a philosophical discipline and consciously distanced himself from contemporary currents of new forms of neopositivism in continental and analytic philosophy. And this truly *is* an outstanding achievement.

But a serious problem, which is at the heart of this essay, remains nonetheless. After everything has been put through the meat grinder of Žižek's dialectical thinking, there is often no theorem left, no basic human conviction, no moral maxim, no liberal-democratic worldview that escapes the dialectical twists and turns of his thought. Or, to put it another way, Žižek's philosophy tends to have unfolded its own genre of negative philosophy. This thinking, both in its readings of Marx, Hegel, and Lacan, and in its references to questions of artificial intelligence, neo-capitalism, and right-wing populist politics, apparently cannot help but repeatedly take up counter-positions, which then also become counter-counter-positions again. And isn't this one of the reasons why Neo-Hegelians like John McDowell and Robert Brandom, with the exception of Robert Pippin (to whom we turn later), refuse to debate, as do many Hegel Scholars in Germany as well, Žižek's many interpretations of Hegel's philosophy? Perhaps they see in a thinking that is committed to a "gappy ontology"[9] or an ontology of negativity—in their view wrongly inspired by Hegel—a general rejection of reason, which then becomes the aforementioned anti-systematic bacchanalian revel? Such a thinking cannot seek a systematics, but possibly only raise the "madness" discovered within Hegel to a program.

This at least is the reproach Robert Pippin makes with regard to "Žižek's Hegel" (in this volume). Žižek betrays the heritage of German idealism by reading into Hegel negative dialectics that, according to Pippin, cannot be found there. Pippin's critique is recalled here and analyzed below, in order to raise subsequently the question of whether Žižek's philosophy has not unconsciously subscribed itself to irony as a philosophical stance.

Irony has been criticized famously in the late nineteenth and early twentieth century by Sören Kierkegaard and Carl Schmitt among others. But before that it was especially Hegel who in his Berlin years criticized the romantic adoption of irony as a confused philosophical stance. But isn't there an elective affinity between Žižek's dialectics and the ironic stance rejected by Hegel? Or, to put it another way, doesn't Žižek's defense of "Hegel's madness" force him time and again to consider justificatory relations of "what exists" from the perspective of irony?[10] In order to explain this thesis, we will have to turn to the concept of reason put forth by Pippin (and Brandom) in their readings of Hegel. For Pippin at least Žižek wants to deliberately undermine a certain conceptual understanding of reason from the legacy of idealism. And the question is, if Pippin is correct in his critique. Maybe Žižek fails to recognize the importance of how Hegel's concept of reason extends Immanuel Kant's *Doctrine of Method* and the Kantian doctrine of reason's postulates.

What distinguishes an idealist in contrast to a dialectical materialist may then not be the belief in an onto-theological divine Spirit behind the frontiers of reality, which governs reality. What distinguishes him may simply be the necessary insight to submit to regulative ideas as an Other of what is this-worldly *because of reason's limits*. And my hunch is that Pippin, as well as Brandom and McDowell submit to this insight dogmatically while Žižek submits to the metaphysics of excess as literally a source of (divine) providence which allegedly saves him from any dogmatic stance. For Pippin and Brandom, the danger of positivism lurks. But in Žižek's case, for his part, the danger of a constitutive contingency-fixed negativism lurks. His "but what if" twists, his almost psychotic ability to intertwine topics and themes of ontology, psychoanalysis, and popular culture, runs the risk of losing a basic concept of reason as a condition of the possibility of coherent thinking. And then this madness may have method, but the charge of irony against Žižek may not be far.

Pippin on Žižek's "Gappy Ontology"

Pippin's critique articulated in his essay "Žižek's Hegel" focuses on the ontological status Žižek ascribes to the Hegelian concept of negativity. Pippin: "What is the ontological status of 'negativity' in Žižek?", he asks.[11] Does it imply the Eleatic enigma of non-being or the observation of a lack of distinct entities? For Žižek, Hegel's concept of negativity deals with nothing of the sort. He is interested in the extent to which Hegel conceptualizes especially in the subject itself an embodiment of negativity, thereby refuting any charge against him of being a pre-Kantian metaphysician. Žižek's proof of his reading lies in the preface to the *Phenomenology*. Here the "True" is not "only as *Substance*, but equally as *Subject*."[12] But what is meant by this proposition is disputed (not only from Pippin's point of view) among Hegel scholars. Is Hegel expressing the insight that the subject as torchbearer of truth embodies the non-coincidence of substance (i.e., the non-coincidence of truth conditions), its gap?[13] Or does the proposition articulate the potential openness of the domain of truth to adapt itself inferentially to all the "commitments and entitlements" (Brandom) reasonable agents will present and make "more explicit" in an open future of their trustful wellbeing?[14]

In the first case, the mentioned subject as embodiment of the True is substance *tout court* and substance subject. The particular is the locus of the universal, and vice versa. The subject does not only participate in substance as synonym of grounding features of reality. It decides from the perspective of its particularity what—seen retrospectively—is due to substance as embodiment of its universal truth practically and theoretically. But does not the order of being lose in this scenario what structures are made of: objective (and not subjective) coherence, inferential and stable relations, the guarantee that— with Brandom—Pittsburgh's location "to the West of Philadelphia" includes the inference that "Philadelphia is to the East of Pittsburgh"?[15] This, at last, is all decisive for the Pittsburgh School's interpretation on behalf of an inferential pragmatism that is explicitly positivistic. And Pippin subscribes to this theory. For him our actions and judgments are anchored in "relations of material consequence and incompatibility," as Brandom puts it.[16] This inferential materiality would implode should, as noted above, the subject as substance be transformed into the instance of substance as substance. Pittsburgh could no longer be safe to be located in an ironic and playful manner east of Philadelphia, and Philadelphia to the west of Pittsburgh. The subject would perceive itself— similar to the romantic genius—"as the absolute." Everything else is vain for it and "all determinations [of what is factual, D.F.] can be destroyed" (Hegel).[17] Here, at least, lies one of the charges that Pippin repeatedly raises against Žižek's interpretation of Hegel's dialectics. The materiality of true relations among concepts would be lost to subjects speaking in the name of their *Gewissen* i.e., in the name of "Antigone," "Vladimir I. Lenin," or "David Lurie," the hero of J. M. Coetzee's *Disgrace* whose fate Žižek comments on repeatedly.[18] As I already said: Who could discourage people from settling Pittsburgh to the east of Philadelphia on *even* days and to the west of Philadelphia on *odd* days and with what arguments? Entitlements and commitments condition historical experience only if "gaps" are excluded— allegedly. Without entitlements and commitments experience collapse under the burden of radical contingency. And this, at least, *appears* to be true. But more alarming is the fact that injustice could elevate itself to the instance of Law. Crime could, as the victor of history, justify its point of arrival as genealogically necessary while the belief in progress and advancement of spirit within bourgeois society (described by Hegel in his *Philosophy of Right*) would only be a vain dream. Instead, Pippin sees in his critique of Žižek's Hegel the imperative of the necessity of rationality tied to Hegel's concept of bourgeois society.[19] It is through this stage, he argues, that the hope of progress through rational insight becomes reasonable.

Pippin underlines that the core of his Hegelianism is rooted in Kant's concept of the transcendental I of pure apperception. It forms the inescapable condition of the possibility of rationality. And even if Pippin's Hegelian stance, compared to Žižek's, actually falls victim to an all too strong rational neopositivism that does not want to admit the limits and aporias of inferential relations of concepts and their contents, his criticism of Žižek remains valid nevertheless—at least to a certain extent which I will delineate below in more detail. For this reason, not only does Texas stand south-east of New Mexico, but rational arguments could, according to Pippin, potentially reform Texas as well into a leftwing "Sweden in the Sixties."[20] Ergo Hegel is, so Pippin, not a thinker of the necessity of contingency and the founding father of a "gappy ontology" Žižek refers to. The genealogy of Spirit's becoming presents a theory of inferential relations necessary for rational agents, in which commitments and entitlements help to ward off unwarranted acts of excessive subjects. Žižek's adherence to contingency by contrast urges all relations to fall potentially into the abysses of excesses (as acts or events), however interpreted, which retrospectively legitimate their conditions of possibility as that what is rational. In this world, Pippin calls it "Hegel's Zoo"; live forms of consciousness have not arrived at what true self-consciousness in the space of reasons stands for. This is why Žižek's theory of the act incorporates Hegelian figures of thought called "The Beautiful Soul, The Knight of Virtue and especially The Frenzy of Self-Conceit."[21] These forms of consciousness adhere to the erroneous belief that they can re-establish the universal in the name of their particularity. But for Pippin this is unwarranted and fundamentally wrong.

For him, the subject that always already cognizes on normative grounds is, as a condition of the possibility of its power of judgment, the subject that always already rationally justifies itself on these normative grounds. Negativity is not explained away. It affects intentional acts of consciousness in acts of cognition, when, for example, we perceive something as wrong; it also affects empirical judgments when we are mistaken, or in actions that turn out to be insufficiently justified. And even if consciousness is without doubt in cases like these never the instance of absolute self-certainty regarding "what there is" or "how we have to act" and so is exposed to the danger of negativity, this does not permit, from Pippin's perspective, to construe the subject as the basic structure of substance and from there, as a gap in substance, the source of truth and reality itself. Wilfrid Sellars has blocked this route of argument. For we know from the co-founder of the Pittsburgh School that epistemological questions carry with them a normative status a priori.[22] Negativity as a basic ontological motif cannot be thought coherently under a priori epistemological conditions if they interchange subject and substance and undermine the "materiality" of truth-values. What norm should be normatively represented in this case anyway, an *anti-norm* as norm? What reason should be given for that which cannot be justified? Questions of meaning are questions about norms, and norms are intelligible in terms of social practices. To be a norm-dominated agent is to have been born into "the space of reasons."[23] This space is missing in

Žižek's Hegel. The symbolic forms in which subjectivity is qua its symbolic investiture wrapped may carry an excess of the symbolic that psychoanalysis reflects upon in its theory of split subjectivity, but in putting too much emphasis on this excess, Pippin argues, the rational framework of commitments and entitlements in the normative character of the investitures is lost. It becomes, so it seems, contingent and with it the basic structures of reality as well. Everything is in danger of becoming sucked into a vortex of negativity of that which is not-identical with itself and forever in becoming via excessive subjects. For Pippin, this explains Žižek's preference for events of political exception, described in Žižek's theory of the act. These cases unveil how the space of giving and asking for reasons is not identical with itself. Spirit is non-identical and comes to bear in subjects the anti-moment of what substance *is*. But, as I said, when the basic structures of reality are construed as ontologically contradictory and/or arbitrary, the game of exchanging rational arguments collapses. A blind struggle analogous to the state of nature prevails and brings us closer to what Pippin calls "Hegel's zoo." Instead of being able to exchange rational arguments in the name of entitlements and commitments, subjects encounter other subjects, each claiming for themselves to be the exception to the norm, an exception that becomes the condition of the future of substance, i.e., the beginning of a better world. And isn't Pippin right at this point in his critique of Žižek's ontology, at least a bit? How should political actions experience motivational force if the "contingency retroactively 'sublates' itself into necessity"[24] and the structure of retrospective justification of events (Žižek's acts) are declared to be the decisive motor of historical processes of progress? (A similar charge is made by Laclau against Žižek in their debate from 2000.)[25] Žižek follows with his negative dialectics in the footsteps of Shakespeare's Hamlet. But while Andrew Cutrofello revalues Hamlet's concept of negativity sociophilosophically and positively distinguishes Žižek's concept of "incomplete determinacy" from Robert Brandom's concept of "complete determinacy,"[26] Pippin sees Žižek's anthropology as well as his ontology, quite in contrast to Cutrofello, as no longer capable of participating in the concept of rationality at all. In that sense, Žižek resembles Heiner Müller's Hamlet who in *Hamlet-Machine* (1977) discards his symbolic role as prince and intellectual with the words: "I stood at the coast and talked with the surf BLABLA at my back the ruins of Europe."[27]

Pippin's criticism repeats the well-known retorsion argument. It was raised, among others, against Derrida's theory of deconstruction. And just as Derrida's concept of differ*a*nce undermines allegedly its own claim to truth, Žižek undermines the discipline of a conceptual-rationalist ontology oriented by Hegel by clinging to dialectics and avoiding dogmatics. Instead of structures of being, structures of non-being apparently dominate. Instead of rational agents, individuals dominate, who—similar the "beautiful soul"—oppose reality with an ultimately *a*rational resistance. But, as I said, in this case, every regime of injustice could be justified if it only reaches the place of a retrospective authentification to "transsubstantialize" its contingent claims to power in the name of necessity. Would we be allowed to think such a thing—for example, with reference to German fascism? Can we think of a fascist space of reasons if World War II would have been won by the Nazi regime? This question came up indirectly in Germany during the so-called *Historikerstreit*. Habermas resisted dogmatically any relativization of the Holocaust in order to be able to phantasmagorically maintain what the space of reasons stands for. And Nazis have—dogmatically speaking—no claim to truth.

But perhaps Pippin's critique could also be interpreted differently. Namely, to the effect that Žižek does not recognize the need to unfold his own transcendental *Doctrine of Method*, i.e., the doctrine Kant develops in the second part of his *Critique of Pure Reason*. And here, I think, lies a valuable difference between Žižek and Pippin (and Brandom), to which Žižek himself pays too little attention. Because I claim that Pippin as well as the Pittsburgh Hegelians cling to a Kantian *Methodenlehre*, even if no trace of such a doctrine may not be found explicitly in their works.

In Need of Dogma?

The reference to Kant's *Doctrine of Method* and the thesis that a doctrine with analogous properties can be found as well in Pippin (and Brandom) may not be immediately obvious. However, one must remember that Kant's doctrine aims to unfold a complete metaphysical system against the background of reason's limits which were measured in the "Transcendental Doctrine of Elements," part one of the *Critique of Pure Reason*. Kant writes: "By the transcendental doctrine of method, therefore, I understand the determination of the formal conditions of a complete system of pure reason."[28] Man's pursuit of truth and knowledge cannot be satisfied by Hume's skepticism and with purely empirical knowledge of what experience offers in the coordinates of space and time. Reason, according to Kant, strives beyond this "flat surface."[29] It seeks an "unconditioned totality"[30] and urges reasonable creatures to always refer to that "which might lie outside this horizon" of spatiotemporal objects of experience.[31] Human reason advances as if this horizon may at best also be "on its borderline [i.e., within the limits of human reason]."[32]

Transcendental philosophy, however, succeeds in this determination only if a priori principles are determined that are irrefutable on the level of *subjective certainty* alone. This may seem paradoxical. After all, subjective certainty must displace the circumstance of not being able to establish its certainty on the objective level of knowledge, neither with the help of the categories of understanding, nor with concepts of mathematics. Only the postulates of God, soul, freedom and the world as totality are available as fantasies to secure subjective certainty *through* subjective certainty. According to Kant, this circumstance does not make this kind of certainty less certain. On the contrary, it is only through subjective certainty that Kant gains, as stated in the B-introduction to the *Critique of Pure Reason*, the "room for faith" religion needs.³³ For Alexandre Kojève, therefore, the *Doctrine of Methods* carries at its center Kant's religious conviction that a moral life in this world is possible only in metaphysical reference to an ultimately dogmatically posited kingdom to come. Kojève states: "Certainly discursive knowledge has no access to this netherworld," this Kingdom of Ends,

> which is the object of a hope and not of a knowledge. But if this hope is subjectively certain, it is faith, which can be rock solid. And even if discursive knowledge cannot vouch for this certainty, it may at any rate not destroy it. [...] It is, then, an irrefutable and indisputable position/stance, i.e., an irrational "existential attitude" expressed discursively by what can be called a "dogma," or an "article of faith" (*Glaubensartikel*).³⁴

Žižek has not developed such an article of faith, as far as I know, nor does he see the need for one. But doesn't that put him in danger of getting lost in the vortex of negative dialectics? According to Kojève, transcendental philosophy, for its part, turns out to be dogmatic. Does this mean that Kant falls back to the level of the dogmatic *Schulphilosophie* of his time? This is not the case, however, since the dogmatics of subjective certainty is a reflected and not an unreflective dogma. My guess now is that a similar form of dogmatic reflective thinking also characterizes Pippin's understanding of Hegel vis-à-vis Žižek's defense of Hegel's madness (as well as the Pittsburgh School's positivism). But, as I mentioned, Žižek does apparently not want to see the value for the necessity of such dogma. The subjective certainty that Kant unfolds as religious with reference to the postulates of pure reason mutates in Pippin (as it does, very roughly speaking, in Brandom and McDowell as well) into a belief in the dogmatic certainty of Sellars' concept of the "space of reasons." This belief cannot be justified discursively. It receives its ground only in subjective certainty.

The Pittsburgh School Hegelians represent in their ontologies unwritten *Methodenlehren* in the tradition of Kant. Žižek gives no account for the deficiency of a *Methodenlehre* and obviously does not want to advocate a secular philosophy of religion, or an unbroken faith in the insights of reason in the "space of reasons." His faith builds on the power of insight in thought alone, even as thought undermines thought. Perhaps, however, Žižek's "gappy" ontology remains nevertheless too hostile to life and the world to be the foundations of hope, argument, and action, and this is because his thinking tends to remove the basis of a phantasmatic illusion into a coherent (rather than incomplete) basic structure of reality, such as any conception of rationality needs. I do not want to claim that Žižek willingly accepted this and—similar to Nietzsche—lives out an ordinary psychosis triggered by the abysses of his theory. My claim is rather that his thinking has not yet confronted this question: How to deal with what thinking itself is not allowed to think? Or differently said: How to deal with dogmas which protect the illusions of thought? Žižek repeatedly criticizes Habermas's philosophy as the offspring of discourse-dogmatic thinking. But perhaps Habermas recognizes his faith in rational discourse only with regard to the dogma of reason in the form of subjective certainty?

Žižek could object that his thinking cannot even endanger the phantasmatic illusory power of human reason. As a condition of the possibility of sociality, illusions return again and again. In every symbolic order they are by definition at work: in form of the phantasmatic belief in values and norms without which not even a single argument could be brought forth in a political debate. Not because individual subjects, like devotees in a sect, adhere to this belief dogmatically, but because the a priori structure of the community makes this belief the condition of the community's possibility in the first place. This argument is valid. And yet one might ask whether Žižek's thinking, described in the introduction to this essay as occasionalist, even ironic, does not reveal the opposite, i.e., the plunge into his self-generated abyss of signifiers. His ontology lays (similarly to Nietzsche's philosophy) the ground of his madness, from which dogmatic philosophers from Habermas to Laclau and Pippin want to protect themselves. And is this not also one of the reasons why he "is not 'violent' enough," (McGowan, Chapter 5 in this volume), and why he is playful and ironic as "Laibach" (Bjerre, Chapter 7 in this volume) and, therefore, cannot become a leader (like Jordan Peterson) for a generation of young women and men in search of their master? His internal compass is dogma-lacking because his dialectical thinking has become all-encompassing and absolute. Žižek apparently chooses not to be a master. But did he truly choose this stance, or is he only the victim of his thought?

Notes

1 Georg W. F. Hegel, *Phenomenology of Spirit*, trans. A.V. Miller (Oxford: Oxford University Press, 1977), § 47.
2 Slavoj Žižek, *The Plague of Fantasies* (London: Verso, 1997), 50.
3 Slavoj Žižek, *The Most Sublime Hysteric: Hegel with Lacan* (Cambridge: Polity, 2014).
4 Slavoj Žižek, *For They Know Not What They Do: Enjoyment as a Political Factor* (London: Verso, 2002).
5 Žižek expressed this opinion on British TV, Channel 4 News, on November 3, 2016.
6 Slavoj Žižek, "Womit Orbán recht hat," in *Die Welt*, 7.8. 2021. See https://www.welt.de/kultur/plus232970669/Slavoj-Zizek-Womit-Orban-recht-hat.html (accessed September 4, 2021).
7 The debate took place at Meridian Hall in Toronto on April 19, 2019.

8   It must be said that this does not concern all works according to the ductus of his thinking depicted here. A work like *Less than Nothing: Hegel and the Shadow of Dialectical Materialism* (London: Verso, 2012), for example, is more systematic compared to *They Know Not What They Do* or *Metastases of Enjoyment*. For this reason, Graham Harman calls it the work with a "deceptively simple structure. Namely, it is organized around Žižek's joint debt to two thinkers whose influence on his thought is widely known" (Chapter 3 in this volume). And of course, there is no dogma of having to practice philosophy systematically at all.

9   Robert Pippin, "Slavoj Žižek's Hegel," Chapter 4 in this volume.

10 For a thinker like Richard Rorty, ironism is desirable (Rorty, *Contingency, Irony and Solidarity*, Cambridge: Cambridge University Press, 1989, 73–140). The ironist embodies the quality of being aware of the contingency of his opinions and convictions, and thus is open to being taught what is new. But Žižek rejects this utopian faith of the political ironist. He criticizes it, among other things, as a basic attitude tending toward cynicism, which goes along with a basic mental state in left-liberal elites: Not taking everything so seriously, branding dogmatic positions as fundamentalist and instead seeking compromises is, as the spirit of the age, for him the new opium for the people. Cynicism as irony, so Žižek has replaced the classical Marxist notion of "false consciousness" and becomes a dominant operational mode of contemporary ideology (Žižek, *The Sublime Object of Ideology*, London: Verso, 1989, 28–30). It gives people, according to Žižek, the deceptive possibility of distancing their convictions from their actions in such a way that responsibility vanishes. Rorty is consequently not an ally of Žižek. But – as I said – on the formal level of his dialectics, the accusation of being an ironist cannot be dismissed. It is precisely in his almost psychotic ability to find occasionalist inspiration for an interesting detour of thought in the detail of a text, in a scene of a movie, or in a product on the market, as it characterizes many of his works, that corresponds to what his thinking is time and again about.

11 Pippin, "Žižek's Hegel," Chapter 4 in this volume.

12 Hegel, *Phenomenology of Spirit*, §18.

13 Žižek, *Less than Nothing*, 359–416.

14 Robert Brandom, *A Spirit of Trust: A Reading of Hegel's Phenomenology* (Cambridge, MA: Harvard University Press, 2019), 5.

15 Robert Brandom, *Making It Explicit: Reasoning, Representing, and Discursive Commitment* (Cambridge, MA: Harvard University Press, 1994), 99.

16 Brandom, *A Spirit of Trust*, 22.

17 "Das Subjekt weiß sich in sich als das Absolute, alles andere ist ihm eitel; alle Bestimmungen, die es sich selbst vom Rechten, Guten macht, weiß es auch wieder zu zerstören." G.W. F. Hegel, *Vorlesungen über die Geschichte der Philosophie* III (Frankfurt am Main: Suhrkamp, 1986), 416.

18 Žižek, *Less than Nothing*, 324.

19 Pippin, "Žižek's Hegel," Chapter 4 in this volume.

20 Ibid.

21 Ibid.
22 Wilfrid S. Sellars, *Empiricism and the Philosophy of Mind*, ed. Robert Brandom (Cambridge, MA: Harvard University Press, 1997) §36.
23 Sellars, *Empiricism and the Philosophy of Mind*, §36.
24 Slavoj Žižek "Da Capo Senza Fine." In *Contingency, Hegemony, Universality: Contemporary Dialogues on the Left*, eds. Judith Butler, Ernesto Laclau, and Slavoj Žižek (London: Verso 2000), 213–62, here: 227.
25 See Ernesto Laclau, "Structure, History and the Political." In *Contingency, Hegemony, Universality*, 182–212.
26 Andrew Cutrofello, *All for Nothing: Hamlet's Negativity* (Massachusetts: MIT Press, 2014), 149.
27 Heiner Müller, *Die Hamletmaschine*. In *Mauser* (Berlin: Rotbuch Verlag, 1978), 89–97.
28 Immanuel Kant, *Critique of Pure Reason*, ed. and trans. Paul Guyer and Allen W. Wood (Cambridge: Cambridge University Press, 1997), A 707/B 735.
29 Kant, *Critique of Pure Reason*, A 759/B 787.
30 Ibid.
31 "The sum total of all possible objects for our cognition seems to us to be a flat surface, which has its apparent horizon, namely that which comprehends its entire domain and which is called by us the rational concept of unconditioned totality. It is impossible to attain this empirically, and all attempts to determine it *a priori* in accordance with a certain principle have been in vain. Yet all questions of our pure reason pertain to that which might lie outside this horizon or in any case at least on its borderline." Kant, *Critique of Pure Reason*, A 759/B 787 – A 760 / B 788.
32 Kant, *Critique of Pure Reason*, A 760/B 788.
33 Kant, *Critique of Pure Reason*, Bxxx.
34 Alexandre Kojève, *Kant* (Paris: Gallimard, 1973), 25–40, here: 38–9.

Response to Finkelde

Slavoj Žižek

Finkelde perfectly formulates what I see as the central issue of our debate: does Hegel remain committed to the Kantian "subjective dogma" (some form of rational-discursive a priori) which sets a limit to dialectical self-questioning, or is every discursive form submitted to ruthless analysis of its immanent failures and inconsistences?[1] In Finkelde's own words:

> After everything has been put through the meat grinder of Žižek's dialectical thinking, there is often no theorem left, no basic human conviction, no moral maxim, no liberal-democratic worldview that escapes the dialectical twists and turns of his thought. [...] What distinguishes an idealist in contrast to a dialectical materialist may then not be the belief in an onto-theological divine Spirit behind the frontiers of reality, which governs reality. What distinguishes him may simply be the necessary insight to submit to regulative ideas as an Other of what is this-worldly because of reason's limits.

If what distinguishes an idealist is his/her submission to "an Other of what is this-worldly because of reason's limits," then Hegel definitely is not an idealist. For Hegel, idealism means precisely that reason has no limits because it is the space of the actual infinity. There is one and only one limit of reason that Hegel concedes, and this limit concerns future: thinking cannot penetrate future, future that awaits us is a blank, thinking can only grasp the notional structure of a life-form which is already in decay. Does this mean that we are in total blindness concerning future? Here, one can risk a step further from Hegel and introduce the domain of poetry and mystic prophecy: a prophetic vision can outline the contours of a possible future. This vision is not knowledge but an obscure prophecy which appears as a glimpse into a possible future. It is obscure because the future itself is obscure, indeterminate. Such visions are risky; they can only be justified retroactively—or be dismissed as nonsense. Maybe, therein resides a possible role of art after the end of art as the medium of Truth.

In an exemplary Kantian way, Finkelde asserts the need for a dogmatic belief into an Other, an "article of faith," which only can save our rational knowledge from disintegrating in the vortex of its self-questioning. However, we should be very careful about what belief means in different ideological constellations. From time to time, we read in our media about the weird claims of the North Korean media: when Kim Il-sung died, even birds descended from the sky and cried at his coffin; their leader doesn't defecate, etc. Our reaction to such claims is double: either we presume that ordinary people secretly laugh at this, well aware that this is all nonsense, or maybe they are so brainwashed that they really believe it. But a third version is much more convincing: what if such stories are propagated by the regime not as literal truths but as something like folkloric tales told with respect although we know they are a fiction. There is, however, a price to be paid for such respect of appearances. A couple of years ago, a young woman who was selling things on a (tolerated, although not legally permitted) flea market, put the money she earned into a plastic bag and buried it in her garden. Police discovered this, she was prosecuted and condemned . . . for what? Not for black-market activity or illegal financial dealings but for a wholly different reason: the plastic bag didn't fully protect the cash, so the banknotes got humid and decomposed—and on the banknotes there are images of the Leader, so the woman was condemned for disrespectfully treating the image of the ruler. One can reasonably claim that the "dogmatic" a priori presupposed by rational thinking has a similar status of a presupposition not meant to be taken quite seriously.

This does not mean that there is no progress in knowledge; what I claim is that the progress of our knowledge cannot rely on any such dogmatic a priori: as Hegel knew it, when we really think, we think in language and simultaneously against language, against the constraints embodied in our discursive rules. Therein resides the big difference between Hegel and Kant's transcendental approach which is followed also by Habermas (who just gives it a discursive turn): Hegel does not presuppose any set of rules or values given in advance, his thought is precisely a continuous questioning of any such set of norms. As he put it at the beginning of his Logic, his only presupposition is the decision to think—there is no need for a set of a priori principles that are "irrefutable on the level of subjective certainty alone." From his Kantian standpoint, Finkelde reproaches me that I have

> not developed such an article of faith, as far as I know, nor does he see the need for one. But doesn't that put him in danger of getting lost in the vortex of negative dialectics? [. . .] Žižek repeatedly criticizes Habermas's philosophy as the offspring of discourse-dogmatic thinking. But perhaps

Habermas recognizes his faith in rational discourse only with regard to the dogma of reason in the form of subjective certainty?

What I find strange is that Finkelde characterizes my nihilistic lack of "dogmatic" foundation as my adherence to the Beautiful Soul: my adherence to contingency "urges all relations to fall potentially into the abysses or excesses (as acts or events), however interpreted, which retrospectively legitimate their conditions of possibility as that what is rational. This is why Žižek theory of the act incorporates Hegelian figures of thought called The Beautiful Soul, The Knight of Virtue and especially The Frenzy of Self-Conceit." But The Beautiful Soul is not simply arational, it just imposes its own contingent standard onto reality as its objective law—and for Hegel, this is exactly what Kant does with his list of a priori categories which should also be dialectically questioned. In his final argument, Finkelde gives his reproach a political twist:

> every regime of injustice could be justified if it only reaches the place of a retrospective authentification to "transsubstantialize" its contingent claims to power in the name of necessity. Would we be allowed to think such a thing—for example, with reference to German fascism? Can we think of a fascist space of reasons if World War II would have been won by the Nazi regime?

My answer is: not only we can, it is already happening—"revisionists" argue that fascism was just an (occasionally exaggerated) reaction to Bolshevism, the more dangerous and true catastrophe. More generally, I am not claiming that ultimately "anything goes" but that ethical progress is never fully assured: things can always go wrong again, that's why a permanent fight is needed just to keep alive what we gained. Of course there is ethical progress—its main indication is that, in a new situation, something is no longer possible to do or to say (publicly, at least). Recall the so-called "parsley massacre," the mass killing of Haitians living in the Dominican Republic's northwestern frontier in October 1937 carried out by the Dominican Army's troops on the orders of the dictator Rafael Trujillo. The name for the massacre came from the shibboleth that Trujillo had his soldiers apply to determine whether or not those living on the border were native Afro-Dominicans or immigrant Afro-Haitians. Dominican soldiers would hold up a sprig of parsley to someone and ask what it was. How the person pronounced the Spanish word for parsley (*perejil*) determined their fate:

> The Haitian languages, French and Haitian Creole, pronounce the r as a uvular approximant or a voiced velar fricative, respectively so their speakers can have difficulty pronouncing the alveolar tap or the alveolar trill of Spanish, the language of the Dominican Republic. Also, only

Spanish but not French or Haitian Creole pronounces the j as the voiceless velar fricative. If they could pronounce it the Spanish way the soldiers considered them Dominican and let them live, but if they pronounced it the French or Creole way they considered them Haitian and executed them.²

When, towards the end of his life, Trujillo was asked which of his acts he is most proud of, he put on the top the parsley massacre which, he claimed, saved the Dominican nation. He did it without shame, celebrating it proudly as an ethical act. Today, hopefully, something like this is no longer possible, or it has at least to be done discreetly, out of the public's eye. This is what I mean by retroactivity and "gappy" reality: yes, we don't live in an arational void, we live in a thick texture of reasons, but this chain is multiple, inconsistent and incomplete, which is why it can always be restructured. Our acts are not "arational," they happen because of gaps in chain of reasons—to quote for the nth time T. S. Eliot:

> what happens when a new work of art is created is something that happens simultaneously to all the works of art which preceded it. The existing monuments form an ideal order among themselves, which is modified by the introduction of the new (the really new) work of art among them. The existing order is complete before the new work arrives; for order to persist after the supervention of novelty, the whole existing order must be, if ever so slightly, altered; and so the relations, proportions, values of each work of art toward the whole are readjusted; and this is conformity between the old and the new. [. . .] the past should be altered by the present as much as the present is directed by the past.³

Let's take the example of Shakespeare: a great staging of *Hamlet* today is not just a new interpretation of the play; in a way it fills the lacks of Shakespeare's original itself—when writing it, Shakespeare didn't know fully what he was saying, the play is full of inconsistencies, open toward the future. And the same holds for politics. When, in 1953, Chou En-lai, the Chinese Prime Minister, was in Geneva for the peace negotiations to end the Korean War, a French journalist asked him what he thought about the French Revolution. Chou replied: "It is still too early to tell." In a way, he was right: with the disintegration of the Eastern European "people's democracies" in the late 1990s, the struggle for the historical place of the French Revolution flared up again. The liberal revisionists tried to impose the notion that the demise of communism in 1989 occurred at exactly the right moment: it marked the end of the era which began in 1789, the final failure of the revolutionary model which first entered the scene with the Jacobins. The battle for the past goes on today: if a new space of radical emancipatory politics will emerge, then the French Revolution was not just a deadlock of history.

Notes

1. Again, in order to avoid repeating myself, I propose that the reader interested in this topic to take a look at my long first chapter, "Hegel: The Spirit of Distrust," in S. Žižek, F. Ruda, and A. Hamza, *Reading Hegel* (Cambridge: Polity Press, 2021), where I deal in detail with Pippin's and Brandom's interpretation of Hegel as well as with other new readings of Hegel (like the one of Rocio Zambrana) which are closer to me.
2. Wikipedia, "Parsley massacre". Available online: https://en.wikipedia.org/wiki/Parsley_massacre (accessed December 20, 2021).
3. T. S. Eliot, "Tradition and the Individual Talent," originally published in *The Sacred Wood: Essays on Poetry and Criticism* (London: Methuen, 1920), 49–50.

CHAPTER THREE

Žižek and the Retroactivity of the Real

Graham Harman

This essay will focus on Slavoj Žižek's *Less than Nothing* (2012), which as his longest book is no doubt one of his least attentively read.[1] Despite the length and apparent complexity of this work, it has a deceptively simple structure. Namely, it is organized around Žižek's joint debt to two thinkers whose influence on his thought is widely known: the German philosopher G. W. F. Hegel and the French psychoanalyst Jacques Lacan, born 131 years apart. It is generally recognized that these two figures are Žižek's major intellectual referents, and that they above all others assist him in developing his own original position. Here I am reminded of an interesting remark by the literary critic Harold Bloom:

> What intimately allies ... [Ernest] Hemingway, [F. Scott] Fitzgerald, and [William] Faulkner ... is that all of them emerge from Joseph Conrad's influence but temper it cunningly by mingling Conrad with an American precursor—Mark Twain for Hemingway, Henry James for Fitzgerald, Herman Melville for Faulkner ... [S]trong writers have the wit to transform [their] forerunners into composite and therefore partly imaginary beings.[2]

Žižek is far from alone in being fascinated by Hegel, Lacan, and both of them simultaneously. In fact, as Žižek himself often notes, a clear Hegel/Lacan parallel suggests itself immediately: just as Hegel implodes Immanuel Kant's thing-in-itself into an immanent space of negativity, so too does Lacan transmute Sigmund Freud's unconscious into an equally immanent space of language and the symbolic order. Yet Žižek's way of combining these two great figures into "composite and therefore partly imaginary beings" is notably different from all other such attempts.

Nonetheless, the primary concern of this article lies elsewhere. Of especial interest is the way in which Žižek's expressed debt to Hegel and Lacan in *Less than Nothing* overshadows an apparently subordinate section near the end of the book devoted to quantum theory. Along with Karen Barad (who is discussed extensively in the book) Žižek is one of the few figures in contemporary continental thought who refers so frequently to recent physics in strengthening his philosophical position.[3] Nonetheless, there is a tension between Žižek's retroactivist (and hence basically idealist) ontology on the one hand, and his concessions to scientific realism on the other. In a brief essay like this one, I can only offer a highly compressed account of arguments that often extend over dozens of pages in the book. But as Lacan put it in his Seminar on the psychoses: "Sometimes too many details prevent the basic formal features from being seen."[4] This has been my experience as well.

Žižek's Retroactive Ontology

While the influence of Hegel and Lacan can be detected on every page of *Less than Nothing*, I will limit myself to Žižek's pivotal Part II on Hegel, running to just under fifty pages, in which Lacan is nearly as present as Hegel himself.[5] This is no introduction to Hegel and Lacan, nor even an introduction to Žižek's Hegel and Lacan, but more like a masterclass that often surprises the reader with a series of diagonal approaches to the heart of his philosophical position. One of the standard clichés of present-day intellectual life is that flux is primary rather than stasis: whereas previous thinkers were duped by petrified things and oppressive essences, today we experience a glorious new dawn of theory in which everything is changing utterly all the time.[6] Žižek begins Part II by countering this thesis. What is truly of interest in the passage of historical time, he claims, is not mere mobility: "after a true historical break, one simply cannot return to the past, or go on as if nothing has happened" (193). Following Arnold Schoenberg's break with Western tonal music, lingering tonal efforts like those of Sergei Rachmaninov have a certain irreducible element of *kitsch*.[7] But not every reactionary response to a historical break takes the form of clinging to the past; often enough, the radical beak is countered by a series of pseudo-breaks that retreat to a previous position despite a surface appearance of novelty. Žižek ventures the controversial claim that this is what happens with three major thinkers who seem to go "beyond" Hegel: F. W. J. Schelling, Søren Kierkegaard, and Karl Marx. These celebrated figures, each in his own way, indulge in a "ridiculous caricature of Hegel the 'absolute idealist' who 'possessed Absolute Knowledge'" (194). Žižek's aim is to isolate the true "irrational" core of Hegel's thought as missed by all of these purported post-Hegelian breakthroughs.

ŽIŽEK AND THE RETROACTIVITY OF THE REAL

What is the most basic principle of Žižek's thinking? Here we seem to face an ambiguity. For on the one hand, "the transcendental standpoint is in a sense irreducible, for one cannot look 'objectively' at oneself and locate oneself in reality" (239). But nearly three hundred pages later, we read the apparently opposite claim: "Hegelian reflection is thus the opposite of the transcendental approach which reflexively regresses from the object to its subjective conditions of possibility" (536). In fact, the word "transcendental" is the closest thing in Žižek to a Derridean *pharmakon*, a term that functions as both poison and cure.[8] Yet in this case the apparent contradiction is easily resolved. Whenever Žižek speaks positively of transcendental philosophy, it is in the sense that he regards Kant's assault on dogmatism as a definitive historical break; we cannot go back to the olden days of Plato and Aristotle, who failed to assess our means of gaining access to the world. As he told Glyn Daly in their fruitful conversation: "Kant was the *first philosopher* . . . Pre-Kantian philosophy cannot think [the] transcendental aspect."[9] Meanwhile, his negative view of the transcendental concerns his preference for Hegel over Kant, in the sense that the human understanding is not just a condition of possibility of the appearance of the world, but is reflexively inscribed in the world itself. While this inscription of thought in the world might seem like an anti-idealist gesture, we note that Žižek retains Kant's view that we cannot talk about the interaction between two non-human things, but only about how this interaction manifests itself to thought. None of Hegel's or Žižek's dialectical modifications of Kant will change this point (which elsewhere I have called "onto-taxonomy") that the thought–world relation is the only relation philosophy can possibly discuss.[10] Further evidence of this can be seen in Žižek's tendency, as early as *The Sublime Object of Ideology* and as late as *Less than Nothing*, to explain ideology as a basically realist phenomenon. To qualify as anti-Semitic, it is not enough to make negative remarks about Jews; one must also say that they have these negative traits *because* they are Jews. That is to say, in true anti-Semitism, Jewishness becomes a mysterious *je ne sais quoi* beneath any explicit qualities: "there is some mysterious ingredient in Jews, an essence of being-Jewish, which causes them to be degenerate . . ."[11] (938). The point seems to be that if we avoid realist essences we also avoid ideology, which is precisely what Žižek aims to do.

He tries to accomplish this with what is probably the key concept of his career: retroactivity. Something in the world was not there all along before I noticed it; rather, it is only through my recognition or positing of it that it appears afterward "to have been there all along." A great deal of Žižek's interpretation of Hegel, and thus of his own philosophy, follows directly from this claim. In one sense retroactivity works against the Aristotelian idea of an essence that lies in things whether we know it or not: Žižek even criticizes the young Marx for adopting this traditional idea (223–4). But more importantly, retroactivity allows Žižek to challenge—often rather mockingly—the usual picture of Hegel as a thinker of absolute knowledge and total reconciliation, in which all conflicts supposedly vanish into a final synthesis. This is because Žižek's idea of retroactivity is coupled with an equally strong commitment to contingency. Freedom, he tells us, is both retroactive and contingent: "it is not simply a free act which, out of nowhere, starts a new causal link, but a retroactive act of determining which link or sequence of necessities will determine us" (213). Only once Caesar chooses freely to cross the Rubicon does he become the one who was destined to do so all along. Whereas Quentin Meillassoux's famous book bears the subtitle *An Essay on the Necessity of Contingency*, Žižek opts in reverse for the contingency of necessity.[12] Indeed, Meillassoux has already had such a debate with Žižek's ally Alain Badiou. As Meillassoux remarked in a 2010 interview: "Badiou sent me a letter in which he clearly distinguished our major point of divergence: I believe in a necessity of contingency, while he upholds a contingency of necessity."[13]

Yet there is an important point on which both notions of contingency agree. No less than Meillassoux, Žižek holds that radical contingency "amounts to a suspension of the Principle of Sufficient Reason: a suspension not only epistemological but also ontological" (229). This, of course, is a radical proposition to make about Hegel. While most readers of the *Phenomenology of Spirit* or the *Science of Logic* will find occasional reasons to quibble with the passage from some dialectical figure to another, most of the time we are suitably impressed by the apparent necessity of each transition.[14] But Žižek holds otherwise: "every dialectical passage or reversal is a passage in which the new figure emerges *ex nihilo* and retroactively posits or creates its necessity" (231). If true, this would reduce the old Hegelian theme of the "end of history" to a myth. At any given moment, the next step of the dialectic would be unforeseeable, entirely subordinate to the workings of contingent freedom. While this might not sound very Hegelian at first, it does permit Žižek to uphold a powerful reading of the image of the Owl of Minerva: it not only flies at dusk, but cannot possibly fly any sooner, and its very flight in some sense produces the dusk. As the leftist Žižek somewhat surprisingly puts it: "there is no place in Hegel for the Marxist-Stalinist figure of the communist revolutionary who understands the historical necessity and posits himself as the instrument of its implementation" (217). Yes, true heroes invent a new form of life, and "operate in a pre-legal stateless zone" (217), but they do so without being able to foresee the consequences of their actions; they are not clear-headed members of an avant-garde consciously leading the masses toward the light. For this reason Marx misses the point of the Owl of Minerva, replacing it with "the singing of the [Gallic] rooster (French revolutionary thought) announcing the proletarian revolution—in the proletarian revolutionary act, Thought will precede Being" (220).

Žižek's emphasis on retroactivity also brings him close in one respect to the structuralist concept of time, which famously favors synchrony over diachrony. In a sense, the long millennia of the past are no longer relevant except insofar as they are retroactively transformed in the present: the

October Revolution is no longer the same thing after the collapse of the Soviet Union in 1991 (218). The vast historical past of humanity is effectively imploded, at each moment, into the time of the present. Here Žižek finds strong support in the literary criticism of T. S. Eliot and Jorge Luis Borges. Eliot's influential essay "Tradition and the Individual Talent" does not just demand that the writer be immersed in the classical tradition, but that they transform that tradition in their own work.[15] As for Borges, we have his clever essay on how Franz Kafka retroactively posited his predecessors without any inherent necessity that they would eventually lead to Kafka.[16] The great writers of the past survive only in their perpetual re-inscription by future authors. In similar fashion, a political revolution also posits its own precursors.

This Hegelian retroactivist departure from Kant's transcendental philosophy has a further important consequence: the value of commitment and of the courage to make mistakes, both of them constant themes in Žižek's intellectual work and arguably even in what we know of his life. The point of Hegel's analysis of the French Revolutionary terror is not that it was too abstract and therefore incapable of establishing an ordered society. Rather, "in spite of the fact that Revolutionary Terror was a historical deadlock, we have to pass through it in order to arrive at the modern rational State" (206). Hegel gives a similar interpretation of the Crusades: yes, it was ultimately meaningless to capture the Holy Land and possess the tomb of Christ. But "only in this disappointment, through this failure-in-triumph, does one reach the insight that in order to 'live in Christ,' it is not necessary to travel to faraway lands and occupy empty tombs, since Christ is already here whenever there is love between his followers" (530). A failed decision creates the conditions for the right decision to be made. More specifically, even if the *content* of an experience is deemed a failure, this very debacle enables our own subjective position toward it to become the content of a new experience: a passage from the constative to the performative (in speech–act terms), or from the the subject of the enunciated to the subject of the enunciation (in Lacanian terms). This sheds further light on Žižek's visceral contempt for the status of the neutral, critical observer: "I hate the position of [the] 'beautiful soul,' which is: 'I remain outside, in a safe place; I don't want to dirty my hands.'"[17] In his political positions, Žižek repeatedly refuses "radical" stances that demand impossible measures. Instead, he seeks more practical measures, as in his critical review of Simon Critchley's book *Infinitely Demanding*.[18] According to Žižek, Critchley's strategy of making infinite and impossible demands on the state gives them an easy alibi for doing nothing. By contrast, as he concludes: "The thing to do is, on the contrary, to bombard those in power with strategically well-selected, precise, finite demands, which can't be met with the same excuse."[19] This was also the spirit of his famous Zuccotti Park address to the Occupy Wall Street gathering in 2011: "remember, carnivals come cheap."[20] None of this will mean anything unless it leads to concrete changes, an attitude also found (for different reasons) in the activism of Michel Foucault. The Hegelian background of Žižek's political positions should be clear enough: to adopt a position of distant moral critique is to repeat the mistake of Kant's transcendental subject, which fails to see that it inevitably becomes embedded in the immanent world in its own right. One should always hate the position of the Beautiful Soul.

This also clarifies Žižek's rejection of the Marxist and Kierkegaardian critiques of Hegel, which claim that the idealist dialectic purports to reconcile everything into perfect harmony, while leaving intact all the class conflicts and existential dilemmas of the actual world in which we live. As Žižek sees it, all of this is already there in Hegel. Above all, the dialectic is saturated with failure: "the failure to achieve the (immediate) goal is absolutely crucial to, constitutive of, this process" (234). Nor does it get any better at the "Absolute" end of the process, since "every universality in its actualization generates an excess which undermines it." The Owl of Minerva can never stop taking flight. The famous Hegelian Whole is "the Whole *plus* its symptoms, the unintended consequences which betray its untruth" (523). Contra Marx, we cannot complete Hegel by noting and then changing these symptoms, since Hegel already recognizes them and addresses them differently, through "a purely formal shift, a change of perspective, which tries to present defeat itself as a triumph" (197). The point is not so much the fabled Hegelian Absolute Knowing, which is governed by the symbolic order (Lacan's Big Other). Beyond all knowing is *truth*, and for Žižek as for Lacan, "the truth that articulates itself is the truth about the failures, gaps, and inconsistencies of the big other" (518). Despite the near-universal view of Hegel as the thinker of completed totality at the end of a string of sublations, this is merely what Freud called a "screen memory": "a fantasy-formation designed to cover up a traumatic truth" (239). That trauma repeatedly reappears at each failed stage of the dialectic, and at the end of the day, no ultimate reconciliation compensates for all these traumas.

Žižek's Semi-Retroactive Theory of Science

To some extent, the section of *Less than Nothing* on quantum theory goes roughly as one would expect.[21] Having already expounded an ontology in which the Subject retroactively posits that which preceded it, it is easy to imagine how the Copenhagen Interpretation of quantum theory would provide additional scientific support for such an ontology: especially in Niels Bohr's more hardline "ontological" stance by contrast with Werner Heisenberg's merely "epistemological" one (924). This plays out further in Žižek's critical engagement with Barad (931–44), though in my view their points of agreement are more extensive than Žižek allows. But if this were all that happened in the pages on quantum theory, they would be more of an anticlimax than they are. Instead, what appears in these pages are several surprising concessions on Žižek's part to standard scientific realism. As one might expect, this creates a fascinating tension between his retroactive ontology and his only semi-retroactive theory of science.

When it comes to the relation between science and reality, one might expect Žižek to follow the occasionally hard line of a different sort of "retroactivist": Bruno Latour. In perhaps Latour's most extreme anti-realist version of the thesis, the verdict that the Egyptian Pharaoh Ramses II died of tuberculosis is impossible, given that this disease was only clinically and then microscopically identified in the nineteenth century.[22] Hence, to say that Ramses II died of tuberculosis is no more convincing than to say that he was killed by a machine gun. In *Less than Nothing* we do catch sight of Žižek making the expected move in a similar direction: "there is no 'objective' reality, every reality is already transcendentally constituted" (907). Later in the book, riffing on a thought of François Laruelle, Žižek goes so far as to declare that "What we call 'external reality' (as a consistent field of positively existing objects) arises through subtraction, that is, when something is subtracted from it—and this something is the *objet a*" (958), or the Lacanian object cause of desire, which has a purely virtual existence posited (retroactively, of course) by the Subject. Žižek continues to cling to a variant of this extreme position in what follows, though I think to an extent he is justified: for even those who insist that scientific knowledge is of a pre-existent real might be willing to admit that there is also the level of *truth* apart from that of knowledge. Namely, there is a sense in which a scientific breakthrough does not just change our factual knowledge about the universe, but also transforms the very position from which we speak about the world: "not through ... *adaequatio rei* but through the way [science] relates to the subject's position of enunciation" (907). Žižek is also right to note that Meillassoux's position—rather surprisingly, for a student of Badiou—is focused entirely on knowledge of the ancestral world and has relatively little to say about "truth" in this sense[23] (907). By contrast, Žižek is willing to risk the claim that one can "define Hegel's (idealist) premise as the claim that all knowledge can be ultimately generated from truth" (907).

Even so, Žižek seems unwilling to go for the jugular and deny any pre-existent, transcendent world at all. For example:

> The epistemological passage from classical physics to the theory of relativity did not mean that this shift in our knowledge was correlated to a shift in nature itself, that in Newton's time nature itself was Newtonian and that its laws mysteriously changed with the arrival of Einstein—at this level, clearly, it was our knowledge of nature that changed, not nature itself (907).

This concession might seem purely anodyne, like when we hear Husserlians and Heideggerians say things such as "but *of course* we do not deny the existence of a world outside the mind!" even while doing nothing philosophically to take such a world into account. But taken in context, Žižek is conceding a severe limitation on his retroactivist ontology, given his evident willingness to confirm that nature itself remained the same in Einstein's time as in Newton's. And this is no mere cursory admission. Žižek not only vaguely accepts the idea of a world that pre-exists retroactivity, he even seems to adopt a specific theory about it: namely, the anti-object standpoint of the analytic philosopher Peter van Inwagen[24] (909). Famously, van Inwagen denies the existence of all intermediate-sized objects, so that at the inorganic level there are only ultimate physical simples arranged "tablewise" or "rock-wise" for an observer. This would entail that Žižek rejects emergent reality at any level beneath that of organisms, and while this makes a good fit with his idea that each figure of the dialectic emerges *ex nihilo*, it would not make a good foundation for a science like chemistry, which as Manuel DeLanda noted requires emergent realities to exist.[25] Rather than a world consisting solely of subjects retroactively positing both themselves and everything else, Žižek makes room for a dualistic model of retroactively positing subjects *and* physical simples: the perfect embodiment of what object-oriented ontology (OOO) calls "duomining," in which only the bottom and top of reality are allowed to exist but nothing in between.[26]

We gain insight into another limitation of Žižek's position from his specific way of describing the dispute between Heisenberg and Bohr. As is well known, Heisenberg's Uncertainty Principle was initially formulated in epistemological fashion: it is impossible to *know* both the position and the momentum (i.e., speed plus velocity) of a particle, since to measure one is to close off possible measurement of the other. Bohr upped the ante on his protégé's theory with his move from Uncertainty to Complementarity: it is not just that we cannot *know* both the position and momentum of the particle simultaneously, it does not even *have* these two qualities prior to their being measured (924). But the way in which Žižek summarizes Bohr's position contains a hidden ambiguity: "particles in themselves do not have a determinate position and momentum, thus we should abandon the standard notion of 'objective reality' populated by things equipped with a fully determined set of properties" (924). The ambiguity concerns the proposed abandonment of "things equipped with a fully determined set of properties." Does Žižek advise abandoning the independent existence of "things" altogether, or only those "with a fully determined set of properties"? After all, the more prudent way to interpret Bohr's Complementarity would be to say that position and momentum do not pre-exist their measurement, but that the particle itself *does*. Philosophically speaking, this would require attention to how we can have a split between objects and their own qualities, which is precisely the concern of OOO, drawing on Husserl's little-noticed demolition of David Hume. For Hume, of course, an object is merely a "bundle of qualities" rather than something over and above those qualities; the same holds for minds, which are defined as nothing but "bundles of perceptions."[27] For Husserl, by contrast, intentional objects are units able to withstand countless variations in their exact set of qualities at any given moment. Ironically, Žižek had nailed Hume earlier in the book on his point about minds: "Hume's famous observation that, no matter how closely or deeply I look into myself, all I will find are respecific ideas, particular mental states, perceptions, emotions, etc., never a 'Self,' misses the point: this non-accessibility of the subject to itself as an object is constitutive of being a 'self'" (539). But for whatever reason, Žižek is unwilling to make the same argument when it comes to objects. Although he allows the subject to be an inaccessible *je ne sais quoi* over and above all the various Humean feelings and perceptions, when it comes to the particle as measured by Bohr, Žižek seems to think that de-realizing its position and momentum empties the particle itself of any intrinsic reality.

Is my point, then, that Žižek is "caught in a contradiction"? To some extent this is true, but it is more interesting to give a Žižekian twist on the situation and say that his position is neither retroactivist nor scientific realist, but only the deadlock or parallax gap between the two. Ironically, this is the same gap that runs through modern philosophy as a whole: is there something outside the mind that we cannot reach, or can everything be immanentized for the Subject? As a general rule, early modern philosophy (from Descartes through Kant) accepts the gap between thought and world and attempts various strategies for mediating the two realms, while late modern philosophy (Hegel, phenomenology, pragmatism) denies such a gap as the very height of naiveté. To some extent Žižek has one leg on each side of the fence, even if his "late modern" side is more pronounced. But here is the point: whether or not we believe in an unbridgeable gap between the two poles of thought and world, in both cases *it is precisely these two terms that are presupposed*.

An analogy from popular culture may be helpful. Some consumers prefer to drink Pepsi while others favor Coke. Yet in a sense there is little difference: both sets of consumers are accepting the premise that they ought to drink a dark-colored sugar water, and their often vehement conflict ultimately boils down to what is called the narcissism of small differences. An even more alarming example is the conflict between the two corn tortilla chip brands Doritos and Tostitos, since it turns out that both of these are owned by the same crushing monopoly, the corporation Frito-Lay. In this respect, the dispute in modern philosophy between the early and late modern approaches, found emblematically in Kant and Hegel (and hence also in Žižek's *pharmakon* word "transcendental"), is a Frito-Lay ontology unaware that it harbors a hidden choice in favor of two and only two terms: thought and world. The avoidance of the Frito-Lay monopoly would come from deciding to try pretzels (or perhaps celery or carrots) rather than corn chips. In similar fashion, the avoidance of the modern philosophical landscape would come from deciding not to focus on the relation between subject and world as the sole homeland of speculation. This was already done by Alfred North Whitehead in *Process and Reality*, where all relations are placed on the same footing.[28] But unsurprisingly, Whitehead is not a mainstream figure in either analytic or continental philosophy (another Frito-Lay oppositon), both of them based largely on the assumption—shared by Žižek—that the transcendental standpoint is the gateway to all rigorous philosophy.

Now, modern philosophers are not stupid, and that includes Žižek himself. If we permit philosophy to talk about object–object relations in the absence of any Subject, is this not the worst form of pre-Kantian dogmatism? Not really. Keep in mind that the critique of dogmatism is essentially a critique of *presence*, of the idea that the inherent character of reality can be placed directly before us given the proper metaphysical arguments. Now, it has seemed to almost everyone in the post-Kantian period that to say anything about the object–object case is an attempt to go beyond what is strictly given, and thereby to lapse into dogmatism. But these are actually two separate issues, as Whitehead saw. To claim that nothing can be directly present is one thing, but to claim that this lack of presence is a matter solely *for the Subject* is quite another. Note that human finitude is not directly given to us, but requires the deductive conclusion that the Subject's conditions of access to the world are something different *in kind* from the thing-in-itself. The same holds if we "Hegelize" or "Lacanize" the situation and say that there is a difference between the content of what is said and the position from which it is enunciated, which is what enables the chain of negativities to unfold in the first place. But there is nothing preventing us from extending the same argument to the level of non-human things: to speculate on the interaction of two non-human entities leads us to a deduction *no different in kind*, to the effect that there is a difference between how these objects manifest to each other, and what they are outside of this interaction. We can thereby avoid dogmatism in the way that Kant wanted, while not accepting an irreducibly "transcendental" position applicable to the Subject alone. That is onto-taxonomy, and unfortunately it is the true core of Žižek's position.

Notes

1 Slavoj Žižek, *Less than Nothing: Hegel and the Shadow of Dialectical Materialism* (London: Verso, 2012). In what follows, all in-text parenthetical page references are to this book.

2 Harold Bloom, *The Western Canon: The Books and School of the Ages* (New York: Riverhead Books, 1994), 11.

3 Karen Barad, *Meeting the Universe Halfway: Quantum Physics and the Entanglement of Matter and Meaning* (Durham, NC: Duke University Press, 2007).

4 Jacques Lacan, *The Seminar of Jacques Lacan: The Psychoses (Book III)*, trans. R. Grigg (New York: Norton, 1997), 76.

5 Žižek, *Less than Nothing*, "Part II. The Thing Itself: Hegel," 193–240.

6 For two unusually intelligent defenses of this view see Thomas Nail, *Being and Motion* (Oxford: Oxford University Press, 2018) and Rein Raud, *Being in Flux: A Post-Anthropocentric Ontology of the Self* (Cambridge: Polity, 2021).
7 Here Žižek advocates an "evental" philosophy of the sort long championed by his close colleague Alain Badiou, *Being and Event*, trans. O. Feltham (London: Continuum, 2005).
8 Jacques Derrida, "Plato's Pharmacy." In *Dissemination*, trans. B. Johnson (Chicago: University of Chicago Press, 1981), 61–172.
9 Slavoj Žižek and Glyn Daly, *Conversations with Žižek* (Cambridge: Polity Press, 2004), 26.
10 For "onto-taxonomy" see Graham Harman, *Dante's Broken Hammer: The Ethics, Aesthetics, and Metaphysics of Love* (London: Repeater, 2016), 237; Graham Harman, "The Only Exit from Modern Philosophy," *Open Philosophy* 3 (2020): 132–46; Niki Young, "Only Two Peas in a Pod: On the Overcoming of Ontological Taxonomies," *Simposia Melitensia* 17 (2021): 27–36.
11 See also Slavoj Žižek, *The Sublime Object of Ideology* (London: Verso, 1989), 6.
12 Quentin Meillassoux, *After Finitude: An Essay on the Necessity of Contingency*, trans. R. Brassier. (London: Continuum, 2008).
13 Meillassoux, in the Interview section of Graham Harman, *Quentin Meillassoux: Philosophy in the Making*, Second Edition (Edinburgh: Edinburgh University Press, 2011), 169.
14 G. W. F. Hegel, *Phenomenology of Spirit*, trans. A. V. Miller (Oxford: Oxford University Press, 1977); G. W. F. Hegel, *Science of Logic*, trans. A. V. Miller (London: G. Allen & Unwin, 1969).
15 T. S. Eliot, "Tradition and the Individual Talent." In *The Sacred Wood: Essays on Poetry and Criticism*. (London: Methuen, 1920).
16 Jorge Luis Borges, "Kafka and his Precursors.". In *Other Inquisitions: 1937–1952*, trans. R. Simms (New York: Simon & Schuster, 1964).
17 Jonathan Derbyshire, "Interview with Slavoj Žižek – Full Transcript," *New Statesman*, October 29, 2009, https://www.newstatesman.com/ideas/2009/10/today-interview-capitalism (accessed November 30, 2021.
18 Simon Critchley, *Infinitely Demanding: Ethics of Commitment, Politics of Resistance* (London: Verso, 2013).
19 Slavoj Žižek, "Resistance is Surrender," *London Review of Books* 29, no. 22, November 15, 2007. https://www.lrb.co.uk/the-paper/v29/n22/slavoj-zizek/resistance-is-surrender
20 Slavoj Žižek, "Slavoj Žižek Speaks at Occupy Wall Street: Transcript," *Impose Magazine*. https://imposemagazine.com/bytes/slavoj-zizek-at-occupy-wall-street-transcript (accessed November 30, 2021).
21 Žižek, *Less than Nothing*, 905–61.
22 Bruno Latour, "On the Partial Existence of Existing *and* Non-Existing Objects." In *Biographies of Scientific* Objects, ed. Lorraine Daston (Chicago: University of Chicago Press, 2000), 247–69.

23 The one exception I can think of is Meillassoux's discussion of how it is not enough to *know* that the virtual God might one day appear: one must also wait *in expectation* of it if the emergence of such a God is to have any meaning. See Quentin Meillassoux, "Appendix: Excerpts from *L'inexistence divine*." In Graham Harman, *Quentin Meillassoux: Philosophy in the Making*, Second Edition (Edinburgh: Edinburgh University Press, 2015), 224–87.

24 Peter van Inwagen, *Material Beings* (Ithaca, NY: Cornell University Press, 1990).

25 Manuel DeLanda, *Philosophical Chemistry: Genealogy of a Scientific Field* (London: Bloomsbury, 2015).

26 Graham Harman, "Undermining, Overmining, and Duomining: A Critique." In *ADD Metaphysics*, ed. J. Sutela (Aalto, Finland: Aalto University Design Research Laboratory, 2013), 40–51.

27 David Hume, *A Treatise of Human Nature* (Oxford: Oxford University Press, 1977).

28 Alfred North Whitehead, *Process and Reality* (New York: Free Press, 1978).

Response to Harman

Slavoj Žižek

Graham Harman's approach is the opposite one to Johnston's: what he finds problematic is not my Spinozism but my Kantianism:

> Žižek retains Kant's view that we cannot talk about the interaction between two non-human things, but only about how this interaction manifests itself to thought. None of Hegel's or Žižek's dialectical modifications of Kant will change this point (which elsewhere I have called "onto-taxonomy") that the thought-world relation is the only relation philosophy can possibly discuss.

Harman concedes that I do not reduce all external objective reality to its interaction with a subject, but what is outside subjective mediation are for me just elementary (and not-specified) "physical simples," a kind of empty remainder filled in by subject's constructions: "Žižek makes room for a dualistic model of retroactively positing subjects and physical simples: the perfect embodiment of what object-oriented ontology (OOO) calls 'duomining,' in which only the bottom and top of reality are allowed to exist but nothing in between." Harman exemplifies this limitation of mine by my reading of quantum physics' complementarity: I claim that position and momentum of a particle do not preexist their measurement, but "the more prudent way to interpret Bohr's Complementarity would be to say that position and momentum do not pre-exist their measurement—but that the particle itself does." Really? Is not the basic thesis of quantum physics also the complementarity of particle and wave—the same entity can act in one measurement as a particle and in another as a wave?

So what do I mean by retroactivity? Let me mention for the nth time the wonderful dialectical joke from Ernst Lubitsch's film *Ninotchka*:[1] the hero visits a cafeteria and orders coffee without cream; the waiter replies: "Sorry, we have run out of cream, but we still have milk. Can I bring you coffee without milk?" In both cases, the customer gets coffee alone, but this One-coffee is each time accompanied by a different negation, first coffee-with-no-cream, then coffee-with-no-milk. And does the same not hold for politics? A situation gets politicized when a subordinated person or group experiences its social position not just as a simple identity but as a "determinate negation." A woman becomes a feminist when she experiences her position as "without" (without freedom, without economic power). We cannot change the past reality, but we can and should make it appear as stigmatized by what it negates. After a woman experiences her identity in a patriarchal society as marked by a "without," all the past is changed: we learn to discover traces of oppression and exploitation in what was previously experienced as an organic stable social order. The ongoing struggle (also between feminists themselves) is the exact nature of this "without": is it predominantly lack of economic and social power, relief from the burden of parenthood, sexual freedom . . .? What this logic of determinate negation implies is the retroactivity of meaning.

My point is not that there is nothing outside subject's mediation, but that we (subjects) cannot step out of ourselves; i.e., as it were stand on our shoulders and draw a clear line of distinction between what only appears to us and what belongs to "things in themselves." "Transcendental" does not signal a superiority of subject but precisely its limitation: everything we experience, interact with, appears within a horizon of meaning or symbolic space into which we are "thrown," as Heidegger would have put it. When Heidegger characterizes a human being as "being-in-the-world," this does not mean that we are an object in the world, it means that, because of our limitation, we cannot ever fully self-objectivize ourselves: we cannot perceive and analyse ourselves as just another object in the world precisely because we are always-already *in* the world.

> Although he allows the subject to be an inaccessible *je ne sais quoi* over and above all the various Humean feelings and perceptions, when it comes to the particle as measured by Bohr, Žižek seems to think that de-realizing its position and momentum empties the particle itself of any intrinsic reality. [. . .] But there is nothing preventing us from extending the same argument to the level of non-human things: to speculate on the interaction of two non-human entities leads us to a deduction no different in kind, to the effect that there is a difference between how these objects manifest to each other, and what they are outside of this interaction. We can thereby avoid dogmatism in the way that Kant wanted, while not accepting an irreducibly "transcendental" position applicable to the Subject alone. That is Onto-Taxonomy, and unfortunately, it is the true core of Žižek's position.

My counter-thesis is here that there is a difference in kind: in contrast to objects, a subject precisely *is* nothing outside its interaction with others (things, subjects, processes); it is a thoroughly "interactional" entity. That's why I oppose the OOO attempt to read the Freudian "Unconscious" as a subject's objective content outside of how a subject appears to itself: the Freudian "Unconscious" is also purely interactional, it resides in the network of symbolic relations that over-determine the subject's direct self-experience. The main candidate for getting close to how reality is "in itself" are formulas of relativity theory and quantum physics—the result of complex experimental and intellectual work to which nothing corresponds in our direct experience of reality. To put it as plainly as possible: of course subjects are part of reality—but what we experience as reality is always already framed by our approach to the world; it is rooted in our active position in the world. Only in this way is interaction between objects subordinated to their interaction with subjects: because we as subjects cannot abstract from ourselves and look at ourselves "objectively." Harman's equation between the way things appear to us (and to each other) and the way things interact with each other is for me by far not obvious: what is beyond appearance is not just isolated "things in themselves" but their interaction itself.

Let me conclude by pointing out that, far from accepting the transcendental dimension as the ultimate frame, my effort in the last years is to outline a dimension beyond the transcendental without regressing to the traditional realist ontology (or, rather, onticology).[2]

Notes

1 I owe this reference to Alenka Zupančič.
2 I deal with this in the Finale of my *Surplus-Enjoyment* (London: Bloomsbury, 2022). See also Slavoj Žižek, "The Two Ends of Philosophy," September 15, 2021. Available online: https://www.philosophy-world-democracy.org/articles-1/the-two-ends-of-philosophy (accessed December 20, 2021).

CHAPTER FOUR

Slavoj Žižek's Hegel[1]

Robert B. Pippin

I

It takes some courage to give a book this size the title *Less than Nothing*.[2] Žižek must know that the first, powerfully tempting phrase that will occur to any reviewer, even before reading the book, will be "Aptly titled." The book has already inspired dismissive reviews in widely read publications, reviews that seem to be reviews (and dismissals) of Žižek himself (or of the Žižek phenomenon, the Symbolic Žižek) and mostly ignore his massive tome. But he has written a serious attempt to reanimate or reactualize Hegel (in the light of Lacanian metapsychology and so in a form he wants to call "materialist"), and in the limited space available to me I want to try to summarize what he has proposed and to express some disagreements.

The question of the possible relevance of Hegel to contemporary concerns divides into two questions and immediately confronts two objections that have long proven deeply compelling for many. There is first the question of what can be said about Hegel's "system." He is taken to be a hyper-rationalist holist whose central claim is that the Absolute (something like what Kant called the unconditioned) is the Idea, and that everything there is can be understood as the actualization, in nature and across historical time, of the Idea. (And, of course, contra Kant, he is thereby claiming to know what Kant had denied we could possibly know.) Second, there is the question of Hegel the *Versöhnungsphilosoph*, the philosopher of reconciliation. On some accounts of this side of Hegel's project, Hegel believed that we had reached the "end of history," both in philosophy (his own position had successfully accounted for all possible philosophical options, in their interconnection with each other) and in politics, art, and religion. Human freedom had been realized in the modern state as described in his *Philosophy of Right*, in the rather doctrinally thin Protestant humanism Hegel championed, and in romantic art, an art form in the process of transcending itself as art, actualizing art in a way that signaled its end as a significant vehicle of human self-knowledge. (The link between the two aspects of Hegel's position is taken to be his theodicy, the role of the Absolute's [or God's] self-actualization in time in accounting for the rationality and culmination of political and intellectual history.)

The objections to both versions of Hegel and Hegelianism are well known. There are a host of objections to Hegelian rationalist holism from the empiricist, scientific naturalist, and analytic approaches to philosophy. (The Anglophone version of that school famously began with the rejection of Hegel.) But in Europe the objections were more often directed at Hegel's uncompromising and supposedly "totalizing" rationalism: his inability, it was charged, to do sufficient justice to the concrete particularity of human existence, the unconceptualizable human individual, the role of unreason in human motivation, the contingency of historical change, and the phenomena of interest to psychoanalysis, like repetition and the death drive. Objections to the second dimension are more varied and more interesting, because Hegel succeeded in convincing even many of his critics (like the "young Hegelians") that philosophy must have a historically diagnostic task (it must be "its own time comprehended in thought"), even while many also rejected Hegel's "idealist" version of that project and his conclusions about "where we are" in any such process. Others simply point to the fact that no one has succeeded in writing *The Phenomenology of Spirit, Part Two*. The historical world that developed after 1831 and after the twentieth century cannot, it is assumed, be properly understood in Hegelian terms, the world of mass consumer societies, postcolonial states, globalized capitalism and therewith greatly weakened nation-states, the culture industry, pervasive reliance on technology in all facets of life, and so forth. Moreover, it is argued, it is not possible to "extend" even a roughly Hegelian analysis to such phenomena, especially to reason-defeating, irreconcilable-with phenomena like Nazism, the Holocaust, Stalin's crimes, or a communist China full of billionaires.[3]

Simply put, Žižek's ambitious goal is to argue that the former characterization of Hegel attacks a straw man, and when this is realized in sufficient detail, both the putative European break with Hegel in the criticisms of the likes of Schelling, Kierkegaard, Nietzsche, Deleuze, and the Freudians will look very different, with significantly more overlap than gaps, and this will make available a historical diagnosis very different from the triumphalist one usually attributed to Hegel. (One of the surprising things about the book is that, despite its size, what interests Žižek, by a very wide margin, is the theoretical presuppositions for such a diagnosis rather than much detail about the diagnosis itself.)[4]

The structure of the book is unusual. It is based on the adage that the second and third most pleasurable things in the world are the drink before and the cigarette after. Hence we get *"the drink before,"* the pre-Hegelian context needed to understand Hegel's option (a lot of attention is devoted to Plato's *Parmenides*, Christianity, the death of God, and Fichte); *"The Thing Itself"* (twice—once with Hegel, once with Lacan); and *"the cigarette after"* (Badiou, Heidegger, Levinas, and a concluding chapter on "the ontology of quantum physics"). A lot of this, especially the occasional digressions about Buddhism and the quantum physics discussion, not to mention the intricacies of Lacan, is well above my pay grade, so I will concentrate in the following on the interpretation of Hegel and the implications Žižek draws from that interpretation.

II

Let us designate the basic problem that the book addresses as the ontological problem of "subjectivity"; *what is it* to be a thinking, knowing, and also acting and interacting subject in a material world? Žižek begins by claiming that there are four main kinds of answers to such a question possible in the current "ideological-philosophical field": (i) scientific naturalism (brain science, Darwinism); (ii) discursive historicism (Foucault, deconstruction); (iii) New Age Western "Buddhism"; (iv) some sort of transcendental finitude (culminating in Heidegger).[5] Žižek's thesis is that these options miss the correct one, which he calls the idea of a "pre-transcendental gap or rupture (the Freudian name for which is the drive)," and that this framework is what actually "designates the very core of modern subjectivity."[6]

This all means that the discussion must proceed at a very high level of abstraction and will require a difficult summary of the basic positions of the "gang of four" (Kant, Fichte, Schelling, and Hegel) that Žižek thinks he needs on the table in order for him to present the core issue he wants to discuss. In the language developed in this tradition, at that high level of abstraction, the problem is the problem of the ontological status of "negativity," nonbeing, what is not (or is not simply the fullness or presence of positive being). In the simplest sense, we are talking about intentional consciousness, say in perception or empirical judgments, and the ontological status of agency. Consciousness is not a wholly *"positive"* phenomenon in this (Kantian and post-Kantian) way of looking at it. If it were it would be something like a mere complex registering and responding device (of the same ontological status as a thermometer). But an empirical judgment about the world ("there is a red book on the table") is not simply wrung out of one by a perceptual episode. One is *not* simply wholly absorbed in the presence of the world to one, and that *"not"* is the beginning of all the German problems Žižek wants to trace out in order to get to his own interpretation. In making any such judgment I "negate" the mere immediacy or givenness of perceptual content, negate it as immediate and putatively given, and take up a position of sorts about what is there.[7] And in agency I am not simply causally responsive to inclinations and desires; there is no fullness of positive being here either. I interrupt or negate merely positive being (what I feel inclined to do, experience as wanting to do) by deliberating and resolving what to do. Any such inclination cannot count as a reason for an action except as "incorporated" within a maxim, a general policy one has for actions of such a type.[8] So when Hegel reminds us in the Preface to the *Phenomenology of Spirit* that we must think "substance" "also as subject," he does not, it would appear, mean for us to think subject merely as an attribute of substance or an appearance of what remains, basically, substance, or an epiphenomenon of substance.[9] The whole point of speculative idealism is to think substance as not-just-substance, the negation of mere substance as such; and to think subject as substance, what is not-mere-subject. A tall order. The closest first approximation of what he means is Aristotelian: subjectivity (thinking and acting according to norms) is the distinct being-at-work (*energeia*, Hegelian *Wirklichkeit*) of the biological life-form that is the human substance; this in the same sense in which Aristotle says, if the eye were body, *seeing* would be its form, its distinctive being-at-work. This being-at-work is how that substantial life-form appears, and not any attestation of the self-negating Gap that is substance. (This is in disagreement with Žižek's Lacanian reading, as at p. 380, inter alia.)[10]

The way Žižek poses the question itself, then, reveals a deeply Schellingian orientation at the beginning and throughout the whole book. (This will not be surprising to anyone who has read *Tarrying with the Negative* or *The Parallax View*.) That is, the question this observation is taken to raise is: What could such a subject with such a negating capacity *be*? And even more sweepingly: What must *being* be, such that there are, can be, "positive" beings and such "negating" ones? For the early Schelling, this led to the conclusion that the distinction between such subjects and objects could be neither an objective distinction nor a subjective one, so the "ground" of the possibility of the distinction must be an "indifference point," neither subject nor object (prompting Hegel's famous, friendship-destroying remark, that this is the night in which all cows are black). And in what could be called the Schellingian tradition, the assumption has long been that neither Kant nor Fichte had, could have, an adequate answer to this question because for them, "being" is "secondary," not primary (an "appearance," or a posited "not-I"),[11] and the "Absolute" is such a "groundless" or putatively (but impossibly) self-grounding subject. The interesting question has always been how to locate the mature Hegel in this field of possibilities.[12] As already noted, for Žižek that position involves a commitment to a "gap" or "rupture" in being. "Speech (presup)poses a lack/hole in the positive order of being."[13] "The void of our knowledge corresponds to a void in being itself, to the ontological incompleteness of reality."[14] There are many such formulations.[15]

This all has deep connections with the original Eleatic problems of non-being (how I could possibly say "what is not" in uttering falsehoods; a problem because what is not is not, is impossible); hence Žižek's sustained attention to the second half of Plato's *Parmenides*. But the German version has a unique, different dimension, and that dimension is the beginning of my deepest disagreement with Žižek. To see the problem (or to see it as I see it, consider what Hegel draws our attention to when he is stating his understanding of his deepest connection to Kant:

> It is one of the profoundest and truest insights to be found in the *Critique of Reason* that the unity which constitutes the essence of the concept is recognized as the original synthetic unity of apperception, the unity of the "I think," or of self-consciousness.—This proposition is all that there is to the so-called transcendental deduction of the categories which, from the beginning, has however been regarded as the most difficult piece of Kantian philosophy.[16]

It is *for this reason*—the apperceptive nature of conceiving, the fact that conceiving is apperceiving—that perceptual awareness, judgment, actions, any determinate intentional awareness, cannot be understood as simply *being* in a mental state (in the fullness or positivity of being, in the manner in which we would say that a computer "is calculating"). For in perceiving, I am also conscious of perceiving, conscious of myself perceiving. In believing anything, I am conscious of my believing, of myself committed to a belief. In acting, I would not *be* acting, were I not conscious of myself acting. (An action is not something that goes on whether I am conscious of it or not, like water boiling. It is only action if I am conscious of myself acting.) There are then two complications in this view that require extensive discussion but can only be noted here. The first: as Sebastian Rödl often notes, the above should not suggest, as the grammar might, that there are two acts of mind involved.[17] There is only one. Action *is* consciousness of action; there is no action unless I am conscious of myself acting.[18] The second: apperception is not a two-place intentional relation. I am not self-conscious in the way I am conscious of objects (or an obvious regress would threaten). One could say that I am conscious of objects apperceptively or self-consciously; never that I am conscious of objects and also conscious of myself as a second object.[19] (This is also why first-order self-*knowledge* is not observational or inferential [not of an object "already there"] but *constitutive*.[20] In any respect relevant to my practical identity [and not any empirical feature], I am what I take myself to be [professor, citizen, social-democrat-liberal]. Or at least I am provisionally; I must also enact what I take myself to be, or it is a mere confabulation or an untested pledge about what I will do. In Žižekian language, there is no self except as posited and enacted, and the apparent paradox [who is doing the positing?] is no paradox.)[21]

When Žižek takes on the apperception claim in his own terms,[22] he notes how implausible it is to think that every act of consciousness is an act of self-consciousness. It seems clearly empirically false. But that is because the supposition concerns two acts, consciousness of the object and consciousness of the subject aware of the object, and the most important claim in the idealist treatment of the issue is that this is not so. There is only one act. Self-consciousness is not consciousness of an object. We do not need Deleuzian "virtuality," or an ontology with an "actuality of the possible." And there is no link in the treatment of this issue by Kant, Fichte, and Hegel to Žižek's own negative ontology, his claim that "what, ultimately, 'there is' is only the absolute Difference, the self-repelling Gap."[23] What there is, in the sense of this inquiry, is a possible space of reasons, into which persons may be socialized and within which constant *self*-correction, self-negation, is possible.

This may all already be "too much information" for a reader interested in how Žižek proposes to offer a renewed version of dialectical materialism and so a critical theory of late-modern capitalism. But this path through German idealism is the path he has chosen, and it is important to know if his version is leading us correctly. With many more pages to demonstrate it, the point of the above formulation would be to suggest a different way of understanding the problem of "negativity" in that tradition, one that will not lead us to gaps or voids or holes in being (or "groundless Acts" in the absence of "the big Other"). I do not fully understand the claims about holes in the fabric of being, and at any rate, we do not need the claim if we go in the direction I am suggesting. For if that formulation of apperception is correct, it means we are able to account for the inappropriateness of psychological or naturalist accounts of such states, all without a gappy ontology (in the sense if not in the same way that Frege and the early Husserl criticized psychologism without an "alternate" ontology). If believing is to be conscious of believing, then it is impossible just to "*be*" believing. For me to be conscious of my believing something is to be conscious of why I believe what I do (however fragmentary, confused, or unknowingly inconsistent such reasons may be). When I want to know what I believe, I am investigating what I ought to believe.[24] Such grounds may be incomplete and may commit one to claims one is unaware of as such, and much belief is habitual and largely unreflective, but never completely so. In such a case, it is just a view I am entertaining, not what I believe. Likewise with action. It is constitutive of action that an agent can be responsive to the "why" question, and that means to be in a position to give a reason for my action. (Again, this is not a possible exchange: "Why did you do that?" "I don't know, I just did it." Your body may have moved, but you didn't do anything.)[25] Doxastic, cognitive, and intentional states are thus "in the space of reasons," and to ask for, say, neuropsychological causes for having come to be in that state is to make a category mistake, to have misunderstood the question, to offer something we cannot use. Such causes are irrelevant to *my* having the reasons I have, and your understanding the reasons I have, all of which must be enunciated and "backed" first-personally. No gaps in being need apply, any more than the possibility of people playing bridge, following the norms of bridge, and exploring strategies for winning need commit us to any unusual gappy ontology to account for the possibility of norm-responsive bridge following. Anyone playing the game is not just acting out responses to cues but is, at the same time as playing and making moves, always "holding open" the possibility of revising strategy, challenging someone on the rules and so forth. This is *what it is* to be following rules, not to be instantiating laws.[26] This capacity is possible because it is certainly actual, and that means that materially embodied beings are able to engage in complex, rule-following practices, the explanation of which is not furthered by reference to their neurological properties. (In his *Phenomenology*, Hegel's formulation of this sort of logical negativity is that consciousness is "always beyond itself," and he frequently, for this reason, characterizes consciousness as a self-negation.)[27]

Now it is possible for Žižek to say just *that*, that possibility for norm-responsiveness, since it is a materially embodied capacity not explicable in material terms, is the gap or void or self-negation he wants to attribute to Hegel's ontology, the "more than material, without being immaterial."[28] But that seems too anodyne for what he wants to say and for the connection he wants to make with Lacan. For, on this way of looking at the matter, there is no need for a paradoxical negative ontology. Of course, it is possible and important that someday researchers will discover why animals with human brains can do these things and animals without human brains cannot, and some combination of astrophysics and evolutionary theory will be able to explain why humans have ended up with the brains they have. But these are not philosophical problems and they do not generate any philosophical problems.[29] (The problems are: What *is* a compelling reason and why? Under what conditions are the reasons people give for what they do "their own" reasons, reasons and policies they can genuinely "identify with"?)[30]

Put another way, Žižek is quite right to note that the importance of the shift from the early to the mature Hegel involves at its core Hegel's realization that "logic" was not a preparation for metaphysics, but that logic *was* metaphysics. But this means that a consideration of being-in-its-intelligibility is the only sort of metaphysics that is possible (to be is to be intelligible, something like the motto of Greek philosophy and so the beginning of philosophy).[31] But this also means that the "movement" in Hegel's *Encyclopedia* from a "logic of nature" to a "logic of *Geist*" has nothing to do with any "materialist evolutionism."[32] Hegel's metaphysics is a logic, and the *intelligibility* of nature at some point, speaking very causally, "runs out," is unable in its terms to account for the complex, rule-governed activities materially embodied beings are capable of. This is not a new, nonnatural capacity that emerges in time, but it emerges in a systematic consideration of the resources for rendering intelligible that are available to accounts of nature.

There is a phenomenological account in Hegel of the context within which materially embodied organic beings, living beings in a minimal self-relation (a self-sentiment necessary to preserve life) can be imagined interacting in a way that "for them" transcends mere self-sustenance, a "move" that will not be comprehensible as a move in the game of mere animal life. That is the famous account in Chapter 4 of the 1807 *Phenomenology of Spirit*. The problematic is to imagine such living beings struggling, perhaps over resources, to the death if necessary, when the possibility is introduced of a participant's indifference to his own life in the service of a demand to be recognized (a "nonnatural" norm), when what one demands is not mere submission but a pledge of service, an acknowledgment of the other's entitlement. "Spirit" emerges in this imagined social contestation, in what we come to demand of each other, not in the interstices of being. This is a phenomenological account (what *it is like* to be and come to be *Geist*), not an encyclopedic logic, but it also introduces the Hegelian account of reason. We see that it is not to be understood as a mere capacity for calculation or merely strategic, but as a sociohistorical practice, what Brandom calls the "game of giving and asking for reasons"[33] to each other, and it introduces the central question of Hegel's historical narrative: Is it plausible to claim that we are getting better at justifying ourselves to each other or not?[34]

One can see this (that the above account is not Žižek's direction) in his very detailed treatment of Fichte.[35] Žižek follows closely the account of Fichte in the recently published undergraduate lectures given by Dieter Henrich at Harvard in the seventies (*Between Kant and Hegel*), and this creates two problems.[36] In the first place, Henrich confuses the problem of apperceptive consciousness in experience and action with the problem of reflective self-identification, how to find and identify my unique self. Those are two different problems, and there is no indication that Fichte confused them and plenty of evidence that he was aware of the difference.[37] Secondly, Žižek accepts Henrich's charge that Fichte confused "logical" with "real" opposition, switching from one to the other, and so could provide no satisfying account of the relation of the I to the not-I. But Fichte was quite clear on the difference, and his remarks track closely the remarks made above about the status of the normative in Kant and the early idealists. A few examples will have to suffice. Here is Fichte in a typical statement of general principles:

> The basic contention of the philosopher, as such, is as follows: Though the self may exist only for itself, there necessarily arises for it at once an existence external to it; the ground of the latter lies in the former, and is conditioned thereby; self-consciousness and consciousness of something that is to be—not ourselves,—are necessarily connected; but the first is to be regarded as the "conditioning" factor, and the second as the conditioned.[38]

But we don't know just from this what "condition" means and especially how it relates to the key term, "positing" (*setzen*), the positing of the *nicht-Ich*.

When he tries to explain what he means, though, he reverts to the "autonomy of the normative" language invoked above. He writes in the 1797 Introduction to the *Wissenschaftslehre*:

> So what then is the overall gist of the *Wissenschaftslehre*, summarized in a few words? It is this: reason is absolutely self-sufficient; it exists only for itself. But nothing exists for reason except reason itself. It follows that everything reason is must have its foundation in reason itself and must be explicable solely on the basis of reason itself and not on the basis of anything outside of reason, for reason could not get outside of itself without renouncing itself. In short the *Wissenschaftslehre* is transcendental idealism.³⁹

In the Second Introduction to the 1796/1799 *Wissenschaftslehre (nova methodo)*, translated as "Foundations of Transcendental Philosophy," he writes: "The idealist observes that experience in its entirety is nothing but an acting on the part of a rational being." The most revealing passage follows this claim about the activity of a rational being, and makes clear what Fichte means by referring to such an "activity." The passage is a gloss on "the viewpoint of idealism."

> The idealist observes how there must come to be things for the individual. Thus the situation is different for the [observed] individual than it is for the philosopher. The individual is confronted with things, men, etc., that are independent of him. But the idealist says, "There are no things outside me and present independently of me." Though the two say opposite things, they do not contradict each other. For the idealist, from his own viewpoint, displays the necessity of the individual's view. When the idealist says, "outside of me," he means "outside of reason"; when the individual says the same thing, he means "outside of my person."⁴⁰

Or, in an even more summary claim from Fichte's notes: "The I is reason."⁴¹ Now this rational self-satisfaction is only something we can "strive" for infinitely according to Fichte, but the larger point is the one of relevance for Žižek's reading. That point concerns the necessary link between the self-conscious character of experience and action, understood this way, and reason, a norm that does not play a prominent role in Žižek's Schellingian account. (The other Hegelian issue that does not play a major role for Žižek is sociality, Geist, and the issues are related, as I will try to show in the next section.) The condition of modern atheism means for Žižek, in Lacanian terms, that there is and can be no longer any "big Other," any guarantor of at least the possibility of any resolution of normative skepticism and conflicts. But no transcendent guarantor is not the same thing as no possible reliance on reason in our own deliberations and in our claims on others. Even a position (like Nietzsche's, say) that held that most conscious appeals to reasons are symptoms, that true reasons lie elsewhere (not the slave's virtuousness but his ressentiment motivated his submission), is committed to the link. (Ressentiment is his reason, counted by him—in self-deceit—as warranting action, submission and moralistic condemnation of the Master.) To claim something or to do something is to offer to give reasons for the claim or the deed, and if there are reasons either to reject the reasons or to reject the claim of sincerity, we are still in, cannot exit, the space of reasons. (An immediate consequence: the first sentence of Žižek's conclusion—"What the inexistence of the big Other signals is that every ethical and/ or moral edifice has to be grounded on an abyssal act which is, in the most radical sense imaginable, political"—makes zero Hegelian sense.[42] Something understood by an agent as an "abyssal" act is a delusion, the pathos of self-inflating and posed heroism, and the gesture belongs in the Hegelian zoo along with the Beautiful Soul, the Knight of Virtue, and especially the Frenzy of Self-Conceit.[43] And if the act is "abyssal," then "politics" simply means "power," power backed by nothing but resolve and will, likely met with nothing but resolve and will.)

To see the relevance of, on the contrary, the connection between self-consciousness and reason to Žižek's project in the book, we need to turn to his long, explicit discussion of Hegel.

III

"In this sense, the post-Hegelian turn to "concrete reality, irreducible to notional mediation," should rather be read as a desperate posthumous revenge of metaphysics, as an attempt to reinstall metaphysics, although in the inverted form of the primacy of concrete reality."[44] Truer words were never spoken in Hegel's voice. In explaining such a claim, Žižek makes a number of salient points about Hegel. For example, one of the most curious things about Hegel's basic position is that it can be fairly summarized by saying that it is no positive position. Rather it is the right understanding of the other logically possible positions. Žižek gets this aspect of Hegel exactly right (cf. p. 387 ff.) and has a number of useful things to say about it and its implications. Moreover, Žižek's interest in Lacan leads him to three other aspects of Hegel that are quite important but often neglected in both conventional (what Žižek calls "textbook") interpretations and more "up-to-date" contemporary reconstructions. This is the dimension, first, of "retroactivity," also sometimes known as "belatedness" (*Nachträglichkeit*), or what Žižek rightly described as Hegel's insistence on the logic of a deed or claim or event that can be said to "posit its own presuppositions" retroactively. (A dream's meaning is constituted by the telling, not "recovered." A trauma becomes the *trauma it is* retroactively, in its interrogation.) In Hegel the notion is most important in his account of act-descriptions and intentions. There is no literal backward causation, but what it is we did and why we did it can be said to come to be what they are only after we have acted (after we have seen what we were actually committed to doing; what others acknowledge, or not, as what we did). Second, in a related claim, Žižek takes much more seriously than most other commentators the unusual and initially paradoxical thesis that Spirit must be understood as a "product of itself." Žižek's discussions of all these topics are, in my view, on the mark and valuable.[46] Moreover, because he does such justice to these themes, especially the latter, he can, third, reject the picture of Hegelian historical action so familiar in critical theory criticisms, especially by Adorno and Adornoitans. This is the picture of *Geist* externalizing itself in its products (its "self-negation"), thereby being alienated from them, until it can "return to itself" in its externality, and so be reconciled with itself in a sublated self-identity (the negation of negation). This is also "the great narcissistic devouring maw" picture of Hegel, devouring and negating otherness in a mad project to become everything, the picture so beloved by Adorno in his dismissal of Hegel as the epitome of "identity thinking" (cf. p. 300). But however right he is in rejecting that caricature, Žižek's own picture seems to me too influenced by his picture of Lacan (not to mention middle Schelling) and so does not allow the true Hegelian alternative in these very abstract possibilities to emerge, especially with respect to the problem of reason (Hegel's "big Other") and sociality.

IV

This brings us, in other words, to the more practical and "critical" question, as Žižek puts it, of "how to be a Hegelian today," whether it is possible, what the implications are of Žižek's interpretation of the notion he places at the center of a Hegelianism—a "self-negating" or "gappy" phenomenal reality. With that ontology as a background, philosophy is supposed to be its own time comprehended in thought. Our time is still the time of bourgeois capitalism and its central institutions: private property, commercial republics, individual-rights-based legal institutions, the privatization of religion and the ideal of religious tolerance, romantic love, love-based marriages, nuclear families, and the (putative) separation of state and civil society. What does "thought's comprehension"—in this case "dialectical" thought—"comprehend"?

One broad-based starting point for such a Hegelianism, shared by Žižek and most "Hegelians": a commitment to the historicity of norms, but without a historical relativism, as if we were trapped inside specific assumptions and cannot think our way out of them. The "universal" for Hegel—the clearest name for which would simply be "freedom"—is always accessible in some way but as the "concrete universal," a universal understood in a way inflected by a time and a place, partial and incomplete, requiring interpretation and reinterpretation and dialectical extension. For example, if we want to understand why gender-based division of labor became so much less credible a norm in the last third of the twentieth century, and exclusively in the technologically advanced commercial republics of the West, one begins to become a "Hegelian" with the simple realization of how implausible it would be to insist that the injustice of such a basis for a division of labor, the reasons for rejecting such a practice, were always in principle available from the beginning of human attempts to justify their practices, and were "discovered" sometime in the early 1970s. And yet our commitment to such a rejection is far stronger than "a new development in how we go on." The practice is irrational and so unjust, however historically indexed the "grip" of such a claim clearly is.

Žižek proposes to defend a Hegel for whom any claim about historical rationality (like this one) is always retrospective, never prospective and predicting, and in this "open-ended" Hegel, he is surely right. (It often goes unnoticed that Hegel's famous claim that the owl of Minerva takes flight only at dusk, that philosophy can begin to paint its gray on gray only when a form of life has grown old, means that he is announcing that the form of life "comprehended by thought" in the *Philosophy of Right* has grown old, is dying, and only because of this can it now be comprehended by Hegel. It is hardly the image one would propose were one trying to claim that we had reached some utopia of realized reason.)[47] Moreover, the retrospective dimension is quite important. It is only after the world-historical influence of Christianity that Greek philosophy could come to seem unable to provide the resources to account for what would eventually come to be understood as Christian inwardness, subjectivity, and so a very different view of agency. There is no World-Spirit puppet master in this picture.

But the alternative to any "shadow of dialectical materialism" must be something like a "dialectical idealism." This of course means simply that there are no "material contradictions."[48] Contradictions result from some self-opposition in an action or practice directed by a subject. This can be in the form of "performative contradictions" in a speech act, or practical contradictions in action. (Hobbes gave us a fine example of the latter: in the state of nature, everyone doing what is maximally rational for the individual's point of view—preemptively striking others—produces what is for everyone the worst possible outcome. Agents contradict themselves by acting rationally.) On the assumption of collective subjectivity (*Geist*) one can imagine how one might try to show that some institutional practice in a form of life "contradicts," in the means it rationally chooses, the overall ends genuinely sought by that society. And all of this depends on what one can show or not; whether a successor social form can be said to be achieving more successfully what a prior social form was attempting or not: hence, determination negation, internal critique, all the Hegelian desiderata. (Gender-based division of labor came to be understood as inconsistent with the already existing ideal of equal protection under the law and meritocratic social mobility, and at a time when changes in the technology of production and the need for many more workers in the greatest period of economic prosperity in history made possible such a realization.)

But we are certainly far enough from the ("dead") particular historical form of bourgeois society that Hegel thought he had comprehended, and our own form of life could plausibly said be said to be growing sufficiently "old" (dysfunctional at least) before our eyes, for us to ask: What *is* the Hegelian account of the large-scale collapse of the state-civil society distinction so crucial to him, the disintegration of the *Stände*, or estates, central to his account of political participation, the emergence of mass consumer societies totally unlike anything in Hegel's political philosophy, the changes in the technology of warfare that make the notion of an occasional war to shake us out of our prosaic complacency suicidal (not to mention the end of citizen armies), the creation of a globalized financial system that renders obsolete even the notion of the "owners" of property, and on and on in such a vein?

Žižek's answer is not surprising, and that answer raises the largest question of all, the one I found the most dissatisfyingly addressed. Like many others, he wants to say that bourgeois society is fundamentally self-contradictory, and I take that to mean "unreformable." We need a wholly new ethical order, and that means "the Act." Its pretense to being a rational form is undermined by the existence of a merely contingent particular, a figurehead at the top, the monarch. (A better question, it seems to me, is why Hegel bothers, given how purely symbolic and even pointless such a dotter of i's and crosser of t's turns out to be.)[49] And, following many others, Žižek claims that the admitted aporia of "the rabble" (der *Pöbel*) in Hegel, what appears to be a permanent underclass of poor, is another mark of the fundamental irrationality of the Hegelian picture of modern ethical life (*Sittlichkeit*). He agrees with the analysis of a recent author, Frank Ruda, and says that Ruda "is fully justified in reading Hegel's short passages on the rabble in his *Philosophy of Right* as symptomatic of his entire philosophy of right, if not of his entire system."[50] In other context, Žižek claims that modern secular bourgeois culture and late capitalism produce their own opposite, evangelical fundamentalism, for example, for which there is no "*Aufhebung*," no return to an elevated form of bourgeois politics and reformed capitalism. (All this in the Lacanian manner in which what is repressed is created by the act of repression itself.)

Whether these relatively brief interludes demonstrate that bourgeois society and a capitalist system of production are fundamentally contradictory (even in the idealist sense sketched above), so that calls for reform would be as absurd as calls for remaining in the state of nature but "reforming it" would be in Hobbes, is too large a topic for this sort of discussion. I can only say that if the basic norm of such a society is, according to Hegel, some institutionally secured state of equal recognitive status, where this also means direct political attention to the material (familial, cultural, economic) conditions for such a possibility, or some egalitarian idea of freedom (no one can be free unless all are), I see no reason to think so, from the occasional remarks given here. The fact that there appears to be ever weakening political will in, for example, the United States for any attention to such a common good (even public schools are now slowly but surely emerging as a target for the ever more powerful far right) is very likely a pathology that needs explaining.[51] Perhaps we need the help of Lacanians to do this (although Hegel was content simply to point out the danger and irrationality of romantic nationalists in his own day), but that great dream of social democrats everywhere—"Sweden in the Sixties!"—does not seem to me something that inevitably produces its own irrational and irreconcilable Unreason, or Other. More lawyers for the poor in Texas, affordable day care, universal health care, several fewer aircraft carriers, more worker control over working conditions, regulated and perhaps nationalized banks—all are reasonable extensions of that bourgeois ideal itself, however sick and often even deranged modern bourgeois society has become. (*Citizens United* was not a logically inescapable result of capitalist logic. It was the result of the ravings of several lunatic judges. We are the only advanced capitalist democracy on earth that allows legalized bribery.) But these are topics for another context (and a soapbox). I will close with a reflection in the Žižekian spirit. Žižek gives us two images, a literary and a cinematic image, to help us understand the dialectical gymnastics involved in his attempt to reactualize Hegel for contemporary purposes. The first concerns the problem of Hegelian "reconciliation," and the example is the mysterious and moving ending of J. M. Coetzee's novel *Disgrace*. Žižek invokes the basic logical structure for rendering "negativity" intelligible that he uses throughout his book. David Lurie appears to have "negated" the status quo, the "big Other" of prudence, trust in the police, holding individuals responsible for their deeds, and seeking to redress wrongs done to individuals (justice), because he has come to see the inadequacy of such a faith for the current, postapartheid reality of South Africa. That is all "negated" by his simply doing whatever he can do to minimize the indignities done to euthanized dogs, satisfied with the gesture of providing for a respectful disposal. That, of course, is, pitiably, not very much in the way of reconciliation. He seems to have accepted his daughter's guilt-burdened acquiescence to her neighbor's complicity in her own rape, and internalized it in his own way, as the price one must pay to continue living with some "ethical dignity" (Žižek's phrase) in South Africa. In the world of unavoidable complicity in the South African crimes, the loss of everything is a "wager" that "this total loss will be converted into some kind of ethical dignity."[52]

But Žižek claims that there is "something missing" in this ending, some gesture of defiance and revolt that could be called the "negation of this negation," some "barely perceptible repetitive gesture of resistance ... a pure figure of the undead drive," by which he means a *Versagung*, a refusal, of the initial or first negation that would not return us to the status quo ex ante, but that would originate the realization of "the fantasmatic status of the *objet a* (the fantasy frame which sustained the subject's desire), so that the *Versagung*, which equals the act of traversing the fantasy, opens up the space for the emergence of the pure drive beyond fantasy."⁵³ The natural thing one wants to say to this suggestion is that any such gesture that would satisfy what Žižek is after would presuppose that everything about David's original position was a "fantasy frame," that there is no "big Other," and by disabusing ourselves of this delusion we would be in a position to open up that space for the emergence of a "pure" drive beyond fantasy. *But just this latter sounds like David's original romantic fantasy itself*, that he is a Byronic servant of eros, can see through the hypocrisy and phoniness of "big Other" conventional morality, and so forth. That is the fantasy *he has disabused himself of*, and why his gesture of wholly symbolic generosity is at once so affirmative and dignified and so pathetic and so limited. There is no Žižekian gesture of defiance because David has seen through the dangerous self-deceit in presuming one is "he who is supposed to know." His assisting Bev in euthanizing the dogs and caring for their remains is done in a different way than that expected by Žižek, a "negation of his first negation," a refusal of mere acceptance of his and his daughter's fate. In the last gesture of the novel, he "gives up" the dog Bev had expected him to save, even as he has "given" *himself* up to his fate, not merely suffered it. Finally, said another way, there is nothing more un-Hegelian than the idea of the "emergence of the pure drive beyond fantasy." David's gesture means he remains the subject of whatever drives he has, not subject to them. The idea of "pure" drives (or "pure" anything) belongs in the Hegelian zoo mentioned before.

The second example is equally interesting. It is Hitchcock's *Vertigo*. Here the idea of a negation, and a negation of negation, is easier to track. Scottie loses Madeleine, or the woman he thought was Madeleine; she dies. But it was all a plot by Elster to murder his wife. Madeleine was not Madeleine but Judy, a working-class woman Elster had enlisted in the plot. When Scottie finds this out, he can be said to *have lost his very loss*, lost the meaning of his first loss. He had not lost Madeleine, because Madeleine was Judy. He discovers the bitterly ironic truth that the woman he was trying to "make up" to look like a fake Madeleine was (is) actually the real Madeleine, because his original Madeleine was a fake. So, as with *Disgrace*, we get an ambiguous ending: Scottie gazing "into the abyss," looking down where Judy has fallen, either a broken man, disabused of all the idealizations and fantasy that sustain love, or a "new" man, freed from his illusions and reconciled with this new realism. Žižek makes use of this structure to suggest a limitation in a Hegelian "negation of negation": that both the suggested readings of Scottie miss something, because they understand the "antagonisms" at issue still too "formally" (what I called before and defended as "dialectical idealism"). Here Žižek insists that we need to do justice to what falls "outside" of either resolution, an "excess," a "contingent remainder," a "little piece of reality." As Žižek goes on to explain what he means by this, he seems to me to come close to reverting to the kind of positivistic, pseudorealist metaphysics he had rightly rejected. (See the quotation at the beginning of section III above.) And the talk of excess and remainders makes it irrelevant that Žižek does not mean something that "simply eludes dialectical mediation" but is a "product of this mediation.[54] Such an excess or remainder still functions in his criticism as "unmediated," and that notion remains profoundly un-Hegelian, for reasons I have tried to present throughout. But there is something quite right about the relevance of the *Vertigo* structure to the German tradition as, I want to say, Hegel would see it. For in that tradition there is certainly the notion of *modernity itself* as "loss." Hölderlin and Schiller come to mind, and the mourning for the lost "beauty" of the Greek world can certainly mirror the sorrow of Scottie over the lost Madeleine-version of Judy. Then one can say that Hegel became Hegel when, for him, that loss was lost, that negation negated, with a more prosaic view of Greek accomplishments. I mean when, under the influence of the Scottish Enlightenment thinkers, he came to see that there was no simple loss in the end of the Greek ideal, and losing that notion of loss was a gain, as he appreciated the development of modern civil society and the error of fantasizing the loss of a more natural harmony.[55] The Helen-like "Madeleine" was really "Judy" all along. (This all in its own way confirms Žižek's insistence that Hegelian mediation does not issue in a "third," synthetic position, but in the right understanding of the antagonism between the "negation" and the "negation of the negation.") This can even be put in terms of Hegel's secularized Christianity—Madeleine *was really Judy*, or Judy had successfully, for Scottie, *become* Madeleine, all prompting her plaintive "Why can't you just love me for who I am?" Every "Judy" is also a "Madeleine," every "Madeleine" really a "Judy" in this egalitarian, Christian vision.

This is of course something Scottie cannot appreciate, and for reasons also relevant to Hegel. For the very structure of the appearance of Judy as Madeleine had been manipulated for gain by Elster, in a way parallel to the ideologically distorted and so false pretensions to achieved equality in contemporary bourgeois societies ("fair exchanges between labor and capital in the marketplace"). The truth of the identity was ruined, made an untruth, because it was *staged*. What Hegel thought was the greatest accomplishment of modern civil society—its ability to educate (as *Bildung*) its citizens to their equal status and profound dependence on each other, and so to educate them to the virtues of civility and trustworthiness—has become a lie (if it ever was the truth), and the shipping magnates and tycoons like Elster "steer" this *Bildung* in a way that ends up wholly theatrical, as in the "theater of Madeleine" put on for Scottie's benefit and to manipulate him. He cannot be educated to the truth of the speculative sentence that "Judy is Madeleine," that essence is its own appearance, because of this distortion. Accordingly, Scottie's attempts to remake Judy into Madeleine, rather than being a way of realizing that Judy already is Madeleine, come off as manipulative and as reifying as Elster's. (Another, more depressing identity: Scottie and Elster, creators of a false Madeleine.)

This forces the question of whether there is much left in contemporary society that provides any sort of material basis for Hegel's aspirations about these potentially transformative and educative potentials of modern civil society. No one can be anything but profoundly pessimistic about this possibility, but the search for such possible "traces of reason"[56] seems to me a more genuinely Hegelian and still possible prospect than anything that could result from "abyssal Acts."

Notes

1 This essay is a reprint. The editors thank University of Chicago Press for the permission: Robert Pippin, *Interanimations. Receiving Modern German Philosophy* (Chicago: Chicago University Press, 2015), 91–116. © Chicago University Press.

2 Slavoj Žižek, *Less than Nothing: Hegel and the Shadow of Dialectical Materialism* (London: Verso, 2012).

3 See Žižek's remarks on Hegel and contemporary finance capitalism in *Less than Nothing*, 244. Perhaps Zadie Smith's trenchant summary is the best: states now "de-regulate to privatize gain and re-regulate to nationalize loss." Zadie Smith, "The North West London Blues." NYR Blog, June 2, 2012, http://www.nybooks.com/blogs/nyrblog/2012/jun/02/north-west-london-blues/ (accessed December 21, 2021).

4 There is a sober, clear statement of what, from a Hegelian point of view, we now need: "breaking out of the capitalist horizon without falling into the trap of returning to the eminently pre-modern notion of a balanced, (self-) restrained society" (Žižek, *Less than Nothing*, 257). But as he goes on to explain this position, the core turns out to be that "the subject has to recognize in its alienation from substance the separation of substance from itself" (258). I have not been able to understand how that helps us do what the sober statement insists on. This is an issue that will recur frequently below.

5 Lots of quibbles and qualifications are possible here. I can't see why anyone would take (iii) seriously. I would include "deconstruction" under (iv), not (ii), would argue for more categories (pragmatism, of the analytic [Brandomian], Rortyean, or Habermasian variety; anomalous monism; phenomenology, which is still alive and kicking in some quarters; Wittgenstein's approach), and I would defend a Hegelian version of compatibilism. But what is important is what Žižek is for; his own position.

6 Žižek, *Less than Nothing*, 6–7.

7 In a more extensive and so more careful discussion, several caveats would be necessary here. The case of perceptual consciousness, while apperceptive, is not of the same logical type as a judgment, an empirical claim to knowledge, and more care would be needed to account for the role of spontaneity. But perceptual consciousness is not mere differential responsiveness, and that is what we need for the "negativity" problem. See my "Robert Brandom's Hegel." In *Interanimations. Receiving Modern German Philosophy* (Chicago: Chicago University Press, 2015), 29–62.

8   The "incorporation thesis," given that name by the Kant scholar Henry Allison in his *Kant's Theory of Freedom* (Cambridge: Cambridge University Press, 1990), emerged as an explicit theme relatively late in Kant's work (in his *Religion within the Limits of Reason Alone* [1793]) and does not mean "causes only affect me insofar as I allow them to affect me" (Žižek, *Less than Nothing*, 169–70). "Only insofar as I count them as reasonable grounds to do something" would be more accurate, and inclinations causally affect me (I can be powerfully inclined to do something); they just cannot be said to produce on their own the bodily movement, if it is to count as an action. There are not many such errors and slips, but they are irritating when they occur. The *Critique of Pure Reason* appeared in 1781, not 1787 (11); Henrich's famous article referred to "Fichtes ursprüngliche Einsicht," not his "Grundeinsicht." And (for me the most significant) the newspaper editor at the end of *The Man Who Shot Liberty Valance* did not say, "When reality doesn't fit the legend, print the legend" (420). He said something much more relevant to Žižek's concerns: "This is the West, sir. When the legend becomes fact, print the legend."

9   I say "it would appear" in order to acknowledge that for Žižek, we *should* say *something like* "substance" negates *itself*, creates a kind of "gap" and incompleteness, and that "space" *is* the subject. (But in what sense could the subject also be said to "substantialize itself"? Negate itself as subject just by being substance?) At any rate, Žižek doesn't mean that a subject is just a kind of property of material substance. I think I understand what the gap or self-negation view would mean in Freudian terms—that natural, even biological maturation *itself* produces a subject divided against itself, unable to realize or satisfy the primary processes—but I don't think that is the problem the post-Kantians were addressing, and I will try to say why below.

10 I have no space to discuss Žižek's interesting parallel reading of substance–subject and id–ego except to agree that in neither case does "wo es war, soll ich werden" amount to a rational appropriation of or control over or simple reconciliation with the "*nicht-Ich*." See Žižek, *Less than Nothing*, 389 ff.

11 Not an unreasonable view. See J. G. Fichte, *Introductions to the "Wissenschaftslehre" and Other Writings*, trans. Breazeale (Indianapolis, IN: Hackett, 1994), 84.

12 According to Žižek (*Less than Nothing*, 144), Hegel's unique position is to deny that we need any "third" to ground both subject and object. "His [Hegel's] point is precisely that there is no need for a Third element, the medium or ground beyond subject and object-substance. We start with objectivity and the subject is nothing but the self-mediation of objectivity." But this simply *is* objective idealism and has not yet differentiated Hegel's view, as I will try to show.

13 Žižek, *Less than Nothing*, 75.

14 Ibid., 149.

15 Cf. Žižek's claim that Marx and Freud can only understand "antagonism" as a feature of social or psychic reality; they are "unable to articulate it as constitutive of reality, as the impossibility around which reality is constructed" (*Less than Nothing*, 250). I am with Marx and Freud (and, I think, Hegel) on

this one. This touches on the most difficult issue for me in the book, what is announced by the title: that "reality" is "less than nothing."

16 G. W. F. Hegel, *Science of Logic*, trans. A. V. Miller (London: George Allen & Unwin, 1969), 515. This quotation alone seems to me to foreclose the gloss given by Žižek on the Kant–Hegel–apperception relation (*Less than Nothing*, 286).

17 Sebastian Rödl, *Self-Consciousness* (Cambridge, MA: Harvard University Press, 2007), 17–64.

18 Cf. Rödl on a "non-empirical knowledge of a material reality" (ibid., 122). See also 131, 133–4, 138.

19 Put another way, the self-consciousness that is a necessary condition of any human doing or thinking adverts to *a way of one's doing or thinking*, as if adverbially, and involves no self-inspection. See my *Kant's Theory of Form*. One does what one does, one is aware of what one is aware of, one thinks what one thinks, all *knowingly*. Apropos the discussion below, cf. Fichte's formulations in the *Wissenschaftslehre*: "The self and the self-reverting act are perfectly identical concepts" (37) and "It is the immediate consciousness that I act and what I enact: it is that whereby I know something because I do it" (38). Or: "Without self-consciousness there is no consciousness whatever; but self-consciousness is possible only in the manner indicated: I am simply active" (41).

20 Žižek makes this same point himself, correctly, in my view, in an approving summary of Lukács (*Less than Nothing*, 220). See also Hegel in the *Science of Logic*: "The most important point for the nature of spirit is not only the relation of what it is in itself to what it is actually, but the relation of what it knows itself to be to what it actually is; because spirit is essentially consciousness, this self-knowing is a fundamental determination of its actuality" (37).

21 It is not because there is no original moment of self-origination. One has always already come to be in some position of self-positing, is always becoming who one is. There is a very great deal more to be said about this problem. For discussions of small subsets of these issues, see my *Hegel's Idealism: The Satisfaction of Self-Consciousness* (Cambridge: Cambridge University Press, 1989), chaps. 3 and 4; and *Hegel's Practical Philosophy. Rational Agency as Ethical Life* (Cambridge: Cambridge University Press, 2008), chap. 3.

22 Žižek, *Less than Nothing*, 347–8.

23 Ibid., 378. And yet, in other contexts, when, for example, he is discussing the "self-consciousness" of the state, Žižek seems to me to state the point being made here in just the way it is made here. See 406 ff.

24 One of the best-known statements and defenses of this "transparency" condition is Richard Moran's *Authority and Estrangement: An Essay on Self-Knowledge* (Princeton: Princeton University Press, 2001). See also Rödl, *Self-Consciousness*, chap. 3.

25 This issue, like every one in this paragraph, is much more complicated than this summary can do justice to. On this last point, the compelling films of the Dardenne brothers make clear how much more has to be said about the issue.

In all of their films, characters certainly *look like* they are acting without being able to say why. What is especially interesting is that they manage to suggest a link between this compelling opacity and the disintegrating fabric of late-capitalist working-class life. They integrate these philosophical-psychological elements with the social seamlessly. See *Le fils* (2002) especially.

26 This is also relevant to how the way animals have representations is different from ours. Theirs are intentional in their way, but they do not have the status of "cognitions," in the way ours do. A dog might see a human figure far away (downwind, let us say) and, seeing an unknown person, begin barking, only later to start wagging her tail as the known person it really is comes into view. *But the dog did not correct herself.* Here we do want to say that a perceptual cue prompted a response (one we can even call a rational response), and then a different perceptual cue (with more detail of visual features in view) prompted a different behavioral response. The fullness of positive being, we might say. (I've never noticed, for example, that my dog ever became embarrassed that she made such a mistake—which she often makes—since she has no way of knowing that she made a mistake that she ought to correct. That is not how she sees; she sees one set of cues, then she sees another. This would be one way of saying she has no unity of apperception.)

27 Here is the formulation from the so-called *Berlin Phenomenology* (my emphasis): "The I is now this subjectivity, this infinite relation to itself, but therein, namely in this subjectivity, lies its negative relation to itself, diremption, differentiation, judgment. *The I judges, and this constitutes it as consciousness*; it repels itself from itself; this is a logical determination." G. W. F. Hegel, *The Berlin Phenomenology*, trans. Michael Petry (Dordrecht: Reidel, 1981), 2.

28 Adrian Johnson, "Slavoj Žižek's Hegelian Reformation: Giving a Hearing to *The Parallax View*," *Diacritics* 37, no. 1 (2007): 3–20. Something like this position is available to Žižek if we understand the space of the Symbolic (in its Lacanian sense) as the space of the normative and so of reason. See his interpretation of Freud's controversial remark about "anatomy" being "destiny," "in other words a symbolic formation," a destiny we must make (*Less than Nothing*, 216).

29 Not that such discoveries could not be relevant to philosophy. They certainly are for Hegel. In §12 of the *Encyclopedia Logic*, Hegel says that philosophy "owes its development to the empirical sciences" (Hegel, *The Encyclopaedia Logic*, trans. T. F. Geraets and W. Suchting et al. (Indianapolis: Hackett, 1991); and in the remark to §246 of the *Philosophy of Nature*, he says that the *Philosophy of Nature* "presupposes and is conditioned by empirical physics" (G. W. F. Hegel, *Philosophy of Nature*, trans. A. V. Miller (Oxford: Oxford University Press, 1977). See also the Addition to §381 in the Introduction to the *Philosophy of Spirit*. These passages are all relevant to the question Žižek raises at 460.

30 When Žižek addresses this issue, he adopts a Nietzschean stance that seems to me unargued for and question begging (*Less than Nothing*, 429): "What kind of power (or authority) is it which needs to justify itself with reference to the interests of those over whom it rules, which accepts the need to provide reasons for its exercise? Does not such a notion of power undermine itself?" He goes on to call such a regime "anti-political" and "technocratic." But appeals to self-interest are only one sort of reason, and the constraints introduced by such

a requirement, if they undermine anything, undermine the notion of mastery and rule. They are not meant to be in the service of such notions.

31 The skeptical anxiety that we would thereby be treating being only as it is intelligible "by our finite lights" is illusory anxiety that Hegel takes himself to have methodically destroyed in the *Phenomenology*, the "deduction" of the standpoint of the *Logic*. The extraordinarily influential Heideggerian anxiety that this all represents the "imposition" of human will "onto" the question of Being is a matter for a separate discussion. See Martin Heidegger, *Nietzsche* vol. 4, trans. D. F. Krell (New York: Harper One, 1991), and my "Heidegger on Nietzsche on Nihilism." In *Interanimations. Receiving Modern German Philosophy* (Chicago: University of Chicago Press, 2015), 179–96.

32 Žižek, *Less than Nothing*, 238.

33 Robert Brandom, *Making It Explicit: Reasoning, Representing, and Discursive Commitment* (Cambridge, MA: Harvard University Press, 1994).

34 In Kantian terms, the role of reason can be said to emerge in any attempt to lead a "justified" life (and so a free one), to seek always the "condition" for anything "conditioned." See my discussion in *Hegel on Self-Consciousness: Desire and Death in the "Phenomenology of Spirit,"* (Princeton: Princeton University Press, 2010), 55–8.

35 It is also the case that this sort of interpretation would mean a disagreement with Žižek's characterization of the beginning of all this in Kant. It is not the case that Kant and the Idealists (certainly not Hegel; see *Belief and Knowledge*, 62–70) conceived the subject as a "spontaneous . . . synthetic activity, the force of unification, of bringing together the manifold of sensuous data we are bombarded with into a unified representation of objects" (*Less than Nothing*, 106; see also 149). It is not the case that "apperception . . . changes the confused flow of sensations into 'reality,' which obeys necessary laws." In the first place, Kant often says this impositionism is exactly the position he rejects, because it would give the "skeptic exactly what he wants" (B168). See also B138, B160n, and the "same function" passage at B105/A79. Nor is it the case that this synthetic activity "introduces a gap/difference into substantial reality" (*Less than Nothing*, 106). The negativity ("not mere being") in question is a matter of the normative dimension of apperceptive experience and action. One could, I suppose, call this a "gap in being," but that seems to me to mystify everything needlessly.

36 Dieter Henrich, *Between Kant and Hegel*, ed. David Pacini (Cambridge, MA: Harvard University Press, 2008). An unusual feature of Žižek's book is his heavy reliance on selected secondary sources. Henrich, Malabou, Miller, and Lebrun are the most heavily relied on, even in disagreements (as with Lebrun).

37 I present this evidence in *Hegel's Idealism*, chap. 3, pp. 42–59.

38 Fichte, "Second Introduction to the *Wissenschaftslehre*," in: *The Science of Knowledge: With the First and Second Introductions*, trans. P. Heath and J. Lachs (Cambridge: Cambridge University Press, 1970), 33.

39 Fichte, *Introductions to the "Wissenschaftslehre" and Other Writings*, 59.

40 J. G. Fichte, *Foundations of Transcendental Philosophy* (Ithaca, NY: Cornell University Press, 1993), 105–6.

41 This is from the notes to his famous *Aenesidemus* review, in *Gesamtausgabe der Bayerischen Akademie der Wissenschaften*, eds. Reinhard Lauth and Hans Jacobs (Stuttgart-Bad Cannstatt: Frommann-Holzboog, 1965), 11, 1, 287. It is important to get this aspect of Fichte right in order to avoid the commitments Žižek makes on p. 283, where we hear again about the *phenomena's* "self-limitation," the "ontological incompleteness of phenomenal reality," and the ground of freedom in "the ontological incompleteness of reality itself." Insofar as I understand these claims, they are regressive and dogmatically metaphysical as the "ineffable particularists," the worshippers of "the Other," that Žižek rightly criticizes. The link between self-consciousness, reason, and freedom is not based on such appeals.

42 Žižek, *Less than Nothing*, 963.

43 When it is described as it is, apparently approvingly, by Žižek on p. 427, a true Badiouian act, the "Act," is said to be a "radical and violent simplification . . . the magical moment when the infinite pondering crystallizes into a simple 'yes' or 'no.'" "Magical" is the right word, close to mystified and unintelligible. One shudders to think how many such Actors gloried in the "infinite" crystallizing itself in *them*. The idea is supposed to be that the founding of a new ethical order must perforce be "abyssal," ungrounded and contingent (460), that you can't have 1789 without 1793 (319), and so forth. But this is a completely non-Hegelian notion of "new" and so of "contingency." See Henrich on *Zufälligkeit*: Dieter Henrich, "Hegels Theorie über den Zufall," *Kant-Studien* 50, no. 1–4 (1950): 131–48.

44 Žižek, *Less than Nothing*, 239.

45 Another vast topic. See my *Hegel's Practical Philosophy: Rational Agency as Ethical Life* (Cambridge: Cambridge University Press, 2008).

46 See his rejection of the "organic model" of Hegelian historical change (*Less than Nothing*, 272).

47 Cf. Žižek, *Less than Nothing*, 263.

48 I see nothing in what Žižek has said to counter the traditional insistence that any claim about such a material contradiction could not be claiming anything, would not be a claim. The argument seems to be: so much the worse for logic, there are such contradictions. But that does not answer the challenge. See Charles Taylor, "Dialektik heute, oder: Strukturen der Selbstnegation." In *Hegels Wissenschaft der Logik: Formation und Rekonstruktion*, ed. D. Henrich (Stuttgart: Klett-Cotta, 1986), 141–53

49 The real problem with Hegel's political philosophy is the absence of any account of political will and the politics of will formation. The legislature just affirms "what's already been decided." See Michael Beresford Foster's invaluable and neglected book *The Political Philosophies of Plato and Hegel* (Oxford: Clarendon Press, 1935).

50 Žižek, *Less than Nothing*, 431.

51 When Žižek gives his list of "what Hegel cannot think" (qualified by a number of "yes, but . . ." suggestions), consisting of such things as repetition, the unconscious, class struggle, sexual difference, and so forth (*Less than Nothing*, 455), I see no reason to think that Hegel would object to such questions and

issues, any more than he needs to provide analyses and diagnoses of various individual and social pathologies. They are not his questions. A plague can completely erode the moral life of some community, and it can stay eroded for centuries. So can ever more frenzied and hysterical consumption, what may be the death spiral of global capitalism (see David Harvey, *The Enigma of Capital* (Oxford: Oxford University Press, 2010), and the beginning of a centuries-long ecological catastrophe.

52 Žižek, *Less than Nothing*, 326.
53 Ibid.
54 Ibid., 480.
55 The indispensable account of this is Laurence Dickey, *Hegel: Religion, Economics, and the Politics of Spirit, 1770-1807* (Cambridge: Cambridge University Press, 1987).
56 Rüdiger Bubner's phrase in "What Is Critical Theory?" In *Essays in Hermeneutics and Critical Theory*, trans. Eric Matthews (New York: Columbia University Press, 1988).

Response to Pippin

Slavoj Žižek

Pippin's text is a reprint of his critical review of my book *Less than Nothing*, and I've already answered it in detail in the "Introduction" to my *Absolute Recoil*,[1] so what follows here is a shortened version of my reply to his critique.

Pippin begins his critique at the most basic level of ontology, problematizing my thesis on the ontological incompleteness of reality:

> I do not fully understand the claims about holes in the fabric of being, and at any rate, we do not need the claim if we go in the direction I am suggesting. For if that formulation of apperception is correct, it means we are able to account for the inappropriateness of psychological or naturalist accounts of such states, all without a gappy ontology (in the sense, if not in the same way, that Frege and the early Husserl criticized psychologism without an "alternate" ontology).

Pippin correctly reads my incompleteness-thesis against the background of the status of subjectivity; he is well aware that I develop the topic of the ontological incompleteness in order to answer the question: how should reality be structured so that (something like) subjectivity can emerge in it? Pippin's solution is different: for him, the Kantian transcendental apperception—the unity of awareness with self-awareness—suffices. Self-awareness means a minimal self-relating on account of which we, humans, have to justify with reasons our acts; Pippin, of course, supplements Kant with the Hegelian account of the (transcendental, not empirical) genesis of self-awareness out of the complex social relations focused on mutual recognition, or, to quote his acerbic critical remark: "'Spirit' emerges in this imagined social contestation, in what we come to demand of each other, not in the interstices of being." There is no need for holes in the fabric of the universe for this.—From my standpoint, the problematic nature of this account is signaled by the fact that Pippin ends up in standard transcendental dualism:

> Of course, it is possible and important that some day researchers will discover why animals with human brains can do these things and animals without human brains cannot, and some combination of astrophysics and evolutionary theory will be able to explain why humans have ended up with the brains they have. But these are not philosophical problems and they do not generate any philosophical problems.

True, but such full scientific (self)naturalization would have consequences for philosophy: if we could fully account for our moral acts in the terms of natural causes, in what sense would we still experience ourselves as free? Kant's notion of freedom implies a discontinuity in the texture of natural causes; i.e., a free act is an act which is ultimately grounded in itself and, as such, cannot be accounted for as an effect of the preceding causal network—in this sense, a free act does imply a kind of hole in the texture of phenomena reality, the intervention of another dimension in the order of phenomena reality. Of course, Kant does not claim that free acts are miracles which momentarily suspend natural causality—they just happen without violating any natural laws. However, the fact of freedom indicates that natural causality doesn't cover all there is but only the phenomenal reality, and that transcendental subject, the agent of freedom, cannot be reduced to a phenomenal entity. Phenomenal reality is thus incomplete, non-all, a fact confirmed by the antinomies of pure reason which arise the moment our reason tries to comprehend phenomenal reality in its totality. One should always bear in mind that this "ontological scandal" is for Kant the necessary result of his transcendental turn.—This brings us to Pippin's second reproach: in his view, the thesis on the ontological incompleteness of reality opens up the space for abyssal acts of freedom, acts not grounded in any rational deliberations, since they are located in the interstices of being.

Now Pippin appears to forget that in his reading of Hegel's ethical thought, he himself insists on the retroactivity of meaning: the meaning of our acts is not an expression of our inner intention, it emerges later, from their social impact, which means that there is a moment of contingency in every emergence of meaning. But there is another more subtle retroactivity involved here: an act is abyssal not in the sense that it is not grounded in any reasons, but in the circular sense that it *retroactively posits its reasons*. A truly autonomous symbolic act/intervention never occurs as the result of strategic calculation, so that I go through all possible reasons and then choose the most appropriate course of action. An act is autonomous when it does not only apply a preexisting norm but, in the very act of applying a norm, creates this norm.

And this brings us to the true focal point of the debate. Pippin's line of reasoning is that since for me bourgeois society is unreformable, a radical change is needed; however, since there is no big Other, this change cannot be a direct enactment of some historical necessity or teleology as in the classic Marxist sense, but an abyssal voluntarist act. Pippin addresses here what he sees as "the largest question of all, the one I found the most dissatisfyingly addressed" in my book: I want

> to say that bourgeois society is fundamentally self-contradictory, and I take that to mean "unreformable." We need a wholly new ethical order and that means "the Act." Its pretense to being a rational form is undermined by the existence of a merely contingent particular, a figurehead at the top, the monarch. (A better question, it seems to me, is why Hegel bothers, given how purely symbolic and even pointless such a dotter of i's and crosser of t's turns out to be.)

Pippin immediately makes it clear in what sense the bourgeois society is reformable—his reference is, as expected,

> that great dream of social democrats everywhere—"Sweden in the sixties!"—does not seem to me something that inevitably produces its own irrational and irreconcilable Unreason, or Other. More lawyers for the poor in Texas, affordable day care, universal health care, several fewer aircraft carriers, more worker control over their own working conditions, regulated perhaps nationalized banks, all are reasonable extensions of that bourgeois ideal itself, however sick and often even deranged modern bourgeois society has become.

As to "unreformability," I am simply claiming that Pippin's list of demands may appear as a series of "reasonable extensions" of the bourgeois ideal, but this appearing is *abstract* in a strict Hegelian way; it ignores the general tendency of today's global capitalism. (Apropos Sweden in the sixties, perhaps Pippin should read a Mankell or Larsson detective novel to get an idea of what Sweden is today, how far it is counter-reformed from the mythic sixties.) But at a more basic level, the claim that bourgeois society is "fundamentally self-contradictory" is a consequence of Hegel's universal thesis—it is a claim which holds for every society:

> The history of a single world-historical nation contains (a) the development of its principle from its latent embryonic stage until it blossoms into the self-conscious freedom of ethical life and presses in upon world history; and (b) the period of its decline and fall, since it is its decline and fall that signalizes the emergence in it of a higher principle as the pure negative of its own.[2]

In this simple and elementary sense, *every* particular form of state and society is by definition "self-contradictory" and, as such, condemned to disappear—or, as Pippin himself points out, the notion of a rational state articulated in Hegel's *Philosophy of Right* also already entered the state of decay, the proof of it is that Hegel was able to articulate its notional structure. (It is in this way that we should read Hegel's last published text, a ferocious polemics against the British reform bill which moved in the direction of universal voting rights, bypassing the mediating role of corporate structures: Hegel reacted in such a panic because the reform bill clearly signaled the outdated character Hegel's idea of state.) This is why the most unHegelian thing imaginable would be here to conceive Hegel's idea of the rational state as a vision which is no longer self-contradictory, but, in a Fukuyama way, in its essence the finally found best possible formula which we, Hegel's successors, only have to gradually improve (and to reform its reality), not to change it in its essence—whatever Hegel stands for politically, it is not the gradual improvement of the bourgeois society. Hegel's vision of social development is, on the contrary, full of unexpected reversals—the promise of freedom turns into the worst nightmare, etc. This is why Hegel would have immediately comprehended the logic of the reversal of the emancipatory promise of the October Revolution into the Stalinist nightmare, of the reversal of the Leninist revolutionary heroic dedication into the Stalinist flattering of the Leader, or, today, the rise of religious fundamentalism in the midst of consumerist permissiveness. As for reformism, the Hegelian stance would have been: yes, but with a twist—one begins with a modest reform which only aims to make the existing system more just and efficient, and one triggers an avalanche which sweeps away the very order of deliberations which made us to propose the modest reform.

A last point of disagreement that I want to mention here: Pippin dismisses my "idea of 'pure' drives (or 'pure' anything)" as something that "belongs in the Hegelian zoo," i.e., something that is definitely superseded, rendered philosophically obsolete, by Hegel's philosophical achievement—however, is war, the way Hegel conceptualizes it, not precisely the (re)assertion of the "pure" essence of state in contrast to its particular content? Is, in this sense, the push-towards-war not an exemplary case of the "pure" death drive (pure negativity)? On can of course argue that war is today more threatening because of catastrophic potentials of new technologies—its result can be the extinction of humanity. This, however, is no way makes Hegel's point outdated; it just compels us to reinvent it for today's conditions.

Notes

1 See Slavoj Žižek, *Absolute Recoil: Towards a New Foundation of Dialectical Materialism* (London: Verso, 2015).
2 G. W. F. Hegel, *Philosophy of Right* (§347), Available online: http://www.marxists.org/reference/archive/hegel/works/pr/prstate2.htm (accessed December 20, 2021).

PART TWO
Ideology

CHAPTER FIVE

Slavoj Žižek Is Not Violent Enough

Todd McGowan

The Violent Issue

Slavoj Žižek is not an advocate of aggressive violence. This is a favorite claim of his most vociferous critics, from Adam Kirsch to John Gray, to name just a few of the many.[1] These critics resort to the most scurrilous methods for tainting Žižek with the stain of violence, not stopping short of quoting his representation of a position he opposes and presenting as his own. That said, violence does play a central role in Žižek's thought. But the fundamental act of violence for Žižek is not one of lashing out aggressively at others and harming them. It involves, instead, striking at oneself. Only by striking at itself can the subject cut into its own ideological investment that prevents it from imagining and actualizing a radical alternative. In this sense, there is violence in Žižek's thought, just not the type of violence that his critics chastise him for.

Despite this widespread critical chastisement, it is my contention—to put it in the style of one of his own formulas—that Slavoj Žižek is not violent enough. He identifies the necessary violence of the radical act, of the act that challenges the givens of the ruling capitalist system, but he makes no sustained attempt to integrate the self-destructive violence of this act into his conception of emancipatory governance. Žižek doesn't theorize how one might turn the form of the political act into a structure of governance, even though he does insist on the necessity of the radical act leading to an alternative form of political power that must be conceived in a new way. In other words, for Žižek, violence is the path to power but doesn't play a clear role within his conception of power. This is the point at which we must take Žižek's conception of violence even further than he himself does.

While he is not an advocate for violence against others, Žižek does not accept the contemporary conception of violence that limits it to its most visible and immediate manifestations. There is a more profound violence in the structure of capitalist relations of production than in the conspicuous violence of the suicide bomber's attack, though we almost always fail to recognize this. What's more, our outrage about the most visible forms of violence can serve to support hidden and objective forms of violence by providing them ideological cover. Theorists decry visible subjective violence while turning a blind eye to the objective violence that sustains the capitalist regime. This is the violence perpetuated against child cobalt miners in the Congo or the workers in Indonesian sweatshops. The distinction between subjective and objective violence enables Žižek to shake up the typical self-assured nonviolence of the liberal democrat who condemns all forms of political violence, especially on the Left, without mentioning capitalism's unrelenting brutality. He points out that the West's outrage about the killings of the *Charlie Hebdo* cartoonists contrasts with the silence about children mining cobalt in the Congo on behalf of Apple.

This is why Žižek disdains the contemporary resistance to any outbreak of violence. Humanitarian concern for the victims of violence—and the theoretical insistence on perpetual humanitarian interventions—is itself part of a larger system of structural violence that he works to challenge. The rejection of violence as such in the name of universal human rights entails an implicit, though seldom avowed, endorsement of the ruling capitalist structure, which is responsible for more violence than any revolutionary agents. By showing the ideological function of our concern for human rights, Žižek hopes to bring the problem of structural violence to the fore of our discussions.

With all of these qualifications, however, one must still assert that Žižek sees violence as a necessary part of his political program. He adopts a leftist and even Marxist political program that envisions revolutionary change as its central idea. He refuses and explicitly denounces any gradualist approach to social change like one finds in the thought of evolutionary socialist Eduard Bernstein.[2] As a champion of rupture, Žižek affirms throughout his work that revolutionary change cannot occur peacefully. It is, by definition, a violent uprooting of existing relations. If it is not violent toward the investment in the current social structure, revolutionary change will not uproot the libidinal investment in this structure and will never be revolutionary. Gradual but steady progress toward a socialist society would strike Žižek as a wholly unacceptable political outcome, which isolates him among contemporary leftist political thinkers, for whom nonviolent progress functions as an unspoken ideal. For Žižek, it is the rupture that makes life worth living because it generates the values that can guide our existence.[3] It is only through the violent uprooting of our symbolic identity that we genuinely find the groundlessness of our subjectivity. Without a fundamental alienation, we remain the prisoners of ideology.

Shoot the Hostage

Violence, as Žižek sees it, is first and foremost a violence performed on oneself. Freedom depends not so much on violently breaking the external chains that hold us but on shattering our own investment in the psychic chains that hold us far more strongly. This is the act that enables us to break the external chains, which is why the political act strikes first at oneself rather than one's political opponent. The rarity of the act is not simply the result of the ideological strength of capitalist society but more the result of our desire to capitulate to the comforts that ideology entails. The act tears us from our ideological comfort zone, and even the most committed partisan of the act experiences this movement as a violent one. But as Žižek sees it, this violence of the act is always a repetition of the origin of subjectivity itself, which comes into being through a complete upheaval.

Every subject is involved with violence through the very assertion of subjectivity, which is a violent break from natural being. The subject separates itself not with violence against natural being but with violence against itself in the form of the death drive. Death drive names the subject's unnatural being, its freedom from the givens of its situation. Death drive casts aside the self-interest that follows from natural being and harms the subject's own good rather than advancing it.

Separation and thus freedom depend on self-inflicted violence. As Žižek notes in the *Parallax View*, "the 'death drive' as a self-sabotaging structure represents the minimum of freedom, of a behavior uncoupled from the utilitarian-survivalist attitude. The 'death drive' means that the organism is no longer fully determined by its environs, that it 'explodes/implodes' into a cycle of autonomous behavior."[4] Self-sabotage, in Žižek's system, is not simply an indication of neurosis; it becomes identical with the birth of subjectivity and the drive that impels the subject out of its ideological comforts. The violence of the death drive and its self-sabotage is the first emancipation that subsequently establishes the pattern for all later political acts of emancipation.

Žižek turns to cinema to find instances that illustrate the emancipatory quality of violence that he embraces. At the end of his first book on Christianity, *The Fragile Absolute*, he finds three filmic examples of violence that he presents as salutary. In *Speed* (Jan De Bont, 1994), *Ransom* (Ron Howard, 1998), and *The Usual Suspects* (Bryan Singer, 1999), we see characters respond to situations in which others have power over them by attacking not the other but what they themselves hold most valuable. It is only the gesture of attacking oneself that frees the subject from the other's hold. In the most infamous of the three from *The Usual Suspects*, Keyser Söze (Kevin Spacey) kills his entire family while a rival criminal gang holds them hostage, or so we hear Söze's alter ego Verbal Kint (also Kevin Spacey) recount it in the film.

To be clear, Žižek does not endorse Söze's actions and hasn't, as far as I know, killed his own family to break from the control that Birkbeck

University has over him. That said, he identifies the impulse behind this act as the truly revolutionary attitude. By striking at himself rather than at his attackers, Söze eliminates the possible psychic hold that his attackers might have on him. He takes away their advantage through the act of self-destruction that eliminates the site of his own psychic investment. This same structure is displayed in each of these films, as they depict characters turning against themselves in order to free themselves from an external threat. Žižek notes, in a situation of forced choice, the subject makes the "crazy" impossible choice of, in a way, *striking at himself*, at what is most precious to himself. This act, far from amounting to a case of impotent aggressivity turned against oneself, rather changes the co-ordinates of the situation in which the subject finds himself: by cutting himself loose from the precious object through whose possession the enemy kept him in check, the subject gains the space of free action. Is not such a radical gesture of "striking at oneself" constitutive of subjectivity as such?[5] It is not so much that Žižek reduces freedom to having nothing left to lose, as Janis Joplin might say, but that he identifies freedom—and the political act—with loss itself. By striking at oneself, one subtracts oneself from the situation and from all its ideological inducements. Žižek's violence has subtraction as its endgame.

This becomes clear in one of Žižek's favorite examples of political violence. To describe the political act, Žižek turns to one of Bertolt Brecht's learning plays that focuses on the sacrifice of an individual for the sake of the collective. In *Die Massnahme* (*The Decision* or *The Measures Taken*), Brecht presents a group of Party members going to a foreign land and organizing on behalf of the Party. While there, a young comrade acts compassionately to help someone and thus endangers their mission. On the return trip, the others decide to kill the young comrade and leave no trace of his existence in order to cover the Party's tracks. If we look at how Žižek responds to this play, his politics of subtraction comes into focus through this drama. But before turning to Žižek himself, let's look at the interpretation of his fellow traveler Alain Badiou, who shares Žižek's appreciation for Brecht's play but interprets it with a wholly different emphasis.

In his commentary on this same play, Badiou discovers an affirmation of the idea that the individual, while not dissolved in the collective, receives its value through the collective. Brecht's play realizes for Badiou the truth that revolutionary political change requires a readiness to sacrifice individuals for the sake of that change. As he puts it, "If you think the world can and must change absolutely; that there is neither a nature of things to be respected nor pre-formed subjects to be maintained, you thereby admit that the individual may be sacrificable. Meaning that the individual is not independently endowed with any intrinsic nature that would deserve our striving to perpetuate it."[6] Brecht's play illustrates, according to Badiou, how the young comrade loses all value when he chooses natural compassion and thereby implicitly abandons fidelity to the event. Allowing morality to trump politics—the contemporary failing par excellence—implicitly involves an abandonment of the ultimate ground for any morality, which is the political decision.[7] His value as a subject immediately resorts to the valuelessness of the natural individual. Fidelity to the event demands his sacrifice, and only a humanitarian—which is to say, in Badiou's terms, a nihilist—would object to the sacrifice, given what's at stake.

Badiou's interpretation is that of a traditional communist, someone who recognizes the priority of the collective struggle over individualist concerns. The play teaches a hard lesson, but Badiou is prepared to accept the extreme cost of collectivist politics. The individual subject, for Badiou, is nothing without the revolutionary event, so giving one's life for this event simply makes sense. Despite the significant political overlap between Žižek's philosophy and Badiou's, this is a point where they diverge considerably.

While Žižek does not object to the group taking the life of the young comrade, what is illustrative about Žižek's political position is just how different his analysis of this play is than Badiou's. Badiou gives a typical communist take on the relationship between the individual and the collective. What is important for Žižek is not the relation between the individual and the group or the violence of the group inflicted on the individual but the subjectivity of the young comrade. Even though Brecht (and Badiou) emphasize the error of the young comrade in giving priority to compassion over political action, Žižek sees the political act occurring in his acquiescence to his own oblivion rather than in the collective activity that the group pursues. Not only must the young comrade die for the cause, he must die without a trace of his existence left behind, and he must will this death himself. When the young comrade does so, he is not simply doing his part for the revolution or functioning as its dupe. He is asserting his subjectivity through an act of self-erasure—an act of striking against himself that repeats the original gesture of subjectivity. Even amid the collectivist act, Žižek's concern is with how subjectivity asserts itself through subtraction. The act is important insofar as it marks the moment of this assertion. Through the repetition of an original violence, the young comrade affirms himself as a subject.

Violence against oneself has priority over violence against others in Žižek's philosophy because the former is more original. Subjectivity—and the split between subject and object—emerges not through the Other's violence toward me (like my mother leaving the room, withholding the breast, hitting me, and so on) but through my violence toward myself. By inflicting a loss on myself in the act of destroying a favorite object, injuring myself, or giving up a privileged activity, I constitute myself as a subject of loss and originate the death drive, which defines my existence through the repetition of loss. Žižek's subject emerges only with loss and its repetition. This is why violence is irreducible for subjectivity.

Žižek theorizes a permanent state of violence because he identifies violence with our subjectivity and with every act that repeats subjectivity's emergence. Žižek's act breaks from the symbolic structure in which it occurs. But this is not the rupture that Žižek emphasizes. The primary rupture of the act occurs within the subject of the act and involves the subject breaking with its own investment in the symbolic structure. The real difficulty of Žižek's act lies not in the physical courage it might require but in the psychic barriers standing in the way. This is why Žižek claims that courage is always a leftist value. The courage of the conservative or reactionary is necessarily faked: it relies on a whole series of capitulations to authority and psychic retreats from horror of our groundlessness that disguise themselves under the mask of physical bravery.[8] Our psychic investment in our job, our home, the good opinion of our friends, the esteem of our colleagues, and our many commodities operates as the ultimate insurance that the situation has against the possibility of our act. In order to act, all this must be thrust aside. Žižek links the radicality of subjectivity itself—its emergence through an absolute subtraction—with the political act. Subjectivity itself provides the paradigm for how we should conduct ourselves as political actors.

The State of Self-Erasure

What Žižek has not done, however, is to integrate his conception of violence into his theory of rule. He imagines revolt in terms of striking against oneself in the manner of Tyler Durden (Brad Pitt) and *Fight Club* (David Fincher, 1999) but he doesn't extend this violence against the self into a conception of anticapitalist governance. If self-destructive violence defines subjectivity itself, its ambit must extend beyond the revolutionary act to the form that emancipatory governance takes. But Žižek himself doesn't fully take this step. There is no theory of governance that violently strikes against itself, although this is what we might expect to see given Žižek's own theoretical propensities.

Žižek is loath to offer prescriptions for what the social order should ultimately look like. This is, as he sees it, one of the idealist missteps that Marx takes relative to Hegel's absolute materialism. Žižek takes Hegel's statement from the preface to the *Philosophy of Right*—"the owl of Minerva takes flight only with the falling of dusk"—as his political watchword.[9] Because Žižek takes up a radical materialist position, there is no possibility for theory or ideas to guide historical processes. Theory always comes too late to give advice for how to arrange the social order. Its only position is one of recognition and critique.

But at the same time, the failure of the Left to imagine an alternative and to articulate its scope rubs Žižek the wrong way. He contends that the emancipatory project of the Left cannot content itself with always fighting against the oppressive ruling power structure but must have the courage to articulate its own alternative. If the Left cannot theorize an alternative to global capitalism, it remains a prisoner of the contemporary capitalist universe. Political exigency seems to demand what Hegel claims is impossible.

The absence of a theory for the return to everyday life after a revolutionary upheaval is one of Žižek's bugbears. The outburst of revolt—Occupy Wall Street, Tahrir Square, the Gilets Jaunes movement in France, Black Lives Matter—promises epochal change in its initial manifestation. But in each case, the promise quickly evaporates as life returns to its prior normality. The revolutionary movement that begins with incredible promise always inaugurates a return to everyday capitalism, not the creation of a new normality. This is because the Left has no coherent alternative to global capitalism that it proffers. The demand for change never includes a concrete vision of the social order that the revolutionaries aim to enact. The celebration of revolt leaves everyday life in the lurch, and it is everyday life that constitutes the real revolutionary terrain.

According to Žižek, this eventual return to normality represents not just a necessary outcome of every revolutionary action but its fundamental justification. If the revolutionary act cannot produce a new and different normality, then there is no reason for engaging in the revolutionary struggle in the first place. And yet, the new normality remains a blank space within today's political struggles. The struggle against capitalist society today includes no vision of what should replace it.

Whereas traditional Marxism has a vision of a future communist society that it aims to unleash, contemporary political groups lack any such ideal. This is, for Žižek, a grave failing. In his talks around the world, Žižek often repeats, "I'm ready to sell my mother into slavery for the film *V for Vendetta Part 2*. What happens the next day?" While one might quarrel with the idea that the first *V for Vendetta* (James McTeigue, 2005) represents a radical film, the point lies elsewhere. Žižek questions the radical act that doesn't produce a new form of normality, that leaves everyday life just as it is after the dust settles. Rightly critical of leftists who celebrate large demonstrations that have no lasting political effect, with the question about the next day that Žižek poses, he insists on the necessity for theorizing what the political upheaval produces. But he himself also leaves the next day largely unthought within his philosophy. Despite all his theorization of the radical act, Žižek's thought has almost no account of the new regime that the radical act will institute.

One thing that we do know is that the next day or the new normality cannot completely eschew violence. Violence inheres in the structure of governance itself, just as it inheres in the structure of subjectivity. There is no imaginable regime—not even one set in the far-off future—that can constitute itself without violence. This is because violence creates the force attached to the law. Without the initial act of violence and the sustained threat of it, law will exist without any compulsion and thus without any constitutive power for the social order.

But when Žižek turns to the relationship between violence and law, he takes up the position of Walter Benjamin, who is drawn to the violence that opposes that of the state and the law. Following Benjamin, Žižek thinks in terms of violence done against the ruling order of things, violence of radical acts. This is what becomes visible when he invokes Walter Benjamin's notion of divine violence. Žižek is careful, as Benjamin is, to distinguish divine violence from the mythic violence that provides support for the state. Divine violence is wholly on the side of those outsiders who act spontaneously against their oppressors. In his treatise *Violence*, Žižek writes, "When those outside the structured social field strike 'blindly,' demanding and enacting immediate justice/vengeance, this is divine violence."[10] There is justice in divine violence, but this justice is not tied to any institutional order.

As both Benjamin and Žižek theorize it, it is impossible for divine violence to provide the basis for a political structure. The ruling apparatus cannot found itself or have recourse to divine violence. Only mythic violence—violence involved in some form of state power—has a clear political bearing. Unlike divine violence, which is "revolutionary violence" or "the highest manifestation of unalloyed violence by man," mythic violence represents the reduction of violence to a means and thus to oppressiveness.[11] Describing mythic violence, Benjamin states, "All violence as a means is either lawmaking or law-preserving."[12] As Benjamin sees it, the fact the mythic violence serves the law as an external end disqualifies it from any political or ethical radicality. It is what the revolutionary thinker and revolutionary party must struggle against, not what they endorse.

Benjamin's reflections on violence lead Žižek away from a possible solution to the question of what happens the next day, which is for him the most pressing political question. Benjamin's conception of divine violence that is always on the side of the revolutionary act and never on the side of power blocks any answer to the problem that vexes Žižek. As long as the focus is on divine violence, Žižek will remain theoretically on the eve of the revolution, never moving to the next day. The step to theorizing the new normality of the next day requires a move away from divine violence and toward violence associated with the state. But as Benjamin sees, this violence cannot be simply a means to accomplishing a good end. This version of mythic violence piles up victims for the sake of a better world. There must be a form of state violence that doesn't just see this violence as a means to an end. There must be a way of theorizing a new mode of governance that integrates the self-destructive violence that Žižek uncovers in the radical act. We can find it in the most unlikely of places, the site of one of the worst outbreaks of mass murder in human history.

The Bright Side of Stalinism

Nothing has gotten Žižek in more hot water with his critics than his positive statements about Stalinism.[13] Not only does Žižek claim that Stalinism has an "inner greatness," but, as an act of provocation, he places a portrait of Stalin conspicuously in his apartment, where visitors and video spectators cannot avoid seeing it.[14] But more important, he rejects Hannah Arendt's attempt to link Stalinism to Nazism under the umbrella term *totalitarianism*.¹⁵ By merging Stalinism and Nazism together, Arendt—and all those who use this term—fails to see that Stalinism belongs to the project of universal emancipation in a way that Nazism does not. Stalinism is the way that emancipation goes awry, but it also holds within it a lesson for the future of the emancipatory project. We can measure the importance of the exploration of Stalinism for Žižek's thought by how much it costs him to sustain it.

The claim that Stalinism has relevance for the Left earns Žižek criticism from both Right, center, and Left, from everywhere on the political spectrum. In his conservative screed against Žižek, Christian Alejandro Gonzales laments that "despite all his writing on Stalinism he cannot muster an unambiguous moral condemnation of Stalin's butchery."¹⁶ This is a right-wing critique that Roger Scruton also advances. Such figures see Žižek's investment in Stalinism as an index of the danger that he poses to the capitalist society that they cherish. The moderate Jonathan Rée sees Žižek's Stalinism as the indication of his proclivity for advocating and even celebrating violence. Žižek's attitude toward Stalinism leaves Rée flummoxed. He states, "Žižek's objection to Stalinism is not that it involved terror and mass murder, but that it sought to justify them by reference to a happy communist tomorrow."¹⁷ From the moderate perspective, the embrace of Stalin disqualifies Žižek as a political authority of any standing whatsoever. The Marxist and anarchist Left sees Žižek's embrace of Stalin as the ultimate sign that Žižek is finally not one of them, not really a thinker of the Left. Writing on the World Socialist Web Site, Stefan Steinberg claims derisively that "Žižek never made a secret of his continuing admiration for Stalin."¹⁸ This, for Steinberg and others, reveals his abhorrence of actual workers and their struggles, as well as an inability to see the democratic bent of Leninism that Stalin subverts. Žižek's embrace of Stalin shows that he shares in Stalin's betrayal of the working class, a betrayal not evident in Lenin.

Given what it costs him in readers and potential friends, Žižek's few positive statements about Stalin and Stalinism, as well as the prominent portrait in his apartment, must have a profound political significance within his thought. Žižek's statements of Stalin cannot just amount to ironic amusements that we shouldn't take seriously. There is something about Stalinism that hints at what the emancipatory project in power must look like. That is, Stalinism points toward a solution to the most intractable problem in Žižek's own thinking—how to theorize the next day without venturing into idealist territory. Obviously, this solution must avoid Stalin's mass murder of the Soviet population and annihilation of all political opponents, but there is nonetheless something instructive in the Stalinist regime.

To suggest that there is something instructive about Stalinism is already to run the risk of being dismissed as a totalitarian, which is perhaps why Žižek doesn't fully elaborate how Stalinism can guide our theorizing about emancipatory governance. Clearly, no one wants a return to Stalinism, least of all Žižek himself, who was born in an actually existing communist country during Stalin's lifetime. But Stalinism, especially in contradistinction from Nazism, contains within it a formal revelation about the project of emancipation in control of state power.

The closest that Žižek comes to conceiving state power in the terms of self-destructive violence—the closest he comes to filling this lacuna in his thought that he believes needs to be filled—comes in his discussion of Stalinism. When he compares Stalinism to Nazism, Žižek insists that both turn life into a nightmare. But there is nonetheless a central point of distinction between them. Although Stalinism subjects people to untold horrors, it still belongs to an authentic emancipatory tradition. Evidence for this, according to Žižek, consists in the different status of the detainees in Nazi concentration camps and Soviet gulags. The detainees in concentration camps were completely excluded from German society, whereas those in the gulag still participated in—and even could feel themselves a part of—the communist project. This is why prisoners in the gulag would sing "Happy Birthday" to Stalin, but one could not imagine a parallel event taking place in a Nazi concentration camp for Hitler.

The difference also concerns the victims of each regime. Nazism ruthlessly attacks and kills those they perceived to be enemies of the Reich—communists, Jews, male homosexuals, Roma, and the disabled. Those who belonged to the Reich, however, live in almost perfect security. Nazi leaders like Reinhard Heydrich may face assassination from political opponents, but they endure no threat from the Nazi regime itself. This situation contrasts utterly with the Soviet Union under Stalin.

Stalinism threatens not just the peasants who stand in the way of collectivization but also members of the ruling class itself. There was no safe space in Stalinist society, no rank high enough immune from suspicion of being a traitor to communist society. In *Trouble in Paradise*, Žižek points out this contrast. Whereas Nazism targets society's outsiders, Stalinism aims at those placed highest in the social order. He writes, "the most dangerous place to be at the time of the terrible 1930s purges in the Soviet Union was at the top of the *nomenklatura*."[19] For Žižek, it is crucial that Stalinism targets those in power more than anyone else in the society.

There is a Stalinist joke that captures this idea. Under Stalin's rule, two NKVD officials come to a first-floor apartment and tell the family living there, "You're all under arrest. We're taking you to the gulag." The mother quickly explains to them, "You've got the wrong apartment. The Communist Party members live upstairs." The joke plays off the actual targets of the NKVD under Stalin. Rather than arrest conservatives or other nonbelievers in the communist project, the secret police target communists themselves. Being a member of the Party doesn't save one from danger but creates it.

In this joke, we can see the clear distinction between Nazism and Stalinism. A joke about the Gestapo trying to arrest members of the SS would not be funny because it wouldn't hit the truth of Nazism. Nazism depends on a clear enemy. Stalinism, even though it represents a perversion of the emancipatory project, nonetheless targets itself rather than an external enemy. As a result, it reveals, albeit in a perverted fashion, what emancipation looks like. Emancipatory rule is a rule in which the form of power targets itself as the object of its violence, not those on the society's margins. In this way, Stalinist violence has something to teach us about emancipation because it points to how the Left might set up a self-critical system of governance.

In fact, we can even imagine Stalin himself coming under suspicion within the constraints of the Stalinist universe. A second joke points in this direction: Wanting to know how ordinary people are getting along, Stalin disguises himself and goes to the cinema. As the newsreel before the film plays, it shows part of one of Stalin's speeches. When the crowd in the theater sees Stalin on the screen, everyone stands up to cheer. Stalin sits quietly eating popcorn, delighted with the reception he receives. But at this point, the man standing next to him leans over and whispers, "For what it's worth, I agree with you, but it's very dangerous not to cheer." This joke works on the reality that even Stalin is not Stalinist enough to avoid altogether suspicion of disloyalty. Through this joke, we can see what Žižek calls the "inner greatness" of Stalinism. Under this ruthlessly oppressive system, those on top, inclusive of Stalin himself, fall victim to the system striking at itself. If we can put credence in theories that suggest some member or members of the Politburo poisoned Stalin and induced the stroke that killed him, then even he wasn't safe from the regime, as this joke suggests. Through its many strikes at itself, the Stalinist regime provides the form for what the emancipatory act in power looks like, although the content must, of course, be radically different. The project of emancipation in power cannot include millions of dead. In this sense, Stalinism is not a model at all.

While Žižek contrasts Stalinism's destructiveness with that of Nazism in order to show that Stalinism belongs to an authentic emancipatory tradition and that Nazism does not, he never builds on this conception in order to theorize the structure of a self-destructive regime. Stalinism offers a hint of how such a regime might be conceived, but Stalinism also represents a profound betrayal of the project of emancipation. Deciphering an emancipatory regime requires another step. The regime that corresponds to the radical political act—emancipation in power—must prioritize striking at itself if it is to remain part of the emancipatory project and not become a new version of oppressive authority.

Let's consider one example of what this might look like. Currently, the Constitution provides the basis for governance in the United States. Its writers function for the American people as the subjects supposed to know. All legislative and judicial decisions refer back to these subjects and the intentions that interpreters derive from the Constitution itself. But the authority of these subjects is not unimpeachable. At key points in American history, the states have approved Amendments to this Constitution that add to or alter its original dictates. The Thirteenth Amendment, for instance, abolishes the slavery that the original Constitution tacitly permits (through three references that never name slavery explicitly but nonetheless permit it legally). The Amendment system allows for changes to the authority of the subjects supposed to know, but it leaves them intact as authority figures. Amendments to the Constitution don't impugn the authority of the Founding Fathers. The sustained authority of these masters divorces this process from emancipatory politics. The blow to oneself that Žižek champions is a blow that reveals the lack in the figure of authority. It is a blow to the authority as a subject supposed to know.

If we replaced the Amendment system with an Emendation system, a much more radical form of democracy, this would come closer to an image of emancipatory governance, to governance that strikes at itself in the way that Žižek himself advocates. Rather than amending the original, we would emend it: the change would be a correction, not a simple addition. This shift of a single letter—*amend* to *emend*—would signal the lack in the subject supposed to know because addition to the original would become correction of an initial error. With each emendation, we would be reminded about how the original writers failed, not about their infinite wisdom. Each emendation would be a blow against the Constitution itself, a way of integrating the radical act of self-destruction into the structure of power. This is one possible version of integrating Žižek's form of violence into governance. It would establish the failure of the authority as integral to the functioning of the authority. This is, of course, just one way of imagining authority that tries to bring the blow to oneself of the radical act into power. But the point is that such thinking is imperative. Even though philosophy is condemned to painting "its grey on grey," to recognizing rather than rejuvenating politics, as Hegel puts it, philosophy can nonetheless propose possible forms that the political structure might take. Hegel's imperative to silence refers only to content.

Žižek himself leaves the emancipatory form of governance blank. But for his few comments on Stalinism, he doesn't attempt to theorize what emancipatory governance might possibly look like. This reticence follows from Hegel's strict warnings about the limits of philosophy in relation to politics, but it leaves Žižek almost silent on what the next day will bring, which, as he rightly sees, is the decisive question for the revolutionary project. And this is what is most troubling, since Žižek is the one leftist thinker who has the courage to refuse the position of pure resistance and to ask the question of what comes the next day. Without a sense of the next day or the new normality, the revolutionary act risks just spinning its wheels, no matter how initially successful it might be.

Žižek rightly sees that the radical act must take *Fight Club* as its model and privilege the blow against itself rather than the blow against the oppressor. But this strategy doesn't have to remain limited to the radical act. We can imagine a form of power that privileges striking against itself. Such a form of governance would translate the violence of the radical act into a rule of violence. Taking a cue from Žižek himself, we can lament: We have yet to invent a form of power violent enough to be adequate for our emancipation. We must imagine a Žižek even more enthusiastic for violence than his detractors imagine him to be.

Notes

1. Adam Kirsch claims that "the curious thing about the Žižek phenomenon is that the louder he applauds violence and terror – especially the terror of Lenin, Stalin, and Mao, whose "lost causes" Žižek takes up in another new book, *In Defense of Lost Causes* – the more indulgently he is received by the academic left, which has elevated him into a celebrity and the center of a cult." Adam Kirsch, "The Deadly Jester," *The New Republic* (December 3, 2008): https://newrepublic.com/article/60979/the-deadly-jester (accessed November 30, 2021). John Gray denounces Žižek just as unequivocally for his purported investment in violence. See John Gray, "The Violent Visions of Slavoj Žižek," *New York Review of Books* (July 12, 2012): https://www.nybooks.com/articles/2012/07/12/violent-visions-slavoj-zizek/ (accessed November 30, 2021. I hope that both would find this essay as risible as Žižek's own works.
2. The problem with Bernstein's conception of evolutionary change is that it explicitly refuses to embrace the event or the act. Even if society did gradually evolve toward the socialism that Bernstein envisions, Žižek would see this as a bad bargain, which separates him from most contemporary leftists, who, even if they aren't explicitly followers of Bernstein (and there are few), nonetheless believe that nonviolent and nondisruptive social change functions as something like an ideal. Žižek insists on the need for the disruption, which is even more important that any better society that might result from it. For Bernstein's description of his gradualist philosophy, see Eduard Bernstein, *Evolutionary Socialism: A Criticism and Affirmation* (New York: Random House), 1961.
3. This is a position that Žižek shares with Alain Badiou, who sees what he calls the event as constitutive of a life worth living. Life outside the bearing of the event is insignificant being, a being in which one is never a subject but just the plaything of the prevailing situation.
4. Slavoj Žižek, *The Parallax View* (Cambridge, MA: MIT Press, 2006), 231.
5. Slavoj Žižek, *The Fragile Absolute, or, Why Is the Christian Legacy Worth Fighting For?* (New York: Verso, 2000), 150.
6. Alain Badiou, *The Century*, trans. Alberto Toscano (Malden, MA: Polity Press 2007), 99.
7. Badiou's criticism of the Nouveaux Philosophes in France (such as André Glucksmann) is that they perfectly embody the young comrade's choice of morality over politics and therefore destroy the ground from which they might launch a moral criticism. In Badiou's eyes, morality is a self-contradicting enterprise, unless it stems from a political decision of fidelity to an event.

8   In this sense (and this sense alone), George W. Bush was absolutely correct to accuse the attackers on September 11, 2001 of cowardice. While liberals such as Bill Maher mocked Bush for this sentiment and claimed they were in fact too courageous, Bush gets it right, from Žižek's perspective. Suicide bombers act without courage because they rely on a hidden substantial Other that supports their act. The suicide bomber does not fly without a net. Or, as Žižek himself puts it, "One should nonetheless insist that there is no 'bad courage': bad courage is always a form of cowardice. The 'courage' of the Nazis was sustained by their cowardice concerning attacking the key feature of their society, the capitalist relations of production; the 'courage' of the terrorists relies on the 'big Other' whose instruments they perceive themselves to be. The true courage of an act is always the courage to accept the inexistence of the big Other, that is, to attack the existing order at the point of its symptomal knot." Slavoj Žižek, *In Defense of Lost Causes* (New York: Verso, 2008), 152. By seeing the cowardice in what appear to be courageous acts—like killing oneself in a plane—Žižek refigures the political terrain. It is only insofar as we recognize the cowardice of the suicide bomber that we can break the spell of the knowing Other for whom this bomber acts.

9   G. W. F. Hegel, *Elements of the Philosophy of Right*, trans. H. B. Nisbet, ed. Allen W. Wood (Cambridge: Cambridge University Press, 1991), 23 (translation modified).

10 Slavoj Žižek, *Violence: Six Sideways Reflections* (New York: Picador, 2008), 202.

11 Walter Benjamin, "Critique of Violence." In *Selected Writings, Volume 1: 1913–1926*, trans. Edmund Jephcott, eds. Marcus Bullock and Michael W. Jennings (Cambridge, MA: Harvard University Press, 1996), 252.

12 Benjamin, "Critique of Violence," 243.

13 Žižek's most straightforward statement of his considered view on Stalinism occurs in *The Ticklish Subject*, where he states, "Stalinism . . . is the point of radical (self-relating) negativity that functions as a kind of 'vanishing mediator' between the 'authentic revolutionary phase of the late 1910s/early 1920s and the stabilization of the nomenklatura into a New Class after Stalin's death." Slavoj Žižek, *The Ticklish Subject: The Absent Centre of Political Ontology* (London: Verso, 1999), 193.

14 "The Inner Greatness of Stalinism" is a section heading in the essay "Afterword: Lenin's Choice," which appears in Slavoj Žižek, ed., *Revolution at the Gates: Selected Writings of Lenin from 1917* (London: Verso, 2002), 167–336.

15 In *Origins of Totalitarianism*, Arendt claims that both Stalinism and Nazism use the concentration camp to cut off dissidents from the rest of society. She states, "The real horror of the concentration and extermination camps lies in the fact that the inmates, even if they happen to keep alive, are more effectively cut off from the world of the living than if they had died, because terror enforces oblivion." Hannah Arendt, *The Origins of Totalitarianism* (New York: Harcourt, 1968), 443. Here, Arendt misses the fundamental difference between the Nazi concentration camp and the gulag. As Žižek insists again and again, the gulag remains part of the communist project, which is why

detainees there can participate in celebrations of the revolution, such as the anniversary of the revolution itself or the leader's birthday. Such celebrations would be unthinkable in a Nazi concentration camp. Arendt blends together the fundamentally Enlightenment project of communism with the reactionary anti-Enlightenment program of the Nazis.

16 Christian Alejandro Gonzales, "Slavoj Žižek, Fashionable Revolutionary," *National Review* (June 30, 2018): https://www.nationalreview.com/2018/06/slavoj-zizek-fashionable-revolutionary/.

17 Jonathan Rée, "*Less than Nothing* by Slavoj Žižek – Review," *Guardian* (June 27, 2012): https://www.theguardian.com/books/2012/jun/27/less-than-nothing-slavoj-zizek-review (accessed November 30, 2021).

18 Stefan Steinberg, *A Right-Wing Rant Against British Youth from Slavoj Žižek*," World Socialist Web Site (August 27, 2011): https://www.wsws.org/en/articles/2011/08/zize-a27.html (accessed November 30, 2021). For his part, Paul Kellogg accuses Žižek of lauding Stalin's terror and wrongly seeing it as the necessary denouement of Leninism. Kellogg writes, "He praises the reign of 'institutional terror' in the Stalin regime as parallel to some kinds of treatment in psychoanalysis." Paul Kellogg, "Slavoj Žižek's Failed Encounter with Leninism," *Links: International Journal of Socialist Renewal* (2008): http://links.org.au/node/1500 (accessed November 30, 2021).

19 Slavoj Žižek, *Trouble in Paradise: From the End of History to the End of Capitalism* (New York: Melville House, 2017), 134.

Response to McGowan

Slavoj Žižek

McGowan's simple but very convincing critical point is that, while I write a lot about violence of a radical act that constitutes a new power, I do not provide a theory of how, once the revolution is done and things return to a new normal, in the new governance also power will have to "violently strike against itself":

> We can imagine a form of power that privileges striking against itself. Such a form of governance would translate the violence of the radical act into a rule of violence. Taking a cue from Žižek himself, we can lament: We have yet to invent a form of power violent enough to be adequate for our emancipation. We must imagine a Žižek even more enthusiastic for violence than his detractors imagine him to be.

I agree with this point, but I was a little bit surprised by how, after the big roar about violence, McGowan ends up with a very modest proposal as a solution: emendation: "Each emendation would be a blow against the Constitution itself, a way of integrating the radical act of self-destruction into the structure of power. This is one possible version of integrating Žižek's form of violence into governance. It would establish the failure of the authority as integral to the functioning of the authority." I can easily imagine versions more pertinent than amendment (which can also be abused by those in power to strengthen their rule, like abortion, etc.). In his last active year, Lenin himself saw this problem. While admitting the dictatorial nature of the Soviet regime, he proposed to establish a Central Control Commission: an independent, educational and controlling body with an "apolitical" edge, consisting of the best teachers and technocratic specialists monitoring the "politicized" CCC and its organs. In "dreaming" (his expression) about the kind of work to be done by the CCC, he describes how this body should resort to some semi-humorous trick, cunning device, piece of trickery or something of that sort. I know that in the staid and earnest states of Western Europe such an idea would horrify people and that not a single decent official would even entertain it. I hope, however, that we have not yet become as bureaucratic as all that and that in our midst the discussion of this idea will give rise to nothing more than amusement. Indeed, why not combine pleasure with utility? Why not resort to some humorous or semi-humorous trick to expose something ridiculous, something harmful, something semi-ridiculous, semi-harmful, etc.?[1]

(Incidentally, CCC was formed, but was immediately neutralized—it had no impact.) A more realist way to organize counter-violence to power is multi-party democracy itself with its basic premise (elaborated by Claude Lefort) that the place of power is primordially empty, that it can be only temporarily occupied by an agent (party) which is always under the threat to be replaced by another. Then there are different forms of popular pressure on state power, and, finally, there is a direct violent rebellion—or, as Thomas Jefferson put it,

> what country can preserve it's liberties if their rulers are not warned from time to time that their people preserve the spirit of resistance? [. . .] What signify a few lives lost in a century or two? The tree of liberty must be refreshed from time to time with the blood of patriots and tyrants. It is its natural manure.[2]

A revolution has to eat its children (or, rather, its children should eat their father). It would be meaningless to commit oneself to one of these forms and to prohibit another.

But today, the question of counter-violence to power (even if it is democratic power) is not just an academic one: it is the one raised by radical leftists and rightists—a clear signal that our (not only) political system is in deep crisis. In the US, we have Black Lives Matter, MeToo, and, on the other side, anti-Covid-measures protests, as well as the rightists' populism. The problem today is not that the state power lacks a counter-violence but that, in its democratic form, it works less and less since it is threatened in multiple ways. Let's reflect upon the following report on what goes on in the US:

> Republican leaders loyal to Trump are vying to control election administrations in key states in ways that could drastically distort the outcome of the presidential race in 2024. With the former president hinting strongly that he may stand again, his followers are busily maneuvering themselves into critical positions of control across the US— from which they could launch a far more sophisticated attempt at an electoral coup than Trump's effort to hang on to power in 2020. In Arizona, another critical swing state, many Trump allies are running for

secretary of state, including Shawna Bolick. She was the architect of a bill introduced to the Arizona state legislature that would have given lawmakers the ability to overturn the will of voters and impose their own choice for president. Under Bolick's bill, legislators would be able to overrule the official count and put forward an alternate slate of electors in the name of the loser by dint of a simple majority vote, no explanation needed.[3]

This means direct violent confrontation, potentially even an outright civil war, without any mediating agency that would translate this antagonism into democratic competition (agonism). No wonder that the specter of communism is rising again. When one mentions the prospect of communism (or even socialism) today, the predominant reaction is the one by Rainer Zitelmann:

> Left-wing intellectuals around the world insist on telling us exactly the same things as they have been saying for 100 years in the wake of every catastrophic socialist experiment: "That was not true socialism." Next time, then, things are sure to work out differently. After every single socialist experiment without exception failed over the past 100 years, it should be clear that the last thing the world needs are any new ones.[4]

There is some obvious power in this argument which is regularly evoked when the prospect of an even modest social change arises—however, why does then the prospect of communism act like a living dead and return again and again? If we dismiss the simplistic explanation that a utopian propensity is immanent to human soul or something similar (like: we are not ready to pay the price for our welfare), the only consistent answer is: because today's situation calls for something like communism. Today, this is becoming more and more obvious: how can we even imagine to cope with ecological crisis without limiting the market and engaging in global solidarity?

Notes

1. V. I. Lenin, "Better Fewer, But Better," *Pravda* vol. 49 (March 1923). Quoted from: *Lenin's Collected Works*, 2nd English edition, trans. David Skvirsky and George Hanna (Moscow: Progress Publishers, 1965), vol. 33, 487–502. Available online: https://www.marxists.org/archive/lenin/works/1923/mar/02.htm (accessed December 20, 2021).
2. Thomas Jefferson, quoted in "The tree of liberty . . . (Quotation)," *Thomas Jefferson Encyclopedia*. Available online: https://www.monticello.org/site/research-and-collections/tree-liberty-quotation (accessed December 20, 2021).
3. Ed Pilkington, "'Terrifying for American Democracy': Is Trump Planning for a 2024 Coup?" *Guardian*, November 14, 2021. Available online: https://www.

theguardian.com/us-news/2021/nov/14/trump-president-2024-election-coup-republicans (accessed December 20, 2021).

4 Rainer Zitelmann, "Will the Lie of Socialism's Success Ever Die?," *The National Interest*, November 12, 2021. Available online: https://nationalinterest.org/feature/will-lie-socialism's-success-ever-die-196127 (accessed December 20, 2021).

CHAPTER SIX

Žižek's Foundationless Building

Ideology Critique as an Existentialist Choice

Hilary Neroni

Slavoj Žižek's most important contribution to contemporary thought is his theory of ideology. He clarifies several aspects of ideology that were implicit but unacknowledged in previous theories—primarily that ideology is effective only when unconscious. This emphasis then allows several other key interventions on his part, especially his theorizing the importance of disavowal and the structuring necessity of the obscene underside of ideology, an underside that gives ideology its libidinal hold on subjects. His theory of ideology reveals that ideology shifts in such a way so as to entrap even the savviest amongst us. These shifts can trap us politically when we fail to recognize the new ideological terrain that has formed. Our relationship toward authority, for example, can often motivate the types of political movements we create. But the ideological valence of authority is not stable. Žižek points out that in the 1960s and 1970s flipping off authority was a radical gesture. But today, it is authority (as embodied in the figures of Donald Trump, Jair Bolsonaro, and Vladimir Putin) itself that flips us off. Authority itself has becomes obscene. This leaves those on the Left befuddled as to how to rebel against an authority that takes up the signs of rebellion itself. How does one create an effective political movement under such conditions? Žižek's point here is that we shouldn't see this as ideology dissolving but rather recognize the situation as one in which ideology takes on a new form. Ideology critique allows us to recognize these shifts and thus respond to the contemporary political situation in potentially more effective ways.

Žižek's theory of ideology and his model of how to critique contemporary ideology has been foundational for his analysis of culture, politics, art, media, and history. In 2021, two years into the Covid pandemic, we find ourselves in an ideologically weighty moment. Oppressive ideological structures abound. Emotional responses have also risen to a fevered pitch, and we seem to be unable to find connection among people that would allow for a coherent political response to contemporary capitalism. Žižek's concept of ideology and his critique of ideology allow us to see the structures we live within and the challenges that the subject has when interacting with these structures. His theory of ideology presents us with a way to address our contemporary quagmire. It does so by thinking ideology in terms of the interaction and overlap between the psychic and the social. When considering the many topics he investigates in his work, there is a thread that runs throughout them all. He consistently attempts what no other theorist has successfully done before: to theorize the social and the psyche together in one concept. Seeing the society in this way often puts him in a precarious position that invites critical responses: one that might be seen as either the canary in the coal mine or a very vocal Sisyphus explaining our relation to the boulder. Žižek's theory of ideology is not only the basis for his own political project. It provides the guidelines—by articulating the inherent limitations—for any contemporary leftist project.

The Ideology of Marx

Even when Žižek turns to topics that seem far afield from the critique of ideology, he constantly returns to the question of ideology as if he can't escape it. This return is often triggered when he hears theorists discussing our post-ideological times. For Žižek, this drives him to intervene with an explanation of how ideology continues to function. But it does raise an important question for any theorist of ideology (one that my students always begin with during every discussion of ideology): Can we ever be free of ideology?

One of Žižek's most significant predecessors in theorizing ideology certainly believes in a moment when we would be free of it. Karl Marx envisioned a society free of ideology after it evolved out of capitalism. Created by capitalism's need to perpetuate itself, ideology, Marx theorized, would no longer be necessary once communism and economic equality arrived. At this point, we would also be free of the need for ideology (which exists, for Marx, to justify relations of inequality). As Marx sees it, ideology is bourgeois ideology, and its purpose was to obscure the relations of production and prevent the proletariat from realizing that they could rise up and challenge these structures. Marx and Friedrich Engels make this clear in a famous passage from *The German Ideology*. They write, "If in all ideology men and their relations appear upside-down as in a *camera obscura*, this phenomenon arises just as much from their historical life-process as the inversion of objects on the retina does from their physical life-process."[1] This conception of ideology has an end point to it. After the proletarian revolution, this ideological inversion of our thinking would no longer be necessary: we could recognize the material origins of our social structures because they would emerge from an egalitarian economic system. No theorist of ideology since Marx has had such a utopian theory nor has thought that we could eventually get rid of it. Of course, explicit in this utopian idea is that the purpose of ideology is to hold together hierarchies of inequality. Once those hierarchies are gone, ideology would also be gone.

Almost no one continues to believe today that there will ever be a time in which the hierarchies of society will be gone.[2] But if we are not striving for an eventual end to ideology, the point of ideology critique seems itself to be in question. One critiques ideology, but to what end, if there will always be some sort of ideological structure. Žižek responds by implying that what is decisive is not overcoming ideology once and for all but rather taking up a certain position within it or with regard to it. For Žižek, the point is to reframe the theory of ideology in order to highlight how the subject relates to the ideological structure that it emerges within. By placing the emphasis on subjectivity, not the economic infrastructure, as the source of ideology, Žižek turns the theory of ideology away from the emphasis on manipulation that it has for Marx.

According to Žižek, to understand ideology you have to understand the subjects that generate ideology. Ideology is not something external to us since each person contributes to its perpetuation. The individual psyche both creates ideology and suffers under it. This leads us to ponder exactly how people are psychically involved with ideology: how do they contribute to its creation, and how does it affect them psychically? Certainly, ideology is largely a term created to address the power of the social order rather than subjectivity. The concept itself points to the larger social structures and the way social expectations, ideals, and cultural practices have a tendency toward keeping hierarchies, dominant ideals, or economic structures in place. But the concept also must take into account each individual's psychic interaction with those larger currents in the social order.

Marx's idea of ideology represents a significant leap forward because he entirely shifts our way of seeing the importance of ideas in relation to the economic structure. He reshapes the understanding of the good and the public sphere by showing the inadequacies of those ideas if the economic system continued as it was. Not everyone had access to the good or the public sphere. Even if they lived in a democracy, it was still radically unequal, if the economic system was capitalist. Marx has to confront in his theory why people participate in a system that is so destructive to their lives. According to the early Marx, ideology is the answer. Marx's theory of ideology considers the people duped by capitalism into thinking that ideas run the world instead of grasping the realities of capital.

For Marx, ideology is false consciousness. Those who don't see the determinative role that capitalism plays in what they think are simply not thinking adequately or clearly. This idea ultimately leads him to argue that once the proletariat becomes aware of the structures of capitalism, they would become aware of their own false consciousness and revolt. This awareness would be achieved by realizing that humanity had the potential to create a different more egalitarian economic system. The result of dissolving their false consciousness is not just propaedeutic to the communist revolution; it is inevitably revolutionary. On the one hand, it seems that for Marx our investment in ideology is simply that we have been convinced of the wrong idea or ideal. On the other hand, the later Marx's concepts of commodity fetishism and reification suggest something more than just false consciousness. He sees fetishism as the vehicle through which capitalist ideology functions (even though he no longer mentions the term *ideology* when he conceives of commodity fetishism in *Capital*).

Both these concepts, however, also evoke a strong emotional and thus psychic investment, which hints at a complexity that is not simply about knowing or not knowing about capitalism. One could say, for example, that as a concept, commodity fetishism hints at the way enjoyment, fantasy, and desire shape the social order. In commodity fetishism, the commodity presents itself and engages the consumer in such a way that they are distracted by the allure of the commodity and in this way the actual conditions of production are obscured. This involvement with the commodity, one so alluring that we forget entirely to think through how it was created, is clearly more about enjoyment than it is about knowledge. It certainly evokes the idea of unconscious investment. Marx, however, does not have a theory of the unconscious. For him the subject is simply a rational being who has been duped by this powerful economic system. He cannot see the importance of considering how the unconscious is an essential component of the social order, ideology, and even the structure of our economic system. This is why he is not able to flesh out the implications of commodity fetishism for the subject.

Similarly, reification as a concept implies desire and non-rational behavior. Marx's theory of reification (as developed by Georg Lukács) suggests that the relationship between people in capitalism mimics the relationship between things.[3] In this way, capitalism perverts or defines the way we interact with each other. Marx deploys the idea of reification to expose the degrading effects of the capitalist system. Most Marxist thinkers just accept the validity of the idea, but in fact people treating each other like things is not a simple gesture. At the very least, it invokes a complex shift in the way people desire and our understanding of our own subjectivity. Marx relies on both these concepts to theorize how capitalism perpetuates itself through ideology, and they remain important explanations to this day. I would argue that the reason these concepts have such longevity as theoretical tools is that they actually signify an unconscious operation, even though Marx himself cannot articulate this. Žižek's theory of ideology opens up both these concepts and reinvestigates them in terms of the desiring subject, revealing that there is even more theoretical potential in these concepts. But to advance the theory of ideology, Žižek must turn Marx's concept of ideology on its head.

For Marx, of course, the material nature of work, poverty, and infrastructure had far more of an impact than ideas. He argues this in many different ways. For example, in *The German Ideology*, he and Engels say, "The phantoms formed in the brains of men are also, necessarily, sublimates of their material life-process, which is empirically verifiable and bound to material premises.... It is not consciousness that determines life, but life that determines consciousness."[4] For him capitalist subjects, especially proletarian subjects invested in capitalism, have to wake up to their predicament, to the actual structure of capitalism. The paradox of Marxism has always been that in order to change these material structures and experiences you have to use ideas to dissolve false consciousness and enact a new structure. Not to mention that just presenting the ideas was not always enough: often political revolutionaries found that they had to whip up emotional fervor in order to create a desire for revolution. Commodity fetishism, reification, the extreme emotion needed for revolt, all seem to be aspects of Marxism that hint at the need for acknowledging the desiring subject with an unconscious, even if Marx didn't theorize this at the time. The fecundity and importance of theorizing these potential complexities of ideology is evident in the theorists who worked to investigate it after Marx.

Marx's concept of ideology has had a lasting effect. It is Louis Althusser who tries to explain how ideology is disseminated in a way that Marx did not. His conception of ideology becomes the ruling definition after he articulates it in 1970. Despite the significant departures from Marx's theorizing about ideology, Althusser actually follows Marx in seeing ideology as a consequence of the economic system.[5] He does expand to focus on the feudal economic system as also generating ideology, thus broadening the conception that Marx initially develops. His main project, however, is to make explicit what Marx left implicit by mapping out where and how ideology is disseminated.

For Althusser, whenever you theorize ideology, you are always attempting to describe the active contours of the social order, which is why he begins his investigation by asking the much larger question: "What is society?" Althusser feels that Marx's metaphor—of a structure in which the economic is the base that everything else rests on and grows out of—is a decisive theoretical move because it forced people to rethink their relation to capital and to each other.[6] Even though he rejects a strict economic determinism for what he calls structural causality, Althusser nevertheless hews to Marx's primacy of the economic when he takes up theorizing ideology.

Althusser adds to this, however, by emphasizing that, as he says, "Ideology represents the imaginary relationship of individuals to their real conditions of existence."[7] For Althusser, ideology represents an imaginary structural realm that allows us to ignore our actual conditions. This ideological realm creates the capitalist subject who then continues to perpetuate this ideology. In what is undoubtedly his most famous formulation, Althusser explains how this happens by saying that "ideology hails or interpellates individuals as subjects."[8] The subject is brought into being by always already understanding ideology as addressing them in particular. In this way, the subject itself only exists within ideology and is, indeed, a product of ideology. Subjectivity is the result of ideological interpellation. Its status is thus wholly illusory and has no capacity for acting as the site for resisting ideology.

The problem is that Althusser's concept of the ideological hail that forms the subject in no way takes into account the subject's unconscious. Despite his debt to Freud and Lacan, Althusser's theory that the subject could be instantiated by ideology as subject relied on a misconception of the unconscious. Although Althusser makes passing mentions of the unconscious in his essay on ideology, he fails to theorize it as operative during the procedure of the ideological hail that supposedly creates the subject. Althusser fails to see how something in the unconscious resists interpellation and that this resistance is subjectivity itself.

The Foundationless Subject

Marx's theory of ideology had no place for subjectivity. This is why one must supplement Marx with Freud, who introduces subjectivity as a figure that doesn't fit in its ideological place, that is *Unbehagen* in the determinations of the social order. Freud's theory of the subject completely upends Marx's conception of ideological determination. Freud's subject not only has no place in this structural theory but in fact thoroughly undermines it.

One symptomatic response to Freud's intervention was to attempt to wrongly make Freud's theory into a structural theory as well. We can see this in the ubiquitous practice of likening the psyche to an iceberg, a metaphor not so unsimilar to Marx's metaphor of the building, in which the ideological superstructure exists on top of the economic base and in which the capitalist class exists on the basis of the work done on the ground floor by the proletariat. Even today, the most widely disseminated images used to illustrate the unconscious, consciousness, and preconscious depict a huge iceberg in which consciousness is only the very tip that sticks out of the water. Most of these depictions suggest that this is actually Freud's metaphor. "Freud's iceberg" is a commonly searched phrase on internet, and popular sources like Wikipedia refer to the iceberg to explain Freud's ideas.[9] Additionally, the iceberg explanation is given in many introductory psychology textbooks as a shorthand for making sense of Freud's conception of subjectivity.[10] In many ways, this makes sense because the metaphor is trying to emphasize the defining importance of the unconscious.

But Freud does not talk about the unconscious as the bottom of an iceberg because this way of envisioning the psyche is completely foreign to his thinking. In an extensive investigation into exactly where this metaphor comes from, Christopher Green concludes, "Some even cite Freud's writings when describing the iceberg metaphor. The problem is that Freud never mentioned the iceberg in his published writings."[11] Green goes on to explain that in fact it was a psychologist during Freud's time, Granville Stanley Hall—who was a proponent of Freud's work and who introduced Freud at his Clark lectures—who often employed this metaphor.[12] Notably, the model that Freud purposefully gives is something that instead looks like an eye ball. In this diagram, Freud maps out where consciousness (residing in what we might think of the cornea), the preconscious (residing next to the cornea), and the unconscious (taking up the rest of the eyeball) fall, and the way the id, ego, and superego interact with these realms. Notably, he refers to consciousness in these diagrams as the "pcpt.-cs." as the "perceptual system."[13]

The shape Freud draws is reminiscent of an eyeball most primarily because he describes consciousness as being at the point of perception. The key here might be to recognize that unlike an iceberg, there is no deep submerged bottom to an eyeball. In fact, the essential aspect to this eye ball-like shape as Freud's metaphor for the psyche is that there is not a foundation at all. Instead, it is a dynamic system that is relational and one in which thoughts move from one area to the other. While the unconscious may take up more space in Freud's diagram, it is not rigid or foundational but rather dynamic and interconnected, even if it is a mystery to the subject.[14]

The absence of a depth model in Freud's conception of the psyche is significant because it suggests that Freud's concept of the structure of the subject is very different from Marx's structure of the social order. Marx's structural theory places the economic infrastructure as the base because he does not believe that anything substantial within the social order can change unless the economic infrastructure changes. We could see the prevalent idea that the psyche is structured like an iceberg as a Marxification of the psyche, an attempt to make Freud's idea into a more rigid theory that gives the psyche a foundation, just as Marx gives the social order a foundation.

The consequence of both these metaphors—society as a building whose foundation is the economic and the psyche as an iceberg whose foundation is the unconscious—is a misunderstanding of the importance of the intersection between society and psyche. Freud himself fears that people might misunderstand his diagram and put too much weight on its divisions. He suggests:

> In thinking of this division of the personality into an ego, a super-ego and an id, you will not, of course, have pictured sharp frontiers like the artificial ones drawn in political geography. We cannot do justice to the characteristics of the mind by linear outlines like those in a drawing or in

a primitive painting, but rather by areas of colour melting into one another as they are presented by modern artists.[15]

His emphasis on the borders melting into one another helps to make his point that this is not a structure in which one thing rests on another, nor one in which there is a foundation. This is a dynamic system.

Althusser doesn't have Freud's reluctance to embrace the metaphor of the building. Instead, he suggests that Marx's metaphor of a building with the economic as the foundation remains productive. He writes, "Like every metaphor, this metaphor suggests something, makes something visible. What? Precisely this: that the upper floors could not 'stay up' (in the air) alone, if they did not rest precisely on their base: that the bottom floor holds up the upper floors."[16] Althusser is certainly correct that these metaphors make something visible, and thus it is important to emphasize that Freud's eyeball-like metaphor actually works against a foundational theory. This metaphor also makes clear that unconscious material is affected by consciousness and the preconscious. While many psychical functions, according to Freud, happen solely in the unconscious, that material is there because of what the subject's consciousness has encountered. Consciousness truly is the lens through which psychic material refracts. What this suggests is that the relationship between the two is dialectical rather than consciousness being held up or undergirded by the unconscious. Of course, initially getting people to believe in the unconscious was difficult. The existence of an unconscious suggested that individuals weren't simply their thinking, conscious mind. Such an insight itself was destabilizing for most who encountered it. Although the unconscious unseats the idea of the conscious mind being in charge, Freud's idea of the psyche does not, in fact, theorize that the unconscious is the solid foundation that grows and determines consciousness. If anything, the unconscious is a shifting, porous set of relations.

In theorizing the psyche and introducing the importance of the unconscious, late in his life Freud feels the need to also introduce another tryptic: the id, superego, and ego. He does this precisely because the place specific description of conscious, preconscious, and unconscious was leading people to make proclamations that seemed to misunderstand his intentions. Freud did not unleash the structural theory of id, superego, and ego to match the topological theory. There is no perfect correspondence between the theories. Their lack of equivalence, in fact, acts to broaden and complicate the understanding of the psyche so that people didn't mistake the categories as a rigid structure, like a building, but rather to see it as a dynamic process— even if it was often inscrutable.

Most people who think about Jacques Lacan at all believe that one of Lacan's important contributions to psychoanalysis was to theorize it with the then contemporary ideas of structuralism. What this produced in Lacan's thought is further investigation into how the subject is situated in the social order and the subject's experience of the relation between their psyche and the social order. Bringing structuralism into psychoanalysis, however, did not produce an idea of Freud's psyche as itself a rigid structure. Instead, structuralism led Lacan in the opposite direction. Lacan never refers to the unconscious as a deep dark foundation. Rather, this theoretical turn to structuralism leads him to see the unconscious as always manifested in the fabric of our experience. For Lacan, we encounter the unconscious in the visual field (in the form of the gaze), and we experience it in the objects that we desire (especially in the disconnect between the object cause of desire and the object of desire). Lacan's own diagram, or metaphor, is three circles that intersect as a representative of our subjectivity. He names these three circles: the symbolic, the imaginary and the Real. The subject resides at their intersection. These three concepts are meant to emphasize the way that every interaction and experience has all the elements of the psyche present. Lacan's impact on our understanding of the subject was tremendous, but the misunderstanding of Freud's theory often continued and informed various modes of thought, including the way that theorists, inclusive of Althusser, conceive ideology. It is Žižek who brings an understanding of the psychoanalytic subject to bear on the theory of ideology.

Žižek's Intervention

Žižek tears open the preceding ideas of ideology to make room for the unconscious and all its implications. His theory of ideology is radically different from previous ones because his theory of the subject is radically different from Althusser's or Marx's concept of the subject, to the extent that either had one. For Althusser and Marx, their "real conditions of existence" are the economic conditions. These are the conditions that shape and create their idea of the subject. While Žižek might also refer to the "real conditions of existence" when discussing the subject and he certainly foregrounds the importance of the economic structure, he would most likely be referring to a different real, one with a capital R. For Žižek, the Real conditions of existence reside in our unconscious, our status as a split subject, and the antagonisms that structure the social order, not in our material economic situation, which is what Marx and Althusser refer to when they use the term *real*. The psychoanalytic subject, which is the subject of the unconscious, has an utterly different way of interacting with and creating ideology. Žižek's concept of ideology turns away from Marx and Althusser and toward Hegel and Lacan. Indeed, throughout his career, Žižek constantly refers to Hegel and Lacan as his theoretical guideposts.

In Žižek's oeuvre, the theory of the subject is intimately tied to a theory of the social order. As much as his subject is that of psychoanalysis, his understanding of the structure of society is tied to Hegel's concept of dialectics. The intersection between Lacan and Hegel, for Žižek, can be found in their understanding of authority. Lacan expands the idea of the superego into the social order by theorizing our need to imagine a Big Other, an authority figure par excellence. Lacan theorizes the Big Other to shed light on our constant desire to capitulate or rebel based on our fantasy of the Big Other. He theorizes the Big Other to broaden psychoanalytic theory so that it can theorize the subject in its relationship to the social order. Certainly, this is often a challenge for psychoanalysis. It is the point where it seems to be incompatible with Marxism or other philosophical traditions. Psychoanalytic theorists constantly confront questions about how they can make statements about a group of people or a whole society, when psychoanalysis is based on observations about the individual psyche. But Freud and Lacan both work to show that not only was it possible to do so but it is imperative. One cannot understand the society without understanding the individual psyche and vice versa.[17] Theorizing the Big Other allows Lacan to show how and why the dominant social structures come into being. Lacan's larger point in creating the concept, however, is to reveal its status as purely symbolic. He famously says, "This Other doesn't exist."[18] The implication here is that the Big Other works only through people's belief in it. It is an authority that functions only on the basis of the obedience that constitutes it and props it up. The subject's oppressive social situation is rooted in its desire to follow the Big Other, to believe in a Big Other. And this is not so easily confronted.

On the basis of this conception of the part the subject plays in its own manipulation, Žižek constructs a theory of ideology that focuses on the relationship between the subject and the social order. For Žižek, Hegel's dialectic helps to create the bridge needed to bring the psyche and the social together. Although Hegel is known for a philosophy that attempts to grasp the structure of thought itself, it is driven by this relationship between the subject and society. Certainly, many theorists—such as Immanuel Kant and J. G. Fichte—work to theorize the larger social through the individual psyche by arguing that society can only be understood as something we fabricate, as structured by our sensibility and our understanding. These theorists stand in opposition to the likes of Marx who emphasized the materiality of the world and its impact on the individual. The key to Žižek's theory of ideology is that it does both. It privileges the individual psyche but also takes seriously the structures of society. This approach is one he finds in Hegel as well.

For Hegel, the movement of history of the social order is also the movement of the individual approaching freedom. One of the key components of Hegel's theory that most influences Žižek's writing about ideology is Hegel's argument that there is no foundational starting point on the path to absolute knowing. In many ways, this is his primary intervention into German idealism—the refusal of any foundation for thought. Other German thinkers of the epoch are more concerned with establishing an origin or a foundation for thought. Their belief is that, without a foundation for one's philosophical system, the system would be immediately suspect. Kant carefully theorizes the conditions for possible experience as the basis for his system, while Fichte, dissatisfied with Kant's weak foundation theorizes a self-positing I as the basis for our knowledge of the world.

In contrast to these forerunners, Hegel contends that the beginning point of any philosophical system is immaterial. He argues, "In my view, which must be justified by the exposition of the system itself, everything hangs on grasping and expressing the true not just as *substance* but just as much as *subject*."[19] In other words, for Hegel, what appears selfsame and autonomous is just as riven with inconsistency and self-division as subjectivity. There is no solid structure, no foundation to the building because the building is at odds with itself in the way that subjectivity is. Rather than starting with a solid foundation and building upward, Hegel takes the reverse approach. He begins with the most obvious inconsistencies and proceeds to the most obscure.

By following this path, Hegel reveals himself to be a philosopher of retroactivity or *Nachträglichkeit*. Although many opponents of Hegel characterize him as an evolutionary thinker of history, this image is completely wrong. Hegel tells history backward. History is always conceived retroactively, so that the present constitutes the past rather than the past shaping the present. This is the point at which the difference between Hegel and Marx becomes most evident (and not in the hackneyed idealism versus materialism conflict). Unlike Hegel, Marx takes an evolutionary and progressive view of history. On this basis, Marx can conceive of a path forward from the contradictions of capitalism to the development of communism. We can have faith in the future, according to Marx, because we know the past. For Hegel, however, history is always in the rearview mirror. We can only see it after it has happened and thus our interpretation of it occurs through the lens of our current moment. This is why Hegel insists that we cannot learn anything from history.

Žižek brings together the nonexistence of the big Other and substance is subject when he theorizes ideology. These two ideas allow Žižek to rip out the solid ground, the ground floor, that ideology rested on in all previous theorizations of it. Importantly, however, this doesn't mean he believes in the lack of structure or some endless social flow. In bringing together Lacan and Hegel, what Žižek finds is a way to theorize the psyche and the social together without the idea of a foundation or an origin. The question might then be: without the building edifice what is ideology perpetuating? Where does it arise from? Here, Žižek intervenes with his theory that ideology in fact arises from antagonism. He argues that it is antagonism that structures the social order. Rather than being the result of the economic system, for Žižek, ideology emerges out of the antagonisms that define our social structure. Ideology arises to cover them over and thus obscure them. Žižek's turn away from the priority of the economy in his theory of ideology gives him a radicality that surpasses that of either Marx or Althusser. By turning the focus to the relation between the subject and the social when theorizing ideology, Žižek makes evident the psychic appeal that ideology has and uncovers the key to its effectiveness, something that neither Marx nor Althusser are able to do.

Antagonism, for Žižek, exists because society is not whole. It is not a complete structure. Instead, it's a failed structure. Antagonism manifests itself through different attempts to address the failure. For Žižek, there are two different approaches to this failure, and these two approaches are inevitably and eternally antagonistic. We can imagine a multitude of different symbolic fictions but there are only two different possible responses to the failure of the social structure. The first attempts to integrate the failure of the social order into its position and to articulate the failure as such by seeing society as divided. The second attempts to overcome the failure and achieve a wholeness that would belie the failure of the social structure. The fundamental antagonism of the social order occurs between these two responses, which can manifest themselves in a variety of ways.[20]

It is essential to note that these responses happen in the larger social order and are therefore external. The external nature of antagonism is essential for Žižek's theory of ideology and where he differs from Hegel. Hegel does not theorize antagonism but instead refers to negativity or contradiction as society's driving force. Hegel's idea is that contradiction is within society and within the subject. Contradiction is internal to the subject or to any entity. For Žižek, antagonism is external—it exists between different forms of subjectivity or between different classes—and in this theoretical move he brings subjectivity and structuralism together.

That said, antagonism cannot act as a foundation for the social order. For Žižek, antagonism is generative but not foundational. That is to say, there is no implied origin in seeing antagonism as what ideology arises out of but rather an acknowledgment of the way the psyche and society impact each other. There is only a dialectical encounter in which the beginning comes to exist out of the process of the encounter itself. For Žižek, society is a dynamic loop that repeats its form but not the content and yet is driven by the constant dialectical relationship between form and content. His theory of ideology allows us to step back and see the form without getting caught up in the content; that is, without letting the content blind us from the form.

One of Žižek's most powerful examples of this that he returns to throughout his work is from structuralist Claude Lévi-Strauss in his work *Structural Anthropology*. Žižek finds Lévi-Strauss's example of the way villagers described their own village the perfect explanation of ideology as such. In this example, the anthropologist asks all the villagers to draw a picture of their village. One group of villagers draws a village in which all the central houses are grouped together in an inner circle. The other group of the villagers draw a village completely divided with one half on one side and the other half on the other. None of the villagers draw the village empirically, as it actually is; instead, they all drew it as they experienced it. Žižek points out that the latter half are in fact correct—even if they might be empirically wrong—because they see the way the social order is an expression of an existing antagonism. These two different drawings reveal, Žižek argues, "a fundamental antagonism the inhabitants of the village were unable to symbolize, to account for, to 'internalize,' to come to terms with, an imbalance in social relations that prevented the community from stabilizing itself into a harmonious whole."[21] Along these lines, one can say that the ideological gesture of the way each group sees the village are also markers of the Real, markers of this antagonism. Žižek's theory of ideology gives us a way to identify these markers and thus to find a way to articulate a truth without becoming caught up in the problem of perspectivism.

Marx's theory of class struggle is another important example. Žižek often points out that in regards to capitalism, Marx takes up the role of Lévi-Strauss in his analysis of the village. Marx sees the way class difference was actually class conflict. In *The Poverty of Philosophy*, Marx uses the term *antagonism* that will later become so fruitful for Žižek. He writes, "No antagonism, no progress. This is the law that civilization has followed up to our days. Till now the productive forces have been developed by virtue of this system of class antagonisms."[22] When he writes "till now," Marx reveals his belief that antagonism is not endemic to the social order but just to capitalist society. He envisions overcoming it. For Marx, antagonism is a solvable problem, which it is not for Žižek. Marx explains, "In a future society, in which class antagonism will have ceased, in which there will no longer be any classes, use will no longer be determined by the *min*imum time of production."[23] Marx's argument that class struggle was ultimately solvable by the victory of the proletariat elided the antagonism that he had uncovered.

In the end, Marx cannot see the centrality of antagonism, because he doesn't have a theory of the unconscious. Lacan, for his part, never addresses antagonism as Žižek theorizes it, because he doesn't have a theory of politicized conflict. In *The Parallax View*, Žižek further explains how he is retooling the Marxist (political) and Lacanian (psychoanalytic) positions. Going back to Lévi-Strauss's example of the village, he explains that the Real, or the antagonism, is evident not in each side of the conflict (each drawing in the case of Levi-Strauss or each class in the case of Marx), but in the shift from one perspective to another. The Real is this gap between the two perspectives. To emphasize his politicization of—and thus departure from—Lacan, Žižek renames the Real here as the "parallax Real" to point out that it is not a Real that always returns to the same place but rather a non-existing kernel through which a multiple of symbolic fictions refract. He argues the Real is "an X which can be reconstructed only retroactively, from the multitude of symbolic formations, which are all that 'there actually is'."[24] In this way, Žižek brings Hegel's gesture of retroactivity to bear on Lacan's theory of the subject and thus politicizes the Big Other while also giving us the tools to be able to see this process.

There are two important components to Žižek's theory of ideology: that ideology arises in response to the antagonism within the social order and that it then serves to hide that antagonism. Within these components, we can see the answer to Althusser's question: What is a society? For Žižek, the subject is not the result of an ideological hail but what this hail obfuscates. Žižek theorizes that ideology is actually what we create and invest ourselves in in order to avoid the trauma of our own desire. This leads Žižek away from the building metaphor and away from all economism. Marx's theory of society as structured like a building with economics at the bottom is completely destabilized by this idea. Žižek's theory of ideology explains why people don't just awaken from their false consciousness and do what is best for themselves and for society.

Žižek's Psyche

The question then remains how does ideology affect us psychically? It is Freud's theory of the unconscious that allows us to see more clearly how the contours of the social order interact with the individual psyche. Namely, we repress desire that is not acceptable, desire that would put us in danger or traumatize us. We can then say that extreme repression, the kind that causes neurosis, is generally caused by ideology. Ideology demands more repression because it is organizing the social order for a particular purpose, a purpose that does not have to do with simple living arrangements but rather with a ruling order created to obscure the structuring antagonism. For ideology to work, it tries to control all aspects of a person's life. What they do with their time, who they love, how and with whom they have sex, what they value, and how they create families and friend groups.

Our proclivity for self-destruction seems aptly expressed in ideology as such. It keeps us constantly hampered, just out of reach of freedom and true equality. Every time we think we have taken a permanent step toward a social order based on equality and freedom for all, we inevitably find ourselves in a new situation that either repeats the ideological status quo or is actually worse than before. This certainly is the case with feminism today. In the 1980s and even the 1990s, there was an assumption that we were on a path finally toward a more equal society. In the United States, the Roe vs. Wade decision had made abortions legal, and it was an accepted standard medical practice. Women sought careers in droves and even Hollywood let a few women direct films. Now in the 2020s with Roe overturned, we find ourselves, in America at least, utterly unable to get an abortion in most states. Even in the most leftist states, like Vermont where I live, where supposedly women are more able to obtain an abortion, the medical schools are no longer teaching students how to perform an abortion.[25] This medical procedure has been so threatened on political grounds that they are too scared to even teach doctors how to do it. Obviously, if medical students are not taught how to do an abortion, then it will very soon be completely unavailable. At the same time, in response to the complicated demands of the pandemic, women have left the workforce in droves to care for their children. Feminists of late have been walking around in disbelief, not understanding how we have come back to an ideological place we thought we had left far behind. Ideology renames things and reshapes them in order to reinforce the structures of society and prevent us from being truly equal or truly free. In other words, it gives us what we want. It gives us the obstacles and impediments that allow us to manifest our self-destructiveness. By doing so, ideology enables us to avoid confronting the structuring antagonism.

One point that Žižek has made since the beginning of his career is that ideology is strongest when we are unaware of it. Additionally, it is generally the case that we don't experience ourselves as steeped in ideology because we believe that our experience is authentic. This is what Žižek means when he says, following Lacan, that emotions lie. Caught up in the throes of emotion we think what we are feeling must be truthful and not simply created by ideology. More than that, we think others are steeped in ideology while we are not. This is an important disavowal that allows ideology to function, which is why Žižek so often brings up the importance of disavowal in the theory of ideology. We can retroactively acknowledge having been embedded in ideology in the past, but we can't see our involvement in ideology in the current moment. The experience of our psyche in the now seems to completely obscure our involvement in ideology. This is partly why people become so irate on the spot when they are accused of being engaged in ideology, since they can't themselves see it in their experience of their own actions. We can see ideology more when we begin to reason through a problem or make a choice that we think through first. At that juncture, where we start to try to make a choice that better represents our ethics, we begin to name the contours of ideology in order to find where we are in that layout.

For example, when considering whether or not you should get married, one might step back and begin to consider the larger institution of marriage, the role it plays in capitalism, and the way that it provides a breeding ground for many modes of the ruling ideology. One might begin to wonder why one needs a marriage certificate to declare one's love or commit to one's partner. Even if you take the cynical approach and admit that the financial benefits of being married might be helpful to a young struggling couple, just acknowledging this forces you to see your choice as embedded in a larger ideology that helps to bolster forces such as capitalism and patriarchy. Even if we step back and evaluate ideology, we often willingly participate nonetheless. The couple who sits and carefully analyzes the ideological pitfalls of marriage and then chooses to get married anyway usually believes that they are the exception: "We will change the marriage institution from the inside out," they say. It is, Žižek's theory of ideology points out, at that very moment when they feel the freest of ideology, the most like an exception, that the couple is actually reinscribing themselves into ideology. Symbolic gestures—like not having the same last name or not wearing wedding rings—might seem like a small place of ideological disruption but may in fact be the very point in which the couple is knitted into the ideology they are trying to eschew.[26]

Žižek's theory of ideology acknowledges that seeing the contours of ideology is not easy, and one needs to put on a certain lens to be able to see it. Žižek is fond of referring to the film *They Live* (John Carpenter, 1988) to explain ideology precisely because it shows the need for putting on one's theoretical glasses in order to see ideology. In this science-fiction film, characters are lulled into accepting their fate with TV commercials, game shows, and enticing billboards of sunny vacations. The world looks completely like the then present-day America. But the characters discover that in fact people are being manipulated by aliens who have infiltrated and run the world. The aliens are simply taking all our resources and keeping us docile while doing it. The main characters discover this when they put on special sunglasses that allow them to see all the subliminal messages under the commercials, shows, and billboards as well as the aliens themselves, some of whom have been masquerading as real people. The subliminal messages encourage people to worship money, obey, and sleep. For Žižek, this film is the perfect example of how ideology functions and how we can become cognizant of it—by putting on the proper pair of glasses.

When the film ends, the characters respond to the deception in an ideological way. They react by killing the aliens with abandon, carrying huge weapons, and attempting to regain the earth by stopping the subliminal signal. In the final moment, John Nada (Rodney Piper) flips off the aliens before he blows up their signal, an act that kills himself at the same time. With the signal ended, the aliens are revealed to everyone, even those without glasses, thus ending the deception and presumably beginning a moment of true revolt when the humans will surely try to take back their world. Clearly, this is an ideological ending because it suggests that a more pure, less docile, less controlled existence is possible if only we can get the aliens off our world. A more radical end to the film might have been to have our hero walk by a mirror when wearing the glasses and see that he, in fact, is also an alien. What would the most ethical act be at that point? To commit suicide, after probably taking down the light beam controlling the world? Or possibly to make the existential choice to live with, and make decisions based on, this knowledge. In a way, we might also see Žižek's theory of ideology as a new theorization of existentialism. It is a theory that allows us to make a choice, to see the relationship between the psyche and the social and then act without the safety net of an origin story. His theory of ideology suggests that it is not an economic revolution that must set us free but a psychic one that will ultimately enable economic transformation. The question might be: what choice do we make now in the face of rising fascism, crushing ideological forces, our extreme political divides, and a stage of capitalism that seems genuinely unending?

Notes

1. Karl Marx and Friedrich Engels, *The German Ideology* (Moscow: Progress Publishers, 1976), 42.
2. In large part, this is because we no longer can imagine the end of capitalism. It's possible that the capitalist gesture par excellence is to say that we are doomed because capitalism will never fail and will never be toppled. This cynicism about capitalism is especially surprising as we watch it crack on a regular basis with the recession of 2008, the supply problems of the pandemic, and the untenable wealth disparity of our current moment. But most people simply say that these failures are part of capitalism's trick.
3. See Georg Lukács, *History and Class Consciousness: Studies in Marxist Dialectics*, trans. Rodney Livingstone (Cambridge, MA: MIT Press, 1971).
4. Marx and Engels, *The German Ideology*, 42.
5. He famously argues, "All ideological State apparatuses, wherever they are, contribute to the same result: the reproduction of the relations of production, i.e., of capitalist relations of exploitation." Louis Althusser, "Ideology and Ideological State Apparatuses." In *Lenin and Philosophy and Other Essays*, trans. Ben Brewster (New York: Monthly Review Press, 1971), 154.
6. This multi-layered approach allows Althusser to point out that, for example a workers' revolution needs to happen on the level of the infrastructure (economic) rather than on the level of the superstructure (ideological/political). He allows, however, for the possibility of workers bringing the struggle into ideology and thus undermining it and forcing it to disrupt itself.
7. Althusser, "Ideology and Ideological State Apparatuses," 165.
8. Ibid., 175.
9. See the Wikipedia entry on Id, Ego, and Superego, for one such example (complete with image as well as description): https://en.wikipedia.org/wiki/Id,_ego_and_super-ego (accessed November 20, 2021).
10. For example, University of Minnesota's *Introduction to Psychology* website says, "For Freud the mind was like an iceberg, with the many motivations of the unconscious being much larger, but also out of sight, in comparison to the consciousness of which we are aware." https://open.lib.umn.edu/intropsyc/chapter/11-2-the-origins-of-personality/ This also includes the iceberg image as well: https://open.lib.umn.edu/intropsyc/chapter/11-2-the-origins-of-personality/§angor-ch11_s02_s01_f01 (accessed November 20, 2021).
11. Christopher Green, "Where Did Freud's Iceberg Metaphor of Mind Come From?," *History of Psychology* 22, no. 4 (November 2019): 369.
12. For a fascinating accounting of the spread of the iceberg metaphor, see Green, "Where Did Freud's Iceberg Metaphor of Mind Come From?," 369–72.

13 Sigmund Freud, *New Introductory Lecture on Psycho-Analysis*, trans. James Strachey, in *The Standard Edition of the Complete Psychological Works of Sigmund Freud*, ed. James Strachey, vol XXII (London: Hogarth, 1964), 78.

14 The only time Freud ever refers to an actual shape to explain the relation is when he describes the relationship between the ego and the id as like the relationship between the germinal disc (as the ego) and the ovum (as the id) that it rests on in an egg. The germinal disc is the area that the sperm enters the egg through, and it contains all the female genetic material. Of course, this could provide more inspiration for analysis, but the dynamic here again is not of a rigid foundation but of an active relation. See Sigmund Freud, *The Ego and the Id*, trans. Joan Riviere, in *The Standard Edition of the Complete Psychological Works of Sigmund Freud*, vol XIX, ed. James Strachey (London: Hogarth, 1961), 24.

15 Sigmund Freud, *New Introductory Lecture on Psycho-Analysis*, trans. James Strachey, in *The Standard Edition of the Complete Psychological Works of Sigmund Freud*, ed. James Strachey, vol XXII (London: Hogarth, 1964), 79.

16 Althusser, "Ideology and Ideological State Apparatuses," 135.

17 The bifurcation between theories of the psyche and theories of the social is itself an ideological gesture.

18 Jacques Lacan, *Le Séminaire XIV: La logique du fantasme, 1966–1967*, unpublished manuscript, session of January 25, 1967.

19 Georg Wilhelm Friedrich Hegel, *The Phenomenology of Spirit*, trans. Terry Pinkard (Cambridge: Cambridge University Press, 2018), 12.

20 This is, of course, an exact description of Lacan's theory of sexual difference and why he claims that there can be no sexual relation. Lacan's formulas of sexuation play a crucial role in the development of Žižek's understanding of social antagonism, as is clear in Slavoj Žižek, *Sex and the Failed Absolute* (London: Bloomsbury, 2020).

21 Slavoj Žižek, *The Parallax View* (Cambridge, MA: MIT Press, 2006), 25–6.

22 Karl Marx, *The Poverty of Philosophy* (New York: International Publishers, 1963), 47.

23 Ibid., 48.

24 Žižek, *The Parallax View*, 26.

25 See https://vtdigger.org/2021/11/26/uvms-larner-college-of-medicine-offers-limited-abortion-training-some-students-want-more/ (accessed November 20, 2021).

26 The preceding is a self-criticism.

Response to Neroni

Slavoj Žižek

With Neroni's text, I have a problem similar to the one I have with Friedlander's text: it is an excellent systematic summation of my dispersed thoughts on ideology, so I am unable to raise any critical points. What I will therefore do is the only way out of this predicament that I see: I will turn criticism toward myself and indicate three points where I think my own standard position should be corrected or balanced, at least.

The first point concerns the idea that the big Other doesn't exist: yes in principle, but the ongoing process of the disintegration of the thick texture of the social big Other is nonetheless something to worry about. One can observe this process at its purest in today's Sweden. When I was a child, Sweden had a mythic status of a country which is so safe that when you left your house you didn't even lock the doors. A last echo of this stance was felt even at the beginning of the pandemic, when Sweden avoided lockdown and other obligatory measures with the justification that Swedes are people with a highly developed sense of community so that legal regulations are necessary. As we have learned from crime writers like Henning Mankel, this image was largely an illusion, but it was an illusion which worked. Now we find in the media headlines such as "Ultraviolent gangs are threatening to subvert the rule of law in Sweden" and we read: "Once one of the most peaceful countries in Europe, Sweden is plagued by the worst rates of deadly gun violence in Europe, 10 times higher than Germany. Its problems offer a warning of what can happen when integration fails." Integration is mentioned here because violence is condensed, even de facto normalized, in ghettos like Hjällbo, a suburb of Gothenburg where

> social exclusion and lack of cultural integration for immigrants provide fertile ground for gangs. Johann Olsson [head of the police's national operation department in Stockholm] says identity is also a driving issue.

The most violent offenders, he says, are seen as occupying "no-man's land." He adds: "They don't obey the rules of their parents' generation and they haven't really integrated into Swedish society. So, they make up their own level of social capital." Hjällbo's segregation is complete, cut off from Gothenburg by forest and hills. Hjällbo is also dominated by the city's most brutal criminal network, an organization that openly challenges the state and whose gangland lifestyle not only threatens to reshape Swedish politics but also to undermine its democracy.[1]

To blame immigrants for their refusal to integrate, as well as to blame the Swedish indigenous white majority for its non-readiness to integrate immigrants, is both wrong and misleading. The basic fact is that immigrant gangs are not just simply criminal—in all its brutality, their community relies on their own ethics, on a set of very stringent norms and prohibitions which are incompatible with the norms and prohibitions of the majority. The problem is that there is no all-encompassing big Other that would regulate the interaction between the two: although we can still talk about the big Other in the sense of a "normal" Swedish society into which gangs are not integrated, the danger is that this big Other is disintegrating, so that if the process of ghettoization will go on. What is awaiting us is a multitude of "tribal" communities less and less held together by a common rule of law.

The second point concerns *jouissance* as a political factor, a topic Neroni is fully aware of: "the intrusion into the political can only be made by recognizing that the only discourse there is [...] is the discourse of *jouissance*."[2] In short, ideology and politics can be explained neither by crude reference to actual class interests nor by discourse-analysis which focuses on the competitive game for discursive hegemony, for which ideology will provide the dominant cognitive mapping of the situation. Even a brief look at racism and sexism suffices to see how, for an ideology to really take hold of us, it has to mobilize the dimension of *jouissance*. Oppression of women is sustained by the fear that, if not controlled, women will explode in excessive pleasures. Racism envies the Other's enjoyments in perceiving this Other as a threat to enjoyments that form our way of life. All such passionate ideological investments are traversed by sadism, masochism, and all their perverted combinations like enjoying one's own humiliation.

The extreme case of *jouissance* today is, of course, the prospect of apocalypse in all its versions (pandemic, ecological catastrophes, nuclear war, dissolution of social order) inclusive of total knowledge itself: wouldn't it be properly apocalyptic to gain direct access to another's stream of thoughts? Lorenzo Chiesa deftly points out that this desire is "manifestly witnessed by our current fascination with virological, ecological, and technological figures of the Apocalypse. Adopting the terminology of *Seminar XX*, we could also call it a desire to be One in order to absolutely enjoy through and in (sexual) knowledge, a desire which instead leads to maximal entropy."[3] Just think about a snuff movie (a pornographic film that shows the actual torture and murder of one of the performers during the sexual interaction)—really, as Lacan put it in a concise way, "everyone's dying to know what would happen if things went really bad."[4] This is why we are so fascinated by the precise features of a dystopian reality, from *The Handmaid's Tale* and stories about European daily life if Hitler won the war up to the future life on a devastated earth. "Dying to know" should be taken here in its ambiguity: it means that I would really like to know it and that this knowledge would bring me to death.

What the notion of fully knowing a catastrophe misses is the fact that, when we get too close to a catastrophe, the distance necessary for knowledge breaks down. We cannot combine the real of a full catastrophe with the safe distance of knowledge (like the idea of entering the sun or a black hole and register what goes on down there). The lesson of Hegel's absolute knowing is exactly the opposite: it is a knowing which includes its own incompleteness. Knowledge is non-all in the Lacanian sense: it is not that something a priori eludes it, there is nothing that eludes it, but for this very reason it cannot be totalized. G. K. Chesterton wrote that Christianity acknowledges one big mystery (God) as the exception which allows a Christian to perceive and understand all other reality as completely rational and knowable. For a materialist, the situation is exactly the opposite: there is no exception, which is why all reality is full of mysteries (just think of the mysteries of quantum physics). We can say that, in the same sense that anti-Semitism is the stupid man's anticapitalism, the full knowledge of an apocalypse is the stupid man's version of Hegel's absolute knowing.

My last point concerns what I consider one of the key lessons of the ongoing pandemic: the need to supplement the standard Marxist view of the state as an instrument of class oppression with a more differentiated view of the state. Álvaro García Linera[5] was the first one who—from a radical leftist stance—approached the question: "Why did, at the pandemic outburst, billions unquestionably accepted the severe limitation of their daily freedoms?" outside the predominant blahblah of state powers using the pandemic as the pretext to strengthen the control over population and discipline it. He begins by pointing out that we were witnessing something absolutely unique—a kind of planetary general strike which hit also the circulation of capital:

> For the first time in human history, vast numbers of people across the world have agreed to abandon their paid activities, to stop attending public gatherings, and confine themselves in their homes for weeks and months. We are living in a kind of general planetary strike which has paralyzed most of the transport, commerce, production, and services. People have accepted confinement when asked to do so by their state institutions which justify the measure as a way to stop the spread of the coronavirus.[6]

So why did people not only accept this but sometimes even demand it? (In the UK, people at some point demanded harsher measures than those enacted by the government.) Linera does not describe this unique situation in order to give rise to our horror in the style of: how could people be so manipulated to voluntarily demand control and servitude? On the contrary, he refers here to the positive function of state: state is not just an agency of oppression and class domination but also the institutional representative of the common interest of the entire population, sustained by

> a common belief in the protection of everybody through public resource. Before, it meant the expectation of collective protection against wars, invasions, violent death, and also the hope of a safeguard against collective misfortunes, economic catastrophes, losing positions. At this moment, the State represents the promise of protection against the risk of death from the virus. It is in collective responses to constitutive fears where we can find decisive clues about the origins and functioning of States. But the State is not the same as fear. The fear of invasions, misery, the loss of possessions, the plague, allows a community of affected people to become a political community when everyone decides to accept a common way of organizing resources that allows to stop, mitigate, defeat imminent or perceived primary fears.[7]

And Linera's point is that, with the pandemic, this role of the state as the ultimate protector of the common good grew stronger than ever—markets were helpless, international cooperation failed, only state remained:

> The pandemic has revealed the basic composition of the state relations by presenting it as the only and last social space of protection against the risk of death and economic catastrophe. International organizations and global markets have abdicated their prerogatives in relation to the State; globalised production is collapsing and companies are lining up to take refuge in public debt. The institutions that once drew on the creation of globalization over the State are now extending their hands in search of government benefits.[8]

In such an extraordinary situation, we became aware of what state is at its most basic: state authority appears and functions as a neutral space above particular groups; this neutrality is illusory, of course, but it is a "real illusion" embodied in a series of material social and ideological apparatuses, from education to health. In short, state is

> not only a belief of collective goods for the common protection; it is also a material reality of organizing a form of management of the common (government, parliament, ministries, legal apparatus, permanent coercive apparatuses); it is a material reality of having resources and common goods for protection (initially taxes, then public goods, services, savings, among others), consequently, it is a way of directing the common; and it

is also discursive ways of territorially delimiting the community of belief (school system, national identity, recognition systems, state legitimacies)." [. . .] It is an illusion, but it is a well-founded illusion objectively sustained by the persistence of these common goods.[10]

The status of this "illusion" is not just objective (it is embodied in a series of material institutions and procedures) but also subjective: in some sense, a state exists only insofar as its subjects believe in it, "take it seriously" even when they oppose it or denounce it as tyranny. That's why state decrees have a performative dimension: they do what they say, they are pronounced from the big Other—there is an invisible gap which separates pronouncements and declarations of even very influential individuals from state declarations. We can feel this distinction in those moments when the state (or its leader) goes on acting as a state but is no longer "taken seriously" since the performativity of its acts is suspended. Let me mention for the nth time the classic scene in cartoons: the cat reaches a precipice but goes on walking, ignoring the fact that there is no ground under its feet; it starts to fall only when it looks down and notices the abyss. When a political regime loses its authority, it is like that cat above the precipice: in order to fall, it only has to be reminded to look down. But the opposite also holds: when an authoritarian regime approaches its final crisis, its dissolution as a rule follows two steps. Before its actual collapse, a mysterious rupture takes place: all of a sudden people know that the game is over—they are simply no longer afraid. It is not only that the regime loses its legitimacy, its exercise of power itself is perceived as an impotent panic reaction. In the book *Shah of Shahs*, a classic account of the Iranian revolution of 1979, Ryszard Kapuscinski located the precise moment of this rupture: at a Tehran crossroad, a single demonstrator refused to budge when a policeman shouted at him to move, and the embarrassed policeman simply withdrew; in a couple of hours, all Tehran knew about this incident, and although there were street fights going on for weeks, everyone somehow knew the game was over.[11]

As a Marxist, Linera is, of course, well aware of how the role of state as representative and protector of all its citizen is always given a specific spin (privileging the rich, a certain religion or ethnic group, oppression of women, etc.), where this spin is (mis)represented as something done for the good of all (rich people are productive and give work to the poor, etc.). However, as he points out, in times of crisis, the state is compelled to privilege its function as the protector of the universal interest of its citizens at the expense of its privileged strata—how far the state is ready to go in this direction depends on the constellation of social struggles and on the popular mobilization. That's why it is crucial not just to dismiss the state as the instrument of domination but to assume state power when possible and use it for the universal welfare—this is what the Bolivian state was doing when Linera was its vice-president. In the situations of natural and health catastrophes, social unrests, etc., it is thus absolutely crucial for the progressive forces to try to grab state power and fully use it, not only in order to adequately react to the fears of ordinary people but also to fight against fears which were artificially created in order to keep the population in check (racist and sexist fears, etc.). The standard Marxist point is that the state as an institution is not just biased in the empirical sense of serving particular interests, but that it is biased in its very form as an institution, independently of which group holds power—again, not just in the sense that state institutions obey their own immanent interests of domination, but also in the sense that the very form in which they "represent" all of society is not really neutral. So, when progressive powers occupy the state, they somehow operate in enemy territory. This very fact, however, is a unique chance to beat the enemy from within. We should also bear in mind that exploitation and domination are not linked to the state: already in the Neolithic period, there was patriarchy and social hierarchy, and since today's civil society is also immanently antagonistic, it is often a fact that civil society resists the state's progressive measures (anti-racism and anti-sexism). So when we are witnessing a rightist populist rebellion, there is no excuse for not ruthlessly using state mechanisms of repression—when the Capitol was invaded by the Trump mob on January 6, 2021 the police should have intervened with all force.

Notes

1. https://www.theguardian.com/world/2021/dec/04/how-the-of-a-swedish-rapper-shocked-a-nation-and-put-police-on-the-back-foot.
2. Jacques Lacan, *The Other Side of Psychoanalysis: The Seminar of Jacques Lacan, Book XVII* (New York: Norton, 2007), 78.
3. Lorenzo Chiesa, "Anthropie: Beside the Pleasure Principle," *Continental Thought & Theory* 3, no. 2 (2021), 189–205.
4. Jacques Lacan, *The Other Side of Psychoanalysis: The Seminar of Jacques Lacan, Book XVII* (New York: Norton, 2007), 176–7.
5. Álvaro García Linera, "The State in Times of Coronavirus: The Pendulum of the Illusory Community," *Crisis & Critique* 7, no. 3 (2020), 161–95. Available online: https://crisiscritique.org/uploads/24-11-2020/alvaro-garci-a-linera.pdf (accessed December 27, 2021)
6. Álvaro García Linera, "The State in Times of Coronavirus," 161.
7. Ibid., 165.
8. Ibid., 180.
9. Ibid., 166.
10. Ibid., 174.
11. See Ryszard Kapuscinski, *Shah of Shahs* (New York: Vintage Books, 1992).

CHAPTER SEVEN

The Subject Is Not Enough

Henrik Jøker Bjerre

Žižek's contribution to the critique of ideology revolves around a tension between the fantasmatic structure of social reality and the subject as the questioning of this very structure. In this relation, the subject has a peculiar status as the condition of possibility of critique and change, *as well as* the condition of possibility of ideology's most smooth functioning. On the one hand, the subject is the Lacanian name for doubt, non-identity with imaginary identifications, and the rupture of old structures and routines. On the other, precisely the subject's non-identity can function as a sense of non-complicity with prevailing ideological formations and thereby as a reason (or an excuse) not to challenge them. This status of the subject creates the problem of how to differentiate between a critique that actually challenges ideology and a critique that merely adds an ironic layer to its interpretation. By analyzing one of Žižek's own favorite examples of interventions into contemporary ideology, the Slovene rock band Laibach, I want to investigate how this ambivalence of the subject works and point toward a dimension of critique that is not very explicitly acknowledged in Žižek's theoretical work, but implicit in his practice as a critical intellectual. In order to avoid the cynical or "merely ironic" attitude, I will claim, Laibach and Žižek both rely on something more than the questioning of ideology—something which must be found in critical praxis in a broader sense. I will begin somewhere else, however, namely with a famous dream reported by the Chinese philosopher Zhuang Zi, because his contemplations highlight some crucial questions about subjectivity, especially in its Lacanian conceptualization. They also, as it will turn out, inadvertently show something about the limitation of a "merely" theoretical approach to critical thought.

Caught in Their Butterfly Net

As it is well known, Zhuang Zi once dreamt that he was a butterfly. It was not the wildest or most complicated of dreams, but it made the ancient philosopher wonder about the nature of being awake in terms that have resonated through a couple of millennia. In the dream, the butterfly that Zhuang Zi dreamt that he was had no awareness that it was really Zhuang Zi. It was merely "flitting and fluttering around, happy with himself and doing as he pleased."[1] Despite the liveliness of the dream, waking up made Zhuang Zi realize quite clearly that it had only been a dream. He did not doubt that it was a dream. Nonetheless, he was struck by another kind of doubt: how could he be sure that he was not now a butterfly dreaming that it was Zhuang Zi? Although he was "back to normal," there was suddenly a realm of doubt connected to this normality itself: his sense of being Zhuang Zi seemed to be no more evident to him than the sense of being a butterfly was to the butterfly. On a first glance, this could seem like a straight forward skeptical paradox: How to know whether the butterfly or the philosopher is real, when they could both be "dreamt" by the other? It seems like both options are equally valid and that there is no way to ensure that one of them is the right one. Nonetheless, there is an asymmetry in the relation between them, which creates a third possible interpretation: The skeptical question occurs only to Zhuang Zi, whilst the butterfly does not ask itself, whether it is not the result of Zhuang Zi dreaming that he is a butterfly. The difference between the two situations thus lies not in a justified sense of certainty that Zhuang Zi is really Zhuang Zi, but in the butterfly's absence of doubt in being a butterfly. In this way, somewhat paradoxically, the best indication of certainty (of one's self) is the presence of doubt.

Jacques Lacan discusses the dream in his eleventh seminar and makes two general points about its implications. First of all, the story shows that Zhuang Zi is not mad, because he "does not regard himself as absolutely identical with Zhuang Zi"[2]—a formulation that resembles Lacan's famous claim that a king who thinks that he is a king is just as mad as the madman who thinks that he is a king.[3] The mark of sanity (and of being the one that is "awake") is that Zhuang Zi does not take his sanity, or his identity, for granted. What can be affirmed about Zhuang Zi is that he doubts about being Zhuang Zi—not that he is unproblematically Zhuang Zi, but this doubt itself is the best indication we can probably get that he is indeed Zhuang Zi (and that he is not mad). What it means to be Zhuang Zi is, however, also complicated (or elaborated) by the contents of the dream as such. There is something more to being Zhuang Zi than that which is captured by his name and public image. He is more right than he thinks, when he "does not regard himself as absolutely identical with Zhuang Zi," because in an important sense he *is* a butterfly. The alternative between being "completely" Zhuang Zi or being "completely" a butterfly is false, because the dream indicates a dimension of "butterflyness" about Zhuang

Zi himself. In his short commentary on the dream, Lacan makes use of a poignant metaphor to make this point: "It is when he is awake that he is Zhuang Zi for others, and is caught in their butterfly net" (ibid., transliteration modified). Zhuang Zi is Zhuang Zi when he is awake, but his identity as Zhuang Zi is that which he is "for others," and in his being-for-others he is "caught in their butterfly net." Notably, it is not a cage or a box or a category that he is caught in, but precisely a butterfly net; i.e., the form of his captivity is a structure particularly suited to captivate the very content that is expressed in his dream. The metaphor of the "butterfly net" thereby encapsulates an essential feature of personal identity, which is not addressed in most usages of this concept: personal identity itself is a way of being caught in a dream. Whether you are aware of it or not, there is a fantasmatic structure in any identity—which is sometimes glimpsed in dreams, erratic behavior, etc. (Identity politics is therefore essentially the politics of wanting to remain captivated by the dream of your own identity. What identity politics fails to see is that the dream of one's identity is simultaneously a way of being "caught in their butterfly net," i.e.. of living up to some particular image that is ultimately derived from the Other.)

Now, the doubt that Zhuang Zi expresses is, in Lacanian terms, another name for the subject. The subject is not the same as that which comprises a certain identity, i.e., the ego; indeed, it is almost its opposite. Unlike so-called poststructuralist accounts of subjectivity as subject-positions, the psychoanalytic understanding of the subject is more like a subject-deposition: a de-centering of the subject, its dethronement, its remainder. If the ego represents a sense of cohesion and recognizability or simply the sense of being the one, one is, the subject is a corrective or a question mark—its commentary is written in the margins of the ego's narration. In the same seminar, *Seminar 11*, Lacan defines the Cartesian cogito as the place where doubt is recognized as certainty.[4] Zhuang Zi's dream has a double potential in this regard: On the one hand, it materializes the unconscious fantasy of Zhuang Zi's own identity: he is in part a butterfly, or the butterfly encapsulates some of the aspects of his own (unconscious) self-perception; on the other hand, the butterfly provokes the question that invigorates a proper subjective stance: "How do I know that I am really Zhuang Zi?"

One of the attractions of Zhuang Zi's dream is therefore that it highlights some of the fundamental ambiguities related to subjectivity in general, and especially those that are related to the critique of ideology in the Žižekian form, since this form of critique relies heavily on a Lacanian theory of the subject. Ideology is a more formal name for what it means to be "caught in their butterfly net." It is the "non-wakefullness" (to use Dominik Finkelde's precise term) that structures everyday life.[5] In other words, there is an element of being not-really-awake in the condition that we otherwise, commonsensically, understand as being awake. This is not to say that there is some condition of being "completely awake" that we have been blocked from by ideology, but rather that what we experience as our normal, everyday life is necessarily conditioned by the culture that we inhabit, the language that we speak, and the images that are available to us. Ideology gives us our social reality itself, as Žižek has put it,[6] and thereby it stiches together a sense of cohesion—not over and against the "true picture of things," but rather as a sense of meaningfulness in the background of whatever we are engaged with. The alternative to ideology is therefore not an objective, unbiased access to the true meaning of the world, but rather the absence of any meaning at all. When we are non-wakeful, we generally accept that the world makes sense, that we can more or less rely on the social infra structure of our society, and that things are more or less rightfully so as they present themselves to us. But although this condition should not be interpreted as a distortion or cover-up of "the real reality" behind it, it is still possible to imagine critiques and changes of the present state of affairs—and the subject is the name of the condition of possibility of such critique. It would be a fallacy, in other words, to infer from the impossibility of a completely unideological state to the futility of any attempt to improve the actual state. Utopia does not have to be a full-fledged vision of a flawless society completely detached from any ideological constraints—indeed, it should much rather be seen as the non-place from within any given configuration which enables a critical stance.

In this context, Zhuang Zi's dream might function as an illustration of the ways in which ideology can be investigated "from within," given that there is no view from elsewhere or "nowhere" from which an objective correlation of its veracity or justification may be given. A dream like the one about the butterfly shows something about the aspects of the condition of non-wakefullness, which we wouldn't otherwise realize. (A little bit like we generally don't notice the blood vessels or inner organs in our body, when it functions more or less normally.) The dream gives us access to the mechanics of non-wakefullness; how it is kept together, how it is organized, such that we may consider it unproblematically normal in our everyday existence. This is not to say that a dream gives us some univocal message that can be directly translated into the language of everyday non-wakefullness or even makes sense to the dreamer. A dream needs analysis, and it is no coincidence that the *interpretation* of dreams was the founding gesture of Freudian psychoanalysis (not, say, their translation or explanation). There is not much interesting knowledge to be gained from the assumption that Zhuang Zi is literally a butterfly (although standard commentary on Zhuang Zi precisely tend to consider the dream as a story about "transition" from one kind of being to another). As a metaphor for the expressions of our mostly unacknowledged, ideological commitments, the dream represents a kind of unconscious manifestation of that which we already are, but the manifest content of the dream is rarely enough to formulate the implications of this manifestation. Similarly, cultural analysis is needed to interpret certain symptomatic events or products. What Žižek's analyses of films, commercials, statements, behavior, rhetoric, etc. reveal, for example, is very often something that we did in a way already know, but didn't know that we knew. Therefore they often contain a surprising sense of recognition in the reader, not unlike the confrontation with a certain "Thou art that!" which might occur in psychoanalysis. Simultaneously, critique of ideology thereby activates what seems to be a more genuine form of subjectivity than the one that mostly dominates the non-wakefullness of everyday life: a possible questioning or distancing from that which we are on the most immediate level of ideology (As it is often the case, Lacan makes use of homophonies to create several possible dimensions to his remarks, when he describes the effort of psychoanalysis to let the subject encounter its own unacknowledged truth. "Tu est ca!" could in French also be heard as "Tuez ca!", i.e., "Kill it"[7].)

Overidentification

We find these elements in one of Žižek's favorite examples of interventions into unacknowledged ideological fantasies: the Slovene rock band Laibach. Laibach appeared in the 1980s in the same wave of intellectual opposition to the power structures of late Eastern European socialism that also counted members like Žižek, Dolar, and others. Since explicit challenges of the regime were potentially dangerous (and for various artistic purposes of course), Laibach developed a peculiar mixture of exaggeration, pompousness, and authoritarian symbolism that has confused audiences and authorities until this very day. Rather than explicitly criticizing power, Laibach put on display its unacknowledged or disavowed totalitarian and nationalist traits and made it possible for people, the subjects of the state, to experience a kind of unheimlich moment of "Thou art that!" Although the early work might have had a more directly subversive impact, the band still manages to formulate new questions to power, even if it has become a well-known and widely interpreted cultural trademark of its own. Besides its original development to mirror or mock the Yugoslav authorities, Laibach has applied similar methodologies more broadly to contemporary capitalist society, and, as late as 2015, they performed in North Korea to the obvious bewilderment of their audience there. This development is maybe not entirely unproblematic, particularly because of the much more generally accepted political signification of Laibach today (clearly, in the first years, their performance was much more enigmatic), but also because of the obviously different ideological formations that the band has intervened into. It would not be completely farfetched to suggest that Laibach has become a kind of inverted version of Beethoven's 9th symphony, which, as Žižek has emphasized, fits remarkably well with remarkably different systems of power in need of an aura of sympathetic neutrality (from Nazi Germany over Maoist China to the contemporary European Union). Is Laibach a one-size-fits all of ideological critique; a kind of "Ode to Authoritarian Enjoyment"? I cannot deal with this question in sufficient detail here, but will have to insist on the nonetheless principal significance of Laibach's invention. Even if one does not accept their intervention in Pyongyang as successful, it would still be a matter of Laibach failing to live up to the standards, which they themselves have set. Their gesture remains relevant for thinking and for new inventions, repetitions in the best, Kierkegaardian sense, although the particular content and communication might have to be reinvented significantly for each case. Laibach's general strategy is one of assuming the underlying and mostly unacknowledged undercurrents in a culture and putting them on display, and I would claim that this strategy does have an important universal applicability. It has been described by Žižek as that of an "overidentification": "it 'frustrates' the system (the ruling ideology) precisely insofar as it is not its ironic imitation, but overidentification with it—by bringing to light the obscene superego underside of the system, overidentification suspends its efficiency."[8] In other words, the more unpleasant parts of the glue that keeps our non-wakefullness together are put on display so that we can no longer secretly adhere to them, while still pretending that they are not there.

To give an example: On their third album, Laibach released a cover version of a 1984 pop hit by the Austrian band Opus with the intriguingly idiotic title "Live is Life" (apparently, it was written on tour as a celebration of live performances). The song was originally played in discotheques and radios across Europe and was generally conceived as a sort of naïve celebration of life, but with Laibach's rendition it acquired an uncanny sense of blind authoritarianism—which, once you noticed it, could suddenly seem to have been already there from the beginning: "When we all give the power / We all give the best / Every minute of an hour / Don't think about a rest." What does it mean that "we all give the power"? Do we possess a power that we give to someone—and to whom? Do we hand over power to someone or something, such that they or it may rule us? And are we thus mobilized to work for this power "every minute of an hour" for perpetuity? Although run-of-the-mill pop songs generally contain similarly empty lyrics, Laibach nonetheless managed to exhibit some unacknowledged dark tendencies—in the song itself as well as in culture at large. All that was needed was a kind of "looking askew" that enabled a completely different picture to emerge, like an anamorphosis in which the spectator is enabled to see what the picture (also) contains. In the official video of Laibach's "Life Is Life," a proto-Nazi aesthetics is on rampant display from the very beginning, complete with a *Sound of Music*-like setting, the rhythm is heavier, the tempo slower, the vocal dark. Even the title itself is twisted just a little bit to fulfill the tautology that was almost there in the original. We recognize Laibach's imagery, because it is there with us already, all around; here, we just get it in the most explicit and unapologetic form.

Laibach's performances have created a lot of discussion of the ambiguity about their own role. Are they really making fun of nationalism or are they themselves part of it? Do they mock the authoritarian techniques—or are they on the contrary promoting them, even literally living off of them? Why don't they just come clean and tell us what the point is? Or, as Žižek himself put it in his early piece on Laibach: people feel at unease, not only because of doubt in Laibach's stance, but also because of a fear that they are playing with fire. "'What if Laibach overestimates their public? What if the public takes seriously what Laibach mockingly imitates, so that Laibach actually strengthens what it purports to undermine?'"[9] Žižek's own answer is to turn the question back to the audience:

> their public (especially intellectuals) is obsessed with the "desire of the Other" [. . .]—what is Laibach's actual position, are they truly totalitarians or not?—i.e., they address Laibach with a question and expect from them an answer, failing to notice that Laibach itself does not function as an answer but a question. By means of the elusive character of their desire, of the indecidability as to "where they actually stand," Laibach compels us to take up our position and decide upon our desire.

So, we have the two elements from Zhuang Zi's dream again. On the one hand, Laibach confronts us with some unacknowledged dimension of our own enjoyment: symbols, emotions and thoughts that we secretly accept, without explicitly admitting it (or even knowing it). On the other, the band functions as a question: "Is this what you want to be?" Are you totalitarian yourself? Is the non-wakefullness of your comfortable identity a way of being "caught in a butterfly net," i.e., of silently accepting the ideological structures that privilege some and hurt others?" The "obsession" with the question of the desire of the Other, i.e., of Laibach's own political stance, of course represents a refusal to confront the question that the band poses.

However, there is another question in Laibach that concerns the critical awareness of those who "understand them right," if you will. What if one actually gets it and understands that "Laibach functions as a question" concerning one's own desire rather than Laibach's? What is the effect of acknowledging one's own secretly (dis)avowed authoritarian traits? Once again, in the terms of Zhuang Zi's dream: Doesn't "getting the question" simply entail that we are not crazy—and that we (come to realize that we) are in part butterflies? What if this critical reflection does not result in the abolition of false consciousness, but simply in a more refined, critical, ironic awareness of certain "dark" tendencies that can be perceived as simultaneously an unavoidable dimension of human subjectivity as such and something which is *not really me*: "I am aware that even I share some of these authoritarian traits, but unlike the true idiots that don't question their allegiance to these traits, I am not fully identified by them!"

I am formulating this, of course, in a way that makes it resemble what Žižek himself would usually say about ironic stances towards ideological formations. Ideology is not exhausted by what Ernesto Laclau described as "the non-recognition [. . .] of the impossibility of any ultimate suture,"[10] almost on the contrary. It is precisely when we can maintain a conscious distance from the ideological commitments that we unconsciously subscribe to, or that we are "objectively" part of, that ideology works best. It works, even if you don't believe in it, like Niels Bohr said about the horseshoe above his summer house entrance. An ideology might in principle function very well, without any single of its subjects actually believing in it, because the vague sense that the others probably believe in it is enough to maintain a sense of normality, even necessity. (Think about the practice of going to church for Christmas for example: the majority of visitors are probably there extremely rarely and don't believe in virgin births, eternal life, etc., but nonetheless they politely play along, because the others seem to believe in it.) The consequence that Žižek draws from this is that "enlightenment" is not enough; ideology cannot be explained away by appealing to the subject's critical and rational sense. Instead, a productive strategy could be overidentification, annulling the critical distance and the subject's hideout, if you will. (In the church example, wouldn't the most disturbing thing in fact be someone who really literally believed in virgin birth and resurrection?) This is what he sees in Laibach. In connection with Laibach's performance in North Korea, Žižek emphasized how the band's achievement is to "bring out" the authoritarian undercurrents and refrain from distancing themselves from them:

> They are deeply aware of the deep ambiguity of even the most democratic power, and they are trying to bring this authoritarian streak out—even with a certain open fascination. There is no distance there. They are not making fun of it. They openly enjoy it. That's the traumatic message of Laibach, staging the Real of power.[11]

But what if we all "enjoy with Laibach"—openly admitting the ambiguity of our own position, partly embracing our dark, authoritarian tendencies, partly distancing ourselves from them or "being deeply aware of the ambiguity of even the most democratic power"? Is enjoyment enough?

Irony

What I am claiming is not that Laibach is in fact authoritarian or support such tendencies, but, almost on the contrary, that Laibach cannot be understood as completely un-ironic. The act simply does not make sense, if it does not contain at least a minimal sense of mockery or some, however vague or indirect, indications of critical distance that might have to be interpreted or very perceptively acknowledged, but which are nonetheless there. (Indeed, the very title of Žižek's early piece on Laibach explicitly says that Laibach are *not* totalitarian, and that it can be explained why.) "Irony is, namely," as Kierkegaard put it, "the first and most abstract qualification of subjectivity,"[12] which is another way of saying (vis à vis the reference to Lacan's theory of the subject) that the subject is in its core ironic: the very ability to question one's own personal or cultural identity and assumptions is a mark of the emergence of a subject at all. Irony in this sense is not to be understood as a safe position from which one can identify and make fun of the weak points of an argument or a cluster of discursive commitments, nor as a modest acknowledgement of the "finality" or "limitation" of one's own stance (which one then nonetheless maintains), but rather as an immanent undermining of a form of life. "Over-identification" can be effective, because it does not postulate some external point of view from which to criticize an ideological formation, but, on the contrary, takes on the logic of the formation itself and brings it to its conclusion. But this gesture is, I would claim, ironic in the best Hegelian and Kierkegaardian sense (and this is one of many cases where Kierkegaard was, if not outright Hegelian, then at least strongly affiliated with Hegel). In other words: If Laibach are not totalitarian, which they are not, they must be ironic, at least in this minimal sense. Jon Stewart has summarized a common understanding of irony in Hegel and Kierkegaard in a way that makes good sense in our context: "The ironic subject is thus one who helps instigate changes in history by bringing to the fore the contradictions present in the world-view of his age."[13] Overidentification is precisely not (merely) identification. It is necessarily "too much" in some sense and this too-much-ness makes possible certain questions and certain ways of relating to them.

Instead of engaging in a discussion about Laibach's "true, political stance," I therefore find it more interesting to use the case of Laibach to highlight an ambiguity inherent in critical subjectivity as such. In order for overidentification to actually have an effect, it needs to produce a kind of estranged subjectivity—like the effect of hearing one's own voice in a psychoanalytic setting: "Is that what I sound like?" Unavoidably, there must be *some* kind of "distancing" towards one's own symbolic and imaginary identity for (any kind of) ideological critique to have an impact—or in his case for Laibach to "function like a question." The paradox is that this effect seems to be the condition of possibility of the critique of ideology and at the same time the condition of possibility of its most effective functioning. So, how do you distinguish between a productive estrangement that challenges unacknowledged, unconscious attachments—and a conscious or ironic distancing from oneself that "knows very well," but nonetheless persists in the same, more or less reactionary patterns?[14] While Žižek eminently describes and analyzes the subject in both of these two functions, he rarely, if ever, directly addresses the question of how to distinguish between them, or, to put it differently, where the two seemingly indistinguishable dimensions of the subject leave us with regard to the critique of ideology: How do we move beyond critique?

The answer, which I will try to sketch, is one that is inherent in Žižek's own thought and practice, but which, as far as I know, is never explicitly related to the question of the critique of ideology. In the best German idealist vein, it implies a shift from the "theoretical" to the "practical" or from a question about knowledge to a question that involves a dimension of doing. A critique of ideology must be seen in the context of its historical and political situation in order to fully appreciate its scope and impact, and it must itself address the situation in a very specific way, in order to "work." The solution, thus, does not lie in an indisputable theoretical proof of the difference between the two dimensions of the subject *in abstracto*, but rather in the concrete analysis of the situation in which a concrete critique is enunciated. Let me first briefly illustrate, how I think the solution must embrace more than epistemological considerations about the status of our knowledge. In the *Sublime Object of Ideology*, Žižek himself refers to the story about Zhuang Zi's dream. He also addresses Lacan's interpretation of it, but turns the screw a round further than Lacan by claiming that the question about his own identity, which Zhuang Zi poses, is *possible* only from the woken condition: "The question, the dialectical split, is possible only when we are awake. In other words, the illusion cannot be symmetrical, it cannot run both ways."[15] This is a more definitive interpretation than Lacan's in which Zhuang Zi's question, like I mentioned in the beginning, "merely" shows that he is not crazy. Although the question, the dialectical split does indeed only occur to the (non-wakeful) woken Zhuang Zi, it is a bit of a stretch to claim that it could only *possibly* occur to him.

Žižek illustrates his point with Alphonse Allais' wonderfully absurd story about the two lovers Raoul and Marguerite, who met at a masked ball and fled to a secret corner for a romantic moment—except that when the masks fell, Raoul realized that he was embracing the wrong woman, and even worse: "Marguerite also finds that the other person is not Raoul but some unknown stranger" (ibid.). This is the "nonsensical situation" that "we would find ourselves in," if the illusion were symmetrical, i.e., if Zhuang Zi could be dreamt just as well as he was dreaming—and thus, Žižek claims, the question is possible only when we are awake. The analogy is illuminating in as far as it shows that Zhuang Zi and the butterfly *cannot both be dreamt* by each other, because there would then be no one to dream them, just like Raoul and Marguerite cannot both be absent in the (failed) encounter. But this does not necessarily imply that Zhuang Zi is the one who is dreaming and not the one being dreamt, even if the appearance of his question does point in that direction. Just because the question doesn't occur to the butterfly, it doesn't mean that it couldn't *possibly* have, like Žižek claims. In principle, anything can be dreamt, even questions and thoughts that play no clear role in the dream. Isn't precisely the inception of certain thoughts a part of the game that the unconscious plays with the subject, as a result, for example, of transference?

Why I am making a big deal out of this? Because it shows that what Zhuang Zi learns about himself is not a matter of "justified true belief," i.e., a kind of certified knowledge arrived at through a logical refutation of doubt. I agree that the appearance of Zhuang Zi's question shows something important, because it adds a specific quality to his usual state of non-wakefulness. The addition, however, is also in a way a subtraction: It adds a lack of certainty (a lack, which the butterfly does not possess), which consists in a kind of awareness of the not-all of the "(non-)wakeful" condition itself. In other words: Zhuang Zi's question does not only concern his own identity, but also the porousness of the net that keeps him captured. There is a sense of the whole, which is different, a way of "orienting oneself" in thought, as Kant would have put it. Rather than a proof of his being Zhuang Zi and awake, the philosopher thus obtains something like a sense that *he could have not been Zhuang Zi*, which also means that he could have not been caught in their butterfly net; i.e., he gets an opening to the possibility of confronting his own "butterflyness," so to say. A similar opening, I would claim, is also at work in the critique of ideology. There is no "pure outside of ideology," as we have established, but there is nonetheless something "more" than the inside (and its immanent/ironic critique), and this "more" represents an opening towards actual change.

Latching On

What I want to suggest is that in order to avoid the critical awareness of one's own ideological attachments leading to a cynical/ironic attitude, the subject needs something else. There must be "more" than the reflective stance. There must be, and can be, a "positive" opening for the subject, besides its critical, "negative" impetus. Even in the case of an overidentification, I would claim, the critical impetus that it might provoke could lead to a cynical or maybe rather resigned attitude. Overidentification could be a joke, literally. With Laibach, on the contrary, wasn't it precisely the general political atmosphere of unrest and reinvention that gave the band its original and genuinely progressive significance? Laibach appeared at a moment and in a general atmosphere that made their intervention *work*. So, rather than the band being a kind of instantiation of a general idea about critique of ideology that found a well-suited occasion for its explication, it was the right, particular answer to the precise conditions of the moment of its emergence—which could then, possibly, be repeated/reinvented in other, different contexts. What functioned in Laibach was thus a "negative" as well as a "positive" aspect: it enabled a critical question about the desire of its spectators, but it also latched on to an emerging sensation of being able to want something else. In Hegelian terms, the negative aspect could be compared to the negative definition of self-consciousness in the *Phenomenology*: "I am not that!"—which creates an impetus to resist the identification of consciousness with anything from the "phenomenal realm" ("life"). The positive aspect of the subject would then be the one that enables it to perform the shift from a certain gestalt or condition into something new, like the transition from subjective to objective spirit for example. Isn't this shift also what is basically at stake in Lacan's "subjectivation without subject" or Badiou's concept of loyalty to the event?

Something changes, which makes it possible for the subject to latch on to something else and shred its former skin. If Laibach functions like a question, much like Zhuang Zi's dream, it does so in a way that enables the negative aspect of the critical subject: I do not want to be that! It does not immediately give us an answer—something to "latch on to," but the question is posed in precisely the right way to create the sensation that there might *be* an answer—that we are somehow already on track of it. Especially in its first phase, Laibach therefore had something more than critique or questions to offer—it took part in something "bigger," which could probably be characterized as a widespread sensation that something new might be on its way. In this perspective, you could even say that the tragedy of Zhuang Zi was exactly that he had nothing else to latch on to—but had to remain a wise old, Chinese philosopher with some intriguing ruminations about his status as dreaming or dreamt.

The close proximity between the "negative" and the "positive" can also be found in psychoanalysis itself. It is often emphasized how the end of analysis to Lacan meant the "fall of the big Other," i.e., a liberation from certain constraints or a sense of necessity, but liberation comes not only in its negative form—it also implies a sense of capability, of *being able to*. When analysis is over, Freud said, the subject may "work and love" again, and this is no small feat, when you consider the kinds of incapacitations, Freud was treating. Indeed, in many cases, having a reflective, critical, sense of the non-existence of the big Other and the absence of a unified meaning of the world could certainly mark the *beginning* of analysis much rather than its conclusion.

So, what is there to latch on to? In an analytic setting, liberation might be characterized as a change of perspective, an opening that makes it possible to latch on to more or less anything. The experience of such a liberation was described by an analysand at the end of the analysis, when he said that "I feel that everything has changed—and yet I am still the same as when I came here the first time."[16] As banal as it may sound, being able to engage in a meaningful conversation with a colleague or, indeed, simply being able to leave the house, might exactly mean "latching on to" something completely new and world-changing in a subject's life. What has changed is not necessarily the "objective" conditions around the subject, but its relation to them, its ability to engage with them and approach them more freely. Something similar might happen in experiences of art or cultural events, when the subject is inspired to give up some of its own reservations or inhibitions towards engagement with the surrounding world. Indeed, critique of ideology itself might have such an effect on the individual, although I will claim that it also, and more importantly, carries with it a potential collective significance as well. The individual experience is ideally expressed in Rilke's poem about the torso of Apollo, where the narrator suddenly feels observed from all sides: "For here there is no place / that does not see you. You must change your life."[17] Politically speaking, however, something more has to change: something about the very conditions themselves. What the subject latches on to in a political event or a widely effective social critique is at the very least a commonly shared sense of an opening towards real, material changes. This super-individual "sense" is a particular phenomenon, which would need an entire, ontological treatment of its own to be adequately presented,[18] but it would be fair to say that it comprises at least two, decisive qualities: a common spirit (from the holy spirit to the Taksim Square) and impending changes of institutions, hierarchies, and structures (from canalization to financial transactions and electoral procedures). This "objective spirit" of some social and political movements somehow knows more than the individuals that take part in them. It knows that change is possible, even when they doubt, and it already contains certain aspirations and ideas, however vague and unclear they might still be, that will become reality, if the movement is successful. What will happen "after the revolution," I would claim, is to some extent already there without the explicit awareness of the members of the movement. More precisely, there is a certain effect of retroactivity: The movement carries a knowledge with it that will (only really) have been there, once it becomes possible to effectuate it.

Laibach and Žižek are of course related to this "collective sense" in different ways. One is a performance and an intervention which asks questions without making them explicit in so many words, while the other is an academic investigation of such and similar interventions that relies on theory, history, and contemporary discussions across various disciplines. In a sense, you could say that Žižek's reading of Laibach, with all its related questions of subjectivity, ideology, fantasy, event, etc., provides a kind of subtext to the band's interventions. (Another question about Laibach: Is Žižek providing their libretto?) Nonetheless, I would claim that they are in an important sense part of the same movement: they seek the points of destabilization within a prevailing structure in order to push their "audiences" to ask themselves certain questions about justice, hegemony, solidarity, etc., and in so doing, they both risk being accepted like ironic gestures, entertainment or empty gestures of critique. They are indeed both forms of critique, although the former of course depends on interpretation more than the latter,[19] and they are both, I would claim, part of a political project that does not shy away from "getting its hands dirty" by engaging with various and shifting actors to further universal political aims that are difficult to describe in very precise terms, but have to do with what Žižek often declares as "communism." And again: In order for both of them to be successful, they need to be more directly affiliated with the movement and what drives it than critics that rather resemble figures like teachers, instructors, or "enlighteners."

A truly progressive critique should therefore ideally address questions that can be translated into the language of a more or less well-established movement, even if the translation is incomplete or the movement is in a porous, undecided state. In fact, I think this is what Žižek himself has more or less systematically been doing from the very beginning—from the presidential elections in then newly independent Slovenia, Occupy Wall Street, Pussy Riot, Syriza, the protests against the persecution of Julian Assange, DiEM25, etc. Analyzing the unconscious dimensions of a political situation could ideally support the momentum of a social actor that has not been adequately recognized as the viable alternative to certain prevailing conditions. In this case, critique could be said to be genuinely dialectical in that it engages with a concrete situation in order to point toward that in the situation itself which transgresses its current frame.

Methodically speaking, there is no secure way toward the right analysis and critique. Precisely because there is no "outside" of ideology, its critique is really effective only when it is articulated exactly in the right way at exactly the right time and place. This certainly makes the effectiveness of critique fundamentally contingent to the extent that one might simply need a bit of luck, before one's critique actually makes a difference, but it also makes it necessary for its practice to become more creative and courageous. The insight, which is one of Žižek's major accomplishments in this field, that ideology is not exhausted by "the non-recognition of the impossibility of an ultimate suture," leaves the critique with a wonderfully concrete analytical task that is very difficult to generalize theoretically. Much like in psychoanalysis, everything hinges on the concrete discourse of the subject/culture, and there is no a priori methodology or set of principles that can be applied to even very similar situations. Each analysis in a way involves a reconsideration of the very theory that it mobilizes. Although Žižek-style critique of ideology of course relies on more or less the entire vocabulary of Lacanian psychoanalysis, it cannot expect to find any cultural constants that can justify identical approaches to different situations ("it is all a question of repressed sexual energy," or something similar). What is right in Madrid might not function in Paris at all (or what was right in Ljubljana might not be right in Pyongyang). Critique might in particularly fortunate cases function like the "straw that broke the camel's back," or it might give a more specific sense of direction and purpose to movements that are already in motion, allowing them to believe in what they already know. Thereby, critique does lose some of its traditional sense, especially in the Marxist tradition, of having "seen through" the superficial or distorted images and rhetoric of an ideological formation, in which the critic is speaking from a genuinely "scientific" or "philosophical" position. Instead, it brings the critic closer to the analyst as someone who must be good at solving puzzles, interpreting concrete expressions and significations, and intervening to lead the analysis to its dialectical conclusion without suggesting a commonsensical or moral alternative.

Such a critique, however, which wants to be effective (and avoid cynicism), must do something more than questioning. It is not enough to reassure readers that they are not crazy, although it is a good idea to exercise their ability to think. A truly dialectical critique comprises both dimensions of "negativity" and of "latching on to," even if the dialectical relation between these two moments as well as the effects of their articulation are to some extent beyond the explicit intensions of their author, because they arise from the unconscious layers of the analyzed material.

Notes

1 Zhuangzi, *The Complete Works of Zhuangzi* (New York: Columbia University Press, 2013), 78.
2 Jacques Lacan, *The Four Fundamental Concepts of Psychoanalysis* (London: Vintage, 1998), 76 (translation modified).
3 Jacques Lacan, *Écrits*, trans. Bruce Fink (New York: W.W. Norton Company, 2007), 139.
4 Lacan, *The Four Fundamental Concepts of Psychoanalysis*, 126.
5 Dominik Finkelde, "Non-Wakefulness. On the Parallax Between Dreaming and Awakening," *The Philosophical Journal of Conflict and Violence* 3, no. 2 (2020): 92–107.
6 Slavoj Žižek, *The Sublime Object of Ideology* (London: Verso, 1989), 45.
7 Lacan, *Écrits*, 100.
8 Slavoj Žižek, "Why Are Laibach and NSK Not Fascists?." In *NSK: From Kapital to Capital* (Ljubljana: Moderne Galerija, 2015), 203.
9 Ibid., 203.
10 Ernesto Laclau, "The Impossibility of Society," *Canadian Journal of Political and Social Theory* 7, no. 1–2 (1983): 21–4, here, 24.
11 Traavikinfo, "Slavoj Žižek Introducing: Laibach in North Korea," November 27, 2018. Available online: https://www.youtube.com/watch?v=NRfgKrmI9Po (accessed August 10, 2021).
12 Søren Kierkegaard, *The Concept of Irony*, trans. Howard and Edna Hong (Princeton: Princeton University Press, 1989), 264.
13 Jon Stewart, *Kierkegaard's Relations to Hegel Reconsidered* (Cambridge: Cambridge University Press, 2003), 168.
14 The immediate answer to this question could be that they are different, because the first implies nothing but the doubt or the question itself (the subject as the mere disturbance of the ego), while the other implies a certain humanist fiction of a "real self" that is not polluted by ideology, but I would maintain that even the humanist version necessarily implies a gesture of non-identity, distance or irony in order to make the move in the first place: "I am not that!"—even if this is then followed by an affirmative: "Because I am really that!" Indeed, as we shall see, the whole thing in a way precisely comes down to *what follows* from the inaugural, critical subjective stance.
15 Žižek, *The Sublime Object of Ideology*, 47.
16 Kjeld H. Enemark, "Den psykoanalytiske akt, 1. Del," *DRIFT –Tidsskrift for psykoanalyse*, no. 1–2 (2003), 69–94, 69.

17 Rainer Maria Rilke, "Archaic Torso of Apollo." In *The Selected Poetry and Prose of Rainer Maria Rilke*, trans. Stephen Mitchell (New York: Vintage International, 1982), 61.

18 We gave it a try in the book *Særklasse: Den tøvende revolution* (Center for Vild Analyse, Copenhagen: Informations Forlag, 2012), which has been partly translated to Slovene (Center za divjo analizo: "Ekspozicija," *Problemi* 7–8, 2016, 143–201), and Žižek himself of course has treated this problem on various occasions—e.g., in "Meditation on Michelangelo's Christ on the Cross," *SPECS Journal of Art and Culture* 1, (2008), article 42, 122–33.

19 Even here they are possibly more alike than might immediately be expected: Žižek's style of writing and public presentation sometimes begs questions not unlike the ones that are asked of Laibach: Did he really support Donald Trump? Is he a Stalinist? Is it all just jokes and make-believe?

Response to Bjerre

Slavoj Žižek

Bjerre begins with the precise thesis that identity politics is "essentially the politics of wanting to remain captivated by the dream of your own identity. What identity politics fails to see is that the dream of one's identity is simultaneously a way of being 'caught in their butterfly net,' i.e., of living up to some particular image that is ultimately derived from the Other." While, of course, agreeing with this thesis, I would just like to supplement it with what is for me its logical implication: there is no pure identity; every identity is based on an underlying exclusion and repression—not of an external enemy or threat but of an immanent excess. A friend from the USA told me of the tragic end of a young woman who wanted to change sex into male; she went through all the procedures and, on the day she got by post the official confirmation that she is now a man, she took her life. It is too easy to speculate about the reasons that pushed her to do it (was realizing her deepest desire too much for her? etc.)—what we should note is just the weight of the symbolic act, of the inscription of my chosen identity into the official big Other. What drew her to suicide was not any change in her bodily or interpersonal reality (her parents and friends were supportive of her decision) but the mere final step of registering what she did.

That's why I am also deeply suspicious of a generalized dismissal of every identity politics as reactionary or even proto-fascist. In a passage of her *Guardian* interview that was censored, Judith Butler attacked the TERFs:

> The trans exclusionary radical feminists and the so-called gender critical writers have also rejected the important work in feminist philosophy of science showing how culture and nature interact [...] in favor of a regressive and spurious form of biological essentialism. So they will not be part of the coalition that seeks to fight the anti-gender movement. The anti-gender ideology is one of the dominant strains of fascism in our times.

I find such use of the term "fascism" all too quick: fascism clearly cannot be reduced to identity as such; it mobilizes national identity in order to obfuscate class struggle—there are strong ethnic identities which in no way imply fascism (Tibetans, Amish, etc.).[2]

This deadlock of identity brings us to Bjerre's critique of my interpretation of Laibach performance as a practice of "over-identification." Apropos Laibach, Bjerre points out how I emphasize that the band's achievement is to "bring out" the authoritarian undercurrents and refrain from distancing themselves from them: "They are deeply aware of the deep ambiguity of even the most democratic power, and they are trying to bring this authoritarian streak out—even with a certain open fascination. There is no distance there. They are not making fun of it. They openly enjoy it. That's the traumatic message of Laibach, staging the Real of power." Bjerre's question: but what if we all "enjoy with Laibach"—is enjoyment enough? My answer is a brutal one: yes. Enjoyment in proto-fascist rituals deprived of their ideological coating is the most efficient way to undermine ideology, much more efficient than complex theoretical analyses. "If Laibach are not totalitarian, which they are not, they must be ironic, at least in this minimal sense." My counter-claim is here that it is the actual "totalitarianism" itself which is not totalitarian in the sense of fully identifying with itself: a minimum of ironic or cynical self-distance is the condition of its functioning. So my answer to Bjerre's question "How do you distinguish between a productive estrangement that challenges unacknowledged, unconscious attachments—and a conscious or ironic distancing from oneself that 'knows very well', but nonetheless persists in the same, more or less reactionary patterns?" is: as Alenka Zupančič pointed out, "I know very well" can itself function as a fetish; i.e., we can only enjoy totalitarian rituals if we "know very well" they are not to be taken seriously, so if we drop "I know very well" (which is what Laibach does) enjoyment itself loses its ideological function.

But now I come to my crucial disagreement with Bjerre's reading of Laibach. He claims that Laibach's "genuinely progressive significance" cannot be accounted for by the immanent features of their performance: it emerged out of the specific socio-political context in which they operated:

> wasn't it precisely the general political atmosphere of unrest and reinvention that gave the band its original and genuinely progressive significance? Laibach appeared at a moment and in a general atmosphere that made their intervention work. [. . .] Laibach therefore had something more than critique or questions to offer—it took part in something "bigger," which could probably be characterized as a wide spread sensation that something new might be on its way.

Bjerre further enumerates two decisive qualities of this "bigger" dimension: "a common spirit (from the holy spirit to the Taksim Square) and impending changes of institutions, hierarchies, and structures (from canalization to financial transactions and electoral procedures)."

I think this was precisely not the case with Laibach. The "bigger" dimension in the air in 1980s was, of course, the gradual disintegration of the communist regime and the prospect of democracy and independence: people expected a lot from multiparty democracy and privatization of economy. Although many perspicuous social analysts were already warning about the dangers of nationalist populism and pointed out that civil society is not just a space for resisting totalitarian state but also harbors proto-fascist tendencies, the overall stance was that of hope—things will get better if we just get democracy and independence. Here Laibach entered the scene: what they staged were not communist rituals but fascist and nationalist rituals; i.e., what popped up as the other side of the transition to democracy. "What will happen 'after the revolution,' I would claim, is to some extent already there without the explicit awareness of the members of the movement." Maybe, but I am tempted to claim that Laibach are to be read precisely as a prescient awareness that "after the revolution," things will go wrong again in another way. Bjerre is right, Laibach "are deeply aware of the deep ambiguity of even the most democratic power, and they are trying to bring this authoritarian streak out"—but that's why they did not ride with the popular desire for change but acted in advance against it. It was punk movement which effectively could be interpreted the way Bjerre interprets Laibach, but that's why Laibach was clearly experienced as a break with the predominant punk wave. So Laibach's answer to "How do we move beyond critique?" is clear: by way of criticizing the predominant democratic mode of critique itself. Laibach's message *is* a dark one: there is no redeeming hope that sustains it.

Notes

1   The *Guardian* published a Judith Butler interview—and then deleted an answer about TERFS. Literary Hub, online: lithub.com.
2   I was told by a friend with links in trans circles that the trans themselves quite like me, but it's the liberal friends of the trans that are responsible for the critiques—so I am loved by many trans and hated by those sticking up for the trans: yet another case of the hypocrisy of the liberals whose protective stance barely conceals a patronizing dismissal of trans as helpless victims.

CHAPTER EIGHT

Žižek and Derrida

Hospitality, Hostility, and the "Real" Neighbor[1]

Zahi Zalloua

Like multiculturalism, deconstruction denies race any ontological validity. If white identity is constituted by and predicated on the negation of other racial identities, the goal of anti-racism, commonly understood, is to contest and denaturalize whiteness as the norm and affirm blackness or brownness, for example, as a positive term, as a source of worth and dignity. Unlike multiculturalism, however, deconstruction (especially as articulated by Jacques Derrida and Emmanuel Levinas) differs in its approach to the other—racialized or not. Against an "insurmountable allergy"[2] to alterity, deconstruction imagines the other in a perpetual state of fragility if not victimization. To think the other is to consider any marginalized figure, any excluded other. Levinas offers his own examples: the stranger, the widow, the orphan, and the Jew.[3] But more generally, we could say that the other *as other* is anyone who resists my identification and domestication. The "face" (*le visage*) of the other "exceed[s] *the idea of the other* in me."[4] This moment of cognitive frustration, which brings into question my autonomy, spontaneity and self-sufficiency simultaneously, is what Levinas famously names "ethics." Affirming the priority of ethics over ontology, Levinas dethrones the authority of reason and the Kantian ideal of autonomy in favor of an enduring state of vulnerability and heteronomy; consequently, freedom is demoted and made to occupy a secondary role to compassion: "to be exposed to sickness, suffering, death, is to be exposed to compassion."[5]

Pursuing a similar line of inquiry, Derrida emphasizes the ethics of unconditional hospitality, which he contrasts with the conditional hospitality informing the rhetoric of many liberals and anti-immigrant nationalists. Unconditional hospitality posits the exposure to the other as a relation of pure singularity—*tout autre est tout autre*, "every other is wholly other"[6]— where the other as event or singularity punctures my horizon of intelligibility and expectations. In short, there is no relation here, no subject–object split, since a relation would introduce and impose a hermeneutic framework on the other and thus neutralize the other's otherness. Conditional hospitality presupposes instead a calculable relation between subject (host) and object (guest). The other, to whom the ethical subject is responding, may be elusive, but their otherness is always relational to me.

Right-wing European politicians often proffer this model of conditional hospitality. They merely gesture to an openness to immigrants, accepting the latter only insofar as they are able to assimilate. According to Derrida, they tolerate and welcome only "what is homogeneous or homogenizable, what is assimilable or at the very most what is heterogeneous but presumed 'favorable': the appropriable immigrant, the proper immigrant."[7] But this is no hospitality:

> Tolerance is actually the opposite of hospitality. Or at least its limit. If I think I am being hospitable because I am tolerant, it is because I wish to maintain control over the limits of my "home," my sovereignty, my "I can" (my territory, my house, my language, my culture, my religion, and so on).[8]

At the same time, Derrida insists that unconditional hospitality is both indissociable from and heterogeneous to conditional hospitality.[9] And here Derrida diverges significantly from Levinas. The other for Derrida never comes fully pre-digested nor is she totally indigestible; Derrida denies the pure or unmediated alterity of the face—whence deconstruction's skeptical hermeneutics of "eating well."[10] This ethico-interpretive injunction answers the *external* call of the other, my interpellation by the other. It readily confronts the aporetic demands of the singular other, where the other is neither fully subdued nor withdrawn, but unruly and hospitable: to be understood, represented, and engaged with, and yet not be reduced to an object of knowledge, not be reduced to its relations, to any schemes of thought. To insist on this double bind is to insist on my paradoxical relationality, characterized by Derrida as a "relation without relation."

Slavoj Žižek, for his part, seems less fascinated with the perplexities of *heterophilia*, and appears to give more weight to conditional hospitality; that is, a qualified love for the refugees. Žižek's detractors have been quick to object to what they see as Žižek's Eurocentric and paternalistic, if not xenophobic and hostile remarks concerning the ongoing refugee crisis confronting Europe. Two particular comments stand out. First, Žižek's claim that it is not in itself racist or proto-fascist for a European host nation to talk of protecting its "way of life"; second, his precondition for "European hospitality": we must "formulate a minimum set of norms that are obligatory for everyone, without fear that they will appear 'Eurocentric': religious freedoms, the protection of individual freedom against group pressure, rights of women, and so on."[11] In comparison with Derrida's call to respect the other in all her unruliness and strangeness (his memorable claim that "monsters cannot be announced. One cannot say: 'Here are our monsters,' without immediately turning them into pets"[12]), Žižek seems to uphold national sovereignty, to want to contain and domesticate refugees, subjecting them to European normativity and thus turning them into European pets.

And yet to stop here would be to fail to grasp the complexity and full force of Žižek's position. What Žižek means by "European" is less than self-evident. His deployment of European is in many ways analogous to Derrida's own use of Europe in his late piece "A Europe of Hope," in which Europe becomes a trope for a deconstructive mode of reading, "a Europe that sets the example of what a politics, a thinking, and an ethics could be, inherited from the passed Enlightenment and bearing the Enlightenment to come, which would be capable of non-binary judgments."[13] "European" is a subject position open to all—to Americans, for example, who draw their hope from the civil rights movement, and to the Haitian revolutionaries who inventively misinterpellated human rights discourse. To read like a "European" is to contest what passes for commonsense or moral clarity today. Likewise, Žižek's Europe functions as a trope for universality, a universality that is "non-all," incomplete and irremediably at odds with the sovereignty and self-transparency of the subject. It is a universality shot through with the unconscious and alterity: "Universality is a universality of 'strangers,' of individuals reduced to the abyss of impenetrability in relation not only to others but also to themselves."[14] Racism arises in no small part from the disavowal of such strangeness: "Racism confronts us with the enigma of the Other, which cannot be reduced to the partner in symbolic communication; it confronts us with the enigma of that which, in ourselves, resists the universal frame of symbolic communication."[15] Racism is one response to this strangeness. Žižek finds in Europe resources for another response.

So it is not a question of crudely applying the European universal to the refugees, as if universality were a civilizing measuring stick. Indeed, a European way of life, as Žižek defines it, is antithetical to apartheid logic and sovereign authority; it rejects rather than upholds global capitalism's divide between Us and Them. It is not the refugees but the anti-immigrant Europeans that pose the greatest threat to Europe: "A Europe where Marine Le Pen [in France] or Geert Wilders [in the Netherlands] are in power is no longer Europe. So what is this Europe worth fighting for?"[16] In this light, we might more productively reformulate Žižek's stance toward the refugee crisis as informed by his own double bind, framed as a resistance to today's "double blackmail": the forced choice between humanist identification with refugees or the racist rejection of refugees, between *heterophilia* (pure hospitality) or *heterophobia* (pure hostility).

Against widespread European "'autoimmune' responses"[17] to the threat of racial and racialized refugees, Žižek turns to the biblical injunction "Love thy neighbor." When (re)politicized and redefined, this command takes the form of an invaluable corrective to "today's 'new reign of ethics,'" to a depoliticized ethical sentimentalism or pious ethics of difference emanating from humanist corners and from what Žižek disparagingly calls the "usual gang of democracy-to-come-deconstructionist-postsecular-Levinasian-respect-for-Otherness suspects,"[18] who object to the racist logic of the Same, seeking out the recognition of the other. "Love thy neighbor" for Žižek stands as a locus of resistance to the immune disorders that are currently besetting Western communities.[19] But in this framing of the problem, Žižek does not sufficiently acknowledge the significant differences between Levinas and Derrida (both deemed founding members of the "gang of democracy-to-come-deconstructionist-postsecular-Levinasian-respect-for-Otherness"). As pointed out above, Derrida's critique of Levinas recasts the desirability of heterology in a way that anticipates Žižek's own critique: *the recognition of pure alterity is an ideological fantasy* and a dangerous one at that. And though Žižek will return to a more generous engagement with Derrida (after the latter's death), he restricts his interest to the earlier Derrida, ignoring the latter's theorization of autoimmunity, since it is presumably guilty by association, part of the same grammar that generated the idea of a "democracy *à venir*." If Žižek laments for good reasons Europe's autoimmune disorders, its increasingly apartheid mentalities when it comes to the refugee question, he misses an opportunity to reengage with Derrida's late work, to ask: How can Derrida's musings on autoimmunity help reconfigure an ethico-politics of the neighbor that starts with the autoimmune self, or the self as *real* neighbor?

Žižek *contra* Levinas

As Žižek's critique suggests, Levinas looms large in anti-racist projects, which draw from his account of "astonishing alterity"[20] to explain racism's functioning. A racist economy of the Same fails to see the racial other as worthy of care and respect. What the racial other lacks is precisely a Levinasian face. Meditating on the association of blackness with evil and criminality, George Yancy notes: "In Levinasian terms, my 'face' does not appear in the form of the imperative 'Thou shall not murder.'"[21] Similarly, Achille Mbembe describes anti-black racism in a Levinasian register as an inability to perceive the face of blacks; lacking depth, a "face"—or a face that is systematically disprivileged—the racialized black other can only be read superficially, at the surface level through a regime of visuality, reduced to what Mbembe calls an "image ontology."[22]

Levinas provides Yancy and Mbembe with a by now familiar and generalized Levinasian framework where the face of the racial other fails to be properly encountered. For these thinkers, racism emerges when there is a breakdown in my exposure to the other's face, when I am confronted with a defaced face—a face that is, or has been, structurally ignored, rendered invisible, or assimilated to the order of the Same. Levinas offers anti-racist philosophers, like Yancy and Mbembe, an explanation for the failure of an ethical encounter with the racial other. While neither Yancy nor Mbembe is following Levinas in a strictly orthodox or sustained fashion, their evocation of his work—the latter's *obdurate* fixation on the face—speaks to the pull of his grammar and its adaptability, as well as his authority in matters of ethics and/as difference. It is on this terrain—the ethics of difference and the primacy of the face—that Žižek confronts Levinas.

Žižek is by no means alone in blaming Levinas for the ethical ideology prevalent today. Alain Badiou argues that the pervasive Levinasian obsession with ethics reduces politics to a series of feel-good platitudes that do little to challenge the status quo:

> Whether they know it or not, it is in the name of this configuration that the proponents of ethics explain to us today that it amounts to "recognition of the other" (against racism, which would deny this other), or to "the ethics of differences" (against substantialist nationalism, which would exclude immigrants, or sexism, which would deny feminine-being), or to "multiculturalism" (against the imposition of an unified model of behaviour and intellectual approach). Or, quite simply, to good old-fashioned "tolerance" which consists of not being offended by the fact that others think and act differently than you.[23]

If Badiou states unabashedly that "the whole ethical predication based upon recognition of the other should be purely and simply abandoned,"[24] Žižek, though not unsympathetic to Badiou's position, pursues a different approach, exposing Levinasian ethics as politically unproductive and, as we shall see, detrimental to an anti-racist critique. To the seemingly timeless Levinasian other, Žižek opposes the protean figure of the neighbor.

If Levinas argues that the concept of the "face," as "a being beyond all attributes,"[25] enabled his philosophy to transcend the realm of sociality and the socialization of the other, Žižek (again, not unlike Derrida), questions this singularization of the face, underscoring instead how Levinas's radical alterity is still subjected to mediation, to the workings of the symbolic order. The face of the other could not be experienced as such, as a face, if it were not always already a discursive product; reading the neighbor as a face thus domesticates the neighbor, making the other's alterity as a resource of infinite responsibility more retrievable. Žižek exposes what he describes as Levinas's "ethical petrification"[26] of otherness, his gentrification of the face (the symbolic neighbor) by juxtaposing it with Primo Levi's account of the *Muselmann*, that living-dead, faceless figure of Auschwitz (the real neighbor. For Žižek, the *Muselmann* discloses the limits of a depoliticizing Levinasian ethics: "When confronted with a Muselmann, one cannot discern in his face the trace of the abyss of the Other in his/her vulnerability, addressing us with the infinite call of our responsibility. What one gets instead is a kind of blind wall, lack of depth."[27] The *Muselmann*, a figure of precarity and bare life, constitutes a disquieting example of the neighbor for whom no relation *as such* is affectively afforded; this "'faceless' face," as Žižek puts it, is a "neighbor with whom no empathetic relationship is possible."[28] Stripped of its symbolic veneer, recalcitrant to one's imaginary projection, denied access to the human realm of intersubjectivity, the *Muselmann* foregrounds the neighbor as real, in which "we encounter the Other's call at its purest and most radical," and "one's responsibility toward the Other at its most traumatic."[29] It is in this context that the ethical injunction to "Love thy neighbor" takes on its full political force.

Setting himself apart from the Levinasian model, Žižek argues that it is not enough to say that I can never account for the other as other, that phenomenologically the other is always in excess of my idea of her. Žižek considers the biblical figure of the neighbor the "most precious and revolutionary aspect of the Jewish legacy," stressing how the neighbor "remains an inert, impenetrable, enigmatic presence that hystericizes."[30] Žižek foregrounds the challenge posed by the injunction "Love thy neighbor!" This injunction confounds universalist thinking; it disturbs ethics as such. The biblical injunction might be better characterized as an "anti-ethics"[31] to the extent that it radically deviates from a humanist orientation, where ethics invests itself in a fetishistic ideal of humanity—a gentrified view of Man as the bearer of rights, endowed with a moral sensibility and so forth—disavowing any knowledge of suffering or man-made evil in the world. Jewish law, for its part, de-gentrifies the other, calling us to confront the Real of the other in its figuration of the neighbor. If Greek philosophy neglected the hysterical presence of this other, Jewish law avows the Real of the neighbor, that is, the neighbor as the "bearer of a monstrous Otherness, this properly *inhuman* neighbor."[32]

The neighbor is a concretization or embodiment of the Lacanian Real, a reminder and remainder of this Real, an intolerable or traumatic stain which remains untranslatable, irreducible to my interpretive mastery, untranslatable in humanist terms. From this vision of the neighbor emerges an ethico-political injunction: "to love and respect your neighbor ... does not refer to your imaginary *semblable*/double, but to the neighbor qua traumatic Thing."[33] The "Real" of the other is impossible but it is an impossibility that paradoxically needs to be sustained:

> The Real is impossible but it is not simply impossible in the sense of a failed encounter. It is also impossible in the sense that it is a traumatic encounter that *does* happen but which we are unable to confront. And one of the strategies used to avoid confronting it is precisely that of positing it as this indefinite ideal which is eternally postponed. One aspect of the real is that it's impossible, but the other aspect is that it happens

but is impossible to sustain, impossible to integrate. And this second aspect, I think, is more and more crucial.³⁴

The real neighbor is neither *assimilable to that which we already know*, nor a radical alterity mysteriously exempt from symbolic mediation.

For Frantz Fanon, similarly, we must guard against the temptation to think the neighbor's singularity outside mediated relation, the temptation to insist on a radical difference that is tantamount to reified sameness, that eschews or denies this encounter, this relation. Singularity comes about through history (through history as "non-all," in Žižek's terms), and to forget this is to mistake history for destiny, to reify being and renounce the possibilities of becoming: "If the question once arose for me about showing solidarity with a given past, it was because I was committed to myself and my neighbor, to fight with all my life and all my strength so that never again would people be enslaved on this earth."³⁵ Fidelity to a "given past" motivates solidarity and action yet also risks arresting this movement. Fanon's neighbor is not *reducible* to a *semblable* (the other with whom I share a colonial past). This neighbor belongs to a different order. The biblical exhortation to love is not grounded in a shared humanity with the other (my imaginary/symbolic counterpart, which always threatens congealing around an identity), but in the acknowledgment of the *inhuman* (the subject's avowed out-of-jointness; the inaccessible, untamable, and anxiety-inducing Real) as the condition of/for universality:

> The most difficult thing for common understanding is to grasp this speculative-dialectical reversal of the singularity of the subject *qua* Neighbor-Thing into universality, not standard "general" universality, but universal singularity, the universality grounded in the subjective singularity extracted from all particular properties, a kind of direct short circuit between the singular and the universal, bypassing the particular.³⁶

Conceptualizing the neighbor in this way undermines the opposition between universality and otherness, denying a familiar talking point of the "leftist-multiculturalist liberals who improvise endlessly on the motif of impossible universality."³⁷ Rather than settling for deference to the other's aseptized particularity, an ethical response to the plight of the real neighbor must pass through universality. Correlatively, we must reconsider who counts as our neighbors, and who has been excluded from that relation.

Racializing the Palestinian Other

Racialization, as the transformation of others into subhuman inferiors, has been and remains a key social and political mechanism by which neighbors are excluded from "the category of the human as it is performed in the modern west,"[38] persecuted, marginalized, barred from love, and thus made disposable, killable without consequences. The Israel–Palestine conflict throws into particularly stark relief the ethical and political challenges of combatting racialization by appealing to a Levinasian notion of the face—or, conversely, by seeing and treating the racialized other as a neighbor. These challenges come into view, importantly, in a radio interview that Levinas, along with Alain Finkielkraut, gave to Shlomo Malka shortly after the massacre of hundreds of Palestinians between September 16 and September 18, 1982 at the Sabra and Shatila refugee camps in West Beirut, Lebanon, at the hands of Lebanese Christian Phalangist militia in Israeli-occupied Lebanon. In this now infamous interview, Levinas makes several comments about the racialized Palestinians that thematize and disclose both the limits and limitations of a philosophy of the face.

The interview starts with a seemingly naïve question by Malka about the relationship between the other, politics, and Israel's failed responsibility toward the Palestinian refugees in the Sabra and Shatila camps: "Emmanuel Levinas, you are the philosopher of the 'other.' Isn't history, isn't politics the very site of the encounter with the 'other,' and for the Israeli isn't the 'other' above all Palestinian?"[39] Levinas's response takes the form of a philosophical lesson in phenomenology:

> My definition of the other is completely different. The other is the neighbor [*prochain*], who is not necessarily my kin [*proche*] but who may be. But if your neighbor attacks another neighbor, or treats him unjustly, what can you do? Then alterity takes on another character, in alterity we can find an enemy, or at least we are faced with the problem of knowing who is right and who is wrong, who is just and who is unjust. There are people who are wrong.[40]

Levinas resists Malka's determination of the Palestinian as Israel's political other. His emphatic "no" to his interlocutor is not only compatible with this phenomenological ethics, but also is required by it. As he says damningly elsewhere: "The best way of encountering the Other is not even to notice the color of his eyes!"[41] In the interview, we quickly learn that difference or alterity is *not* relational. Race, racism, and racialization are strictly speaking ontic matters, better addressed in sociology rather than in ethics. Even the conflict of duties (which of my neighbors [fellow Jews or Palestinians] am I [more, first] responsible to?) is about justice, which falls under the jurisdiction of politics. And yet by insisting that ethics—not politics—is first philosophy, Levinas assigns the Palestinian question (Malka's own question, "Is the Palestinian the other of the Israelis?" and the more general question, "How to address and redress the wrongs committed to the Palestinian people?") to at best a secondary consideration. Operating at a high level of abstraction ("There are people who are wrong"—who? why?), Levinas seems to default to a register where the Jews of Auschwitz are humanity's timeless victims, making the Palestinian, in turn, the Israeli's political victimizer. Difference here is ironically relational, an ontical designation; the enemy is historicized and culturalized (that is, racialized).

Faced with the Palestinian question, Levinas's rhetoric of alterity falls flat. "What Levinas is basically saying," according to Žižek, "is that, as a principle, respect for alterity is unconditional (the highest sort of respect), but, when faced with a concrete other, one should nonetheless see if he is a friend or an enemy. In short, in practical politics, the respect for alterity strictly means nothing."[42] What is at stake in Žižek's critique of Levinas is the latter's *substantialization* of the other; the fascination with the Levinasian other blinds us to the structural suffering of concrete others: "The true ethical step is the one beyond the face of the other, the one of suspending the hold of the face, the one of choosing against the face, for the third."[43] True emancipatory ethics, then, resists the lure of "subjective violence," and steps back to attend to the "objective violence"; it transcends the dyadic moment of the face-to-face encounter (the ethical proper) to an incorporation of the other's others (the political proper).

Deciding "who is right and who is wrong, who is just and who is unjust' and recognizing that "there are people who are wrong" are not what disqualifies Levinas. Žižek does not have misgivings about determining enemies. On the contrary, he repeatedly asserts the need for the Left to identify its true enemy: "What we need is *even more hatred*, but proper *political* hatred: hatred directed at the common political enemy."[44] What is problematic in Levinas's response is the ideological structure of priority. All things being equal (everyone is my neighbor), attachment to Israel tips the scale. Not unlike liberal Zionists, Levinas cannot see that the racialization of the Palestinians co-existed with the creation of the state of Israel. Israel's violence toward the Palestinians was and continues be constitutive of Israeli existence. To be sure, all nations engage in forms of what Walter Benjamin describes as state-founding violence (of which the racialization of the Indigenous people is one prevalent model). But as Žižek critically observes, what makes Israel's case unique today is that this violence is ongoing and contested, and thus its memory is still very much alive. Israel "hasn't yet obliterated the 'founding violence' of its 'illegitimate' origins, repressed them into a timeless past. In this sense, what the state of Israel confronts us with is merely the obliterated past of every state power."[45]

An anti-racist critique of Israel must attend not only to the current abhorrent realities of life under Occupation but also to Israel's "original sin"—the Nakba, the Arabic word for "catastrophe," denoting the forced expulsion of 800,000 Palestinians between 1948 and 1949. The work of anti-racism must keep this link between "founding violence"—the arbitrary and groundless division of the social field between Jews and non-Jews (of which the Palestinians are the lowest manifestation)—and "objective violence"—the rules and practices that sustain the existence of the Zionist status quo—visible.

De-Racializing the Palestinians, or the Palestinians as Neighbors

If Levinas lacked the moral courage to tackle the problems of a messianic Zionism, Žižek boldly calls for abandoning any mythic or trans-historical pretensions of origins and exclusionary claims of rooted-identity:

> The lesson is simply that every form of legitimization of a claim to land by some mythic past should be rejected. In order to resolve (or contain, at least), the Israeli–Palestinian conflict, we should not dwell in ancient past—we should, on the contrary, forget the past (which is in any case basically constantly reinvented to legitimize present claims).[46]

Seeing that "Zionism was a historical construction,"[47] as Gianni Vattimo and Michael Marder point out—and not the realization of Israel's Manifest Destiny—is a first step to deconstructing Zionism, to seeing it as an ideological concept. Zionists constantly argue that the connection between Jews and the land of Israel is both intrinsic and essential, that Jews dwelling in Israel is a necessity that had to happen. But the historical record of Zionism is more complicated: Palestine was by no means the only option for the Promised Land considered by early Zionists. Uganda, Azerbaijan, and Argentina were also some of the destinations seriously explored. A second step to deconstructing Zionism is to address and redress the injustices committed against Zionism's victims, who are "not only the Palestinians . . ., but also . . . the anti-Zionist Jews, 'erased' from the officially consecrated account of Zionist history."[48]

Žižek turns to the figure of the *refuseniks*, Israeli soldiers who refuse to complete their compulsory military service in the Occupied Territories, for a *critique of Zionism from within*. The *refuseniks*, like any Israeli citizen, inherit a racist ideology that instructs them to treat Palestinians "not *as if* a racial group, not simply *in the manner* of a racial group, but *as* a despised and demonic racial group." Goldberg calls this "racial Palestinization."[49] What can only emerge from this racist ideology is the bestialization of the Palestinian, the genocidal view that *a good Palestinian is a dead Palestinian*. But the *refuseniks* decline such interpellation into the Zionist social body. Refusing to serve as instruments of Israel's brutal necropower, the *refuseniks* reject blind allegiance to the nation-state, opting for a more just Israel. *Refusenik* Haggai Matar spoke in the early 2000s against Israel's disproportionate response to the second Palestinian *intifada* or uprising in the following words:

> Today, militarization and racism among the Jewish population have reached a fascist level. The repression of critical thinking, the total acceptance of the occupation's crimes, the idolization of the army and the gradual acceptance of the principle of "ethnic cleansing"—all these

constitute only part of our society's collapse. To this list one should add the systematic mistreatment of the Palestinian citizens of Israel, the hateful violence addressed at peace demonstrators, and the heartless attitude towards the abnormal and the weak.[50]

These conscientious objectors intervene in the politics and ethics of Jewishness. Declining to perpetuate Israel's state of exception—that is, its sovereign power to remove Palestinians from the protection of the law—the *refuseniks* seriously take up, if not fulfill, the injunction to "Love thy neighbour":

> What the *refuseniks* have achieved is the passage from *Homo sacer* to "neighbour": they treat Palestinians not as "equal full citizens," but as *neighbours* in the strict Judeo-Christian sense. And, in fact, that is the difficult ethical test for Israelis today: "Love thy neighbour!" means "Love the Palestinian!" (who is their neighbour *par excellence*), or it means nothing at all.[51]

After their act, Zionist life is out of joint, even if temporally. Palestinian lives are transfigured from *homines sacri* (individuals stripped of their rights, and deprived of the means of articulating their very exclusion or demanding redress) into neighbors (individuals who solicit an ethical response despite, or because of, their racialized otherness). The *refuseniks*' treatment of Palestinians calls for a reinvention of the Symbolic—infusing doubt into the racial separation of Jews and Arabs, which, in turn, unsettles the phantasm of a pure racial Zionist identity. It constitutes an anti-racist "ethical act," something of a "miraculous moment in which eternal justice momentarily appears in the temporal sphere of empirical reality."[52] As a virtually contagious miracle, though "downplayed"[53] by the mainstream media, the *refuseniks*' "No!" holds a genuinely emancipatory promise.

Dominik LaCapra criticizes Žižek's jubilant reading of the *refuseniks* for its idealism and ahistoricity:

> Žižek can offer the totally speculative, implausible interpretation of the acts of refuseniks in Israel, refusing to fight in the occupied territories, not only as a move away from seeing Palestinians as Agamben's *homo sacer* toward a vision of them as Judaeo-Christian neighbors (what happens to Islam here?), but also as designating "the miraculous moment in which eternal justice momentarily appears in the temporal sphere of empirical reality"—in effect as acts of transcendent grace conflated with (or incarnated in) this-worldly miracles.[54]

LaCapra's disciplinary preference for situating causality and the possible within a particular historical framework forecloses the very possibility of an *act*, of that which makes the impossible possible.

Žižek is not saying *refuseniks* are all revolutionary subjects calling for the destruction of the Zionist order of things. It is very likely that most of the *refuseniks* fall under the category of liberal Zionists (they are only refusing to serve *in the Occupied Territories*), continuing to believe in Israel as a Jewish state living side by side with a free Palestine one. Still, in the act of refusal, Žižek perceives a disturbing excess that reveals the lack in the Symbolic, a gap whose revolutionary potential he seeks to exploit, challenging Israelis to live up to their own ideal, to exert pressure on their Zionist communal life, and treat the Palestinians as neighbors.

To treat the Palestinians as neighbors is, of course, not simply to acknowledge their ontological opacity, to acknowledge, that is, the truth that "we are all opaque subjects"—*it is that and more*. It is to underscore and attend to their historical racialization, their state of precarity, or, in other words, the symbolic order's contingent distribution of vulnerability and unfamiliarity (an unfamiliarity increasingly taken as bestial and threatening). The *refuseniks*, on Žižek's account, also decline the liberal or humanist remedy, which would mean conceiving of the neighbors through a limiting framework as "equal full citizens." The injunction to "Love the Palestinian" goes further in insisting on the challenges posed by the other. The Palestinian as a neighbor—the Palestinian stripped of her symbolic veneer via Israeli racialization—continues to arouse anxiety, compelling a different kind of affective relationality, a relationality that exposes the limits of relationality: when confronted with Palestinians, the *refuseniks* encounter "a blind wall, a lack of depth"[55] and act ethically toward them. Acting on the neighborly injunction de-racializes the Palestinians, decompletes Zionist reality and its apparatus of racial classification: *Zionist ideology is not all*. "Love the Palestinian" produces an affective excess, a visceral ethical feeling, that is, a non-coincidence between a compulsory hatred of Palestinians (what cultural norms tell soldiers they should feel for the enemy, for the racialized other) and how they actually respond to the (real) Palestinians: to de-racialize the Palestinians is to insist on treating them on equal footing.

To treat and relate to the Palestinian as a neighbor is, however, also to reject the faux universality of an "equal full citizen" model, a model that relies on a logic of sovereignty, a structure through which a sovereign power dictates who is included in Israel's modern state (applying the Law of Return), and who is excluded from it (denying the right of return). The enlightened sovereign self decides on the exception; the liberal Zionist is driven to act by a masculine logic. That self would make the Palestinian other grievable on the basis of an implicit identification with the formerly excluded, now brought fully into the polity and the "privileges" of humanity, into the realm of intersubjectivity and sameness, controlled and contained under the umbrella of an inclusive humanism (a false universalism). By contrast, if there is identification, we might say that the *refuseniks* identify with Zionism's symptom: the Palestinians as symptoms, the excluded "part of no-part." Israel's racialized other here is never ontologized or divorced from the economic and political field of power. Quite the opposite, the example of the *refuseniks* repoliticizes the Symbolic, opening up new possibilities and modalities. It challenges Zionism as the unquestioned and ultimate horizon of Jewish political practice, delegitimizing the Zionist colonizer settler narrative that racially frames or structures Israeli knowledge and experience of the Palestinian people, that decides "who matters and who does not, who is *disposable* and who is not."[56]

The *refuseniks*' important disidentification with the state of Israel inscribes them in a rich Jewish tradition, aligning them with the cosmopolitan Jew who, as Žižek observes, always kept a critical distance vis-à-vis his or her community:

> The privileged role of Jews in the establishment of the sphere of the "public use of reason" hinges on their subtraction from every state power. Theirs is this position of the "part of no-part" in every organic nation-state community, and it is this position, not the abstract-universal nature of their monotheism, that makes them the immediate embodiment of universality. No wonder, then, that, with the establishment of the Jewish nation-state, a new figure of the Jew emerged: a Jew resisting identification with the State of Israel, refusing to accept the State of Israel as his true home, a Jew who "subtracts" himself from this State, and who includes the State of Israel among the states towards which he insists on maintaining a distance, to live in their interstices.[57]

As the "part of no-part," the cosmopolitan Jew stands for "the empty principle of universality."[58] Praise for this "uncanny Jew,"[59] of course, comes with a risk. Non-Jews who offer such praise risk the charge of anti-Semitism, while Jews risk the charge of pathological self-hatred. Contemporary Zionists treat Jews (like the *refuseniks*) who do not fully identify with Israel and accept its racial regime as a "foreign excess disturbing the community of the nation-state."[60] In declining organicist attachment, this universalist Jew experiences a new form of racism and racialization, which Žižek aptly dubs "Zionist anti-Semitism."[61]

Bruno Chaouat dismisses Žižek's claim of "Zionist anti-Semitism," seeing in the idea of an "uncanny Jew"—the Jew who does not (want to) belong to his or her given community—"a mirror of the antisemitic topos": "the common trope of antisemitism, the trope that traverses Western history, is that Jews ... are never where they ought to be, they are always in an awkward, somewhat anachronistic position vis-à-vis the dominant ideology—cosmopolitan in a nationalistic Europe, capitalist in communist Russia, Bolsheviks in Nazi Germany, nationalist in post-national Europe, etc."[62] Žižek and other post-Heideggerian theorists are blamed for "Jew-splitting," for creating a mythic, dichotomous caricature: the good uncanny Jew versus the bad Zionist Jew. But there is an irony here in that Chaouat is guilty of creating his own split: the good Jew who appreciates Israel's historical necessity and the bad Jew, like Judith Butler, who fetishizes diasporic Judaism and falsifies the history of Zionism. In fact, Chaouat never really deals with Žižek's characterization of "Zionist anti-Semitism," that there is anti-Semitism at work when Jews who courageously disidentify with the state of Israel are vilified, described as traitors to their own race. Chaouat draws instead a facile analogy between the old racist anti-Semites who malign Jews as outsiders and Žižek (the new anti-racist anti-Semite) who privileges the Jew as an outsider.

If the creation of Israel was supposed to put an end to, or at least curtail, this anti-Semitic topos (since all Jews in principle can claim Israel as their home), Žižek's insistence on this "uncanny Jew" is read as a desire to prolong the life of anti-Semitism. What Žižek is saying is quite the opposite. Žižek is not phantasmatically projecting anti-Zionist Jews. What he is pointing out is the ironic situation in which supporters of Israel are themselves recycling anti-Semitic topoi—you don't belong in our community, you collaborate with our enemies, you are a threat to our way of life, etc. Žižek's sympathies clearly lie with Jews who object to Israeli policies toward the Palestinians, who question an aggressive Zionism that silences opposition at home and abroad. This does not stem however from a desire to perpetuate anti-Semitism—the hatred of Jews in the guise of a noble defense of the marginalized, excluded, and dispossessed other—but from what Judith Butler has called "a passion for justice," a genuine desire to see, and fight for, universal equality and freedom (*égaliberté*) for Jews and Arabs alike.[63]

Žižek with Derrida

In light of the example of the *refuseniks*, we can return to the refugee crisis with which we opened the essay and now ask, paraphrasing Žižek: isn't the difficult ethical test for Europeans today precisely to see the refugees as neighbors? "Love thy neighbor!" means "Love the refugee!", or it means nothing at all. As a corollary question: what kind of hospitality does justice to the biblical injunction? Here, thinking Žižek with Derrida might prove resourceful.

While Žižek is often critical of deconstruction, seeing it as failing to confront today's true antagonisms, he does perceive a convergence between Derrida's early notion of *différance* and his own account of "minimal difference":

> Since I have written many pages in which I struggle with the work of Jacques Derrida, now—when the Derridean fashion is fading away—is perhaps the moment to honor his memory by pointing out the proximity of this "minimal difference" to what he called *différance*, this neologism whose very notoriety obfuscates its unprecedented materialist potential.[64]

What both ideas have in common is the insistence on an internal division in the thing itself, "the constitutive noncoincidence of a thing with itself."[65] Žižek couples his praise for the materialist potential of *différance* with a dismissal of the late Derrida's rhetoric of the messianic. When "radical" liberals advocate open borders in order to let in all the refugees, an idea Žižek rejects, we can hear in their call an echo of Derrida's discussion of openness to the other:

> Let us say yes *to who or what turns up*, before any determination, before any anticipation, before any *identification*, whether or not it has to do with a foreigner, an immigrant, an invited guest, or an unexpected visitor, whether or not the new arrival is the citizen of another country, a human, animal, or divine creature, a living or dead thing, male or female.[66]

Derrida may have increased the range of the "face"—it is no longer restricted to living humans and also includes racial others (the other as immigrant or foreigner)—but what we have here from a Žižekian vantage point is more of the same, more Levinasianism, more fascination with difference—the endless awaiting of the other. The messianic other looks a lot like the Levinasian other, plagued with similar political problems. Deconstruction is, at best, a remedy for subjective violence; at worst, it ignores objective violence, consigning the other's others to oblivion.

But this is to ignore Derrida's critical distance from Levinas and his rejection of Levinas's "*dream* of a purely *heterological* thought."[67] Against what we might call the Levinasian blackmail, Derrida insists that the question is not one of choosing between "the opening and the totality,"[68] that is, between infinity and sameness. Derrida keeps returning to the *relationality* of the other/the face. Though there is always something surprising about the other, something "wholly other [*tout autre*],"[69] a pure or unmediated encounter with the other remains something of a *phantasm*. And to be sure, we find Derrida, at times, all too captivated by this *phantasm* of a "pure ethics":

> Pure ethics, if there is any, begins with the respectable dignity of the other as absolute *unlike*, recognized as nonrecognizable, indeed as unrecognizable, beyond all knowledge, all cognition and all recognition: far from being the beginning of pure ethics, the neighbor as like or as resembling, as looking like, spells the end or the ruin of such an ethics, if there is any.[70]

Yet we must attend carefully to Derrida's self-puncturing moments of doubt here, to moments such as the one above, where Derrida entertains thoughts of a pure ethics while qualifying such observations with the repetition of the words, "if there is any"—thematizing, as it were, the phantasmatic character of such a notion.

We can reread Derrida's account of the other in terms of the Lacanian Borromean knot, which unites the three orders of the Real, the Imaginary, and the Symbolic. When Derrida evokes "the neighbor as like or as resembling, as looking like," he is referring to the imaginary-symbolic neighbor. His account of the other aligns with the real neighbor, the neighbor as a "monstrous Thing"—unaltered or domesticated by the symbolic order. Unfortunately, Žižek tends to foreclose such a reading of Derrida. Yet there is much convergence here between the two. Both would agree that the injunction "Love thy neighbor" is about loving the real neighbor, not the decaffeinated other of liberal multiculturalism. Derrida is equally critical of "the idealized Other who dances fascinating dances and has an ecologically sound holistic approach to reality."[71] This neighbor disturbs me at my core. The challenge is how to politically and ethically engage the (non-European) other.

Of course, not all monsters are created equal. Evoking the "monster" for Derrida is about resisting the reduction of the other to the already known (the other is without abyss, phantasmatically transparent); it is to maintain a relationless relation with the other. Each other is radically monstrous, and yet each other shares the identity of monstrosity. Conceptualizing the relation to the other as a "relation without relation" renders problematic the choice between pure otherness or pure sameness, and serves to block or forestall the (illusory) hermeneutic security that the "is" (the other is . . .) might provide.

And there is the monstrosity of the refugees. This monstrosity is doubled: it is constituted by racist fantasies of intruding foreigners (of course, referring to them as "monsters" can easily play into the hands of racist right-wing populists) and by the neighbor's anxiety-producing unknowability and unpredictability: Who are the refugees? What do they want from me? To consider refugees as real neighbors is not to dehistoricize or ontologize their condition, nor is it to minimize their racially dehumanized condition. On the contrary, "Love thy neighbor" takes up the difficult—even traumatizing—task of identifying with society's/globalism's desubjectivized others, those others whose faces fail to disclose their humanity. It is also to avow and come to terms with the fact that "refugees are the price humanity is paying for the global economy."[72] Today's large migrations in Europe are the direct result of Western interventions and neocolonial expansions. Most refugees originate from "failed states," severely lacking "public authority."[73] If some in the West conveniently promote timeless explanations of the unrest in Syria, Iraq, Libya and elsewhere ("ethnic warfare fuelled by old passions"), Žižek locates the source for the failed states in the global economy, as "the result of international economics and politics."[74]

The refugees desperately need their own *refuseniks*, Europeans citizens and politicians who will refuse to serve the interests of global capitalism. Žižek praises German chancellor Angela Merkel's 2015 "invitation to accept the refugees—more refugees than any other European state," considering it "a genuine ethical miracle, one that cannot be reduced to the capitalist strategy of importing cheap labor force."[75] Merkel knew that she would take a political hit for her decision—and increase the popularity of anti-immigrant right-wingers—but still did it because it was the right thing to do. At the same time, Žižek knows that it is going to require the election of more than liberal politicians to change the current path of the global economy. More "radical" liberal politicians only fuel the fantasy of a capitalism with a human face; that is, a postracial capitalism capable of accommodating the occasional influx of refugees and still function as "efficiently" as before. In his exchange with John Caputo, Žižek throws into starker relief the fault lines separating a Marxist critique from its liberal deconstructive counterpart. Caputo first responds to Žižek and Badiou's alarming concern about the spread of global capitalism with the following patronizing reassurance:

> I would be perfectly happy if the far left politicians in the United States were able to reform the system by providing universal health care, effectively redistributing wealth more equitably with a revised IRS code, effectively restricting campaign financing, enfranchising all voters, treating migrant workers humanely, and effecting a multilateral foreign policy that would integrate American power within the international community, etc., i.e., intervene upon capitalism by means of serious and far-reaching reforms.... If after doing all that Badiou and Žižek complained that some Monster called Capital still stalks us, I would be inclined to greet that Monster with a yawn.[76]

Žižek counters that this "Monster" is precisely untamable within the existing economic structures. Cosmetic reforms that pretend to stabilize capitalism can only prolong the disastrous reign of the postpolitical:

> The problem here is not Caputo's conclusion that if one can achieve all that within capitalism, why not remain within the system? The problem lies with the "utopian" premise that it is possible to achieve all that within the coordinates of global capitalism. What if the particular malfunctionings of capitalism enumerated by Caputo are not merely accidental disturbances but are rather structurally necessary? What if Caputo's dream is a dream of universality (of the universal capitalist order) without its symptoms, without any critical points in which its "repressed truth" articulates itself?[77]

Caputo's universality is a universality without refugee crises, a universality that exists alongside the fantasy of a "frictionless"[78] capitalism.

Žižek sees the mainstream Left as critically impoverished—abandoning its call for "the ruthless critique of all that exists,"[79] tacitly acquiescing to the permanent reality of today's global economy. He ironically labels them "leftist Fukuyamaists." Žižek urges the Left to shift focus back to the material realities that brought us this refugee crisis. Humanitarian aid is a *pharmakon*; it is "both cure and poison."⁸⁰ It does address the suffering of the refugees. But, the point here is to redress their suffering. This will not happen merely by increasing humanitarian intervention, which prolongs the exposure and suffering of the refugees by obfuscating the global causes of the crisis and prolonging. Nor do lofty proclamations suffice, as when leftist liberals, or "Beautiful Souls," assert that "Europe should show solidarity, should open its doors widely."⁸¹ Such claims smack of fake radicalism. The call for open borders is an empty act.

What prevents a confrontation with the problem at hand is a series of distortions about what the problem is. We (Europeans and the rest of the Western world) are asked to choose between terrorism or anti-terrorism, a humanist identification with refugees or a racist rejection of refugees, the defense of Western values or the rejection of Western values, Islam or a critique of Islam, and so on. This binary logic confuses the refugee problem. What is needed is more lucidity over the Left's short-term and long-term goals:

> The political consequence of this paradox [when it is the religious fundamentalists or right-wing populist factions, and not Western, or Western-backed, liberal forces, who are dealing with class matters] is the properly dialectical tension between long-term strategy and short-term tactical alliances: although, in the long-term, the very success of the radical-emancipatory struggle depends on mobilizing the lower classes that are today often in thrall to fundamentalist populism, one should have no problems with concluding short-term alliances with egalitarian liberals as part of anti-sexist and anti-racist struggles.⁸²

Long-term humanitarian help is for this reason detrimental for both the refugees and the Europeans: "The more we treat refugees as objects of humanitarian help, and allow the situation which compelled them to leave their countries to prevail, the more they come to Europe, until tensions reach boiling point, not only in the refugees' countries of origin but here as well."⁸³ For Žižek, the long-term solution for Europe is to fundamentally rethink hospitality as solidarity:

> Don't just respect others: offer them a common struggle, since our problems today are common; propose and fight for a positive universal project shared by all participants. [. . .] So let's bring class struggle back— and the only way to do it is to insist on the global solidarity of the exploited and oppressed. . . . Maybe such global solidarity is a utopia. But if we don't engage in it, then we are really lost. And we will deserve to be lost.⁸⁴

At a time when both the Left and the Right are (re)turning to the nation-state (as a means of resisting global capitalism by minimally subtracting yourself from it), global solidarity would make the impossible possible. Only such solidarity can effectively deal with populist hostility. Only such solidarity can counter Europe's hitherto "'autoimmune' responses."[85] But here we might also want to give the term "autoimmune" a Derridean twist. As with *différance*, the notion of autoimmunity embodies for Derrida a certain "minimal difference" as Žižek understands the term. Autoimmunity entails a process through which, as Derrida puts it, "a living being, in a quasi-*suicidal* fashion, 'itself' works to destroy its own protection, to immunise itself *against* its 'own' immunity."[86] Yet while autoimmunization refers to the attempt to gain pure immunity, the attempt to wall off the self—an individual, a community, a nation—from external forces and influences, autoimmunity also names the condition of the self, that introduces a non-coincidence between the self and itself, that makes such attempts at self-enclosure impossible.

In describing the self as autoimmune, Derrida redefines the term, understanding it not as an illness or disability to lament or overcome, but rather as a condition of malleability and openness—a condition that involves vulnerability to harm but that also makes intersubjective contact and relation possible. Derrida cautions against the dangerous fantasy of a pure community, insisting that for a community to stay "alive," it must remain "open to something other and more than itself."[87] European communities are living in a state of paranoia, which compulsorily fuels the immunitary attitude. "Everywhere we look, new walls, new blockades, and new dividing lines are erected against something that threatens, or at least seems to, our biological, social, and environmental identity," writes Roberto Esposito.[8] The refugee crisis has triggered and is triggering such immune disorders in one European nation after another.

What is Europe? And what is happening to it? The liberal Left, ashamed of its colonial past, adopts a generous humanitarian perspective vis-à-vis the refugees, willing to assimilate them in an ever-expanding capitalist Europe. The anti-immigrant populist Right wants to shrink Europe, to deglobalize it; the extreme Right fully endorses the virtues of the immunology paradigm. European lives ought to be immunized, purified, and protected, whereas refugee lives ought to be left disposable, exposed, and precarious. The Right's message is clear: *Europe for Europeans—or even better, France for the French, Germany for the Germans, Italy for the Italians, and so on.*

Both the Left's and the Right's responses are to be rejected. We must go beyond humanitarian concerns or security concerns. Against this depoliticization of violence, where one talks about refugee suffering without needing to address the world's economic and political landscape, the Left must reorient its critical focus on the *causes* of global injustice and inequalities. The refugee crisis provides Europe "a unique chance to redefine itself."[89] Here we might ask: Why does Žižek not enlist Derrida? Doesn't this crisis expose to the world Europe's "pervertability"?[90] Does it not show how, on the one hand, Europe's universal image as the defender of human rights and its practices (treatment of the refugees) hardly coincide, and, on the other, how Europe's "strange illogical logic"[91] of autoimmunity, its self-destructive propensity, is also what enables Europe to improve, to endlessly perfect itself? Doesn't Žižek's intervention presuppose a kind of autoimmune Europe, a Europe whose being (autoimmunity involves a process "from which no region of being, *phúsis* or history would be exempt"[92]) and universality is precisely in question, a universality that ought to foreground its various communities' "part of no-part"?

An autoimmune Europe casts "Love thy neighbor"—Žižek's bold advice for Europeans—in a new light. To love the refugees is to decline an embrace of the other based on charity, sentimentalist humanism, or empathy. There is no "friendly neighbor"[93] behind the mask of cultural difference. "Love thy neighbor" means acknowledging the radical alterity of the neighbor, the refugee's singular form of *jouissance*, accepting that "most of the refugees are *not* 'people like us.'"[94] There is no "harmoniously indifferent coexistence."[95] But as if to block the impulse to reify this difference (Us versus Them), Žižek is quick to add, "not because they are foreign, but because *we* ourselves are not 'people like us.'"[96] This point is crucial. The "we" is always already irreducibly inconsistent. The same holds for *jouissance*: "It is not only that different modes of *jouissance* are incongruous with each other without a common measure; the other's *jouissance* is insupportable for us because (and insofar as) we cannot find a proper way to relate to our own *jouissance*."[97] The fundamental division is not between Europeans and refugees—rather, the division exists within each one of us. We share with the neighbor an inhuman core, an "abyss of impenetrability."[98] Avowing this impenetrability is to come to terms with one's autoimmunity. But here it is not simply a question of recognizing our autoimmunity or constitutive inhumanity—accounting for the fact that we are not whole, which, in turn, always risks producing nostalgia, a yearning for a "lost" wholeness that never existed. The Derridean (and Žižekian?) lesson is: *what disables enables*. Without an autoimmune self—or an autoimmune Europe—nothing would happen; there would be no presence, no dialogue, no experience of the Real, no event of any kind. Europe's universality would be reducible to its abstract, ideological projections; no contestation of the status quo, the established order's positivity, would take place. No politics as such would be possible.

With absolute immunity, without any experience of the self as neighbor, we would be forever anchored in the postpolitical, free of "the space of litigation in which the excluded can protest the wrong or injustice done to them."[99] The postpolitical is of course a space where the liberal Left thrives. And Žižek emphatically rejects the patronizing respect or soft racism that emerges from this camp. Suspending critical judgment of the refugees and other marginalized groups, refusing to treat them on equal footing, keeping them at a comfortable distance, betrays rather than sustains this ethical relation. Žižek obviously does not want to add to their suffering by joining the chorus of the anti-immigrant populist right. But, at the same time, he does not want to speak for the other; he does not want a toothless depoliticized respect of the other that only fetishizes the racialized refugees and their way of life. This homogenized other makes liberal Europeans feel good about their anti-racism—which is nothing but the flipside of the extreme right's enjoyment of hating the refugees. If the Left wants to bring about genuine change in Europe, in the lives of the refugees, and the rest of the world, it must seek out "the global solidarity of the exploited and oppressed."[100] What prevents this "global solidarity" from becoming yet another leftist empty gesture is internal critique. The Left must reaffirm and reclaim its commitment to anti-capitalism—and carefully tie its struggle against racism and other forms of oppression to that commitment—which it has inadvisably all but surrendered to the extreme right populist movements. Pure hospitality or pure hostility is ultimately a false choice in the refugee crisis. Of course, what is happening to the refugees is catastrophic. They need immediate protection from xenophobic groups, and they need to be afforded hospitality, but this cannot become an end in itself; this is not a problem solvable by humanitarian aid alone. The Left must also engage critically and honestly with the refugees and other oppressed groups. Don't fetishize the (non-European) other! As Edward Said used to say, "never solidarity before criticism."[101] The Left must insist (and strive to convince others) that some European values and ideas—egalitarianism, human rights, the welfare state, and so on—are worth saving and (collectively) fighting for.

Notes

1. This chapter draws on material originally published in *Žižek on Race: Toward an Anti-Racist Future,* by Zahi Zalloua (Bloomsbury Academic, 2020).
2. Emmanuel Levinas, "The Trace of the Other." In *Deconstruction in Context: Literature and Philosophy*, ed. Mark C. Taylor, trans. Alphonso Lingis (Chicago: University of Chicago Press, 1986), 346.
3. Levinas, *Totality and Infinity: An Essay on Exteriority*, trans. Alphonso Lingis (Pittsburgh: Duquesne University Press, 1969), 78.
4. Levinas, *Totality and Infinity*, 50.
5. Levinas, *Otherwise than Being, or, Beyond Essence*, trans. Alphonso Lingis (The Hague: Martinus Nijhoff, 1981), 195 n. 12.
6. Derrida, *Aporias*, trans. Thomas Dutoit (Stanford: Stanford University Press, 1993), 22.
7. Derrida, *Negotiations: Interventions and Interviews 1971–2001*, ed. and trans. Elizabeth Rottenberg (Stanford: Stanford University Press, 2002), 102.
8. Derrida, "Autoimmunity: Real and Symbolic Suicides : A Dialogue with Jacques Derrida." In *Philosophy in a Time of Terror: Dialogues with Jürgen Habermas and Jacques Derrida*, ed. Giovanna Borradori (Chicago: University of Chicago Press, 2004), 127–8.

9   Derrida, *Of Hospitality: Anne Dufourmantelle Invites Jacques Derrida to Respond* (Stanford: Stanford University Press, 2000), 27.
10 Derrida, "'Eating Well,' or the Calculation of the Subject," trans. Peter Connor and Avital Ronell. In *Points. . .: Interviews, 1974–1994*, ed. Elisabeth Weber (Stanford: Stanford University Press, 1995), 282.
11 Žižek, *Against the Double Blackmail: Refugees, Terror and Other Troubles with the Neighbors* (London: Penguin Random House, 2016), 99.
12 Derrida, "Some Statements and Truisms about Neologisms, Newisms, Postisms, Parasitisms, and Other Small Seismisms." In *The States of "Theory"*, ed. David Carroll (New York: Columbia University Press, 1989), 80.
13 Derrida, "A Europe of Hope," *Epoché* 10, no. 2 (2006): 410.
14 Žižek, *Against the Double Blackmail*, 79.
15 Žižek, "Love Thy Neighbor? No, Thanks!" In *The Psychoanalysis of Race*, ed. Christopher Lane (New York: Columbia University Press, 1998), 155.
16 Žižek, *Like A Thief in Broad Daylight: Power in the Era of Post-Humanity* (New York: Allen Lane, 2018), 98.
17 Slavoj Žižek, Eric L. Santner, and Kenneth Reinhard, *The Neighbor: Three Inquiries in Political Theology, with a New Preface* (Chicago: Chicago University Press, 2013), ix.
18 Žižek, *The Parallax View*, 341, 11. See also Žižek, "Preface: Burning the Bridges." In *The Žižek Reader*, eds. Elizabeth Wright and Edmond Wright (Oxford: Blackwell, 1999), ix.
19 Žižek, Eric L. Santner, and Kenneth Reinhard, "Preface, 2013." In *The Neighbor: Three Inquiries in Political Theology, with a New Preface* (Chicago: Chicago University Press, 2013), ix.
20 Levinas, *Entre Nous: On Thinking-of-the Other*, trans. Michael B. Smith and Barbara Harshav (New York: Columbia University Press, 1998), 101.
21 George Yancy, *Black Bodies, White Gazes: The Continuing Significance of Race in America* (Lanham: Rowman & Littlefield, 2008), xxxv.
22 Achille Mbembe, "Raceless Futures in Critical Black Thought," *Archives of the Nonracial* (June 30, 2014). Available online: https://www.youtube.com/watch?v=VkqmAi1yEpo (accessed January 21, 2022).
23 Badiou, *Ethics*, 20.
24 Ibid., 25.
25 Levinas, "The *I* and the Totality." In *Entre Nous: Thinking of the Other*, trans. Michael B. Smith and Barbara Harshav (New York: Columbia University Press, 1998), 28.
26 Žižek, *In Defense of Lost Causes* (New York: Verso, 2008), 165.
27 Žižek, "Neighbors and Other Monsters." In *The Neighbor: Three Inquiries in Political Theology*, eds. Slavoj Žižek, Eric L. Santner, and Kenneth Reinhard (Chicago: University of Chicago Press, 2006), 161.
28 Žižek, "Neighbors and Other Monsters," 162.
29 Ibid., 162.

30 Ibid., 140–1.
31 Žižek, *In Defense of Lost Causes*, 16.
32 Žižek, "Neighbors and Other Monsters," 162.
33 Ibid., 140.
34 Žižek and Daly, *Conversations with Žižek* (Cambridge: 2004, Polity), 71.
35 Frantz Fanon, *Black Skin, White Masks*, trans. Richard Philcox (New York: Grove Press, 2008), 202, translation modified.
36 Žižek, *In Defense of Lost Causes*, 16–17. See also Žižek, *Less than Nothing*, 831.
37 Žižek, *Less than Nothing*, 831.
38 Alexander G. Weheliye, *Habeas Viscus: Racializing Assemblages, Biopolitics, and Black Feminist Theories of the Human* (Durham: Duke University Press, 2014), 3.
39 Levinas, "Ethics and Politics." In *The Levinas Reader*, ed. Seán Hand (Oxford: Blackwell, 1989), 294.
40 Ibid., 294.
41 Levinas, *Ethics and Infinity: Conversations with Philippe Nemo*, trans. Richard A. Cohen (Pittsburgh: Duquesne University Press, 1985), 85.
42 Žižek, *Organs without Bodies: On Deleuze and Consequences* (New York: Routledge, 2004), 106.
43 Žižek, "Neighbors and Other Monsters," 183.
44 Žižek, *The Fragile Absolute*, 11.
45 Žižek, *Violence*, 117.
46 Žižek, "Whither Zionism?" *In These Times* (March 2, 2015). Available online: http://inthesetimes.com/article/17702/slavoj_zizek_zionism (accessed January 21, 2022).
47 Gianni Vattimo and Michael Marder, "Introduction: 'If Not Now, When?'" in *Deconstructing Zionism: A Critique of Political Metaphysics*, eds. Gianni Vattimo and Michael Marder (New York: Bloomsbury, 2013), xiii.
48 Vattimo and Michael Marder, "Introduction: 'If Not Now, When?'" xii.
49 Goldberg, *The Threat of Race*, 139.
50 Peretz Kidron, *Refusenik! Israel's Soldiers of Conscience* (New York: Zed Books, 2004), 76.
51 Žižek, *Welcome to the Desert of the Real*, 116.
52 Ibid., 116.
53 Ibid., 116.
54 Dominick LaCapra, *History and Its Limits: Human, Animal, Violence* (Ithaca: Cornell University Press, 2009), 43.
55 Žižek, "Neighbors and Other Monsters," 161.
56 Mbembe, "Necropolitics," *Public Culture* 15, no. 1 (2003): 27.
57 Žižek, "Anti-Semitism and Its Transformations." In *Deconstructing Zionism: A Critique of Political Metaphysics,* eds. Gianni Vattimo and Michael Marder (New York: Bloomsbury, 2013), 1–13, 6.

58 Žižek, "A Leftist Plea for 'Eurocentrism'," *Critical Inquiry* 24, no. 4 (1998): 988.
59 Žižek, "Anti-Semitism and Its Transformations," 6.
60 Ibid., 6.
61 Ibid., 6.
62 Bruno Chaouat, *Is Theory Good for the Jews? French Thought and the Challenge of the New Antisemitism* (Liverpool: Liverpool University Press, 2016), 66, 8–9.
63 Judith Butler, "Foreword." In *On Anti-Semitism: Solidarity and the Struggle for Justice* (Chicago: Haymarket Books, 2017), x.
64 Žižek, *The Parallax View*, 30.
65 Ibid., 30.
66 Derrida, *Of Hospitality*, 77.
67 Jacques Derrida, "Violence and Metaphysics," *Writing and Difference*, trans. Alan Bass (Chicago: University of Chicago Press, 1978), 151.
68 Derrida, "Violence and Metaphysics," 84.
69 Derrida, *Aporias*, 22.
70 Derrida, Rogues: *Two Essays on Reason*, trans. Pascale-Anne Brault and Michael Naas (Stanford: Stanford University Press, 2005), 60.
71 Žižek, *Welcome to the Desert of the Real*, 11.
72 Žižek, *Against the Double Blackmail*, 101.
73 Ibid., 46.
74 Ibid., 46–7.
75 Žižek, "The Need to Traverse the Fantasy," *In These Times* (December 28, 2015). Available online: http://inthesetimes.com/article/18722/Slavoj-Zizek-on-Syria-refugees-Eurocentrism-Western-Values-Lacan-Islam (accessed January 21, 2022).
76 John Caputo and Gianni Vattimo, *After the Death of God*, ed. Jeffrey W. Robbins (New York: Columbia University Press, 2007), 124–5. Quoted in Žižek's *First as Tragedy, Then as Farce* (New York: Verso, 2009), 77–8.
77 Žižek, *First as Tragedy*, 77–8.
78 Žižek, "Nobody Has to Be Vile," *London Review of Books* 28, 7 (April 6, 2006). Available online: https://www.lrb.co.uk/v28/n07/slavoj-zizek/nobody-has-to-be-vile (accessed January 21, 2022).
79 Karl Marx, "Letters from the Deutsch-Französische Jahrbücher." In *Collected Works of Marx and Engels*, Vol. 3 (New York: International Publishers, 1975), 142.
80 Kelly Oliver, *Carceral Humanitarianism: Logics of Refugee Detention* (Minneapolis: University of Minnesota Press, 2017), 15.
81 Žižek, *Against the Double Blackmail*, 7–8.
82 Ibid., 62–3.
83 Ibid., 9.

84 Ibid., 100, 110.
85 Žižek, Santner, and Reinhard, "Preface, 2013," ix.
86 Derrida, "Autoimmunity," 94.
87 Derrida, "Faith and Knowledge." In *Acts of Religion*, ed. Gil Anidjar (New York: Routledge, 2002), 87.
88 Roberto Esposito, *Terms of the Political: Community, Immunity, Biopolitics* (New York: Fordham University Press, 2013), 59.
89 Žižek, *Against the Double Blackmail*, 10.
90 Derrida, *Rogues*, 34.
91 Derrida, *Rogues*, 123.
92 Derrida, *Politics of Friendship*, trans. George Collins (New York: Verso, 1997), 76.
93 Žižek, "Neighbors and Other Monsters," 144.
94 Žižek, *Against the Double Blackmail*, 82.
95 Žižek, *Disparities*, 181.
96 Žižek, *Against the Double Blackmail*, 82.
97 Žižek, *Disparities*, 181.
98 Žižek, *Against the Double Blackmail*, 79.
99 Žižek, "A Leftist Plea for 'Eurocentrism,'" 997.
100 Žižek, *Against the Double Blackmail*, 110.
101 Edward Said, *Representations of the Intellectual* (New York: Vintage, 1996), 32.

Response to Zalloua

Slavoj Žižek

I immensely admire Zalloua's contribution for a simple reason: while basically sympathetic to my approach, he never abandons cold judgment and pointedly brings out some pertinent observations. He noted that, in my critique of deconstruction, I do not "sufficiently acknowledge the significant differences between Levinas and Derrida (both deemed founding members of the 'gang of democracy-to-come-deconstructionist-postsecular-Levinasian-respect-for-Otherness')." What I miss here is that, in contrast to Levinas, Derrida is much closer to my position since he emphasizes that "the injunction 'Love thy neighbor' is about loving the real neighbor, not the decaffeinated other of liberal multiculturalism. Derrida is equally critical of 'the idealized Other who dances fascinating dances and has an ecologically sound holistic approach to reality.'" (I fully accept his critique, although my stance towards Derrida remains basically critical—I've written about this extensively elsewhere.) In a very subtle analysis, Zalloua then deploys "how Europe's 'strange illogical logic' of autoimmunity, its self-destructive propensity, is also what enables Europe to improve, to endlessly perfect itself": "Doesn't Žižek's intervention presuppose a kind of autoimmune Europe, a Europe whose being (autoimmunity involves a process 'from which no region of being, phúsis or history would be exempt') and universality is precisely in question, a universality that ought to foreground its various communities?" This, I think, is the core question: how to think the universal dimension of European emancipatory legacy without falling into a new form of Eurocentrism? The answer is a notion of dislocation. Let's take a case from twentieth-century music. Bernard Herrmann's clarinet quintet "Souvenirs de voyage" (1967) opens up with the same melodic line that he used a decade earlier in the beginning of the most famous piece (scene d'amour) from his score of Hitchcock's *Vertigo* (1958). This is dislocation: an element (a melodic line, in this case) is torn out from its context and placed into a new context in which it is subordinated to a space regulated by a different logic. The same melodic line is first (in *Vertigo*) the opening moment of a movement that inexorably leads towards a romantic crescendo, heavily relying on Wagner's *Tristan*, while its reprisal in the quintet remains firmly within the pre-Wagnerian space of a theme and its variations. The surprising element here is the regressive direction of this shift: first a romantic push towards a climactic crescendo, then the step back to a more classical space in which such crescendos are excluded.

Such a notion of dislocation is a key dialectical concept whose proper understanding enables to dispel some key misunderstandings that haunt Hegel's notion of *Aufhebung* (sublation). Let's take a different case from the sphere of politics. Rejecting the idea of the Haitian Revolution as the true consummation of the ideals of the French Revolution, Jean Casimir argues in his *The Haitians: A Decolonial History* that "Haiti dislocates rather than consummates the project of modernity."[1] Casimir's critique is directed at all those (me included) who see in the Haitian Revolution the universalization and radicalization of the French Revolution: only through its repetition in Haiti does French Revolution really become a world-historical event with universal meaning. In this sense, the Haitian Revolution is the *Aufhebung* of the French Revolution: the full actualization of its potentials, its repetition at a higher level. From the standpoint of the predominant post-colonial thought, such a view is all too "Eurocentric": if the Haitian Revolution is reduced to the deployment of the immanent potentials of the French Revolution, then—to put it in Hegelese—the French Revolution, a European phenomenon, is the over-reaching notion and the Haitian Revolution remains a subordinate moment of its self-deployment. Even if Haitians were "more French than the French themselves," even if they went further and were more consequent than the French, they were part of the European dynamic process.

Dislocation, on the contrary, means that elements are thoroughly recontextualized, integrated into a new symbolic and social space which confers on them a new meaning unrelated to the original meaning—one can in no way "deduce" this new meaning from the original one. Let's take equality, a notion which originates in modern European thought. Although many advocates of equality worked to expand this notion also to women, other races, etc., such an expansion remains within the scope of the Western notion of equality. When a true other (black slaves, exemplarily) appropriates equality, this notion is not just expanded but transposed in a different domain which radically affects its functioning—the unease with Black Lives Matter proves this abundantly. Furthermore, is the entire history of Marxism and communist revolutions not a history of dislocations? In spite of Lenin's abundant quotes from Marx, Lenin effectively transposes Marx into a radically different historical situation in which the revolution was executed by a narrow party of professionals and won by addressing non-proletarian issues (land and peace). Mao Zedong did something even more radical: against Marx and Engels vision, he moved from workers to farmers in the countryside as the revolutionary force—something unimaginable for Marx and Engels. Again, in each of these two cases, we are not talking about a continuous expansion but about a radical dislocation—no wonder that in both cases, orthodox Marxist opposed the reorientation (the basic reproach of Mensheviks to Lenin was that, in a non-Marxist way, he wants a revolution before the circumstances for it are ripe).

We should also bear in mind that capitalism as such involves a process of continuous dislocation. Capitalism originated in Europe but then gradually expanded into a global economic order, and this expansion was not continuous, it involved radical dislocations. Not only was capitalism from the very beginning linked to colonization and new rise of slavery, but it also changed with the emergence of strong non-European capitalism countries like Japan, India and now China. Incidentally, it is interesting to note how the same post-colonial leftists who decry every expansion of equality and democracy as a dislocation and not a continuous development always insist that capitalist is "Eurocentric," attributed to Europe: even if it appears in China, India, etc., capitalism remains European. The underlying premise is clear: when a progressive idea like equality and democracy is expanded into a Third World, it involves a radical dislocation and is no longer European, but the "bad" capitalism remains a foreign (European) intruder. This mistake is serious because it misses the key fact that capitalism is actually universal, trans-cultural, indifferent toward particular cultures: it is not dislocated from one culture and then appropriated by another; rather, it stands for a universal dislocation from cultural space as such.

At this point, we can return to the relationship between the Hegelian sublation and dislocation: the approach which opposes the two (as we have seen with Casimir apropos Haiti) misses a key feature of the Hegelian dialectical process, it reduces subject to a dynamized Substance. The critics dismiss the Hegelian notion of democracy-and-equality as an all-encompassing substantial entity which gradually actualizes its immanent potentials, passing from one to another particular figure but remaining the same ground of the entire process. Let us imagine, the state goes through the stages of Asiatic despotic state, ancient slave-owning democracies, feudal monarchies, modern authoritarian state, etc., but all the stages mentioned are particular formations which emerge as the immanent deployment of the same notion of State. Now can this be the case?

If we remain at this abstract level, we have to add at least two points. First, for Hegel, the full consummation of an idea (when reality fits its idea) always implies the self-negation of this idea itself; say, the reality of states never fully fits the idea of state—when this happens, we no longer have a state but we pass into a religious community. Second, and more important, in a dialectical process the predicate always passes into subject: what was at the beginning a subordinate particular moment of the process asserts itself as its subject and retroactively posits its presuppositions as its own moments ("predicates"). So, again, it is not the same Subject which goes from one to another particular figure, remaining the same agent which pulls the strings and controls the entire movement: what Hegel calls "Absolute" is the very process in which radical reversals happen and a predicate turns into a new Subject. Every dialectical passage is thus a form of dislocation: the previous Substance is dislocated into a new encompassing universality. It is not the same Universality which passes from one to another particular form—in each passage, Universality itself is dislocated, it is reduced to a subordinate moment of a new Universality.

Let's take the passage from money to capital described by Marx: in pre-capitalist market exchange, money is a mediator of the exchange between producers which disappears in the final result (when I sell what I produce and buy what I need); with capitalism, however, money becomes capital, the subject (active agent) of the entire process. Although, from my individual standpoint, I produce (and sell) things so that I will get (other) things that I need (or desire) for my life, with capitalism, the true goal of the entire process is the expanded self-reproduction of capital itself—my needs and their satisfaction are just subordinated moments of capital's self-reproduction. In this sense, social production is radically dislocated, reduced to a subordinate moment of the capital's reproduction.

Back to Haiti, what further complicates the picture is that the tension between imitating Europe and breaking out of European modernity is inscribed into the very heart of the revolutionary process itself. Toussaint l'Ouverture, the first leader of free Haiti, insisted on the equality of all races and rejected any privileging of the blacks, plus, although he formally abolished slavery, he simultaneously imposed obligatory work (plantation workers had to remain at their post so that production was going on). The two leaders who came after him, Dessalines and Christophe, enacted the anti-white turn (all non-blacks with the exception of Poles who supported the revolution were massacred), but mandatory work remained, so that for ex-slaves things didn't change a lot. During Christophe's reign, Haiti was divided into two states: Christophe ruled as the emperor the northern part and Alexandre Petion the republic in the southern part. While the North turned into a half-feudal authoritarian imitation of a European modern state focused on boosting production and wealth (concentrated in the hands of the ruling black elite), in the republic in the South land was distributed to small farmers who survived in a self-subsistent economy with low productivity. Although some commentators celebrate the South as an attempt to develop new communal forms of life as an alternate outside to European modernity, the experiment soon failed. A further paradox to be noted here is that the anti-white shift from equality of races to black domination which occurred with Dessalines coincided with the rise of authoritarian class structure with the Emperor at the top which imitated the worst of European authoritarian modernity.

Similar paradoxes are already discernible in the case of Paraguay: before it was destroyed by the Spanish–Portuguese intervention, Paraguay under the domination of the Jesuit order which organized indigenous tribes into "reducciones" (missions) was not only an early form of communism but was also much closer to cultural independence than Argentina or Brasil. Jesuits were already printing books in Guarani language (which is even today spoken by the majority in Paraguay), so if Jesuits were not thrown out, the history of Latin America would take a different turn, with the aboriginal language becoming one of the official state languages. Throughout modern history, Jesuits were as a rule much more progressive than Franciscans, although (or precisely because) Jesuits were organized as dogmatic fanatics while Franciscans emphasizes poverty and spiritual inner life. Even today, Jesuits are the bastion of the Catholic Left while many Franciscans are neo-fascists. Brecht was right to copy ("dislocate") Jesuits sacred propaganda theatrical pieces in his communist "learning plays."

There is an important paradox in the distinction between Guarani spoken outside of the missions and the Jesuit Guarani: Jesuits constructed new words in Guarani to translate European notions while ordinary people simple incorporated hispanicisms:

> By and large, the Guarani of the Jesuits shied away from direct phonological loans from Spanish. Instead, the missionaries relied on the agglutinative nature of the language to formulate calque terms from native morphemes. This process often led the Jesuits to employ complicated, highly synthetic terms to convey Western concepts. By contrast, the Guarani spoken outside of the missions was characterized by a free, unregulated flow of hispanicisms; frequently, Spanish words and phrases were simply incorporated into Guarani with minimal phonological adaptation. A good example of that phenomenon is found in the word "communion." The Jesuits, using their agglutinative strategy, rendered this word "Tupârahava," a calque based on the word "Tupâ," meaning God. In modern Paraguayan Guaraní, the same word is rendered "komuño."[2]

We encounter something similar in many of today's languages (the state protects their purity, prohibiting anglicisms, etc.), but in the Jesuit Paraguay, foreign colonizers themselves played this role.

The point of these remarks apropos Zalloua's text is a very simple one: to complicate the standard binary of Eurocentrism versus postcolonial thought. What if the two are inextricably linked? What if European influence is not only an obstacle to decolonization, what if it can help it? As Zalloua knows very well, when we dream about post-colonial future, it is crucial that we take into account such paradoxes.

Notes

1 Jean Casimir, *The Haitians: A Decolonial History* (Chapel Hill: University of North Carolina Press, 2020). I rely here on Rocio Zambrana's "Hegelian History Interrupted" (to appear in *Crisis and Critique*).
2 Wikipedia entry on "Guarani language," see: https://en.wikipedia.org/wiki/Guarani_language (accessed January 27, 2022).

CHAPTER NINE

The Politics of Incompleteness
On Žižek's Theory of the Subject

Nadia Bou Ali

Slavoj Žižek's main objective since the 1990s has been to combine Lacanian psychoanalysis with German idealism in order to rectify what he perceives as the "fatal flaw of Western Marxism," which, because it is "constrained by the transcendental role of social practice as the ultimate horizon of our experience [...] cannot adequately take into account radical negativity as the crack in the Real which renders possible the rise of subjectivity."[1] Simply put, Žižek's entire project revolves around arguing for the political relevance of the Lacanian subject. But I want to suggest he never quite spells out in concrete terms how and where we can locate the Lacanian subject. This subject is the point of intersection between the Real, as an absent cause, and the symbolic, as a non-totalizable realm. The symbolic in Lacan's account is constituted by a chain of signifiers that is in turn inaugurated or grounded in a missing signifier, a traumatic kernel—as Žižek often maintains—that is part of the Real and cause of the symbolic. Furthermore, the relation of causality, between the Real and Symbolic, is of a peculiar kind: the Real is a cause but not a law as such; it is not part of a chain of causal determinations but rather "the cause qua the Real intervenes where the symbolic determination stumbles, misfires—that is where a signifier falls out."[2] It can "never effectuate its power in a direct way ... but must always operate immediately, under the guise of disturbances within the symbolic order."[3] The Real in Žižek's account is not simply immanent to the Symbolic, but is a cause that eludes "the grasp of the symbolic": it is neither immanent nor is it a transcendental condition of experience. Rather, the Real qua cause is a "redoubling" of a constitutive negativity of the Symbolic, reproduced through a *Nachträglichkeit*: it is a re-constitution of trauma based on a present deadlock. The Real, maintains Žižek, presents itself as a cause through a redoubling act: it is a "retroactive product of its own effects."[4] It is crucial to point out here that the trauma is not simply an event *in the past*, which the subject has to work through *in the present*: "the trauma has no existence of its own prior to symbolization; it remains an anamorphic entity that gains its consistency only in retrospect, viewed from within the symbolic horizon."[5]

Thus, the symbolic is fundamentally inconsistent and it folds or redoubles its inconsistency in the subject. The subject is thus the answer to the Real. Throughout his oeuvre, Žižek argues that this is not to be understood in terms of a linear determinism, or an essence/appearance or depth/ surface problem, but rather through a topological account that can represent the *extimate* status of the subject to structure. The object-cause is neither inside nor outside symbolic structure; it is *extimate* to structure and requires a topological model to cognize it. Furthermore, "the subject is strictly correlative to this real *qua* Cause."[6] By "correlative" Žižek means that the subject emerges as a response to the object cause, *objet a*, which in turn resists symbolization and subjectivization. The subject has to wrestle itself from its "shadow among the objects, a kind of stand-in for the subject, a pure semblance lacking any consistency of its own."[7]

In Žižek's account then, *objet a* is an uncanny double of the subject, it is the subject "itself in the mode of objectivity: an object which is the subject's absolute otherness precisely in so far as it is closer to the subject than anything the subject can set against itself in the domain of objectivity."[8]

And here resides what we could call the stakes of Žižek's account of subjectivity: on the one hand, he rejects the claim that this negativity—that is, the subject—can be ontologized, while, on the other hand, he refuses to simply reduce it to the transcendental-noumenal object. Žižek proposes to do this by reading Hegel through Lacan. Simply put, Žižek argues that in Hegel we have a similar version of the instability of the symbolic in the account of absolute necessity and the dialectical synthesis of necessity and contingency. Žižek argues that we can read Hegel's "substance as subject" as the retroactive becoming of contingency as necessity: the subject emerges when the contingent Real is retroactively narrativized as a necessity. The radical claim here is that rather than perceiving the subject as the site of exposition of the absolute in the particular, it is the other way around; the subject is the external point from which the inherent determination of the absolute occurs. There is no room here to engage at length with the complexity of Hegel's account of absolute knowledge and the problematics that are associated with it, not to mention Žižek's own singular reading of Hegel's corpus. But it's important to note that this account of the dialectic is rendered through the Lacanian understanding of causality discussed above, which can be summarized in Lacan's oft-quoted statement: "there is a cause only in something that doesn't work." The subject is the correlative of this object-cause. This is a fundamental Žižekian pillar, which he has maintained across his numerous works; one could even argue that his books all in one way or the other revolve around addressing this crucial question of the subject as non-ontological point of negativity in the *extimate* folds of unstable structures of signification.

In the *Sublime Object of Ideology*, which remains perhaps one of Žižek's most important books because it is the one where he grounds his analysis in Marx's notion of commodity fetishism, he argues that the subject emerges precisely at the site of failure of interpellation, where the law breaks down rather than succeeds. This subject is not equal to a homeostatic liberal individual, a self-transparent ego: "Subjects are not the 'effective' presence of 'flesh-and-blood' agents that make use of language as part of their social practices, filling abstract language schemes with actual contents: 'subject' is, on the contrary, the very abyss that forever *separates* language from the substantial life process."[9] So the subject is incomplete, and its incompleteness implies a non-ontological politics. Furthermore, this "incompleteness" of the subject poses the question of sex or the problem of sexuality.

In *Sex and the Failed Absolute*, Žižek argues that psychic life turns around repetition, which cannot be totalized. There is no exception to the pleasure principle; it is compelled by a drive that has no other purpose to it but the compulsion itself. For Žižek, Lacan maintains, contra Badiou, a universality (the problem of sex) as a non-All that has no exception. Moreover, while Badiou's subject, for Žižek, is the masculine exception to the human animal, for Lacan the subject is feminine, a "self-sabotaging withdrawal that undermines from within the smooth functioning of the human animal."[10] Like Alenka Zupančič, Žižek maintains that the universality of the question of sexual difference is not the difference between two sexes (feminine and masculine) but the "same difference which cuts from within each of the two sexes, making each of them thwarted, unequal-to-itself." It is not a difference between two identities, masculine and feminine, but a difference between identity and difference as such, a "pure difference." However, although sexual difference is its own "meta-difference" without it having a meta language, there is a further difference to the "two functionings of sexual difference."[11] Although the masculine and feminine are not identities, there is a difference between them as "modes of sexual difference": "between masculine human universality and its feminine exception and from the feminine standpoint a difference between feminine non-all and masculine non-exception."[12]

Žižek explicates this difference *in* difference through Lacan's formulas of sexuation, which he reads as a different iteration of Kant's antinomies of pure reason.[13] Lacan's claim *there is no sexual relation* is homological to Kant's premise that our knowledge cannot correspond to reality in-itself. If we try to establish this correspondence, we end up totalizing reality and falling into irreconcilable antinomies. Like the antinomies of pure reason, the formulas of sexuation arise from the impasse that presents itself when the subject attempts to symbolize its sexuality. In this attempt to symbolize its sexuality, or, in other words, identify its desire, the subject stumbles upon a mode of enjoyment, the *jouissance* that drives it. While Kant's claim is that the moral law is established through the triumph of the supra-sensuous over the sensuous, such that reason and morality have to harness nature and pathological drives, Lacan maintains that the gap lies not between the supersensuous and the sensuous but within the sensuous itself, which is a non-All: "There is no exception to the sensuous order, but we nonetheless cannot totalize it, i.e., this order remains non-all. In other words, insofar as the sensuous is overcome here, it is not overcome into another, higher dimension but from within, caught into its own inconsistency—this is the immanent tension that characterizes what Lacan calls *jouissance feminine*."[14]

It is important to note here that there is nothing about sex that is natural. In this perspective, the sensuous is immanently divided, cut through by an antagonism within itself, and not simply with the higher moral order of the supra-sensuous. The Kantian transcendental is itself divided; it is "antinomic, traversed by immanent inconsistencies."[15] Despite many vulgar accounts of psychoanalysis, there is nothing natural or biological about sex or sexuation. Freud before Lacan pointed to the impasse of sexuality for the human subject; simply put, sex poses the problem of identification for the subject. However, this is where the problem with Žižek lies from the perspective of transgender studies: if sex is an imperative, it opens up the problem of the Real in subjective experience; but why must the Real still be symbolized according to the feminine/ masculine divide; or, stated otherwise, why is it important to name the difference within difference as either feminine and masculine? In other words, why does Žižek maintain the feminine and masculine as an antinomical pair of sexuation? This is the fundamental objection that Žižek has received from gender theorists like Judith Butler. While the Lacanian account of the feminine and masculine is that they are inherently unstable structures, Žižek is seen to maintain a heterosexual account of the familial complex. Thus there is much at stake in how we assess Žižek's account of sexual difference.

The entire wager of post-Lacanian theories of the subject lies here: sexual difference is the incompleteness of the subject (Slavoj Žižek and Mladen Dolar's term, sex for Alenka Zupančič, etc.), it is the opening and the site for any emancipatory politics. Judith Butler, on the other hand, maintains that the site of negativity bears on the problem of universality insofar as it flags an exclusion: in other words, the empty form of the universal for Butler flags "the evidence"[16] of the processes of exclusion by which universality is constituted. Contra Žižek, Butler maintains that the "constitutive lack" of subjectivity must be offered an adequate social constructivist account lest it remain an empty form. Butler holds the view that the negativity in question, which she designates using the term "foreclosure," cannot be assumed to precede the space of the social and is not "explicable through the recourse to structuralist accounts of kinship."[17] So while she agrees with Lacan that negativity is constitutive of the social link, she takes issue with its nomination as "incest taboo" or "castration." The main point of contention here concerns the nomination of trauma: as "Real," "point of exclusion," or "constitutive lack." If all identity emerges from trauma (a point on which Butler and Žižek agree, if we disregard for the sake of our argument here some major disagreements), the main point of contention is: why does the trauma have to be retroactively interpreted via a "transcultural structure . . . that presupposes a sociality" that pre-assumes the heterosexual family as the model of kinship? Butler claims that sexual difference is the name for subjective trauma: "sexual difference is distinguished from other struggles within hegemony precisely because those other struggles—'class' and 'nation,' for instance—do not simultaneously name a fundamental and traumatic difference and a concrete, contingent historical identity."[18] Taking issue with what she considers to be Žižek's empty formalism of sexual difference, Butler invokes Hegel's objections to the emptiness of Kantian formalism: "the empty and formal structure is established precisely through the not fully successful sublimation of content as form. It is not adequate to claim that the formal structure of sexual difference is first and foremost without content, but that it comes to be 'filled in' with content by a subsequent and anterior act."[19] Although there is much to say about the Žižek–Butler debate, I want to focus on this specific problem of sublimation, or failed sublimation, that is at work in the positing of universality as a form that subsumes its content but is irreducible to it; a whole that is in excess of its parts, or more than their sum. Sublimation is not restitution, à la Melanie Klein where the subject is driven by the *restitution* of the mother's body that has been lost; rather, sublimation is fundamentally about social recognition; it is, simply put, about what society finds satisfying. Žižek maintains that sublimation is "not the opposite of sexualization but is equivalent."[20] Sublimation is our way of making sense of the not-all of sex *and* ontology:

> Reality is not-One, which doesn't simply mean that it is multiple: not-One, the impossibility of being One, is inscribed into it as its own innermost condition of (im)possibility. What this means is that a deontological tension is inscribed into the very heart of ontology: reality is in itself thwarted, it cannot be what it should be immanently. Or, in more Hegelian terms, One emerges as One only through a self-relating which opposes its one-ness to all its particular properties shared by others, so it has to divide itself into One in contrast to its properties.[21]

Žižek insists that every self-identity is predicated on a failure to identify it via its predicates:

> The assertion of self-identity is thus the assertion of the difference itself: not just the difference of the thing from all other things (in the sense of differentiality), but the difference of a thing with regard to itself, the

difference which cuts across a thing, the difference between the series of its predicates (defining its positive features)—"A rose is a rose" means the rose cannot be reduced to the series of its predicates. In a nice case of the link between identity and failure, every self-identity is thus grounded in a failure of predicates.[22]

The masculine position fails in its position to be masculine, as does the female position. This failure to differentiate the self or the difference in its becoming precedes and undercuts the difference between two positions and it is this differentiation in difference that is sexual difference. It is the Real of sex which undercuts the subject from within. This *extimate* status of sex, however, does not justify why we need to maintain these two positions of difference. If the masculine and feminine are indeed disrupted internally by their own difference to themselves, why do we need to maintain them as opposite poles of the antinomy of sex? Furthermore, if sexuation is sublimation, as Žižek maintains, then how would a different sublimation look concretely? I.e., if the paternal function or the crisis in the symbolic, by which Žižek characterizes modernity, is followed by the logic of multiplicity (1 + 1 + 1 + 1), what would a proper sublimation of the not-All of sex be like? How does this connect to the culture of capitalism? Žižek's resort to Christian theology and to love of the neighbor does not provide us with a sustained engagement with the question of how the problem of sexuation relates to the real abstractions of capitalist society. Is the real enemy the logic of multiplicity everywhere in the same way? Must we not ground it in its relation to law and to conditions of labor in different contexts of capital?

Another objection to add here is that while the account of sexual difference proposed by Žižek is crucial it does not go all the way to engage with how the body becomes the *extimate* site of intersection of language and enjoyment for the subject. Žižek's "gap in reality" has to be extended to engage with the question of the body and how it is conceived psychoanalytically. It is not enough to assert that the feminine and masculine position are inherently unstable; the body itself has to be theorized as the site of a cut and an instability, insofar as it is subjected to the work of the signifier and is the very site of the splitting of the subject. This is Lacan's fundamental move away from Freud's Oedipal horizon. There is no question that despite his radical claims about sexuality (as being originally polymorphous) Freud remained limited to his Oedipal account of castration, whereas Lacan proposed that the symbolic is constituted via a cut. The signifier introduces a cut into the body; a cut that is pre-ontological, beyond the division between what is and isn't yet constitutive of it.

Samo Tomšič's framing of this problem provides a valuable supplement to Žižek here:

> The signifier, this basic unit of language itself, stands for the cut, which produces a redoubling within the same "extended substance," a symbolic

body in the living body. The notion of the signifier thus complicates the conception of the body, since it stands for the material cause of the *bodily* split, in which the biological is reworked and provided a different type of extension from the Cartesian one.[23]

Žižek takes the problem of sexual difference, the main question pertaining to the subject of the unconscious, to underlie fundamental questions in post Hegelian philosophy. But he grounds it all in the space opened up by the Cartesian cogito. The move that Žižek makes by replacing the Kantian antinomies with the antinomies of sexuation is aimed toward the central thesis he repeats throughout his work: the incompleteness of the subject and its retroactive positing through an unconscious structure of repetition.[24]

This claim about subjectivity is what drives Žižek's materialism; a materialism forged along the internal limits of idealism as a torsion in the self-positing subject. Many scholars have objected that Žižek's materialism is actually an idealism.[25] While these criticisms are worth engaging with, the most crucial question remains: what politics is adequate to the psychoanalytic concept of the incomplete subject? What kind of politics can speak to the anxious subject of psychoanalysis and how is it different from the fascist liberal bind in which we find ourselves in the present moment? In other words, how can the sexed incomplete subject be the subject of emancipatory politics? If the incomplete subject lends itself both to a liberal politics of recognition and to a reactionary politics of identification, what is it after all that is so radical about the Žižekian subject, beyond the undeniably important correctives it offers to traditional ontology and philosophy?

Žižek often resorts to theology to answer this question, through a Kierkegaardian return to Hegel via Schelling and Fichte. Although he insists his is a Marxist materialism, à la dialectical materialism via quantum physics, Žižek persists in thinking of the (failed) absolute without shoring up a concrete theory of politics or critical social theory. It is true that Marxism requires supplementation for its shortcoming with regards to the transcendental account of social practices that it offers—which as Žižek maintains falls short of the constitutive negativity that is the subject—but what are the concrete determinations of this overcoming? Žižek, and the Slovenian school more generally, expose the complicity between liberal and reactionary ideologies and the fantasies that sustain them. They also offer a serious and welcome corrective to the Millerian co-optation of Lacan into a liberal conservatism. However, the fundamental social forms of capitalism beg consideration if we are to develop a theory of subjectivity that is adequate for emancipation. These forms have to be named: property or ownership of means of production (and its relation to particular religions), bourgeois law, and productive activity. This is not to say that the Žižekian account of subjectivity (as non-relational) does not bear on these crucial aspects of the social relation, but it is important to note that his account remains tethered to the most speculative moment of Marx's exposition of capital, commodity fetishism.[26] Žižek does locate this moment as the site of contradiction between subject and substance or the misrepresentation of actuality as consciousness. However, there is no account of *bildung* of culture beyond capitalist culture, or of a possible re-formation of subjectivity. What Žižek, unlike Lacan, leaves us with is a subject that is destitute but full of anxiety. What we need for emancipation are more subjects who are capable of working through anxiety towards certainty. This certainty about what kind of world we wish to have and be in can only succeed in its aims if it has a determinate ethical and political content beyond an abstract act of conversion, or a declaration of a belief in a (lost) cause.

There are two implications that develop from Žižek's corpus: 1) an ethics of psychoanalysis (rather than a politics of psychoanalysis) grounded in 2) an act that concretizes the actuality of freedom as the recognition of constraint *and* the realization of a logic of causality that is non-linear or determinate. This is not too far from Marx's own position in relation to consciousness: Marx after all maintained that there is no structural change possible in capital without a change in consciousness. Žižek maintains that there is no structural change possible in capital without an avowal of the unconscious as the unacknowledged "change in consciousness" that is already there. But how can the subjective act, or the retroactive self-positing of the split that is the subject, become revolutionary practice? What is political about the incomplete subject? The question is important because the relation between capitalism and politics "is not an abstract question about the relation between theory and practice, but a phenomenological question about the relationship between acknowledgement of actuality and the possibility of change."[27] The utopian answer of the Frankfurt School is surely no longer satisfying alone. However, Marcuse's notion of repressive desublimation, which should be contrasted with Lacanian surplus-enjoyment, did at least construct a Utopian idea which kept real the possibility of an alternative, a stubborn negation of what is. With Žižek, we have a diagnosis of postmodern culture, one of generalized perversion as he claims, in the wake of collapse of parental authority and the transformation of the individual from a self-reflexive subject to a narcissistic subject of enjoyment.[28] Although Žižek is an astute diagnostician of the postmodern condition, of the dismantlement of the social bond by capitalism, he sometimes comes dangerously close to the neo-conservative Right that also blames our current crisis on the decline of paternal authority. The rise of populist figures of authority in our contemporary moment is a response to the crisis in the symbolic. As Mladen Dolar put it once: "it turns out Trump is a Lacanian". The reason why we are so anxious about figures of authority like Trump is because they fill the lack in the symbolic, create a lack of lack.

The symbolic crisis engendered by capitalist modernity requires, according to Žižek, a "radical anti-humanism" which can deal with the death-drive that is constitutive of subjectivity. Žižek resorts to a Christian ethics of neighborliness as what is capable of suspending the disavowal of monstrosity in the subject. His anti-liberalism and Romanticism lead him toward a flirtation with the "irrationalist reactions to modernity."[29] Žižek's most interesting critics have hoped that he would not reject political rationalism all together.[30] I am reminded here of Jean Claude Milner's statement in *L'oeuvre claire* that Lacan somehow realized that *politics is destined to be out of sync with the modern universe*, in which the unconscious has already been discovered. The modern universe, in which signifiers [of science] have real material effects, is the one after all within which the subject of the unconscious is located. In it, on the one hand, politics always falls short of the revolutions in thought that characterize modernity, plagued by repetition compulsions and the return of the repressed. The ego itself is an avatar of all that has passed and haunts our modern condition. And it is also in modernity that the field of psychoanalysis forms, which since Freud is very much characterized by a stated indifference to politics, yet completely steeped in political questions from the start identity, sex, group formations, etc.

Lacan's claim that all of history is fallacious has to be taken to mean that the unconscious isn't only specific to capitalist society. However, it emerges as a (un)concept within the purview of the modern scientific episteme which in turn is coincidental to the rise of modern capitalism. The unconscious has implications for how we consider the universe entirely, or, as Milner puts it, "the word 'unconscious' stands for the inexistence of anything that might be considered beyond-the-universe." Lacan's claim—with which Žižek agrees— is that God is unconscious and that while modern science attacks precisely this God and the world of antiquity, psychoanalysis attacks the Ego, whose avatars (or super-egos for Žižek) we see parading in a society organized around commodity production. If the unconscious stands for the inexistence of anything that maybe considered beyond the universe, then how can we ensure that sexual difference, or the incompleteness of the subject, is not hypostasized as an abstract form devoid of content? Not in the sense of Butlerian exclusion discussed above, but rather from a purely speculative position? Does not the ethical and theological act of self-positing of subjectivity, albeit always incomplete, not fall short of the transformation of ethical life, or actual world as property, which is in turn also subjective and not fully objective? Why does revolution have to be conceived according to the model of theological conversion, a point of lawless exception, whereas the revolution could be a "concept that commands" the lawless world of capital?

This missing element in the Žižekian account of subjectivity, is perhaps not surprising. Perhaps it is easier to get rid of capitalism than to get rid of psychoanalysis. The former may be necessary and desirable while the latter is not. Perhaps the real question is: will there ever be a time when psychoanalysis will no longer be necessary for the speaking being ... how can we get rid of psychoanalysis? The political question is lacking in both Lacan and Marx, but remains un-addressable without putting the two together. The overcoming of capitalism cannot but go by way of a revolution in consciousness, beginning from its inner torsions and negativities, but neither psychoanalysis nor Marx alone can offer an alternative symbolic, a new S1 that can reorganize discourse and re-knot subjectivity.

Notes

1. Slavoj Žižek, *Sex and the Failed Absolute* (London: Bloomsbury, 2019), 93.
2. Slavoj Žižek, *Metastases of Enjoyment: Six Essays on Women and Causality* (London: Verso, 2006), 30.
3. Ibid.
4. Ibid., 31.
5. Ibid.
6. Ibid., 32.
7. Ibid., 33.
8. Ibid.
9. Žižek, Slavoj, *For They Know Not What They Do: Enjoyment as a Political Factor* (London: Verso, 1991), 201.
10. Žižek, *Sex and the Failed Absolute*, 330.
11. Ibid, 256.
12. Ibid.
13. Joan Copjec pointed to this before Žižek in "Sex and the Euthanasia of Reason." In *Supposing the Subject* (London: Verso, 1994), 16–45.
14. Žižek, *Sex and the Failed Absolute*, 183.
15. Ibid, 187.
16. Judith Butler, Ernest Laclau, and Slavoj Žižek, *Contingency, Hegemony, Universality: Contemporary Dialogues on the Left* (London: Verso, 2000), 137.
17. Ibid.
18. Ibid., 143.
19. Ibid.
20. Žižek, *Sex and the Failed Absolute*, 180.
21. Ibid., 189–90.
22. Ibid.
23. Samo Tomšič, "The Ontological Limbo." In *Extimacies: Encounters between Psychoanalysis and Philosophy*, edited by Nadia Bou Ali and Surti Singh (forthcoming).
24. Refer to Peter Osborne, "More than Everything: Žižek's Badiouian Hegel." In *Radical Philosophy* 177 (January/February 2013), 19–25.
25. Refer to Mathew Sharpe and Geoff Boucher, *Žižek and Politics: A Critical Introduction* (Edinburgh University Press, 2010) and Matthew Sharpe, Geoff Boucher, and Jason Glynos (eds,), *Traversing the Fantasy: Critical Responses to Slavoj Žižek* (Ashgate, 2005).

26 Refer to Gillian Rose's discussion of Marx in *Hegel Contra Sociology* (Athlone Press, 1981), 210–20.
27 Ibid., 218.
28 Geoff Boucher and Mathew Sharpe trace this development well in *Žižek and Politics*.
29 Ibid., 218.
30 Mathew Sharpe and Geoff Boucher in *Žižek and Politics: A Critical Introduction*, 204.

Response to Bou Ali

Slavoj Žižek

I am grateful to Nadia Bou Ali for providing a precise and rigorous résumé of the basic critical point that Judith Butler made against my (Lacanian) notion of sexual difference. Butler accuses me of ahistorical Kantian formalism: of elevating sexual difference into a trans-historical a priori, i.e., of ignoring how Lacan's notion of sexual difference is grounded in a specific patriarchal historical constellation. But Bou Ali does not just recapitulate Butler's line of argumentation; she also endeavors to draw the political implications of the psychoanalytic notion of an incomplete subject, expressing her doubt that the incompleteness of the subject is "the opening and the site for any emancipatory politics": for Bou Ali, incompleteness alone just reproduces the anxiety of a contemporary subject, and this anxiety alone is not enough to break the "fascist/liberal bind in which we find ourselves in the present moment"—more is needed, a passage from anxiety to certainty, to a new positive emancipatory project that clearly formulates what we want. (Incidentally, I think the term "incomplete subject" is not enough to characterize the subject implied by psychoanalytic theory: every evolutionary liberal would agree with it and emphasize that emancipation is an endless process, there is nothing specifically Freudian or Lacanian about it; Butler herself comes all too close to such liberal "incompleteness," advocating the infinite process of the subject's performative reconstruction, of gradually gaining more and more freedom.)

But let's begin at the beginning: against what she rejects as the formal universalism of Lacan's notion of sexual difference, Bou Ali makes the Butlerian point that every universality, every universal form, is constituted through an exclusion, and that this exclusion is not an ahistorical a priori but "must be offered an adequate social constructivist account lest it remain an empty form. Butler holds the view that the negativity in question, which she designates using the term 'foreclosure,' cannot be assumed to precede the space of the social." If (as Lacan does) we call this constitutive exclusion "symbolic castration," we already elevate into a trans-historical a priori a phallocentric notion of castration that pertains to patriarchal order. My point is here exactly the opposite one: every and any "space of the social" is based on some grounding "foreclosure" (I prefer Freud's name *Ur Verdraengung*, "primordial repression," since "foreclosure" stands for psychotic exclusion). This "primordial repression" is not preceding historical processes, it is their pre-supposition, their retroactively posited ground. So can we break out of it? Yes, but then this will no longer be sexuality as we understand it, it will be a totally different economy of pleasures. The dream of another sexuality without "castration" is the same as the dream of "alternate modernity" without capitalism: there is no modernity outside capitalism, outside capitalist antagonisms.[1]

In contrast with Butler for whom some part of content is always excluded from (what claims to be) the universal form, I maintain that the very gap between content and form is to be reflected back into content itself, as an indication that this content is not all, that something was repressed/excluded from it. So universal form is not primarily the agency of censorship which excludes some content, it is simultaneously the return of the repressed. Recall the classic case of universal human rights: their first formulation, of course excluded (or reduced to a marginal place, at least) women, other races, the poor, etc.; however, the very fact of the universal form, of its excess over particular content, simultaneously opened up the space for the expansion of the content of human rights—why not also women (Mary Wollstonecraft), why not also blacks (Haiti revolution), why not also poor workers (socialism)? Butler is aware of this, but, in her very radical historicism, she is not historical enough; she de facto advocates an ever-expanding liberal universality. For Butler, since every universal form implies an excluded part of its content, the task of the emancipatory politics is to engage in the endless process of opening up the universality so that it will include these repressed elements: all the different forms of non-patriarchal sexuality, etc. But the question to be raised here is: is what one cannot but call her anthropological constant (sexual identity is not a natural or ideal fact but the result of the permanent process of performative social process of construction) not her own universal premixes? In contrast to her, I think that the notion of the plasticity of sexuality as a contingent process of performative construction is not simply a universal fact but is also rooted in our late-capitalist society in which subjective identities appear as contingent constructions. We can, of course, say that the sexuality of first humans was also discursively constructed but we can say this only retroactively, from the perspective of today's late capitalism which dissolves all fixed forms of identity. In short, in the same way Marx wrote that the universal concept of work, although present in all human societies, becomes social reality only with capitalism in which the actual worker experiences their work as an abstraction (they can in principle permanently change profession), the same goes for sexuality.

I would only add two qualifications to this point. First, what Butler presents as the emancipatory project is for me a fact of today's global capitalism, its hegemonic ideology which persists in spite of all temporary setbacks. Marx and Engels wrote more than 150 years ago, in the first chapter of *The Communist Manifesto*: "The bourgeoisie, wherever it has got the upper hand, has put an end to all feudal, *patriarchal*, idyllic relations."[2] These lines are still ignored by those leftist cultural theorists who focus their critique on patriarchal ideology and practice. Is it not the time to start to wonder about the fact that the critique of patriarchal "phallogocentrism," etc. was elevated into a main target at the very historical moment—ours—when patriarchy definitely lost its hegemonic role, when it is progressively swept away by market individualism of rights? What becomes of patriarchal family values when a child can sue his parents for neglect and abuse, i.e., when family and parenthood itself are *de jure* reduced to a temporary and dissolvable contract between independent individuals? (And, incidentally, Freud was no less aware of this: for him, the decline of the Oedipal mode of socialization was the historical condition of the rise of psychoanalysis.) In other words, *the critical statement that patriarchal ideology continues to be today's hegemonic ideology* is today's hegemonic ideology—its function is to enable us to evade the deadlock of the hedonist permissiveness which is effectively hegemonic.

Second qualification: the idea that every universality is based on an exclusion is one of the basic Lacan's insights, but he opposes it to the "feminine" mode of non-all field with no exception. So why two modes—or, to quote Bou Ali: "If the masculine and feminine are indeed disrupted internally by their own difference to themselves, why do we need to maintain them as opposite poles of the antinomy of sex?" My answer: because they are disrupted in a thoroughly different way, i.e., because what Lacan calls the "masculine" and "feminine" side of the formulas of sexuation is not a fixed identity but the name of an irreducible deadlock, impasse. Sexual difference, although a fact of the symbolic order, is nonetheless a sublimation of what is ultimately a biological fact of reproduction. However, the term "sublimation" is to be used here in a precise Lacanian sense: not sublimation in the sense of the transposition of some raw real into a socially acknowledged symbolic form but, on the opposite, the elevation of a rather common biological fact to the level of an impossible Thing.

What Lacan calls "symbolic castration" is not a universal form which represses (fails to sublimate) some content which remains outside (like non-Oedipal sexualities). It is a cut which establishes the entire field of public sphere and its specific repressed. So when Bou Ali approvingly quotes Butler: "the empty and formal structure is established precisely through the not fully successful sublimation of content as form," I disagree with the notion of sublimation used here—sublimation as a censoring agency which permits content to pass through only if it fits the criteria of what is publicly acceptable: "sublimation is fundamentally about social recognition; it is, simply put, about what society finds satisfying." Here, again, I disagree: what society in its public discourse doesn't find satisfying is its specific repressed—unwritten rules, obscene supplements which are socially not recognized but necessary. This is what I call the structure of inherent transgression: a social space is not just the space of what is permitted but also the space of what is repressed, excluded from public space, and simultaneously necessary for this public space to reproduce itself. Here is an old example of mine. When Bill Clinton's administration resolved the deadlock of gays in the US Army with the compromise of "Don't ask, don't tell!" (i.e., soldiers are not directly asked if they are gay, so they are also not compelled to lie and deny it; although they are not officially allowed in the army, they are tolerated insofar as they keep their sexual orientation private and do not actively endeavor to engage others in it), this opportunist measure was deservedly criticized for basically endorsing homophobic attitudes: although the direct prohibition of homosexuality is not to be enforced, its very existence as a virtual threat compelling gays to remain in the closet affects their actual social status. In other words, what this solution amounted to was an explicit elevation of hypocrisy into a social principle, like the attitude toward prostitution in traditional Catholic countries—if we pretend that gays in the army do not exist, it is as if they effectively do not exist (for the big Other). Gays are to be tolerated, on condition that they accept the basic censorship concerning their identity. While fully justified at its own level, the notion of censorship at work in this criticism, with its Foucauldian background of Power which, in the very act of censorship and other forms of exclusion, generates the excess it endeavors to contain and dominate, nonetheless seems to fall short at a crucial point: what it misses is the way in which censorship not only affects the status of the marginal or subversive force that the power discourse endeavors to dominate, but, at an even more radical level, splits from within the power discourse itself. One should ask here a naive, but nonetheless crucial question: why does the army universe so strongly resist publicly accepting gays into its ranks? There is only one consistent answer possible: not because homosexuality poses a threat to the alleged "phallic and patriarchal" libidinal economy of the army community, but, on the contrary, because the libidinal economy of the army community itself relies on a thwarted/disavowed homosexuality as the key component of the soldiers' male-bonding.

From my own experience, I remember how the old infamous Yugoslav People's Army was homophobic to the extreme (when someone was discovered to have homosexual inclinations, he was instantly turned into a pariah, treated as a non-person, before being formally dismissed from the army), yet, at the same time, everyday army life was excessively permeated with the atmosphere of homosexual innuendos. For example, while soldiers were standing in line for their meal, a common vulgar joke was to stick a finger into the ass of the person ahead of you and then to withdraw it quickly, so that when the surprised person turned around, he did not know who among the soldiers behind his back sharing a stupid obscene smile did it. A predominant form of greeting a fellow soldier in my unit, instead of simply saying "Hello!", was to say "Smoke my prick!" ("Pusi kurac!" in Serbo-Croat); this formula was so standardized that it completely lost any obscene connotation and was pronounced in a totally neutral way, as a pure act of politeness.

The key point not to be missed here is how this fragile co-existence of extreme and violent homophobia with thwarted, i.e., publicly non-acknowledged, "underground" homosexual libidinal economy, bears witness to the fact that the discourse of the military community can only be operative by way of censoring its own libidinal foundation. Do we as well not encounter outside the confines of military life, a strictly homologous self-censoring mechanism in the contemporary conservative populism with its sexist and racist bias? Against the image, all-present in cultural criticism, of a radical subversive discourse or practice "censored" by the Power, one is even tempted to claim that today, more than ever, the mechanism of censorship intervenes predominantly to enhance the efficiency of the power discourse itself.

This ambiguous status of homosexuality in the Yugoslav army is also a perfect example of what Marcuse called "repressive desublimation." However, if we follow Lacan's precise definition of sublimation, then Marcuse's idea of "liberated persons" who are able to experience "the non-repressive desublimation of resexualizing their polymorphously perverse bodies" is a utopian nonsense—why? For Lacan, "repressive desublimation" cannot be opposed to non-repressive desublimation because *desublimation is* as such *repressive*, which is why perversion in which the subject actualizes its dirtiest fantasies is, as Lacan pointed out, the hidden part of any oppressive power. For Lacan, sexual drive as such relies on sublimation: sublimation elevates an ordinary worldly object to the level of the impossible Thing—this is how sublimation sexualizes an ordinary object. Lacan reads sublimation in the Kantian way: what is prohibited in sublimation is not the direct object but the impossible Thing—that's the basic paradox here: what is prohibited is already in itself impossible to reach. In sublimation, we shift from one to another object to catch the elusive Thing which eludes already the direct object.

To make this crucial point in a more precise way, a brief excursus into identity and difference is needed. For Hegel, identity is the most radical form of difference, difference brought to its self-reference, not just in the obvious sense that a thing's identity is defined by the difference from all other things but above all in the sense that "identity" names the difference of a thing with itself, a thing's difference from all its particular properties (each of which can be shared by other things): a thing "is" not its properties, it "is" a unique receptable of its properties. This is why, for Hegel, identity and difference are moments of the logic of essence, reflexive determinations—this reflexive structure is absent in the logic of being, i.e., when we talk about, say, a quality, this quality does not have an "identity" in the described sense.

However, we have to add another reversal here: not only is identity difference brought to its self-reference (or, rather, self-relating); difference itself (at its most radical, as an impossible-real that cannot be reduced to symbolic differentiality) also acquires its own identity as a separate entity which cannot be reduced to the difference between the two terms it differentiates. We thus have three elements at work in such a difference: the two opposed elements *and* their difference "as such" existing apart from the two as a separate entity. Let's take the two obvious cases: sexual difference (for a Lacanian) and class difference (for a Marxist). Class difference (or its political expression, Left and Right) is "real" in the sense that every determination of the difference is already partial, "colored" by one of the two sides—there is no "neutral" determination of class difference, and this is what Lacan means by "there is no meta-language": we cannot take a look at class difference from a neutral standpoint exempted from class difference. But—now comes the paradox we are aiming at—class struggle means precisely that a society is never clearly differentiated into two classes (the ruling one and the subordinated one): there is always "at least one," a third element which doesn't fit this opposition ("middle classes," "rabble")—if there were just two classes, we wouldn't have a struggle but just a stable co-existence of the two classes. (Or, a more problematic case, in anti-Semitism, the figure of the Jew stands for class antagonism as such: without the Jew, society would be a harmonious hierarchic order, and the Jew is the foreign intruder which triggers antagonism and class struggle—what anti-Semitism disavows is that social hierarchy is already in itself antagonistic.) This third element, in its very positive existence, works as a stand-in for the difference as antagonistic, irreducible to symbolic differentiality—in short, there is no original plurality (multiple positions) which then is then reduced to two fixed identities plus something that remains, what is primordial is the antagonism itself. In sexuality, this third element which gives body to sexual difference as such (as the real of an antagonism) are *trans-subjects*: they are not external to sexual difference, a remainder of some primordial polymorphous-perverse multiplicity; they are constitutive of sexual difference as such, the privileged point of its positive existence.

Back to our central line: the exclusion which establishes the form itself is the "primordial repression / *Ur-Verdrängung/*," and no matter how much we bring out all the repressed content, this gap of primordial repression persists—again, why? The immediate answer is the identity of the repression with the return of the repressed, which means that the repressed content does not pre-exist repression, but is retroactively constituted by the very process of repression. Through different forms of negation/obfuscation (condensation, displacement, denegation, disavowal, etc.), the repressed is allowed to penetrate the public conscious speech, to find an echo in it (the most direct example from Freud: when one of his patients said, "I do not know who this woman in my dream is, but I am sure she is not my mother!", mother entered the speech)—we get here a kind of "negation of negation," i.e., the content is negated/repressed, but this repression is in the same gesture itself negated in the guise of the return of the repressed (which is why we are definitely not dealing here with the proper Hegelian negation of negation). The logic seems here similar to that of the relationship between sin and Law in Paul, where there is no sin without Law, i.e., where the Law/prohibition itself creates the transgression it tries to subdue, so that, if we take away the Law, we also lose what the Law tried to "repress," or, in more Freudian terms, if we take away the "repression," we also lose the repressed content. Is the proof not provided by today's typical patient whose reaction to the same dream would have been: "I do not know who this woman in my dream is, but I am sure she has something to do with my mother!" He says this, but there is no liberation, no truth-effect, no shift in his subjective position—why? Again, what remains "repressed" even when the barriers preventing the access to the repressed content fall down? The first answer is, of course: the form itself. That is to say, both the positive and the negative form ("This is my mother" and "This is not my mother") move within the same field, the field of the symbolic form, and what we should focus on is a more radical "repression" constitutive of this form itself, what Lacan (at some point) called symbolic castration or the prohibition of incest, a negative gesture which sustains the very symbolic form, so that, even when we say, "This is my mother!", mother is already lost. That is to say, this negative gesture sustains the minimal gap between the symbolic and the real, between (symbolic) reality and the impossible real.

However, insofar as we are dealing here with the properly dialectical mediation between form and content, one should not reduce primordial repression only to the form of a gap: something insists, a weird positivity of an excessive "content" not only impervious to negation, but even produced by the very process of redoubled (self-relating) negation. Consequently, this something is not simply a remainder of the pre-symbolic real that resists symbolic negation, but a spectral X called by Lacan *objet a* or surplus-enjoyment. One should mobilize here Lacan's key distinction between pleasure (*Lust, plaisir*) and enjoyment (*Geniessen, jouissance*): what is "beyond the pleasure principle" is enjoyment itself, it is drive as such. The basic paradox of *jouissance* is that it is both impossible *and* unavoidable: it is never fully achieved, always missed, but, simultaneously, we never can get rid of it—every renunciation of enjoyment generates an enjoyment in renunciation, every obstacle to desire generates a desire for obstacle, etc. This reversal provides the minimal definition of the surplus-enjoyment: it involves the paradoxical "pleasure in pain." That is to say, when Lacan uses the term *plus-de-jouir*, one has to ask a naive, but crucial question: in what does this surplus consist? Is it merely a qualitative increase of ordinary pleasure? The ambiguity of the French expression is decisive here: it can mean "surplus of enjoyment" as well as "no enjoyment"—the surplus of enjoyment over mere pleasure is generated by the presence of the very opposite of pleasure, i.e., pain; it is the part of *jouissance* which resists being contained by the homeostasis, by the pleasure principle. Or, it is the excess of pleasure produced by "repression" itself, which is why we lose it if we abolish repression.

To get the paradoxical logic of "less is more," it is crucial to distinguish symbolic castration from the real castration (a penis—or testicles—is actually cut off) and the imaginary castration in which the loss is just imagined (as in the case of a woman imagining she once had a penis and lost it). In the symbolic castration, nothing happens in (bodily) reality, all that happens is that phallus itself (as the moment of bodily excess) becomes a signifier of "castration," of its lack/impotence. In this sense, social authority really is "phallic" insofar as it exerts the effect of symbolic castration on its bearer: if, say, I am a king, I have to accept that the ritual of investiture makes me a king, that my authority is embodied in the insignia I wear, so that my authority is in some sense external to me as a person in my miserable reality. As Lacan put it, only a psychotic is a king who thinks he is as king (or a father who is a father) by his nature, as he is, without the processes of symbolic investiture. This is why being-a-father is by definition a failure: no "empirical" father can live up to his symbolic function, to his title. How can I, if I am invested with such an authority, live with this gap without obfuscating it through psychotic direct identification of my symbolic status with my reality?

And this is why, from the strict Freudian standpoint, the human finitude (symbolic castration) and immortality (death drive) are the two sides of the same operation; i.e., it's not that the substance of life, the immortal *Jouissance*-Thing, is "castrated" by the arrival of the symbolic order. As in the case of lack and excess, the structure is that of parallax: the undead Thing is the remainder of castration, it is generated by castration, and vice versa, there is no "pure" castration, castration itself is sustained by the immortal excess which eludes it. Castration and excess are not two different entities, but the front and the back of one and the same entity; that is, one and the same entity inscribed onto the two surfaces of a Möbius strip.

What are the implications of this parallax structure for our emancipatory engagement? Here we come to what is probably the ultimate difference between Bou Ali and my position: her view is that

> what we need for emancipation are more subjects who are capable of working through anxiety towards certainty. This certainty about what kind of world we wish to have and be in can only succeed in its aims if it has a determinate ethical and political content beyond an abstract act of conversion, or a declaration of a belief in a (lost) cause.

In Adorno's words, negative dialectics is not enough; we need a clear vision of what we are fighting for, "an alternative symbolic, a new S_1 /Master-Signifier/ that can reorganize discourse and re-knot subjectivity." My Hegelianism prohibits me from accepting this prospect. Of course we are involved all the time in projects about the future we want, but since all thinking is deeply historical, we must always take into account that our projects of a better future are always overdetermined by our present—we cannot step on our own shoulders.

Notes

1 I have elaborated this point repeatedly in many of my works – see, for example, Chapter 11 of my *Less than Nothing* (London: Verso, 2013).
2 Quoted from Manifesto of the Communist Party (marxists.org).

PART THREE
Psychoanalysis

CHAPTER TEN

Reading the Illegible
On Žižek's Interpretation of Lacan's "Kant with Sade"

Dany Nobus

During the early 1980s, Slavoj Žižek belonged to the chosen few who had been personally invited by Jacques-Alain Miller to participate in his closed seminar on Lacan's "Kant with Sade."[1] Even though I shamelessly admit that, at the time and for a long time afterwards, I was deeply envious of this small privileged circle's weekly opportunity to enter into a direct discussion with Miller, this is not to say that I simultaneously felt that Žižek was undeserving of his place in this private cenacle of luminaries. Given Žižek's legendary loquacity and his deep familiarity with the Western philosophical tradition, not to mention his razor-sharp wit and his habitual penchant for the counter-intuitive insight, Miller should have counted himself lucky that Žižek was available to enliven and enlighten the debates. To all intents and purposes, Žižek's calling was an entirely justifiable act, in the sense that Miller could not have wished for a better interlocutor. To the best of my knowledge, no record (recording and/or transcription) of this special confluence of minds survives, yet I have always imagined those historical exchanges to follow the same format as that adopted (or arising) during Miller's two famous lectures on "Kant with Sade" at Kent State University in Ohio at the end of May 1989—Miller taking charge of the proceedings and presenting his views very much "with Žižek," who incessantly interrupts and occasionally steers the master's discourse with his own observations, questions, and illustrations.[2] Hence, if many years later Žižek would concede that it was during his Parisian years that he truly discovered and came to appreciate Miller's pedagogical genius, Miller himself also undoubtedly benefited tremendously from Žižek's unstoppable barrage of disruptive, dispersed critical comments, which would not have been a paragon of pedagogical genius, but indicative of a certain genius all the same.[3]

Irrespective of what really happened during those mythical, most exclusive, private gatherings on Lacan's "Kant with Sade" in Paris—and of which Miller would give us, his general public, only a little snippet at his weekly Wednesday lectures—one cannot overestimate the importance Lacan's essay would come to acquire for the development of Žižek's own thought. If, as Žižek claims in *The Indivisible Remainder*, "Kant with Sade" is "the theme which, perhaps, provides the key to the entire Lacanian theoretical edifice," I feel equally justified in positing that "Kant with Sade" constitutes the linchpin of Žižek's own entire philosophical oeuvre.[4] From Žižek's seminal 1989 monograph *The Sublime Object of Ideology* to his most recent major theoretical interventions, such as the treatise *Sex and the Failed Absolute*, i.e., during a period of more than thirty years covering more than seventy single-authored and edited books in English, there are very few volumes in which "Kant with Sade" is not invoked in one way or another as part of Žižek's argumentation, be it in the context of highly charged, polemical discussions about political ideology, or as part of more light-hearted reflections on the "dark obscene dialectical underside" of popular culture.[5] In addition, as any cursory reader of Žižek's books will easily ascertain, and as he himself underscored at the very beginning of *The Most Sublime Hysteric*—his Parisian doctoral dissertation originally published in French in 1988—the methodology of reading an author, or an established body of ideas, with an ostensibly antagonistic, seemingly irreconcilable correlative is a standard Žižekian rhetorical strategy that runs through his entire intellectual project, and which endows it with its well-known, irresistible incongruity: Hegel is read with Lacan, Lacan is read with Hitchcock, ideology is read with dirty jokes, and so on.[6] Finally, for all I have been able to establish through my reading of roughly 25,000 pages of Žižek's works, "Kant with Sade" is the only *écrit* by Lacan that comes with its own unequivocal categorical imperative: in an "early" text, whose origin more or less coincides with the publication of *The Sublime Object of Ideology*, Žižek insists that "one must read 'Kant with Sade'."[7] The point not to be missed, here, is that Žižek does not exhort his readership to read Kant with Sade, as he had done in *The Most Sublime Hysteric*, but that he emphasizes one's ethical duty to read "Kant with Sade," i.e., the infamous essay by Lacan whose first version dates back to 1962 and which was subsequently revised for publication in *Écrits*.[8]

Of course, the fundamental problem with fulfilling one's ethical duty, as Kant himself remarked in his *Critique of Practical Reason*, is that no human being, however rational it may be, is really up to the task, and that the asymptotic approximation of this endlessly postponed, full compliance with the moral law may in itself come at the cost of a great deal of pain, which is supposed to be endured as much as possible in favour of the realization of the highest, transcendental good.⁹ In other words, the ethical duty to read "Kant with Sade," non-negotiable as it may be, constitutes a radical impossibility, for the pure and simple reason that "Kant with Sade" is totally unreadable. I am not saying this because on various occasions Miller opined that this essay is one of the most difficult texts in *Écrits*—a huge selection of Lacan's writings whose 'mainstream' papers are already widely considered to be distinctly and infuriatingly cryptic—but because Lacan himself admitted as much at a press conference in Rome on October 29, 1974: "[N]o one has ever sent me any remarks on that article ['Kant with Sade']. It is true that I am incomprehensible [in it]."¹⁰ I am also saying it, because I myself bear the indelible marks of the horrendous pain I had to put up with when, for reasons that should not concern us here, I agreed to comply with the ethical duty not only to read "Kant with Sade," but to describe and explain each and every aspect of its totally impenetrable contents.¹¹

Hence, if there is a discernible center to the Žižekian universe, this indispensable nucleus, around which his entire constellation of thoughts revolves, constitutes a radical impossibility which, as will become clear from my exposition below, is not to be understood as an impossibility per se, but rather as the retroactive configuration of the impossible as "what did happen"—as Žižek himself accentuates in *Iraq: The Borrowed Kettle* and elsewhere.¹² The implication can only be that any serious critical analysis of Žižek's works needs to focus on this impossible reading of Lacan's "Kant with Sade"; every other approach, every commentary that moves away from this focal point is de facto ancillary—what the Germans tend to refer to as "*ein Kriegsnebenschauplatz*," an imaginary accessory to the actual battleground, where the real war is taking place. It would be disingenuous of me not to confess, though, that my reason for tackling Žižek's impossible reading of Lacan's "Kant with Sade" is also conditioned by more "pathological" motives and is thus not nearly as pure as it may seem. The fact that "Kant with Sade" constitutes the beating heart of Žižek's intellectual body is an extremely welcome opportunity to seek compensation and indemnify myself for the intolerable pain I endured when trying to make sense of the most incomprehensible of Lacan's *écrits*.

At this point, I should also disclose that I see my own essay as a critique rather than a mere criticism. Its main purpose is to question Žižek's answers rather than to provide another (alternative, purportedly better) answer to the questions he raises. In the process, I shall highlight some factual errors and omissions in Žižek's reading, yet these infelicities may be less important than my critical reconstruction of the coherence and consistency of Žižek's numerous interpretations of "Kant with Sade" as they appear throughout his works, whereby I intend to "stress-test" his arguments and conclusions against Lacan's (and Sade's) own propositions, evaluating the concrete repercussions of Žižek's dialectical engagement with this most abstract of texts, and opening up some new perspectives on how (not) to read Lacan. Inevitably, my critique will eventually take me beyond the boundaries of "Kant with Sade," into a brief reconsideration of Žižek's interpretation, portrayal and eventual re-writing of Sophocles' *Antigone*.[13] In Žižek's works, "Kant with Sade" is never far removed from *Antigone*, and so it is next to impossible—in this precise assignment of locating and evaluating the impossible burning core of Žižek's thought—not to engage with *Antigone*, the play as well as its eponymous heroine. Of course, this should not surprise anyone who has read Lacan's (eminently readable) *Seminar VII, The Ethics of Psychoanalysis*, in which the detailed commentary of *Antigone* follows his "primal" association of Kant and Sade.[14] In fact, Miller's own initiative to run a private seminar on "Kant with Sade" during the early 1980s probably would not have occurred if he had not decided to select *The Ethics of Psychoanalysis*, the only seminar Lacan himself intended to turn into a monograph, as the first seminar to be released after Lacan's death.[15]

As I indicated above, "Kant with Sade" traverses Žižek's work from the beginning, which is generally situated in *The Sublime Object of Ideology*, to its (provisional) end. The challenge of articulating a solid critique of his reading of Lacan's text is thus almost exactly the opposite of the challenge of reading Lacan's text itself. Whereas the latter is only possible by unleashing and allowing oneself to become totally absorbed by a ferocious centrifugal force, which takes the reader into the widest and most diverse sphere of philosophical, literary and other references, against which Lacan's exceptionally dense "arguments" slowly begin to acquire a certain meaning, the former requires the creation of an equally mighty centripetal force, which condenses Žižek's scattered, iterative yet persistently thought-provoking comments on "Kant with Sade" into a more or less manageable shape. Much like those of all serious scholars, Žižek's reflections on "Kant with Sade" represent thought-in-motion, which not only implies that a thorough critique can only proceed from a sustained process of restoration, whereby the various "philosophical fragments" are brought together into some form of temporary unity, but more importantly that one cannot single out a particular assertion for critique, without taking account of the meaning, or indeed the lack thereof, it acquires retrospectively, when it is repeated (often *verbatim*) in a different context, for different purposes, and with a different agenda.

Having embraced this methodology, and borrowing Derrida's intellectual metaphor in *Life Death*, I propose that Žižek's reading of "Kant with Sade" is conceived as an itinerary of three rings.[16] The first ring, which shall be the main focus of my essay, entails the circular movement between Kant and Sade. In the second ring, which I shall only briefly address owing to restrictions of space, the apparent deadlock of this movement between Kant and Sade is then transcended and resolved through the figure of Antigone and, more precisely, the metaphysical dimension of Antigone's act. Finally, in the third ring, the ethics of Antigone's act is employed as a paradigm for articulating the "conditions" of socio-political change. In my essay, I shall present the third ring alongside my succinct presentation of the second, and it will be primarily articulated as a set of questions, partly because I believe that at this stage of his itinerary Žižek's own answers are less forthcoming and more ambiguous, partly because my own questions may give him an opportunity to clarify and concretize the practical recommendations for transformational change that emanate from his ethico-political thought. However, unlike the three rings of Lacan's notorious Borromean knot, this set of rings is both strictly hierarchical and impossible to untie.[17] The hierarchy is to be situated in the fact that the first ring, which lies at the centre of Žižek's theoretical edifice, is the *conditio sine qua non* for the second ring, and that the latter equally conditions the third. At the same time, the rings are impossible to untie, because (as I shall demonstrate) the "concrete universality" around which the third ring revolves is already at stake in the first and also occupies a key aspect of the second.

As regards the movement between Kant and Sade (the first ring), Žižek argues that the most innovative contribution of Lacan's text is not to be found in his statement that Sade is the truth of Kant, i.e., that there is a sadistic dimension to the Kantian categorical imperative, but is rather to be situated in the much more implicit and much more disturbing proposition that Kant is also the truth of Sade.[18] Insofar as Sade represents the truth of Kant, Žižek often moves beyond Lacan—whose assertion is generally restricted to the observation that Kant's principal aim (in the *Critique of Practical Reason*) of formulating a moral law that is entirely devoid of empirical, "pathological" objects inadvertently descends into a rational justification for sacrifice and murder—because he tends to formulate a whole panoply of reasons as to why the categorical imperative harbours an element of sadism, yet he ultimately comes to the conclusion that presenting Sade as the truth of Kant is just stating the obvious and as such blatantly self-evident, if not to say utterly banal.[19] The wide array of reasons Žižek adduces starts with Lacan's own declaration that the strict formality of Kant's imperative generates a new, obscene injunction to enjoy, but gradually crystallizes into the idea that the Sadean perversion erupts as a result of Kant's unwillingness to acknowledge the ultimate consequences of his own ethical system, which coincides with Žižek's contention that Sade is effectively the symptom of Kant.[20] Sade thus appears as the "pathological" result of Kant's (unconscious) self-betrayal, which occurs when he himself compromises on his desire to draw the ultimate conclusion from his aspiration to articulate a purely formal ethical system. From the late 1990s, however, Žižek has consistently constructed this obscene, symptomatic, Sadean truth of Kantian ethics as a glaringly banal truism, whereby his countless remarks to that effect are commonly preceded with the question: "What's all the fuss about?"[21] It is important to emphasize, here, that Žižek does not associate the underlying sadism of the categorical imperative with Arendt's "banality of evil," whose revelation will return further on, in a different context, but that he judges Lacan's first principle of "Kant with Sade"—Kant as "a flower of sadism"—to be palpably trite and patently feeble.[22] Still, I would consider Žižek's value judgment, here, to be primarily a cunning rhetorical strategy, which is mainly designed to give more weight to the second principle, of Sade secretly adhering to Kantian ethics. Were the principle to be as banal as Žižek claims it to be, we probably would not have had to wait almost exactly 100 years for Nietzsche to expose it, and another fifty or so for Horkheimer and Adorno to unfold it. Were it to be as banal as Žižek claims it to be, Lacan's "Kant with Sade" would probably be much less impenetrable than it effectively is.

As mentioned above, the second proposition is much more implicit in Lacan's essay, insofar as he never explicitly proclaims in it that Kant is also the truth of Sade. In "Kant with Sade," Lacan concludes that the libertine's obstinate ambition to set desire free, to liberate it from all constraints, is a law upon itself and that Sade (his libertine heroes) remains therefore in a state of "submission to the Law." However, it is only retrospectively that Lacan reformulates this conclusion as Sade being a Kantian.[23] It is no doubt fair to say, here, that Žižek is much more categorical than Lacan, yet in this case his unequivocal insistence helps us coming to grips with an easily overlooked aspect of Lacan's essay: Sade is a closet Kantian.[24] At this precise point, Žižek's reading of "Kant with Sade" displays a first inconsistency, which relates specifically to the nature and the effect of Sade's hidden Kantianism.

In *The Indivisible Remainder*, Žižek argues that the Kantian quality of the libertines' desire, which translates into an absolute "will to *jouissance*," is tantamount to its purification: "Lacan 'purifies' Sade: the sadist Will-to-Enjoy is the exemplary case of a pure, non-pathological desire."[25] This inference is re-stated in "Kant with (or against) Sade" as Lacan recognizing (in the Sadean libertines' law of desire) "'a pure faculty of desire,' since desire *does* have a non-pathological, a priori object-cause," notably "what Lacan calls *objet petit a*."[26] In my reading of Žižek's reading, he also acknowledges this "pure, non-pathological desire" as what supports the objective of the "second death" in the so-called "system of Pope Pius VI," which constitutes one of the longest philosophical disquisitions in Sade's *Juliette*.[27] Lacan first adumbrates the libertine pontiff's vision in Chapter 16 of his seminar *The Ethics of Psychoanalysis*, whereby he underscores his Holiness's ultimate wish to secure a more absolute form of destruction than that which merely takes away a living organism's earthly existence (the so-called "first life"), through which the remnants of the substance's body would still re-enter a new natural cycle of regeneration.[28] What Sade's Pope Pius VI aspires to accomplish is a much more radical annihilation, which breaks the endless alternation between life and death.[29] It is this supreme obliteration that Lacan designates as the "second death" and which Žižek glosses as "the destruction, the eradication, of the cycle itself, which then liberates nature from its own laws and opens the way for the creation of new forms of life *ex nihilo*."³⁰ It is crucial to highlight, here, that the concept of the "second death" is Lacan's own invention, because throughout his extended sermon the Pope only ever refers to the need for the extinction of the second life.³¹ This nuance is less important for Lacan than it is for Žižek, because (as the quote shows) Žižek sees in the second death a necessary precondition for what he initially terms "materialist creationism" and later captures as "the zero-level starting point out of which the fragile/inconsistent reality emerges."³² I shall return to the latter development at the very end of my essay, yet the "second death" is clearly an index, here, of another type of purification—a perfect cleansing which coincides with the complete liquidation of the most fundamental (constraining) law of all, i.e., that of Mother Nature itself.

Elsewhere, however, Žižek acknowledges that the Kantian law which continues to underpin the Sadean will to *jouissance* limits its implementation and renders it fundamentally impure. The Sadean libertine is thus not nearly as autonomous as she or he thinks, or as the Kantian categorical imperative would bestow upon his or her ideology. All in all, Žižek formulates two main reasons in support of this ineluctable return of the impure in Sade's libertine philosophy. First, he avers that Sade's vision of an emancipated desire and its associated unconditional will to *jouissance* can only be realized at the level of particularity. As he puts it in *Looking Awry*: "[A]ny attempt to give to the 'right to enjoyment' the form of a universal norm in conformity with the 'categorical imperative' necessarily ends in a deadlock," because it "excludes reciprocity."³³ Of course, what we encounter here is a prototypical example of having your cake and eating it. One cannot maintain that Sade is a closet Kantian and then proclaim that his Kantianism fails at the point where he cannot be a Kantian. Either Sade's law of *jouissance* meets the conditions of the categorical imperative or it doesn't. Yet from the late 1990s, Žižek develops another reason as to why the purity of the Sadean enterprise is effectively a massive illusion. In "Kant with (or against) Sade," he argues that the Sadean libertines, much like Kant before them, compromise on their grand dream of setting desire free, because they remain ineluctably enslaved to the voice of Nature, which is first conceptualized as a fundamentally capricious, external structure, and then reconfigured as an ethical force in its own right.³⁴ For Žižek, this also explains why the Sadean libertine is never cold enough: "his 'apathy' is a fake, a lure concealing the all too passionate engagement on behalf of the Other's *jouissance*."³⁵ Žižek's second reason for doubting the purity of the Sadean desire comes closest to Lacan's own emphasis in "Kant with Sade" on the flaw in the Sadean universe, yet it only scratches the surface of Lacan's profound skepticism as to the absolute freedom of the libertines. I do not want to go so far as to claim, here, that Žižek himself compromises on his desire to articulate the limitations of Sade's heroes, yet he definitely could have done more to explicate Lacan's critique of Sade in "Kant with Sade," which revolves around four distinct observations.

First, the libertines' desire is always already mediated by another desire, which not only manifests itself in the (ethical) voice of Nature, but much more crucially in the fact that they cannot realize their vision without singling out victims for torture and sacrifice. In this respect, Lacan rekindles his own classic formula that "desire is the Other's desire," but he also (implicitly) repeats an argument made by Maurice Blanchot in his pathbreaking 1949 essay "*La raison de Sade*" (Sade's Reason): "When 'being the master' of myself means 'being the master of others,' when my independence does not come from my autonomy, but from the dependence of others on me, it is obvious that I forever remain connected to others and that I need them, even if only to obliterate them."[36] Second, the libertines persistently fail in realizing their desire, because they do not succeed in bridging the constitutive gap between knowledge and desire. Time and again, they think they know what it means to desire like a libertine, yet every so often they have to admit, occasionally to their own downfall and sacrifice, that their knowledge was on the side of virtue rather than in the service of vice. The most striking illustration of this disparity between knowledge (of libertine desire) and desire (for libertine knowledge) is provided by the hideous Saint-Fond, who gladly shares with his brothers-in-arms his deepest wish that the suffering he inflicts upon his victims lasts forever and continues to haunt them in the afterlife, without thereby realizing that in harboring this wish he has broken one of the foundational rules of the libertine ideology, namely that each and every concept of an afterlife needs to be destroyed at its root.[37] And so the great Saint-Fond inadvertently presents himself as a secret proponent of the libertines' enemies, which leads to his being unmasked as a fake libertine and condemned to death. Third, when all is (philosophically) said and (sexually) done, the libertines constantly have to admit that all their criminal acts—extreme as they may be, both in terms of the number of sacred principles that have been violated and the number of virtuous people that have perished in the process—are but a mediocre semblance of the ultimate act of destruction they fantasize about. Some libertines, such as Belmor, are more vocal about this failure than others, yet at the end of the day it is as if all the libertines have to concede: "I always thought that I would be able to do and be this, but now I'm not so sure anymore that I have what it takes."[38]

In "Kant with Sade," Lacan attributes this irreparable disparity between libertine fantasy and libertine deed to the fact that, *à la limite*, the libertines are enslaved to the inescapable fact that, as human beings of flesh and blood, their *jouissance* is forever contaminated by pleasure: "[T]he [Sadean] executioner's *jouissance* . . . does not spare his *jouissance* the humility of an act in which he cannot help but become a being of flesh and, to the very marrow, a slave to pleasure."[39] Contrary to what Arendt claimed in her reports on the Eichmann trials, the radical evil of the Sadean libertines is therefore not buttressed, much less enhanced, but rather stymied to the point where they become desperate, by the fact that they can only *imagine* themselves to be superhuman gods. No matter how hard they try, time and again they have to accept that they are just banal human beings compared to the heroes they portray themselves as in their fantasy. Ironically, perhaps, the only space the libertines finally identify as being conducive to the preservation of radical, absolute freedom, insofar as the truth of their desire will never be compromised in it, is that of (creative) writing.[40] I shall return to this point at the end of my essay, because it probably constitutes one of the most advanced arguments in "Kant with Sade"—with other than merely literary repercussions—and it is almost completely absent from Žižek's interpretation of Lacan's essay. Fourth, Lacan suggests that, for all their exhaustive (and exhausting) attempts at championing the libertine cause, Sade's heroes never succeed in converting anyone and, more importantly, many of the victims somehow miraculously succeed in retaining their features after they have been subjected to the most horrible bodily tortures.[41] Hence, virtue is never transformed into vice, and virtue's extraordinary capacity to survive constantly throws the libertines off-guard. Even the exquisitely delicate, virginal, and aptly named Eugénie in *Philosophy in the Boudoir* does not exchange her virtuousness for vice. As Madame de Saint-Ange discloses at the beginning of the play, she had met the young girl at a convent sometime before and noticed how the venom of immorality was already circulating in her heart.[42] Eugénie is not another Justine; she is rather a young Juliette, whose inborn proclivities merely require a little more education for them to come to full fruition.

Much more than Žižek, Lacan thus underlines the fundamental bankruptcy of the libertines' ideology of absolute destruction.[43] However, this is also where Lacan stops and where Žižek continues to seek a workable solution to the deadlock. Whatever he may ascribe to Lacan by way of desire to rupture the vicious cycle between Kant and Sade by insisting on the necessity of a "critique of pure desire," or the identification of a "pure faculty of desire," Lacan never compromises on the observation that there is no way to escape the deadlock: every subject's alienation (to the symbolic moral law) leads to a return of the (pathological) object and every subject's attempt to separate him or herself from this alienation by adopting the position of the object invariably leads to a new alienation, unless the separation exceeds the boundaries of the subject's earthly life and results in physical death.[44] For Lacan, this is not only how the (neurotic) fantasy operates, but it is also the fundamental, inescapable truth of the (neurotic) human condition. However, whereas Lacan accepts the deadlock, Žižek is adamant that an escape route can be found. In this way, he transforms Lacan's constitutive constellation of forces into a largely incidental, situational set of variables. In Žižek's works, Lacan's necessity becomes a new contingency, which can be resolved through a reconceptualization of the act. In Žižek's view, the key paradigm for this new ethical act that breaks the vicious cycle of Kant and Sade is Antigone, which represents the second circle in his intellectual itinerary.[45] The hinge between the first and the second circle is thereby to be found in the motto, "Do not give up on your desire!"

Žižek's proposed integration of Antigone and the Sadean libertines is already detectable in *The Sublime Object of Ideology*, in which he aligns "the dignified Antigone sacrificing herself for her brother's memory" and "the promiscuous Juliette giving herself over to enjoyment beyond all limits."[46] However, as his thought progresses and he comes to accept that the Sadean libertines, including Juliette, remain bound to the ethical voice of Nature, in whose name and on whose behalf they commit their atrocities, Antigone starts to appear as a purer version of Juliette. For example, in *The Metastases of Enjoyment*, Žižek avers that Antigone is "the exemplary case of a pure ethical attitude," because (as he puts it elsewhere) "Antigone does *not* obey a command that humiliates her, a command effectively uttered by a sadistic executioner."[47] The first thing to note, here, is that Žižek's prime motive for aligning Antigone and Juliette, and for eventually abandoning Juliette in favour of Antigone, is the ethical precept "Do not give up on your desire!" which is also the hinge between the first and the second circle of Žižek's intellectual itinerary.[48] However, even though Žižek consistently attributes this axiom to Lacan, it has absolutely no basis whatsoever in Lacan's work. The only passage in Lacan's oeuvre in which a version of this formula appears is the final lesson of *Seminar VII*, in which he proposes to outline the psychoanalytic paradoxes of ethics.[49] But the transcription of Lacan's words, which has been verified and deemed accurate, reads: "I propose then that, from an analytical point of view, the only thing of which one can be guilty is of having given ground relative to one's desire [*Je propose que la seule chose dont on puisse être coupable, au moins dans la perspective analytique, c'est d'avoir cédé sur son désir*]."[50] Nowhere in his seminar, nor elsewhere in his lectures and writings, does Lacan employ the last part of this phrase with a negative, as in "*not* giving up on one's desire." And nowhere does Lacan elevate this (already absent) negative phrase into an ethical imperative.[51] On the contrary, after having formulated the first psychoanalytic paradox of ethics, Lacan insists that it is the subject's inexorable fate to *always* give up on his or her desire and that this structure of self-betrayal is fundamentally inscribed into the subject's destiny.[52] Žižek's interpretation of this passage from Lacan's *Seminar VII* thus constitutes a fundamental misreading, although it has to be said that, over the years, he has not been alone in "perverting" Lacan's words in this way.[53] Of course, there is nothing intrinsically wrong with "giving up on Lacan," that is to say with abandoning his current of thought, or taking it into a different direction, yet in that case one should also have the courage to state that Lacan was wrong and why.[54]

Let us assume, however, that Antigone really does succeed where Juliette and her fellow libertines fail. How should we interpret Antigone's act, then? At this point, a second inconsistency appears in Žižek's work. Whereas the first inconsistency destabilizes the integrity of the first ring (see above), this inconsistency jeopardizes the solidity of the second. In an attempt to account for the nature and function of Antigone's act (of burying her brother

Polynices against Creon's prohibition), Žižek depicts Antigone as a figure who performs an autonomous ethical act, which renders her uncannily terrifying (in accordance with Heidegger's interpretation of the word δεινόν in the second choral ode of Sophocles' play), and which allows her to exceed and transform the structure of the symbolic order.[55] Yet Žižek oscillates here between situating this autonomy in Antigone's embodiment of a pure signifier, which would take her desire in the direction of the drive, and her transcendence of the unresolvable dialectic between authoring the moral law and obeying its principles by incarnating the excess that is the object a. [6]

Beyond this inconsistency, Žižek nonetheless continues to emphasize that Antigone's act is ethical, exemplary, and pure, despite the fact that her stubborn refusal to comply and her unconditional insistence on her own moral authority also turns her into a proto-totalitarian figure, i.e., the historical antecedent of what Žižek designates as "ontological totalitarianism."[57] However, what enables Antigone to leverage her transgressive deed as an effective conduit for "reconsidering the symbolic Law as a set of contingent social arrangements open to change" is the absolute contingency of her act, which coincides with a "momentary suspension of the big Other" and which creates its own (new) rationality, away from the abstract universality of the law (as a categorical imperative) toward the concrete universality of a transformational intervention.[58] Apart from the fact that I do not doubt that Lacan would have radically disagreed with almost every element of Žižek's argument, quite a few aspects of it cannot but strike anyone familiar with Sophocles' *Antigone* as fundamentally at odds with the substance of the narrative. Space prevents me from listing all the points where Žižek's depiction of Antigone does not chime with Sophocles' portrayal of her, so I shall restrict myself to just one instance of disparity, although this particular instance may very well dislodge the foundations of Žižek's entire construction. What allows Žižek to continue to rely on Antigone as a paradigm for effectuating (socio-political) change is the radical contingency of her act, which acquires both its status and its transformational power from the fact that it proceeds from and incorporates the lack in the Other. Drawing on Lacan's formulation in his essay on logical time, Antigone's act thus derives its contingency from its being structured by a subjective logic of anticipated certainty.[59] However, even though it is true that Antigone is thrown into a state of debilitating turmoil after she has committed the deed, one cannot say that her act was contingent, insofar as it was accidental, unexpected, or unplanned. Antigone shares her plan to defy Creon's orders with her sister Ismene from the very beginning of the play and she effectively undoes the initial act, which one could indeed perceive as a spontaneous, momentary lapse of reason, by performing the burial rites on her brother twice. Hence, Žižek's claim that Antigone's act is radically contingent crumbles purely on the basis of an attentive reading of Sophocles' text.[60] Reading *Antigone*, one is tempted to rephrase Freud's own famous "ethical" axiom "Where id was, there ego shall be" ("*Wo Es war, soll Ich werden"*) as "Where contingency was, necessity shall be."⁶¹ Were Žižek to retort that contingency and concrete universality correspond exactly to a sudden emergence of subjectivity, I would reply that, from a Lacanian standpoint, this does not preclude the necessity of the structural circularity between alienation and separation. Even though the two operations are non-reciprocal (alienation does not undo separation and vice versa), they are strictly concordant (the one always leads to the other, *ad infinitum*).

This issue is all the more important since the concrete universality of Antigone's contingent act also constitutes the hinge between the second and the third circle of Žižek's itinerary, which entails the articulation of the conditions for socio-political change. As I announced at the beginning of my essay, I shall simply describe this third circle in the form of a series of questions, in part because I am not so sure that, at this stage, Žižek provides the answers, in part because, if he does have them, I would like to give him the opportunity to present them in a more coherent, synthetic account. If, as Žižek puts it in *Iraq: The Borrowed Kettle*, "*only such an 'impossible' gesture of pure expenditure* [as it is to be found in Antigone's contingent, concrete universal act] *can change the very co-ordinates of what is strategically possible within a historical constellation,*" how can we reasonably expect, or encourage ordinary (banal) human beings of flesh and blood to enact this risk and to take their chances that a "fragile/inconsistent (new) reality" *may* emerge as a result of the zero-level starting-point they have unwittingly created?⁶² Antigone's act may be less of a fantasy than the Sadean libertines' ideology of absolute destruction, yet she is still a fictional character. Wherein lies the inspirational value of the contingency of Antigone's act for the concrete universality of real-life individual and social protest, especially in light of the fact that, more than ever before it seems, the transformational potential of every form of risk-taking is crushed by the brutal force of established discursive power structures (see the protests against the coup in Myanmar, the protests against the rigged elections in Belarus, the protests against the extrapolation of Chinese law to Hong Kong, the attempt to orchestrate the downfall of Erdogan, etc.)?

When, at the very end of *Absolute Recoil*, Žižek posits that "the rise of a new Master-Signifier is not the ultimate definition of the symbolic event: there is a further turn of the screw, the move from S_1 to $S(A)$, from new harmony to new disharmony, which is an exemplary case of subtraction" and then goes on to call for a politics of radical emancipation "which practices subtraction from the reign of a Master-Signifier," I agree with him, and I know how this could be facilitated within the confines of a clinical psychoanalytic setting, but how does one put this into practice in the socio-political arena?⁶³ If, as Žižek has intimated in various public lectures and podcasts, this effectively involves a transition from acting to thinking, then what kind of thinking might enact this process of subtraction?⁶⁴ Isn't it the case that thinking might only acquire the status of a contingent, concrete universal act after a long, laborious process of narrative re-framing, which

Freud called "working-through" and Lacan termed the "traversal of the fantasy"?[65] And wherein lies the power of writing in all of this? As Lacan suggested in "Kant with Sade," the Sadean libertines persistently fail in realizing their fantasy of absolute destruction, yet Sade-the-man did not stop writing. Something in his desire did not stop being written, so that it was in his writings that he himself came closest to transcending the limitations of the symbolic order and to occupying the position of object a, *pace* his performing this act of writing from the confines of a prison-cell or the constraints of a madhouse.[66] Could the pen indeed be mightier than the sword? What is the role of the public intellectual under conditions of global capitalism? What does Žižek intend to achieve with his unstoppable series of books, essays, commentaries, and criticisms? Given the three circles of his intellectual itinerary, what is Žižek's answer to the three famous Kantian questions that underpin the interest of our reason? What can I know? What ought I to do? What may I hope?[67]

Notes

1 Slavoj Žižek and Glyn Daly, *Conversations with Žižek* (Cambridge: Polity Press, 2004), 34. See also Slavoj Žižek, *Slavoj Žižek on Jacques-Alain Miller*, November 6, 2015, available at https://www.youtube.com/watch?v=9eMbN7pqNMA (accessed August 12, 2021).

2 Jacques-Alain Miller, "A Discussion of Lacan's 'Kant with Sade'." In *Reading Seminars I and II: Lacan's Return to Freud*, eds. Richard Feldstein, Bruce Fink, and Maire Jaanus (Albany, NY: State University of New York Press, 1996), 212–37.

3 Žižek and Daly, *Conversations with Žižek*, 34.

4 Slavoj Žižek, *The Indivisible Remainder: An Essay on Schelling and Related Matters* (London: Verso, 1996), 172.

5 Slavoj Žižek, *The Sublime Object of Ideology* (London: Verso, 1989); Slavoj Žižek, *Sex and the Failed Absolute* (London: Bloomsbury, 2020).

6 Slavoj Žižek, *The Most Sublime Hysteric: Hegel with Lacan*, trans. Thomas Scott-Railton (Cambridge: Polity Press, 2014), 2. For the original French text of Žižek's dissertation, see Slavoj Žižek, *Le plus sublime des hystériques. Hegel passe* (Paris: Point Hors Ligne, 1988).

7 Slavoj Žižek, "The Limits of the Semiotic Approach to Psychoanalysis." In *Interrogating the Real*, eds. Rex Butler and Scott Stephens (London: Bloomsbury, 2005), 105. In an editorial comment, the editors of this anthology point out that they "revised the translation and made corrections to certain grammatical and terminological errors" in Žižek's original text, yet the phrase in question appears in exactly the same form in the original version. See Slavoj Žižek, "The Limits of the Semiotic Approach to Psychoanalysis." In *Psychoanalysis And . . .*, eds. Richard Feldstein and Henry Sussman (New York: Routledge, 1990), 95.

8   Žižek, *The Most Sublime Hysteric*, 100; Jacques Lacan, "Kant with Sade" (1962). In *Écrits*, trans. Bruce Fink (New York: W. W. Norton & Company, 2006), 645–68.
9   In Book 2 of his *Critique of Practical Reason*, Kant wrote: "Complete conformity of the will with the moral law is, however, *holiness*, a perfection of which no rational being of the sensible world is capable at any moment of his existence." See Immanuel Kant, *Critique of Practical Reason* (1788), trans. and ed. Mary Gregor (Cambridge: Cambridge University Press, 1997), 102. For Kant's reflections on pain and displeasure, see Immanuel Kant, *Critique of Practical Reason*, 52–5.
10 See Jacques-Alain Miller, "Sobre 'Kant con Sade.'" In *Elucidación de Lacan: Charlas brasileñas* (Buenos Aires: Paidós, 1998), 201; Jacques-Alain Miller, "A Discussion of Lacan's 'Kant with Sade,'," 212; Jacques Lacan, "The Triumph of Religion." In *The Triumph of Religion, preceded by Discourse to Catholics*, trans. Bruce Fink (Cambridge: Polity Press, 2013), 83.
11 See Dany Nobus, *The Law of Desire: On Lacan's 'Kant with Sade'* (Basingstoke: Palgrave Macmillan, 2017).
12 Slavoj Žižek, *Iraq: The Borrowed Kettle* (London: Verso, 2004), 80. See also Slavoj Žižek, "What Some Would Call . . .: A Response to Yannis Stavrakakis," *Umbr(a): A Journal of the Unconscious* 4 (2003), 132.
13 Sophocles, *Antigone*, in *Antigone/Women of Trachis/Philoctetes/Oedipus at Colonus*, ed. and trans. Hugh Lloyd Jones (Cambridge, MA: Harvard University Press, 1998), 1–127; Slavoj Žižek, *Antigone* (London: Bloomsbury, 2016).
14 Jacques Lacan, *The Seminar. Book VII: The Ethics of Psychoanalysis (1959–1960)*, ed. Jacques-Alain Miller, trans. Dennis Porter (New York: W. W. Norton & Company, 1992).
15 For Lacan's (failed) intention to publish *The Ethics of Psychoanalysis* as a monograph, see Jacques Lacan, *The Seminar. Book XX: On Feminine Sexuality, the Limits of Love and Knowledge (Encore) (1972–1973)*, ed. Jacques-Alain Miller, trans. Bruce Fink (New York: W. W. Norton & Company, 1998), 1, 53. As to Miller's reasons for choosing *The Ethics of Psychoanalysis* as the first seminar to be published after Lacan's death, see Jacques-Alain Miller, *Entretien sur Le Séminaire avec François Ansermet* (Paris: Navarin, 1985), 33; Jacques-Alain Miller, *Del síntoma al fantasma. Y retorno (1982–1983)*, ed. Silvia Elena Tendlarz, trans. Silvia Baudini (Buenos Aires: Paidós, 2018), 144–6.
16 See Jacques Derrida, *Life Death (1975–1976)*, eds. Pascale-Anne Brault and Peggy Kamuf, trans. Pascale-Anne Brault and Michael Naas (Chicago: University of Chicago Press, 2020); Jacques Derrida, "To Speculate—On 'Freud'." In *The Post Card: From Socrates to Freud and Beyond*, trans. Alan Bass (Chicago: University of Chicago Press, 1987), 259 note 1.
17 See Jacques Lacan, *The Seminar. Book XIX: . . . or Worse (1971–1972)*, ed. Jacques-Alain Miller, trans. A. R. Price (Cambridge: Polity Press, 2018), 75; Lacan, *The Seminar. Book XX*, 124.
18 With very few exceptions, when Žižek invokes Sade he does not refer to the extraordinary life of the Marquis de Sade, but to a sub-section of Sade's

voluminous writings, notably his so-called libertine novels, the most famous of which are (the unfinished) *The 120 Days of Sodom, Justine or the Misfortunes of Virtue, Philosophy in the Boudoir*, and the monumental *Juliette*. See Marquis de Sade, *The 120 Days of Sodom*, in *The 120 Days of Sodom and Other Writings*, trans. Austryn Wainhouse and Richard Seaver (London: Arrow Books, 1990), 181–674; Marquis de Sade, *Justine or the Misfortunes of Virtue*, trans. John Phillips (Oxford: Oxford University Press, 2012); Marquis de Sade, *Philosophy in the Boudoir or, The Immoral Mentors*, trans. Joachim Neugroschel (London: Penguin, 2006); Marquis de Sade, *Juliette*, trans. Austryn Wainhouse (New York: Grove Press, 1968).

19 Lacan's own, most succinct formulation of his thesis actually appears at the very end of *Seminar XI* rather than in "Kant with Sade" itself. See Jacques Lacan, *The Seminar. Book XI: The Four Fundamental Concepts of Psychoanalysis (1964)*, trans. Alan Sheridan (Harmondsworth: Penguin, 1994, 275–6.

20 For Žižek's (re)formulation of Lacan's argument, see, for example, Žižek, *The Sublime Object of Ideology*, 81 and Slavoj Žižek, *For They Know Not What They Do: Enjoyment as a Political Factor* (London: Verso, 1991), 232. For the argument that Sade is the symptom of Kant's philosophical compromise, see Slavoj Žižek, "Afterword: Lenin's Choice." In *Revolution at the Gates: Selected Writings of Lenin from 1917*, ed. Slavoj Žižek (London: Verso, 2002), 243; Slavoj Žižek, *The Puppet and the Dwarf: The Perverse Core of Christianity*, (Cambridge, MA: MIT Press, 2003), 54; Slavoj Žižek, *The Parallax View* (Cambridge, MA, 2006), 94; Slavoj Žižek, *In Defense of Lost Causes* (London: Verso, 2008), 209; Slavoj Žižek, "Dialectical Clarity versus the Misty Conceit of Paradox." In Slavoj Žižek and John Milbank, *The Monstrosity of Christ: Paradox or Dialectic?*, ed. Creston Davis (Cambridge, MA: MIT Press, 2008), 238; Slavoj Žižek, *Less than Nothing: Hegel and the Shadow of Dialectical Materialism* (London: Verso, 2012), 817. In an essay from the late 1990s, Žižek also correctly points out that Lacan's thesis had already been anticipated by Adorno and Horkheimer in "Excursus II" of their *Dialectic of Enlightenment*, yet he forgets to mention that the first to intimate the potential inhumanity of Kant's categorical imperative (without therefore bringing in Sade) was actually Nietzsche, who stated in *On the Genealogy of Morals*: "the categorical imperative gives off a whiff of cruelty [*der kategorische Imperativ riecht nach Grausamkeit*] ..." See Slavoj Žižek, "Kant with (or against) Sade." In *The Žižek Reader*, eds. Elizabeth Wright and Edmond Wright (Oxford: Blackwell, 1999), 283–301; Theodor W. Adorno and Max Horkheimer, "Excursus II: Juliette or Enlightenment and Morality." In *Dialectic of Enlightenment*, trans. John Cumming (London: Verso, 1997), 81–119; Friedrich Nietzsche, *On the Genealogy of Morals (1887)*, trans. Douglas Smith (Oxford: Oxford University Press, 1996), 47.

21 See Slavoj Žižek, "Kant and Sade: The Ideal Couple," *Lacanian Ink* 13 (1998), 12; Žižek, "Kant with (or against) Sade," 288; Slavoj Žižek, "Author's Afterword: Where Do We Stand Today?" In *The Universal Exception*, eds. Rex Butler and Scott Stephens (London: Bloomsbury, 2006), 382; Slavoj Žižek, *Disparities* (London: Bloomsbury, 2016), 332; Slavoj Žižek, *Sex and the Failed Absolute* (London: Bloomsbury, 2020), 113.

22 See Hannah Arendt, *Eichmann in Jerusalem: A Report on the Banality of Evil (1963)* (London: Penguin, 1977). For the phrase "flower of sadism," see Lacan, *The Triumph of Religion*, 83.
23 For Sade's "submission to the Law," see Lacan, "Kant with Sade," 667. For Lacan's retrospective reformulation of "Kant with Sade" as Sade being a Kantian, see Jacques Lacan, *Le Séminaire XIV: La logique du fantasme (1966–1967)*, lesson of June 14, 1967, unpublished; Lacan, *The Seminar. Book XX*, 23.
24 For the antecedents and the explicit promotion of this formula in Žižek's oeuvre, see Slavoj Žižek, *Tarrying With the Negative: Kant, Hegel, and the Critique of Ideology* (Durham, NC: Duke University Press, 1993), 70; Žižek, "Kant with (or against) Sade," 288; Slavoj Žižek and Mladen Dolar, *Opera's Second Death* (London: Routledge, 2002), 141; Žižek and Daly, *Conversations with Žižek*, 131–2; Žižek, "Author's Afterword: Where Do We Stand Today," 382; Slavoj Žižek, *Violence: Six Sideways Reflections* (London: Profile Books, 2008, 165); Žižek, *Disparities*, 332; Žižek, *Sex and the Failed Absolute*, 113.
25 Žižek, *The Indivisible Remainder*, 173.
26 Žižek, "Kant with (or against) Sade," 299. This point is restated almost verbatim in Žižek's most recent volume *Sex and the Failed Absolute*: "Lacan asserts the necessity of a 'critique of pure desire': in contrast to Kant, for whom our capacity to desire is thoroughly 'pathological,' Lacan claims that there is a 'pure faculty of desire'." In other places, Žižek refers to the Sadean perversion as "pure reason." See Žižek, *Sex and the Failed Absolute*, 114; Žižek and Daly, *Conversations with Žižek*, 62.
27 Throughout his works, i.e., from beginning to end, Žižek erroneously situates this disquisition in Book 5 of *Juliette*, because it actually occurs at the end of Book (Part) 4. See Marquis de Sade, *Juliette*, 765–98; Žižek, *The Sublime Object of Ideology*, 134; Žižek, *For They Know Not What They Do*, 261; Žižek, *The Most Sublime Hysteric*, 174; Žižek, *Disparities*, 334; Žižek, *Sex and the Failed Absolute*, 50. Now, I would prefer not to think that Žižek has never read *Juliette*, and this error may seem like a minute, inconsequential infelicity, yet given the significance Žižek himself attributes to numbers in his works—see, in this respect, the second (expanded) edition of Slavoj Žižek, *Enjoy Your Symptom! Jacques Lacan in Hollywood and Out* (London: Routledge, 2001), x— and the fact that the error is repetitive, the psychoanalyst in me is tempted to interpret 5 as the number of Žižek's (unfulfilled) desire, which would in this case represent a desire to exceed the fundamental quadripartite structure of Lacan's theory. However, in a more serious vein, I should also point out that the way in which Žižek "quotes" the system of Pope Pius VI in his most recent works, such as *Disparities* and *Sex and the Failed Absolute*, borders on the unforgivable, at least from a scholarly perspective. In both of these books, the long quote "from Sade" that is set apart from the rest of the text is in fact a literal quote from a book by Aaron Schuster, which is only mentioned directly at the start of the chapter in the first volume and as an unpublished manuscript after the quote in *Sex and the Failed Absolute*, whereby Schuster's own attributed citations from Sade in this paragraph are no longer referenced. See Žižek, *Disparities*, 334–5; Žižek, *Sex*

and the Failed Absolute, 50; Aaron Schuster, *The Trouble with Pleasure: Deleuze and*, (Cambridge, MA: MIT Press, 2016), 39–40. For the logic of the quadripartite structure in Lacan's oeuvre, see Jacques-Alain Miller, "1, 2, 3, 4 (1984–1985)," available at http://psicoanalisisdigital.wordpress.com/2012/05/22/1-2-3-4-1984-1985/ (accessed November 20, 2021).

28 See Lacan, *The Seminar. Book VII*, 210–17.
29 The qualification that it concerns *Sade*'s Pope Pius VI is important, because he is the only character in *Juliette* that is not entirely fictional. Also, when the novel was first published (in 1797) Pope Pius VI (Count Giovanni Angelo Braschi) was still very much alive and would have been abhorred by the "philosophical system" of his fictional persona.
30 Lacan first mentions the notion of the second death three weeks after his initial discussion of the system of Pope Pius VI, i.e., during his seminar session of May 25, 1960, which is also the first session of his commentary on *Antigone*. See Lacan, *The Seminar. Book VII*, 248. For Žižek's gloss on the second death, see Žižek, *The Sublime Object of Ideology*, 134. For similar glosses in Žižek's works, see Žižek, *The Most Sublime Hysteric*, 74, 175; Žižek, *Enjoy Your Symptom!*, 161 note 6; Žižek, *Disparities*, 335.
31 See de Sade, *Juliette*, 770. The reason as to why Pope Pius VI does not refer to a second death, but to a second life is not immaterial to the essence of his philosophical system: what is at stake is the absolute, total, irreversible extermination of all traces of life.
32 For "materialist creationism," see Slavoj Žižek, *Did Somebody Say Totalitarianism? Five Interventions in the (Mis)use of a Notion* (London: Verso, 2001), 173. Note the first word of the book's subtitle. For the subsequent formulation, see Žižek, *Disparities*, 335.
33 Slavoj Žižek, *Looking Awry: Jacques Lacan in Hollywood and Out* (Cambridge, MA: MIT Press, 1991), 167–8. For a similar argument, see Slavoj Žižek, "The Fetish of the Party." In *The Universal Exception*, eds. Rex Butler and Scott Stephens (London: Bloomsbury, 2006), 102.
34 Žižek, "Kant with (or against) Sade," 295.
35 Ibid., 298. For similar statements, see Žižek, *Did Somebody Say Totalitarianism?*, 113; Žižek, *The Parallax View*, 93. In various places, Žižek writes that Lacan designated the ethical force of Nature in the Sadean universe as the Supreme-Being-in-Evilness, yet the latter notion (*l'Être suprême en méchanceté*) is actually part of what one could call the "system of Saint-Fond" in *Juliette*, which is explained at the end of Part 2 of the book. See de Sade, *Juliette*, 399; Žižek, "Kant with (or against) Sade," 295; Žižek, "Author's Afterword: Why Hegel is a Lacanian," 343 note 7; Žižek, *The Parallax View*, 93; Žižek, *In Defense of Lost Causes*, 475–6 note 21; Slavoj Žižek, *Absolute Recoil: Towards a New Foundation of Dialectical Materialism* (London: Verso, 2014), 82, note 35.
36 Maurice Blanchot, "Sade's Reason." In *Lautréamont and Sade*, trans. Stuart Kendall and Michelle Kendall (Stanford, CA: Stanford University Press, 2004), 23. Blanchot's essay is not mentioned by Lacan in "Kant with Sade," yet he recommends its study to his audience during his seminar session of March 30

1960. See Lacan, *The Seminar, Book VII*, 200–1. The principle that "desire is the Other's desire" has its roots in Lacan's work from the early 1950s and it is repeated on no less than three occasions in "Kant with Sade." See Lacan, "Kant with Sade," 652, 658 and 662.

37 de Sade, *Juliette*, 395–406. It is worth mentioning that Saint-Fond's discourse occurs in response to a previous libertine lecture by Clairwil, which he believes to be insufficiently libertine. In "Kant with Sade," Lacan invokes the disparity between knowledge and desire in two different ways. First, he posits that "desire is not the subject, for it cannot be indicated anywhere in a signifier of any demand whatsoever, for it cannot be articulated in the signifier even though it is articulated there [*pour n'y être pas articulable encore qu'il y soit articulé*]." Second, he adduces it by way of a rhetorical question pertaining to his own reading of Kant: "But if the credence we lent to the *Critique* due to the alacrity of its argumentation owed something to our desire to know where it was heading, can't the ambiguity of this success [of our desire to know] turn the movement back toward a revising of the concessions we unwittingly made?" See Lacan, "Kant with Sade," 653, 662.

38 In the words of Belmor: "[A]ll the deeds ambitioned by all the most infernal and the most malignant spirits that ever were, in their most disastrous effects were nought compared to what we dare desire . . ." See de Sade, *Juliette*, 522.

39 Lacan, "Kant with Sade," 652.

40 See, for example, de Sade, *Juliette*, 525, 1193.

41 Lacan, "Kant with Sade," 665, 654. Žižek mentions the unassailable beauty of the Sadean victims in various places, but he tends to see it as an avatar of their immortality, which would then in itself constitute the Sadean correlative of Kant's postulate of the immortality of the soul in his *Critique of Practical Reason*. See, for example, Slavoj Žižek, *The Metastases of Enjoyment: Six Essays on Woman and Causality* (London: Verso, 1994), 213; Žižek, "Kant with (or against) Sade," 290; Slavoj Žižek, "Welcome to the Desert of the Real (Reflections on 11 September 2001)." In *The Universal Exception*, eds. Rex Butler and Scott Stephens (London: Bloomsbury, 2006), 304; Žižek, *Absolute Recoil*, 334.

42 de Sade, *Philosophy in the Boudoir*, 7–9.

43 Lest I be accused of poor scholarship, I should mention that Lacan's critique of Sade is not limited to the four areas I described, yet his additional criticisms are less germane to the philosophical (in)consistency of the libertines' ideology and more attuned to Sade's qualities as a writer. For example, Lacan insinuates that, for all the transgressive contents of his libertine novels, Sade's style in it remains rather conventional and he also deplores the author's lack of wit. On at least two occasions, Žižek expresses his agreement with Lacan with regard to the latter point, yet I cannot bring myself to sanction Lacan's and Žižek's opinion here. Apart from the fact that some authorial comments in *Philosophy in the Boudoir* and *Juliette* are absolutely hilarious, Sade's entire libertine corpus could definitely be constructed differently—as one, sprawling political satire—and his place in André Breton's *Anthology of Black Humour* could therefore be well deserved and indisputable. See Lacan, "Kant with Sade," 664–6; Žižek, *For They Know Not What They Do*, 234; Žižek, "The Limits of

the Semiotic Approach to Psychoanalysis," 105; André Breton, *Anthology of Black Humour*, trans. Mark Polizzotti (San Francisco, CA: City Lights Books 1997), 45–58.

44 See Žižek, "Kant with (or against) Sade," 298; Žižek, *Sex and the Failed Absolute*, 114. In "Kant with Sade," Lacan never considers the possibility of a critique of pure desire. In fact, after having formalized the libertines' "utopia of desire," he playfully suggests that the Kantian universality is rewritten as a *Critique of Impure Reason*. See Lacan, "Kant with Sade," 653–4. For alienation and separation as the two constitutive operators of the fantasy and the neurotic psychic structure, see Lacan, *The Seminar. Book XI*, 203–15; Jacques Lacan, "Position of the Unconscious," in *Écrits*, trans. Bruce Fink (New York: W. W. Norton & Company, 2006), 703–21. In the latter text, Lacan employs Empedocles' act of throwing himself into the crater of Mount Etna as an example of a successful separation. See Lacan, "Position of the Unconscious," 715.

45 I would prefer not to think, here, that Žižek has thereby fallen into the trap of the logical fallacy of *post hoc ergo propter hoc*. Just because it is true that, in *Seminar VII*, Lacan's discussion of *Antigone* follows his explanation of the vicious cycle between Kant and Sade, this does not imply that Antigone appears in this place *because of* this vicious cycle, even less that Sophocles' heroine might provide us with an answer to the questions Kant and Sade failed to resolve.

46 Žižek, *The Sublime Object of Ideology*, 117. See also Žižek, "Author's Preface: The Inhuman." In *Interrogating the Real*, eds. Rex Butler and Scott Stephens (London: Bloomsbury, 2005), xxvi.

47 Žižek, *The Metastases of Enjoyment*, 69; Žižek, "Kant with (or against) Sade," 298–9.

48 See, for example, Žižek, *The Metastases of Enjoyment*, 70; Žižek and Daly, *Conversations with Žižek*, 163; Žižek, *The Puppet and the Dwarf*, 54; Žižek, *The Parallax View*, 94; Žižek, *Disparities*, 334.

49 Lacan, *The Seminar. Book VII*, 319–22.

50 Ibid., 319. Dennis Porter's English translation of the phrase is rather clumsy and unnecessarily verbose. A better, more straightforward rendition could be: "the only thing one can be guilty of is having given up on one's desire."

51 It is therefore quite painful to see Žižek mention on two separate occasions that "do not compromise your desire" "was never used again by Lacan in his later work." See Žižek, *The Puppet and the Dwarf*, 54; Žižek, *The Parallax View*, 94. The point is not that the formula was never used again by Lacan, but that it was never used! I should also remind the reader here that, on January 26, 1983, Jacques-Alain Miller devoted an entire session of his own public seminar to the danger of turning Lacan's ethical paradox into a negative imperative, evidently to no avail. See Miller, *Del síntoma al fantasma*, 193–204.

52 Lacan, *The Seminar. Book VII*, 321. The reason as to why Lacan presents the quandary as a paradox is that guilt is generally associated with the opposite of "giving up on one's desire." Giving up on one's desire suggests that one did not

do what one thought one was supposed to do, whilst the common conception of guilt is that it emerges when one has done something one thought one was *not* supposed to do.

53 For similar misinterpretations, see Alain Badiou, *Ethics: An Essay on the Understanding of Evil*, trans. Peter Hallward (London: Verso, 2001), 47; Alenka Zupančič, *Ethics of the Real: Kant, Lacan* (London: Verso, 2000), 250–1; Mari Ruti, *The Singularity of Being: Lacan and the Immortal Within* (New York: Fordham University Press, 2012), 71; Simon Critchley, *Tragedy, the Greeks and Us* (London: Profile Books, 2019), 130; Deborah Anna Luepnitz, "Antigone and the Unsayable: A Psychoanalytic Reading," *American Imago* 77, no. 2 (2020), 355. For a detailed critical analysis of this misreading in all its logical inconsistencies and spurious ramifications, see Marc De Kesel, "The Real of Ethics: On a Widespread Misconception." In *Unconscious Representations: Psychoanalytic and Philosophical Perspectives on the Body*, eds. Brian W. Becker, John Panteleimon Manoussakis and David M. Goodman (Abingdon: Routledge, 2018), 76–93.

54 Both in *The Puppet and the Dwarf* and in *The Parallax View*, Žižek posits that Lacan's *Seminar VII* is "the point of deadlock" for Lacan, because he comes "dangerously close to the standard version of the "passion for the Real." See Žižek, *The Puppet and the Dwarf*, 54; Žižek, *The Parallax View*, 94. However, the deadlock that Žižek identifies here is artificial, because it is the corollary of his own misreading of Lacan's seminar as ending in the imperative "Do not give up on your desire!"

55 Sophocles' *Antigone* contains the first recorded instance in history of the word αὐτόνομος, which could be rendered literally in English as "by virtue of one's own law." See Sophocles, *Antigone*, 81. Owing to this, scholars have often depicted Antigone as the historical paragon of humanism, because she is held to epitomize the indomitable power of the human spirit. It is in the same context that Hegel referred to *Antigone* for the first time in his own works, notably as a marginal note to a manuscript from 1796 that is known by its incipit *Jedes Volk* . . . See Georg Wilhelm Friedrich Hegel, "Jedes Volk . . . ." In *Gesammelte Werke, Band 1: Frühe Schriften 1*, eds. Friedhelm Nicolin and Gisela Schüler (Hamburg: Felix Meiner Verlag, 1989), 368. Heidegger's interpretation of *Antigone* appears in his 1935 lecture course *Introduction to Metaphysics*, but primarily in his 1942 lectures on Hölderlin's hymn "The Ister." See Martin Heidegger, *Introduction to Metaphysics* (1953), trans. Gregory Fried and Richard Polt (New Haven, CT: Yale University Press, 2000), 112–26; Martin Heidegger, *Hölderlin's Hymn 'The Ister'*, trans. William McNeill and Julia Davis (Bloomington, IN: Indiana University Press, 1996), 51–122. When Žižek refers to Heidegger's reading of the play, he only ever mentions the *Introduction to Metaphysics*. See Žižek, *On Violence*, 59–60; Žižek, *Less than Nothing*, 832; Žižek, *Absolute Recoil*, 401. I should also emphasize that throughout his commentary on *Antigone*, Lacan steers away from all suggestions that Sophocles' heroine is really acting autonomously, according to her own law. See, for example, Lacan, *The Seminar. Book VII*, 273.

56 For Antigone's act as the emergence of a pure signifier, see Žižek, *Enjoy Your Symptom!*, 106; Žižek, *Less than Nothing*, 84; Žižek, *Antigone*, xv. For

Antigone as the autonomous subject who transcends the dialectic between authorship of and obedience to the moral law via the object *a*, see Slavoj Žižek, *On Belief* (London: Routledge, 2001), 138–40.

57 See Žižek, *Did Somebody Say Totalitarianism?*, 157–60.

58 For "reconsidering the symbolic Law as a set of contingent social arrangements," see Žižek, *Welcome to the Desert of the Real! Five Essays on September 11 and Related Dates* (London: Verso, 2002), 99. Note the first word of the book's subtitle. For "absolute contingency," see Žižek, *In Defense of Lost Causes*, 309. For "momentary suspension of the big Other," see Slavoj Žižek, *The Ticklish Subject: The Absent Centre of Political Ontology* (London Verso, 1999), 263. For the act as creative of its own (new) rationality, see Žižek, *Revolution at the Gates*, 243. For the transition from abstract to concrete universality, see Žižek, *Less than Nothing*, 567. The argument that I have summarized in one sentence originates in a vehement and often caustic discussion between Žižek and Yannis Stavrakakis, which starts in the pages of a 2003 issue of the journal *Umbr(a)* and culminates in a long section in Žižek's 2008 volume *In Defense of Lost Causes*. See, in this respect, Yannis Stavrakakis, "The Lure of Antigone: Aporias of an Ethics of the Political," *Umbr(a)* 4 (2003): 117–29; Žižek, "What Some Would Call . . .," 131–5; Žižek, *In Defense of Lost Causes*, 304–33.

59 See Jacques Lacan, "Logical Time and the Assertion of Anticipated Certainty: A New Sophism." In *Écrits*, trans. Bruce Fink (New York: W. W. Norton & Company, 2006), 161–75.

60 Apart from this fundamental disparity between the text of Sophocles' *Antigone* and Žižek's representation of its eponymous heroine, I should draw the reader's attention to two additional misreadings, which are less significant but nonetheless indicative of a certain sloppiness in Žižek's engagement with Sophocles and Lacan. First, in at least three places Žižek associates Antigone's ἄτη with the zone between-two-deaths, in which she lingers after she has been sentenced by Creon and before she takes her own life. See Žižek, *The Fragile Absolute*, 155–6; Žižek, *Less than Nothing*, 512; Žižek, *Antigone*, xxiii, note 1. However, for Lacan, ἄτη is the real barrier Antigone intends to cross and, as such, that which truly conditions her entering the zone between-two-deaths. For Lacan, Antigone's desire to bury her brother is therefore just a pretext, a welcome opportunity to fulfil another desire, namely the eradication of the curse (ἄτη) that has devastated the House of Labdakos since time out of mind This is also why Lacan does not see Antigone's desire to bury her brother as a pure desire, but rather as a desire that is already conditioned by another desire. See Lacan, *The Seminar. Book VII*, 263. Second, in *Absolute Recoil*, Žižek argues that the tragedy of Antigone's act turns into comedy in the first antistrophe of her final "argument" with Creon, notably where she invokes mythical examples of eternal damnation. See Žižek, *Absolute Recoil*, 335; Sophocles, *Antigone*, 81. However, this "theatrical" moment is far less comedic than Antigone's final lament, in which she directly addresses the corpse of Polynices and whose authenticity remains disputed to this day precisely for this reason, as Goethe famously conceded to Eckermann on March 28, 1827: "In Antigone, for example, there is a passage [verses 909–12] that always jars with me, and I would give a great deal for some eminent scholar to come

along and prove that it is not original, but a later interpolation by somebody else," because it is quite unworthy of Sophocles and "verges on the comical." See Johann Peter Eckermann, *Conversations with Goethe (1823–1832)* trans. Allan Blunden (London: Penguin, 2022), 507–8. Žižek quotes these verses (909–12) in *Less than Nothing*, yet only to demonstrate that Antigone's act generates its own norm and therefore acquires a dimension of concrete universality. See Žižek, *Less than Nothing*, 567. Interestingly, in *Absolute Recoil*, which succeeds *Less than Nothing*, Žižek also refers the reader back to Chapter 5 (note the number) of *Less than Nothing* "[f]or a more detailed analysis of the comical turn in Antigone [sic]," yet in this chapter there is literally "less than nothing" about comedy in *Antigone*. In it, Žižek merely announces what he himself would realize in 2016 in his own re-writing of *Antigone*, namely the option of an alternative ending of the tragedy, in which both Creon and Antigone are punished and the Chorus takes control of the polis. See Slavoj Žižek, *Absolute Recoil*, 335 note 18; Žižek, *Less than Nothing*, 323–4; Žižek, *Antigone*, xxiv. The principal section on *Antigone* in *Less than Nothing* occurs in Interlude 4 (note the number): Žižek, *Less than Nothing*, 566–8.

61 Sigmund Freud, "New Introductory Lectures on Psycho-Analysis. Lecture XXXI: The Dissection of the Psychical Personality." In *The Standard Edition of the Complete Psychological Works of Sigmund Freud*, Vol. 22, ed. and trans. James Strachey (London: The Hogarth Press and the Institute of Psycho-Analysis, 1964), 80. On numerous occasions, Lacan too reformulated Freud's phrase, whereby he generally replaced the term "ego" with "I" (*je*) or "subject" (*sujet*). See, for example, Jacques Lacan, "Science and Truth (1965)," in *Écrits*, trans. Bruce Fink (New York: W. W. Norton & Company, 2006), 734.

62 Žižek, *Iraq: The Borrowed Kettle*, 81. The italics are Žižek's.

63 Žižek, *Absolute Recoil*, 411.

64 See, for example, Slavoj Žižek, *Don't Act, Just Think* (2012), available at https://www.youtube.com/watch?v=IgR6uaVqWsQ (accessed 18 May 2021).

65 See Sigmund Freud, "Remembering, Repeating and Working-Through (Further Recommendations on the Technique of Psycho-Analysis II)." In *The Standard Edition of the Complete Psychological Works of Sigmund Freud*, Vol. 12, ed. and trans. James Strachey (London: The Hogarth Press and the Institute of Psycho-Analysis, 1958), 145–156; Lacan, *The Seminar. Book XI*, 273.

66 The link between Sade's writings and the object *a*, which is part of Lacan's second schema in 'Kant with Sade', is no longer identifiable in the English edition of *Écrits*, because the letter '*a*' was considered a typographical error and therefore deleted. See Lacan, "Kant with Sade," 657. To the best of my knowledge, the only place where Žižek engages with this specific part of "Kant with Sade," which may very well be one of its most original and thought-provoking features, is in a rarely quoted 1992 essay. See Slavoj Žižek, "In His Bold Gaze My Ruin Is Writ Large." In *Everything You Always Wanted to Know About Lacan (But Were Afraid to Ask Hitchcock)* (London-New York NY: Verso, 1992), 222. Surprisingly, perhaps, the most perspicacious champion of Lacan's idea – even though Lacan did not receive a single

mention – was Michel Foucault who, in his 1970 lectures on Sade at the State University of New York in Buffalo, situated the truth of the Sadean enterprise in Sade's incessant act of writing. See Michel Foucault, "Lectures on Sade," in *Language, Madness, and Desire: On Literature*, eds. Philippe Artières, Jean-François Bert, Mathieu Potte-Bonneville & Judith Revel, trans. Robert Bononno (Minneapolis MN-London: University of Minnesota Press, 2015), 93–146.

67 See Immanuel Kant, *Critique of Pure Reason (1781)*, ed. and trans. Marcus Weigelt (London: Penguin, 2007), 635.

Response to Nobus

Slavoj Žižek

One has to admit that Nobus did a tremendous scholarly work in his critical reading of my interpretation of Lacan's "Kant avec Sade." However, I stick to my interpretation—why? Let's begin with Nobus's claim which appears just to resume Kant's position:

> Of course, the fundamental problem with fulfilling one's ethical duty, as Kant himself remarked in his *Critique of Practical Reason*, is that no human being, however rational it may be, is really up to the task, and that the asymptotic approximation of this endlessly postponed, full compliance with the moral law may in itself come at the cost of a great deal of pain, which is supposed to be endured as much as possible in favor of the realization of the highest, transcendental good.

While this claim is correct, I think it stands only for one side of the much more ambiguous Kantian position. For Kant, freedom is real in the most radical (Lacanian) sense: freedom is an inexplicable, "irrational," unaccountable "fact of reason," a Real which disturbs our notion of (phenomenal) spatio-temporal reality as governed by natural laws. For this reason, our experience of freedom is properly traumatic, even for Kant himself, who tends to confuse the Real as the impossible which *happens* (that which "I cannot not do") with the Real as the impossible-to-happen (that which "I cannot ever fully accomplish"). In Kantian ethics, the true tension is not between the subject's idea that he is acting only for the sake of duty, and the hidden fact that there was effectively some pathological motivation at work (the vulgar psychoanalysis); the true tension is exactly the opposite one: the free act in its abyss is unbearable, traumatic, so that when we accomplish an act out of freedom in order to be able to sustain it, we experience it as conditioned by some pathological motivations. One is tempted to refer here to the key Kantian concept of schematization: a free act cannot be schematized, integrated into our experience, so, in order to schematize it, we have to "pathologize" it. And Kant himself as a rule misreads the true tension (the difficulty to endorse and assume a free act) as the standard tension of the agent who cannot ever be sure if his act effectively was free, not motivated by hidden pathological impetuses. Kierkegaard was here more consequent than Kant when he put it that the true trauma is not our mortality, but our immortality: it is easy to accept that we are just a speck of dust in the infinite universe; what is much more difficult to accept is that we effectively are immortal free beings who, as such, cannot escape the terrible responsibility of their freedom. In other words, in contrast to the individual caught in the standard skeptical despair, i.e., the individual who knows he will die but cannot accept it and hopes for eternal life, we have here, in the case of "sickness unto death," the individual who desperately wants to die, to disappear forever, but knows that he cannot do it, i.e., that he is condemned to eternal life.

The reason for this ambiguity of Kant is another compromise which brings us close to Sade. Kant gets involved with a difficult predicament when he distinguishes between the "ordinary" evil (the violation of morality on behalf of some "pathological" motivation, like greed, lust, ambition, etc), the "radical" evil, and the "diabolical" evil. It may seem that we are dealing with a simple linear graduation: "normal" evil, more "radical" evil, and, finally, the unthinkable "diabolical" evil. However, upon a closer look, it becomes clear that the three types are not on the same level, i.e., that Kant confuses different principles of classification. "Radical" evil does not designate a specific type of evil acts, but an a priori propensity of the human nature (to act egotistically, to give preference to pathological motivations over universal ethical duty) which opens up the very space for "normal" evil acts, i.e., which roots them in human nature. In contrast to it, "diabolical" evil does designate a specific type of evil acts: acts which are not motivated by any pathological motivation, but are done "just for the sake of it," elevating evil itself into an apriori non-pathological motivation—something akin to Poe's "imp of perversity." While Kant claims that "diabolical evil" cannot actually occur (it is not possible for a human being to elevate evil itself into a universal ethical norm), he nonetheless asserts that one should posit it as an abstract possibility. Interestingly enough, the concrete case he mentions (in Part I of his *Metaphysics of Morals*) is that of the judicial regicide, the murder of a king executed as a punishment pronounced by a court: Kant's claim is that, in contrast to a simple rebellion in which the mob kills only the person of a king, the judicial process which condemns to death the king (this embodiment of the rule of law) destroys from within the very form of the (rule of) law, turning it into a terrifying travesty—which is why, as Kant put it, such an act is an "indelible crime" which cannot ever be pardoned. However, in a second step, Kant desperately argues that in the two historical cases of such an act (under Cromwell and in the 1793 France), we were dealing just with a mob taking revenge. Why this oscillation and classificatory confusion in Kant? Because, if he were to assert the actual possibility of "diabolical evil," he would find it impossible to distinguish it from the Good—since both acts would be non-pathologically motivated, the travesty of justice would become indistinguishable from justice itself.

For this reason I still "maintain that Sade is a closet Kantian and then proclaim that his Kantianism fails at the point where he cannot be a Kantian." As for Sade's inconsistency, i.e., as for the fantasmatic nature of Sade's dream of the second death, Lacan made it clear what is wrong with this dream of a radical pure negation which puts a stop to the life-cycle itself. In a superb display of his genius, he provided a simple answer: "It's just that, being a psychoanalyst, I can see that the second death is prior to the first, and not after, as de Sade dreams."[1] (The only problematic part of this statement is the qualification "being a psychoanalyst"—a Hegelian philosopher can also see this quite clearly.) In what precise sense are we to understand this priority of the second death—the radical annihilation of the entire life-cycle of generation and corruption—over the first death, which remains a moment of this cycle? Aaron Schuster points the way: "Sade believes that there exists a well-established second nature that operates according to immanent laws. Against this ontologically consistent realm he can only dream of an absolute Crime that would abolish the three kingdoms and attain the pure disorder of primary nature."[2] In short, what Sade does not see is that there is no big Other, no Nature as an ontologically consistent realm—nature is already in itself inconsistent, unbalanced, destabilized by antagonisms. The total negation imagined by Sade thus does not come at the end, as a threat or prospect of radical destruction, it comes at the beginning, it always-already happened; it stands for the zero-level starting point out of which the fragile/inconsistent reality emerges. In other words, what is missing in the notion of Nature as a body regulated by fixed laws is simply subject itself: in Hegelese, the Sadean Nature remains a Substance. Sade continues to grasp reality only as Substance and not also as Subject, where "subject" does not stand for another ontological level that is different from Substance, but for the immanent incompleteness-inconsistency-antagonism of Substance itself. And, insofar as the Freudian name for this radical negativity is death drive, Schuster is right to point out how, paradoxically, what Sade misses in his celebration of the ultimate Crime of radical destruction of all life is precisely the death drive.[3]

Nobus concludes his text with a series of Kant's questions:

> What is the role of the public intellectual under conditions of global capitalism? What does Žižek intend to achieve with his unstoppable series of books, essays, commentaries, and criticisms? Given the three circles of his intellectual itinerary, what is Žižek's answer to the three famous Kantian questions that underpin the interest of our reason? What can I know? What ought I to do? What may I hope?

My answers are straight and simple. I can know not-all in the Lacanian sense (which is different from Kant's limitation to phenomenal reality) there is no external limit to our knowledge, and for this very reason it remains not-all. There is no transcendent thing-in-itself, the very inconsistencies of our knowledge enable us to gain access to truth. What may I hope? Nothing, absolutely nothing. What ought I to do? I think this is a wrong question, this is not what Lenin meant with his title. Lacan said "Ne demande que faire, que celui dont le désir s'éteint" ("Only the one whose desire is waning asks what is to be done").[4] Is Lacan's wonderful formula to be read as an implicit critique of Lenin? No. Although Lenin's title is a question, the book is a clear answer; it provides precise guidelines of what is to be done. The title works like similar titles of introductory textbooks: "What is Quantum Physics?", "What is Biogenetics?", etc. When today's post-Marxists write treatises where they ponder endlessly on what to do, on who could be the agent of radical change, their desperate doubt and search effectively bears witness to the waning of their desire to really embark on a radical change: they do not really desire change, they rather enjoy the endless self-critical pondering which, as they know well, will not lead to any clear result. This was never my problem: in my political engagements, I simply reacted when I felt my intervention would be pertinent, never pondering what should I do. Plus, I never accepted to be terrorized by the motto that thinking should contribute to social change: I naively accept that there is an emancipatory aspect in reflexive thinking as such, in its distance toward so-called reality.

Notes

1 Jacques Lacan, *The Seminar. Book XVII: The Other Side of Psychoanalysis (1969–1970)*, ed. Jacques-Alain Miller, trans. Russell Grigg (New York NY: W. W. Norton & Company, 2007), 67.

2 Aaron Schuster, personal communication.

3 I will ignore here the topic of Antigone's act; I just want to signal that too much focus on Antigone is misleading: in the seminar that follows the seminar on the ethics of psychoanalysis (where he reads Antigone), Lacan provides a detailed reading of Claudel's Sygne de Coûfontaine, and I think this move from Antigone to Sygne is to be read as Lacan's autocritique.

4 Jacques Lacan, *Television*, in *Television: A Challenge to the Psychoanalytic Establishement*, ed. Joan Copjec, trans. Denis Hollier, Rosalind Krauss and Annette Michelson (New York NY: W. W. Norton & Company, 1990), 42.

CHAPTER ELEVEN

Raising a Mundane Object to the Dignity of the Thing

When Desire Is Not the Desire of the Other

Mari Ruti

Throughout his elaborations of Lacanian theory, Slavoj Žižek draws a firm distinction between the normative subject of desire and the antinormative, even revolutionary, subject of the drive. According to Žižek, the subject of desire is incapable of dissociating itself from dominant sociosymbolic commandments because its desire is merely a reflection of the hegemonic desire of the big Other: the Other seduces the subject into submission by appropriating its desire to the extent that, even on an unconscious level, it desires exactly what it is culturally conditioned to desire. In contrast, the subject of the drive is able to "traverse" the unconscious fantasies that have been domesticated by the Other; it is able to bypass the ruses of desire in ways that enable it to dive into the rebellious energies of the drive and therefore to attain some "real"—rather than merely imaginary—satisfaction. The subject of the drive, in short, is capable of the ethical "act" of rejecting the Other's desire even if, in extreme cases, doing so means destroying itself. On this reading, ethics is aligned with the drive whereas desire, despite Lacan's insistence that the ethics of psychoanalysis is a matter of not giving ground on one's desire, stands in direct opposition to ethics.

Žižek describes the distinction between desire and the drive as follows:

For Lacan, desire and drive are opposed with regard to their formal structure: desire drifts in an endless metonymy of lack, while drive is a closed circular movement; desire is always unsatisfied, but drive generates its own satisfaction; desire is sustained by the symbolic Law/Prohibition, while drive remains outside the dialectic of the Law. Desire and drive thus form a parallax unity of mutual exclusion: each is irreducible to the other, there is no shared space within which we can bring them together.[1]

In Žižek's rendering, if desire can never escape symbolic law, the drive does so automatically. If desire is always dissatisfied, the drive finds satisfaction—hits its "aim"—by repeatedly missing its goal of reaching its object. If desire idiotically pursues objects as substitutes for the originary non-object, the Thing, that the subject fantasizes having lost, the drive, as Žižek puts it, "takes lack itself as object, finding a satisfaction in the circular movement of missing satisfaction itself."[2] In other words, if desire is motivated to pursue objects that falsely promise satisfaction, "the drive is not the persisting attachment to the lost object, but the repeating enactment of the loss as such—the object of the drive is not a lost object, but loss itself as an object."[3] One of the advantages of the drive over desire, then, is that it bypasses the disappointments of object cathexis by ignoring objects altogether and instead finding its *jouissance* in the incessant repetition of loss.

I want to begin by saying that I have a degree of appreciation for Žižek's reasoning and have even explicitly defended it.[4] Like Žižek, I believe that, in Lacanian terms, the only "cure" for the subject's lack-in-being is to accept that there is no cure, that there is no object of desire can that definitively fill its lack. I also understand that at the background of Žižek's distrust of desire resides a legitimate concern with the manner in which consumer capitalism, the critique of which is crucial to Žižek's theoretico-political intervention, exploits the fact that the subject attempts to evade the realities of its ontological condition of lack by investing its desire in the sparkling attractions displayed at store windows, billboards, television screens, online sites, and other settings designed to catch its eye.

There is no doubt that capitalism thrives on the subject's hopeless quest to heal its lack and that the world is saturated by objects of desire that deceptively promise satisfaction. I have always been compelled by Žižek's claim that Western societies are driven by an "injunction to enjoy," which, instead of curtailing our pleasure through restrictions, such as rules of appropriate sexual behavior, in the manner that earlier societies did, deliberately encourages us to enjoy ourselves to the fullest.[5] This results in a situation where we are constantly worried about not enjoying ourselves enough. Yet the more we "enjoy," the more capitalism profits. Indeed, if in the past it made sense to strive to unshackle our desire from authoritarian social injunctions, we have now reached a point where every newly "liberated" desire gets appropriated by the Other, thereby merely augmenting the Other's hold over us.

Capitalism is so effective in manipulating desire that even the subject's disappointment with the commodities that it acquires does not lead to any lasting disillusionment regarding the system's capacity to satisfy it. As Todd McGowan has dexterously illustrated, it merely feeds the impression that the subject simply has not yet chanced upon the right object; it feeds the hope that just around the corner—or in the next department store—lies in wait an object that will finally grant the subject the satisfaction it deserves.⁶ Consequently, the possibility that we are capable of having desires that are independent of the Other's desire has admittedly become increasingly difficult to envision.

Given this reality, I understand the appeal of thinking that if it is the case that the drive does not need objects for its satisfaction—that it experiences loss itself as satisfying—we may manage to outwit the lures of capitalism by replacing desire with the drive. After all, a subject that has no need for objects has no need for capitalism;⁷ such a subject walks past an elaborate Macy's window display without even registering it. I love this idea—I truly do. However, the attempt to valorize the drive at the expense of desire—as Žižek repeatedly does—leaves me with the gnawing feeling that this solution to the evils of capitalism and the disenchantments of object cathexis discards important components of human psychic experience, especially the fact that beyond the deceptive satisfaction offered by commodities, we are capable of desiring objects—people, ideals, and principles—that fall outside the capitalist paradigm and, more generally, the Other's desire.

When Žižek categorically elevates the drive over desire, he fails to distinguish between objects that do not merit our attachment and others that do. He implies that desire is *intrinsically* erroneous and politically regressive, that our objects of desire are invariably tainted by capitalist normativity. In contrast, I believe that there are objects that not only deserve our attachment but also genuinely satisfy and enrich us, and that sometimes ethics is a matter of defending our commitment to such objects, either because we cherish them so much that nothing can shake our loyalty to them or because we feel that justice demands that we stand by them no matter what the risk of doing so might be.

This chapter is designed to illustrate that Žižek's distinction between desire and the drive is too strongly drawn—that the subject, at least in some circumstances, is perfectly capable of desiring in ways that have nothing to do with, or that may even directly challenge, the Other's desire. More specifically, I want to propose that the ethical "act" would be extremely unlikely to take place without the presence of an object of desire—a person, ideal, or principle—that captures, and hence *arrests*, the subject's *jouissance* to such an extent that it feels compelled to act against its own interests. If the drive, as Žižek claims, "is a closed circular movement," by itself it would never be able to induce the subject to undertake an act of any kind; it would happily keep going around solipsistically, without any regard for anything outside of itself. That is, the subject needs something beyond itself—beyond its drive—to motivate it to act. My wager is that only an object that activates the subject's desire on a level that is non-negotiable is capable of providing such an incentive.

A Case for Sublimation

Rethinking the ethical potential of desire entails making a case for the centrality of sublimation in Lacanian theory. Sublimation is the dimension of Lacan's thinking that most interests me but that appears to least interest Žižek. I think that considering Lacanian ethics through the lens of sublimation—of Lacan's commentary on raising a mundane object to the "dignity of the Thing"[8]—can result in a productive reassessment of significant aspects of Lacanian theory, perhaps even moving this theory in a more affirmative direction than Žižek's theorization of the destructive ethical act—which by now has become paradigmatic in Lacanian studies—is able to provide. Simply put, I wish to put pressure on the following statement made by Žižek:

> With regard to this relation between drive and desire, we could perhaps risk a small rectification of the Lacanian maxim of the psychoanalytic ethic "not to cede one's desire": is not desire as such already a certain yielding, a kind of compromise formation, a metonymic displacement, retreat, a defense against intractable drive? "To desire" *means* to give way on the drive—insofar as we follow Antigone and "do not give way on our desire," do we not precisely step out of the domain of desire, do we not shift from the modality of desire into the modality of pure drive?[9]

Let me state my disagreement plainly. First, the "rectification" that Žižek proposes is far from being "small," for it would have immense ramifications for the way in which we theorize not only Lacanian ethics but also the very structure of subjectivity and the subject's relationship to the world. Second, I do not believe that Lacan's decision to associate ethics with desire rather than the drive is a lapse of reasoning that we should rush to correct, nor do I believe that desire is "already a certain yielding, a kind of compromise formation." In committing her act, Antigone does not "shift from the modality of desire into the modality of pure drive." Rather, Antigone's act reflects her non-negotiable loyalty toward Polyneices or, alternatively, toward her principles. Whether she sacrifices herself because she loves Polyneices or because she values the ideal of offering him a dignified funeral is unimportant. What matters is that she acts for the sake of *someone* or *something*. Simply put, there would be no Antigone's act without Polyneices or without the principles that she holds dear.

Although it is true that desire functions as a defense against the full (annihilating) force of *jouissance*, I do not agree with Žižek that "desire and *jouissance* are inherently antagonistic, exclusive even."[10] I also do not believe, as he states in the passage that I quoted at the beginning of this chapter, that desire and the drive are "irreducible to each other," that "there is no shared space within which we can bring them together." I want to show that sublimation is precisely the "shared space" where it is possible—at least to some degree—for desire to appropriate some of the drive's *jouissance*. In other words, I wish to propose that desire, at least the kind of desire that is capable of inducing the subject to act, consists of sublimated *jouissance* which has become attached to people, ideals, and principles.

Žižek himself offers an account of the matter that initially seems to accord with my interpretation when he writes: "How is it possible nonetheless to couple desire and *jouissance*, to guarantee a minimum of *jouissance* within the space of desire? This is made possible by the famous Lacanian object a that mediates between the incompatible domains of desire and *jouissance*."[11] I could not agree more, for as I illustrate shortly, I also believe that it is the *objet a* that holds the key to the kind of desire that "guarantees a minimum of *jouissance* within the space of desire." It is therefore possible that my disagreement with Žižek is merely a matter of emphasis rather than of a complete divergence of interpretations.

Žižek correctly specifies that the *objet a* is not what we desire but rather what sets our desire in motion: it is the "formal frame the confers consistency on our desire."[12] Žižek therefore acknowledges that despite all the metonymic displacements of desire from one object to the next, there is a degree of idiosyncratic consistency to our desire that has to do with our fundamental fantasy, with the deepest layers of our singular structure of desire. In other words, given that there is no universal formula for desire, each of us invents our "private" formula, which then gives our desire an automatic valence in the sense that this desire attaches itself to objects that fit our "pre-given fantasy."[13] All this makes perfect sense. However, my interpretation departs from that of Žižek in the sense that I am interested in the sublime aspects of the *objet a* rather than solely in its "uncanny," even "horrifying" dimensions—dimensions that, according to Žižek, "dispossess" the subject, reducing it "to a puppet-like level beyond dignity and freedom."[14]

In this context, Žižek gives an example of an ad campaign which depicts a series of well-tanned women's behinds in tight bathing suits to market a sun-tanning lotion with the slogan, "Each has her own factor."[15] The ad is premised on a vulgar, misogynistic objectification of women: each woman can be "had" if you can figure out her "factor." Žižek uses this ad to demonstrate that, generally speaking, each subject has its own "factor," its own fundamental fantasy. I agree. However, I do not agree that it is invariably the case that there "is nothing uplifting" about this factor.[16] Rather, I believe that Lacan proposes that there are situations where the "factor" in question takes on a sublime rather than a debasing hue: the *objet a* is not always mortifying or demeaning, but may instead point to a kernel of sublimity within the object of the subject's desire. Consequently, the *objet a* does not always rob the subject of its "dignity and freedom," but rather—as I aim to show—contributes to its ability to experience both. Sublimation is the mechanism that accomplishes this feat.

Sublimation, Jouissance, and "Real" Satisfaction

As I see it, both the drive and desire pursue the *objet a* as an emissary of the Thing, the difference being that desire goes about the task more obliquely. Neither the drive nor desire are natural—the drive is not instinct—but desire has undergone a greater degree of socialization, which obviously *can*, but does not *always*, mean that it is socially complacent. Although I readily admit that most forms of desire reflect the desire of the Other, I believe that the kind of desire that approaches the drive—and therefore sublimates *jouissance*—rather than imitates the Other's desire gives the subject a degree of "real" satisfaction. It is precisely the additional layer of socialization, of sublimation, that desire has undergone that creates the distance between the subject and the Thing that is necessary for this type of satisfaction; it is because sublimation acts as a shield against self-destruction that the subject has access to bits of satisfaction—morsels of the real—that it would not otherwise be able to attain. This is one way to understand what it means to raise a mundane object to the dignity of the Thing: the people, ideals, and principles that desire pursues have been infused with a tolerable amount of the *jouissance* that the Thing (fantasmatically) embodies; sublimation retains a smidgeon of *jouissance* without allowing it to overwhelm the subject.

The drive and desire are therefore not two mutually exclusive entities but instead related, and at times even slightly overlapping, ways of generating *jouissance*. Both circle the Thing without attaining it. When it comes to the drive, two options seem possible: either the drive enjoys never attaining its object—which, if you ask me, is an anemic form of enjoyment—or it gets so deeply sucked into the Thing's orbit that the subject self-destructs. Desire, in contrast, offers the subject the possibility of experiencing *jouissance* in manageable doses. On my reading, this is what Lacan has in mind when he claims that the Thing is "found at the most as something missed. One doesn't find it, but only its pleasurable associations."[17] "If the Thing were not fundamentally veiled," Lacan continues, "we wouldn't be in the kind of relationship to it that obliges us, as the whole of psychic life is obliged, to encircle it or bypass it in order to conceive it."[18] In other words, it is precisely because we have to "encircle" or "bypass" the Thing at a safe distance that we attain the kinds of "pleasurable associations" that give us a little taste of *jouissance*. Such pleasurable associations may be mere muffled echoes of the Thing, yet they still manage to satisfy us by transmitting its muted imprint.

Lacan's commentary on desire as the foundation of the ethics of psychoanalysis only makes sense if we accept the notion that he operates with two different conceptions of desire: the first is the kind that Žižek (correctly) demonizes because it yokes the subject to the desire of the Other; but the second is the kind that, in touching something about the "truth" of the subject's sinthome, about its fundamental fantasy as the deepest level of its desire, draws close to the drive in order to capture some of its *jouissance* without thereby fully merging with it. This second kind of desire evades the Other's dictates by bringing the subject to the proximity of the drive (which is not the same thing as translating desire into the drive): it allows the subject to attain the kind of satisfaction that is more closely associated with its sinthome than with the Other's desire.

I believe that it is this second kind of desire—the kind of desire that absorbs some of the drive's vitality—that Lacan strives to protect when he advises the subject against yielding on its desire. Because there are critics who have claimed that Lacan never actually says anything about not ceding on one's desire,[19] let us recall a key statement from *The Ethics of Psychoanalysis*:

> It is because we know better than those who went before how to recognize the nature of desire ... that a reconsideration of ethics is possible, that a form of ethical judgment is possible, of a kind that gives this question the force of a Last Judgment: Have you acted in conformity with the desire that is in you? ... I propose then that, from an analytic point of view, the only thing of which one can be guilty is of having given ground relative to one's desire.[20]

Lacan clearly states that, from an analytic viewpoint, the only thing one can be guilty of is "having given ground relative to one's desire." To me, this sounds more or less identical to the idea that one should not cede on one's desire. This maxim, which represents the basis of Lacan's "reconsideration of ethics," relies on a psychoanalytic, secular version of the Last Judgment, urging the subject to ask itself whether it has acted "in conformity with" its desire. Later in the text, Lacan specifies: "What I call 'giving ground relative to one's desire' is always accompanied in the destiny of the subject by some betrayal": the subject betrays its desire in order to "return to the common path."[21] "Giving ground relative to one's desire"—ceding on one's desire—is here plainly presented as a form of self-betrayal that ushers the subject back into the folds of the Other's desire, which Lacan definitely does not wish to endorse.

It is hence impossible that Lacan, in this instance at least, equates the subject's desire with the Other's desire. In positing that the ethics of psychoanalysis is an ethics of not giving ground on one's desire, he refers to the kind of desire that animates the subject by allowing it to tap into the reservoir of energy that *jouissance*—the overagitation of the drives— represents. For this reason, I believe that it is misleading to propose, as Žižek does, that to desire "*means* to give way on the drive." Even if desire is a "compromise formation," "a defense against the intractable drive," it is not a matter of "giving way"—of yielding in the sense of giving up or discarding—but of arresting the incessant movement of the drive for long enough to make satisfaction possible. This satisfaction is by necessity always temporary and partial, but this does not in any way diminish its value. If anything, it is precious because it is the only "real" satisfaction that the subject is capable of beyond the lackluster satisfaction that it attains from continuously reliving its loss.

The Dignity of the Thing

Who, in all honestly, wants the latter? I readily accept my loss, my status as a being of lack. However, if the only thing I can expect from life is the experience of endlessly reliving this loss, I might as well end it now. There must be *something*—some Thing—that makes life worth the pain that it entails. In my opinion, this "something" has to do with the fact that, as human beings, we possess the capacity to raise mundane objects to the dignity of the Thing; we possess the sublimatory capacity to (extraordinarily selectively) imbue certain people, ideals, and principles with a special significance, a sublime glow, that gives us genuine satisfaction, thereby making it meaningful for us to keep living.

Alenka Zupančič expresses the matter perfectly when she states: "To raise an object to the dignity of the Thing is not to idealize it, but, rather, to 'realize' it."[22] In other words, sublimation is what makes the real "appear" within reality: it "realizes"—renders tangible—a little piece of the Thing. This is why Zupančič asserts that when we insist on an unbridgeable chasm between the Thing and all worldly things—which is exactly what Žižek seems to do—we remain perpetually dissatisfied. We become dedicated to a hopeless fidelity "to a lost enjoyment" in the sense that we spurn everyday objects because we imagine that only the missing Thing can grant us "authentic" fulfillment: "in the name of the lack of the True object, we reject all other objects and satisfy ourselves with none."[23] When we focus on the fantasmatic nature of all ordinary objects, we fail to appreciate the partial satisfactions offered by worldly things, thereby evacuating our existence of all possibility of non-destructive *jouissance*.

I do not think that it makes any sense to suggest, as Žižek does, that when we refuse to "give way" on our desire, we automatically switch from the register of desire to that of the drive. I would instead claim that whenever we do not give way on our desire, we choose the singularity of our *jouissance*, our sinthome, over collective definitions of desirability. We walk past the Macy's window display without even noticing it because we are preoccupied with a person, ideal, or principle that consumes us so intensely that the Other's desire becomes utterly irrelevant. We have not entered "the modality of pure drive,"[24] for we are still able to walk down the street without getting arrested. However, the main thing that matters to us is the person, ideal, or principle that has taken possession of our being. This, I want to argue, is what happens when we raise a mundane object to the dignity of the Thing. It is why I believe that Lacanian ethics is not merely a matter of destructive acts of rebellion but also—and I do not want to portray this as an either-or situation—of sublimation, of paying passionate attention to the gleam of the Thing that permeates the objects we most value and for the sake of which we are willing to sacrifice a great deal, including our symbolic and imaginary supports.

In *The Ethics of Psychoanalysis*, Lacan offers two examples of what it means to raise a mundane object to the dignity of the Thing—of what it means for an ordinary object to become invested with extraordinary value—that I have used in my previous work because I find them compelling.[25] The first is his depiction of the ornamental string of matchboxes that his friend has hung around his mantelpiece:

> This arrangement demonstrated that a match box isn't simply something that has a certain utility, that it isn't even a type in the Platonic sense, an abstract match box, that the match box all by itself is a thing with all its coherence of being. The wholly gratuitous, proliferating, superfluous, and quasi absurd character of this collection pointed to its thingness as match box. Thus the collector found his motive in this form of apprehension that concerns less the match box than the Thing that subsists in a match box.[26]

Lacan here asserts that his friend's collection of matchboxes reveals the "thingness"—rather than the utility or even the Platonic "type"—of the matchbox: it illustrates that a matchbox "is not simply an object, but that, in the form of an *Erscheinung*, as it appeared in its truly imposing multiplicity, it may be a Thing."[27] Despite its "quasi absurd character," the assemblage of matchboxes illuminates the trace of the Thing that "subsists" in the matchbox: it makes the sublime appear in the most commonplace of objects; it prompts the Thing's aura to materialize within the fabric of daily life. Although Lacan admits that the matchbox "is a thing that is not, of course, the Thing"—that the ordinary object that his friend has elevated to the nobility of the Thing remains a substitute that does not yield the Thing-in-itself—he claims that the example demonstrates "the sudden elevation of the match box to a dignity that it did not possess before."[28] That is, the matchbox, in this particular instance, serves as an instance of sublimation: it grants its creator a tiny bit of *jouissance* that connects him to the luster of the Thing.

Lacan proposes that something similar occurs when we admire an apple painted by Cézanne: "everyone knows that there is a mystery in the way Cézanne paints apples, for the relationship to the real as it is renewed in art at that moment makes the object appear purified; it involves a renewal of its dignity."²⁹ When Cézanne paints an apple, he "renews" its dignity. Insofar as his art reaches toward the real—toward the dwelling place of the Thing—he taps into a mystery that resides beyond his skill at portraying his object. Cézanne's apple is never merely a simple depiction of an apple, for the deeper goal of his art is a dimension that exceeds mere imitation: the singularity of his art resides in the fact that it "makes the object appear purified," that it manages to capture something about the enigma—and even the sublimity—of the Thing in its representation of an utterly banal object.

One could argue that the string of matchboxes and Cézanne's apples are less objects of desire in the usual sense of the word than they are objects of sublimatory admiration. However, I want to propose that the dynamic of desire—when it touches the real of *jouissance* rather than merely replicates the Other's desire—is identical to the dynamic of sublimation that Lacan outlines through his discussion of the matchboxes and Cézanne's apples. Like these objects of sublimatory admiration, "real" objects of desire contain a trace of the Thing, something that is "more in them than them," to paraphrase Lacan's famous dictum. In other words, they contain the *objet a*, the object-cause of desire. While the *objet a* is often a purely imaginary entity that we place in the object of our desire, it can, sometimes at least, also be an emblem of the trace of the Thing that "subsists" in, and even "renews," the object.

Žižek himself comes close to this interpretation when he notes, in *The Sublime Object of Ideology*, that the *objet a* is the "surplus" of the real "over every symbolization."³⁰ In *The Plague of Fantasies*, in turn, he specifies that the *objet a* "designates what which remains of the Thing after it has undergone the process of symbolization."³¹ Although it is true that we are the ones who deposit the *objet a* in our object, this does not mean that our desire is invariably mistaken or that it can always be reduced to the illusions of narcissistic fantasy.

The Psychoanalytic Object and the Truth of Desire

Let us recall that, far from shunning the *objet a*, Lacan considers it as one of Freud's greatest discoveries. He in fact draws a distinction between regular objects and "the psychoanalytic object," which is, precisely, the *objet a*: the partial object. As opposed to regular objects that enter into an economy of equivalence, objects that can be substituted for each other, the psychoanalytic object "is the aim of desire as such, the something that emphasizes one object among all the others as incommensurate with the others."³² The *objet a* is therefore linked to the kind of desire that renders objects unique so that it becomes impossible to exchange one object for another. Lacan furthermore proposes that this uniqueness—or incommensurability—of the object makes it "weighty," which means that we discern this uniqueness "in a being *only* when we truly love."³³ In this manner, the *objet a* connects us to the truth of our desire, to our sinthome, which is why Lacan criticizes those who attempt to replace it with a whole object, to transform it "into a flat, round, total object . . . the other as a whole person."³⁴ "We had a real find there," Lacan specifies in relation to the *objet a*, namely "that of the fundamentally partial nature of the object insofar as it is the pivotal point, crux, or key of human desire."³⁵ However, because it is disturbing to think that our desire may not have much to do with the beloved as a whole person, analysts—like the rest of society—engage in a process of totalization that erases the *objet a* in favor of the ideal of the desired other as a full subject in its own right. As an ethical approach, this is undoubtedly compelling. However, Lacan suggests that the attempt to conjure away the *objet a* by replacing it with a whole person is a mistake because, as we have seen, it is the *objet a* within the other that renders this other "incommensurate": incomparable and irreplaceable.

Lacan offers a concrete account of the essential place that the *objet a* holds in his theory in his seminar on transference when he discusses the fierce erotic dynamic between Socrates and Alcibiades at the end of Plato's *Symposium*. This seminar, delivered a year after *The Ethics of Psychoanalysis*, makes explicit aspects of Lacan's theory of desire that remain implicit in his discussion of his friend's matchboxes and Cézanne's apples. I offer a detailed commentary on this seminar in *Distillations*.³⁶ Here I merely wish to pull out a few strands of this commentary that are relevant to my attempt to demonstrate that the subject's desire is not always equivalent to the Other's desire and that Žižek's tendency to favor the drive over desire may obscure the gist of Lacanian ethics as an ethics of sublimation.

Lacan's analysis of Socrates and Alcibiades allows him to sharpen his concept of the *objet a* through the Greek word *ágalma*, for when Alcibiades declares his undying love for Socrates at the end the symposium, he specifies that the reason he is so hopelessly obsessed with Socrates is that Socrates contains this *ágalma*, or *agálmata* in the plural. Lacan notes that the word *ágalma* may mean "ornament" or "jewelry," but that in the context of Alcibiades's desire for Socrates, it "means above all a gem or precious object."³⁷ Lacan paraphrases the speech Alcibiades delivers in an attempt to explain why his love for Socrates is non-negotiable as follows: "I saw them, the *agálmata* that are . . . divine—they're wonderful, they're golden—totally beautiful."³⁸ For Alcibiades, the *agálmata* within Socrates are magnificent, like a gleaming treasure. As Lacan specifies: "It is enough to indicate that *ágalma* has to do with the meanings *brillant* [sheen] and *galant* [gallant], the latter coming from *gal*, meaning *éclat* [sparkle or gleam] in Old French. In a word, what is at stake here if not the function we analysts have discovered that is designated by the term 'partial object'?"³⁹ The *ágalma* here equals the *objet a*, the partial object. And, importantly for my argument, we are here far from well-tanned female behinds: we are in the realm of the sublime dimensions of the *objet a*.

Socrates rejects Alcibiades's advances for reasons that at first glance make him an exemplary Lacanian: because he understands the fantasmatic structure of desire, he knows that he does not contain the golden treasure—the *objet a*—that Alcibiades sees in him. Because Socrates "knows the score in matters of love," he comprehends that "there is nothing in him that is lovable," that his essence is "emptiness or hollowness."[40] Socrates knows that it is Alcibiades who has deposited the *agálmata* in him, which is why he responds by stating, "Pay attention—where you see something, I am nothing."[41] If this were where Lacan left things, we would merely have a good example of the imaginary and intrinsically narcissistic structure of desire. I would be forced to agree with Žižek's denigration of desire.

However, Lacan claims that if Alcibiades is misguided in not grasping the illusory nature of desire, Socrates is equally mistaken in not recognizing that even though he does not contain the treasure that Alcibiades sees in him, Alcibiades's desire for him is nevertheless "real," worthy of respect (and perhaps even reciprocation); Socrates does not recognize the simple fact that he does not need to be "lovable"—full of glistening gems—to be loved. That is, it is insofar as Socrates is excessively committed to insisting on the imaginary structure of desire that "he is doomed to be mistaken—namely to misrecognize the essential function of the targeted object constituted by *ágalma*."[42]

Note that it is precisely because Socrates is hollow that Alcibiades is able to place the *agálmata* in him, is able to raise him to the dignity of the Thing, in the first place. From this point of view, Socrates's mistake is to question the very fantasmatic structure of desire that renders him irreplaceable to Alcibiades, that transforms him from an exchangeable object to an unexchangeable ("incommensurate") one; his mistake is not to discern that the route to the "real" of desire can, sometimes at least, be forged through fantasy.

As is the case with the string of matchboxes and Cézanne's applies, the *agálmata* that Alcibiades finds in Socrates emit something about the Thing's aura; they offer bits of *jouissance*. These *agálmata* elevate Socrates to the nobility of the Thing, which explains why Alcibiades's desire for Socrates is unassailable, impervious even to the embarrassment of being publicly rejected. As Lacan points out, when it comes to Socrates, Alcibiades says something like, "I want it because I want it, whether it's for my own good or not."[43] In other words, Alcibiades wants Socrates regardless of how dearly he might have to pay for his desire. The parallels with Antigone should be obvious.

Salvaging Our Dignity

In *The Ethics of Psychoanalysis*, Lacan leaves little ambiguity about his commitment to the ethics of desire, for he claims that the allegiance to the

Thing that we showcase through our sublimatory efforts introduces a code of ethics that is drastically different from what he describes as "the morality of the master, created for the virtues of the master and linked to the order of powers."[44] At the core of the master's morality is a work ethic that sidelines desire, repeatedly asking desire to wait for its turn (which never arrives). To this morality, Lacan opposes the ethics of desire: "There is another register of morality that takes it direction from that which is to be found on the level of *das Ding*; it is the register that makes the subject hesitate when he is on the point of bearing false witness against *das Ding*, that is to say, the place of desire."[45] It would be difficult to state the matter more clearly: the ethics of psychoanalysis is an ethics of desire, of faithfulness to the Thing as the arbitrator of the kind of desire that is related to *jouissance* (rather than the Other's desire or the master's morality).

Here I have reached the crux of my disagreement with Žižek: I see desire as an ethical force insofar as it, as we have seen, renders certain objects so incomparable and irreplaceable that we are willing to do a great deal—sometimes even sacrifice ourselves—for the sake of these objects. The objects that substitute for the lost Thing and that we endow with special significance hold value for us. They may fall short of the Thing, yet to the degree that they evoke it, they lend meaning to our lives. Lacan expresses the matter evocatively when he explain that the *objet a* has the power to interrupt the sliding of desire along the signifying chain.

Under normal conditions, the constant sliding of the signifier constitutes our daily reality. Translated into the universe of normative desire, this means that desire moves from one object to the next in ways that feed the goals of capitalism and therefore reflect the Other's desire. In this scenario, objects are largely interchangeable, so that if one does not work out, another can easily take its place. However, Lacan specifies that when the *objet a* enters the scene, it arrests this sliding of desire, fixing our attention in the way that the string of matchboxes, Cézanne's apples, and Socrates's "treasure" do. The result is that suddenly only *this* object matters, only *this* object is worth our attention.

It is impossible to find a replacement for an object that vibrates on the frequency of the Thing in this manner. Here it is worth quoting Lacan at length:

> An object can thus assume, in relation to the subject, the essential value that constitutes the fundamental fantasy. The subject himself realizes that he is arrested therein, or, to remind you of a more familiar notion, fixated. We call the object that serves this privileged function *a*. . . . This object is overvalued. And it is insofar as it is overvalued that it serves the function of saving our dignity as subjects—that is, of making us something other than subjects subjected to the infinite sliding of the signifier. It makes of us something other than subjects of speech, turning us into something unique, inestimable, and irreplaceable in the final analysis, which is the

true point at which we can designate what I have called the dignity of the subject.... Individuality consists entirely in the privileged relationship in which we culminate as subjects of desire.[46]

Far from robbing the subject of its "dignity and freedom," the *objet a* salvages both: because the object of desire that seems to contain the *objet a* fixes the subject to a spot, it rescues both its dignity and freedom by turning it into something other than a subject subjected to the infinite sliding of the signifier. Insofar as the *objet a* connects the subject to its fundamental fantasy, it—for a moment at least—ceases to function as a wholly symbolic creature, a creature enslaved to the signifier, let alone the Other's desire. It individuates itself through the specificity of its desire. Lacan in fact implies that this kind of desire renders not only the object, but also the subject, "unique, inestimable, irreplaceable."

Conclusion

I want to conclude by emphasizing that Lacan's commentary on the ethics of desire—on the importance of the Thing in guiding our desire to the point of giving us our destiny—explains why our object choices are sometimes so surprising, why we are capable of the kind of desire that defies the happiness narratives and economic objectives of our society. That is, our desire is far too idiosyncratic, far too unpredictable to be instrumentalizable in terms of our society's dominant values. For instance, the fixations of our desire frequently war against the neoliberal creed of efficiency and high productivity, sometimes paralyzing us to the extent that we cannot even perform the routine tasks of everyday life, let alone "accomplish" things in the sense that this creed demands.

This alone demonstrates why our desire cannot always be explained by capitalist brainwashing, why it does not always coincide with the Other's desire: it is surely not in the interest of neoliberal capitalist society to distract us to the point that we become incapable of participating in its performance principle. Moreover, as I have illustrated, the idiosyncratic cathexes of our desire can thwart our culture's ethos of consumerism by focusing our attention on a particular object to such a degree that we become uninterested in all other objects: inasmuch as a special object outshines all others, it ruptures the logic of capitalism that invites us to glide from one object to the next without hesitation.

In addition, our desire can attach itself to objects, including people, that mainstream society deems worthless. Even more enigmatically, we sometimes find ourselves drawn to objects that actively harm us. Although the kind of ideology critique that Žižek engages in when he establishes a connection between our desire and that of the Other explains how we are taught to desire certain objects, it cannot explain the irrational manner in which we at times remain devoted to objects that we *know* are likely to make us miserable, sometimes because they are unavailable (already lost) and sometimes because they are obviously injurious (such as hurtful lovers). In other words, even though Žižek's approach clarifies why we attach ourselves to objects that promise happiness without delivering on this promise, it fails to explain why we attach ourselves to objects that do not even bother to promise happiness, that are frank about the fact that they will never make us happy. In the context of our culture's ethos of positivity, which demands cheerfulness, there is something mysterious about the kinds of desires that can only prolong our pain. In contrast, Lacan's theory of desire as a residue of the lost Thing sheds some light on such counterproductive attachments by illustrating the psychic mechanisms that render some relational ties, however damaging, virtually unbreakable.

Notes

1 Slavoj Žižek, *Less than Nothing: Hegel and the Shadow of Dialectical Materialism* (New York: Verso, 2013), 900.
2 Žižek, *Less than Nothing*, 899.
3 Žižek, *Less than Nothing*, 579.
4 See Mari Ruti, *Distillations: Theory, Ethics, Affect* (New York: Bloomsbury Press, 2018).
5 See Mari Ruti, *Penis Envy and Other Bad Feelings: The Emotional Costs of Everyday Life* (New York: Columbia University Press, 2018).
6 See Todd McGowan, *Capitalism and Desire: The Psychic Cost of Free Markets* (New York: Columbia University Press, 2016).
7 McGowan argues along these lines in *Capitalism and Desire*.
8 Jacques Lacan, *The Seminar of Jacques Lacan, Book VII (1959–1960): The Ethics of Psychoanalysis*, ed. Jacques-Alain Miller, trans. Dennis Porter (New York: Norton, 1997), 112.
9 Slavoj Žižek, *Looking Awry: An Introduction to Jacques Lacan through Popular Culture* (Cambridge, MA: MIT Press, 1992), 172.
10 Slavoj Žižek, "Desire: Drive = Truth: Knowledge," *Umbr(a)*, 1997. Available online: https://www.lacan.com/zizek-desire.htm (accessed July 7, 2021).
11 Ibid.
12 Ibid.
13 Ibid.
14 Ibid.
15 Ibid.
16 Ibid.
17 Lacan, *The Ethics of Psychoanalysis*, 52.
18 Ibid., 118.

19 See Marc De Kesel, "The Real of Ethics: On a Widespread Misconception," *Unconscious Incarnations: Psychoanalytic and Philosophical Perspectives on the Body*, ed. Brian Becker, John Manoussakis, and David Goodman (New York: Routledge, 2018).
20 Lacan, *The Ethics of Psychoanalysis*, 314.
21 Ibid., 321.
22 Alenka Zupančič, *The Shortest Shadow: Nietzsche's Philosophy of the Two* (Cambridge, MA: MIT Press, 2003), 77.
23 Alenka Zupančič, *Ethics of the Real: Kant and Lacan* (New York: Verso, 2012), 240.
24 Žižek, *Looking Awry*, 172.
25 See Mari Ruti, *The Singularity of Being: Lacan and the Immortal Within* (New York: Fordham University Press, 2012) and Ruti, *Distillations*.
26 Lacan, *The Ethics of Psychoanalysis*, 114.
27 Ibid., 114.
28 Ibid., 117–18.
29 Ibid., 141.
30 Slavoj Žižek, *The Sublime Object of Ideology* (New York: Verso, 1997), 50.
31 Slavoj Žižek, *The Plague of Fantasies* (New York: Verso, 1997), 105.
32 Jacques Lacan, *The Seminar of Jacques Lacan, Book VIII (1960–1961): Transference*, ed. Jacques-Alain Miller, trans. Bruce Fink (New York: Polity, 2017), 146.
33 Ibid.,148.
34 Ibid., 143.
35 Ibid.
36 See Ruti, *Distillations*.
37 Lacan, *Transference*, 135, 137–8.
38 Ibid.,138.
39 Ibid., 143.
40 Ibid., 153, 155.
41 Ibid., 154.
42 Ibid., 159.
43 Ibid., 157.
44 Lacan, *The Ethics of Psychoanalysis*, 314–15.
45 Ibid., 109–10.
46 Lacan, *Transference*, 170.

Response to Ruti

Slavoj Žižek

The last three texts all turn around the same problem: the relationship between *das Ding* and *objet petit a*. Ruti links this relationship to the one between drive and desire: drive is fixated on the impossible Thing around which it circulates, while *a* is the cause of desire which endlessly eludes the subject's grasp. Based on this distinction, her reproach to me is that I wrongly privilege drive over desire, which is why I get caught in the debilitating alternative of superficial metonymy of desire versus deadly obsession with the Thing.

> When Žižek categorically elevates the drive over desire, he fails to distinguish between objects that do not merit our attachment and others that do. He implies that desire is intrinsically erroneous and politically regressive, that our objects of desire are invariably tainted by capitalist normativity. In contrast, I believe that there are objects that not only deserve our attachment but also genuinely satisfy and enrich us, and that sometimes ethics is a matter of defending our commitment to such objects, either because we cherish them so much that nothing can shake our loyalty to them or because we feel that justice demands that we stand by them no matter what the risk of doing so might be.

What can save us from this deadlock is sublimation in which a mundane object is raised to the dignity of the Thing:

> The people, ideals, and principles that desire pursues have been infused with a tolerable amount of the *jouissance* that the Thing (fantasmatically) embodies; sublimation retains a smidgeon of *jouissance* without allowing it to overwhelm the subject. [. . .] It is hence impossible that Lacan, in this

instance at least, equates the subject's desire with the Other's desire. In positing that the ethics of psychoanalysis is an ethics of not giving ground on one's desire, he refers to the kind of desire that animates the subject by allowing it to tap into the reservoir of energy that *jouissance*—the overagitation of the drives—represents.

A desire fixated on a sublime object thus provides a minimal determination of the ethical act which is

> extremely unlikely to take place without the presence of an object of desire—a person, ideal, or principle—that captures, and hence arrests, the subject's *jouissance* to such an extent that it feels compelled to act against its own interests. [...] If the drive, as Žižek claims, "is a closed circular movement," by itself it would never be able to induce the subject to undertake an act of any kind; it would happily keep going around solipsistically, without any regard for anything outside of itself. That is, the subject needs something beyond itself—beyond its drive—to motivate it to act. My wager is that only an object that activates the subject's desire on a level that is non-negotiable is capable of providing such an incentive.

My question here is: "non-negotiable" for whom? For the desiring subject itself? If "there would be no Antigone's act without Polyneices or without the principles that she holds dear," these "principles" are obviously symbolic norms, part of the big Other. But what is non-negotiable for, say, a pervert can be a specific obscene act, or, for an obsessional neurotic, a stupid compulsive gesture which also compels the subject to "act against its own interests." This fact alone makes very problematic Ruti's attempt to give sublimation an anti-capitalist twist: "beyond the deceptive satisfaction offered by commodities, we are capable of desiring objects—people, ideals, and principles—that fall outside the capitalist paradigm and, more generally, the Other's desire." Agreed, but is, say, a passionate and destructive racist desire also not "beyond the deceptive satisfaction offered by commodities"? "There is no doubt that capitalism thrives on the subject's hopeless quest to heal its lack and that the world is saturated by objects of desire that deceptively promise satisfaction." Is, then, capitalist consumerism inherently hysteric? Are we by definition disappointed after we buy a product, the mysterious ingredient is never there, "ce n'est pas ça," the thing we buy is never "it," so we pass to the next object in the metonymy of desire? Not really—in consumerism, the hysterical stance is effectively re-appropriated by a perverse libidinal economy: as consumerists, we know well in advance that we will not get what we desired, so we are never really disappointed, the properly hysterical drama of deceit fails to take place, and it is this knowledge-which-neutralizes-the-hysterical-drama that defines perversion. Hysteria is a subjective stance of questioning (What do I really desire? What does my Other see or desire in me, i.e., what am I for the Other?), while a pervert knows, he is not haunted by questions. Today's consumerist is a cynical pervert who knows—in this way, desire is neutralized, nothing happens when we get the object of desire, no event of a true encounter, when we love there is no *falling* in love.

My next point: *jouissance* is also the Other's *jouissance*, and in many ways: it is not just structured by the big Other, it can also be supposed to exist in the Other (the subject supposed to enjoy—recall the racist secret mode of enjoyment of the Other). Today the supreme case of this is precisely consumerism: consumerism is not just desire determined by the big Other but it definitely "taps into the reservoir of energy that *jouissance* represents," it evokes all the time the enjoyment promised by the object, and it makes us enjoy the very repetitive search for the object that would bring enjoyment. There is nothing noble or ennobling in *jouissance*—Lacan repeatedly insists on the immanent stupidity of enjoyment, and he also insists the true message of every superego injunction is: "Enjoy!" *Jouissance* has nothing to do with ennobling principles or values; it is much more a set of dirty small pleasures, more often disgusting than not (like smelling one's sweat). *Jouissance* is in no way limited to "base" material needs: the domain of spiritual experiences is today more commodified as ever—the pandemic gave a big boost to a new profession, that of "spiritual concierge," like Aree Khodai in New York who "curates private experiences of transcendence for the residents of luxury apartments":

> The advent of "spiritual concierges" makes clear that luxury has mutated but not completely transformed under covid. In the Before Times, a hotel concierge would enhance your luxury travel experience by granting you access—to a sold-out play, perhaps, or a hot new restaurant. Today, a spiritual concierge also grants you access, but to pandemic-proof pleasures that are more metaphysical than physical, enhancing travel that occurs not over land or sea, but inwardly, in the realms of soul and spirit—without leaving your apartment.[1]

One should resist here the temptation to dismiss "spiritual concierge" as providing only an "inauthentic" experience: in itself it may be exactly the same as the "true" spiritual experience; there is no way to distinguish the two immanently. There is a long tradition of "commodification" even in Zen Buddhist mediation: after World War II, D. T. Suzuki, the great master of Zen, organized in Japan paid meditation trainings for top managers. The problem I see here is nicely rendered by the second part of the title of Ruti's text: "When Desire Is Not the Desire of the Other." "Desire of the Other" cannot be reduced to a desire whose object is predetermined by the social Other—Lacan's formula "desire is the desire of the Other" can be read at (at least) three levels. First, imaginary—it points towards the irreducible intersubjectivity of desire in the sense of subjective and objective genitive: my desire is the desire for the other's desire (I desire to be desired by the other, I desire what the other desires). Then, symbolic—it means what Ruti implies: what I desire is overdetermined by the big Other, by the symbolic space into which I am thrown. Finally (and most importantly), real—the Other is never just a neutral symbolic structure, it is in itself inconsistent, enigmatic, harboring an obscure desire, and the lack Lacan speaks of is not my (subject's own) but the lack in the Other itself, so that I am a desiring subject only with regard to this obscure point in the Other. That's what I find missing in Ruti's line of thought: "I readily accept my loss, my status as a being of lack. However, if the only thing I can expect from life is the experience of endlessly reliving this loss, I might as well end it now. There must be something—some Thing—that makes life worth the pain that it entails."

My rejoinder to these lines is quadruple. First, the lack is not just or primarily minor; it is the lack of/in the Other itself. Second, lack is strictly correlative with excess—there is always something that adds itself to reality, that is in excess with regard to it: human life never coincides with itself; to be "really alive" means to be "larger than life," and the morbid denial of life is not the denial of life itself, but, rather, the denial of this excess. Third, neither the Thing nor *a* are "something that makes life worth the pain that it entails": *a* is not what we desire but the cause that determines what we desire, and the Thing is not a Cause, it is the horror of an abyss. Fourth (a point I don't have space to develop here), the Thing and *a* are not in any sense correlative, they do not form a couple, they move in different spaces. That's why I reject the idea that *a* is a "smidgeon" of the Thing, a kind of minimally gentrified (domesticated) Thing, the Thing reduced to a tolerable feature within the symbolic space.

I thus definitely do not prioritize drive over desire. I think the two are co-dependent since each of them can be understood as a reaction to the other. Desire is metonymic, always sliding from one to another object, again and again experiencing that "this is not that," and drive resolves this endless movement of desire by way of elevating the endless circulation around a lost object into a source of satisfaction. Drive is a circular movement, caught in its closed cycle, and desire breaks out of this closure, bringing fresh air into the situation, externalizing the object and sending the subject on a quest for it. Such a situation is a parallax at its purest: none of the two terms are more primordial than the other. The third term is not any synthesis of the two but just the pure gap itself, and desire and drive are the two reactions to this gap: desire externalizes the lack into a cause-object, drive circulates around the object. In desire, the gap appears as lack; in drive, it appears as an excess that derails the circulation of life.

The best case of the porosity of the distinction between desire and drive is the case of Antigone. Antigone's desire remains the desire of the Other—not of the social Other (law of the city) embodied in Creon but of the Other of immemorial Laws—it is definitely not directly "her own" desire. In his seminar on the ethics of psychoanalysis, Lacan proposed that "the only thing one can be guilty of, at least in the analytic perspective, is having given up on one's desire." His motto is thus: *ne pas ceder sur son désir*—but here ambiguity enters immediately: since desire is hysteric and metonymic, since it targets the gap beyond or between demands, so what "not giving up on one's desire" amounts to is precisely the readiness to pass from one to another object because no determinate object is "that"—or, as Lacan put it in his seminar *Encore*: "Je te demande de refuser ce que je t'offre parce que c'est pas ça":[2] "I demand from you (ask you) to reject what I offer you because it is not that." But does Antigone not function in the exactly opposite way? Her act expresses the unconditional fidelity to a deep law, not its transgression—in short, she unconditionally insists on her demand—to bury properly her brother; there is no metonymic desire here, no compromise. Now we can understand why Lacan's formula of drive is $-D, a subject attached to a demand—and this is what Antigone does. Is this also not why Lacan's formula of ethics (do not compromise your desire) is pronounced only once, it never returns, in clear contrast with Lacan's other formulas to which he always returns in new variations?

Notes

1 Rhonda K. Garelick, "How Luxury Survived the Pandemic," *The Washington Post Magazine*, November 17, 2021. Available online: https://www.washingtonpost.com/magazine/2021/11/17/how-luxury-survived-pandemic/ (accessed December 20, 2021).

2 Jacques Lacan, *Le Séminaire, Livre XX, Encore*, ed. Jacques-Alain Miller (Paris: du Seuil, 1975), session of February 9, 1972.

CHAPTER TWELVE

Hoping Against Hope
Žižek, Jouissance, and the Impossible

Jennifer Friedlander

Based on the titles of his works—*The Courage of Hopelessness*, and "The Liberal Utopia: Against the Politics of *Jouissance*"—Žižek might seem an unlikely figure upon whom to pinpoint a politics of hope with *jouissance* at its core. Yet, the aim of this essay is to make the case that Žižek's development of a radical politics depends upon both hope (with an emphasis less on the future than on the potential of the past and present) and *jouissance* (figured in terms of repetition). In developing this claim, I highlight the key roles that temporality and lack play in Žižek's formulation of both hope and *jouissance*. I ultimately contend that Žižek enables us to appreciate how both hope and *jouissance* emerge not only in response to the "impossible," but also can bring about the impossible. I then shift to considering Žižek's argument for embracing hopelessness as a radical political strategy in conversation with José Esteban Muñoz's celebration of hope's utopian capacity to unleash the transformational potentiality of the past. Reading Žižek's work within this context prompts a two-fold argument: 1) that Žižek's work offers new insight into the discussion surrounding hope as it is staged within this subsection of queer theory; and 2) that reading Žižek's thinking in relation to this work from queer theory sharpens Žižek's position that hope and *jouissance* work together in the service of a radical politics.

Hopelessness and Jouissance: Repetition and Lack

Considerable critical debate centers on whether, as Geoffrey Boucher succinctly characterizes it, Žižek's call to "embrace the 'courage of hopelessness'" should be interpreted as "an endorsement of despair," or (as Boucher does) a "provocation to articulate a new kind of utopia."[1] I argue, alongside Boucher, in favor of interpreting Žižek's argument as one in which hopelessness can be seen itself as a form of hope, which plays a vital role in radical politics. I bolster this position by reading it alongside Žižek's criticism of Yannis Stavrakakis's formulation of a "politics of *jouissance*" (which Žižek develops in response to Stavrakakis's criticism of his work). Such an approach opens a way of appreciating the interrelation of hope and *jouissance* in Žižek's politics.

Particularly illuminating for the purpose of this account is Žižek's response to Stavrakakis's accusation that Žižek posits a political "Act without After"—and specifically that Žižek "ignore[s] the effects of the act."[2] Žižek counters this criticism by attesting not only that he attends continually to the question of "the day after" but also, more crucially, that the temporality of the Act should be understood as a "retroactive causality."[3] As Žižek explains, "an act proper is not just a strategic intervention into a situation bound by its conditions, it retroactively creates its own condition."[4] This retroactive temporality, for Žižek, operates in terms of the psychoanalytic structure of repetition, rather than return. Here Žižek follows Lacan who adamantly distinguishes repetition (which operates at the level of the drive) from return/reproduction (which operates at the level of the symptom): "in Freud's texts," Lacan tells us, "repetition is not reproduction. There is never any ambiguity on this point: *Wiederholen* is not *Reproduzieren*."[5] Žižek inflects this distinction with a political dimension, within which repetition works to unleash an unactualized potential of the past. Thus rather than aim directly for a better future—one as far removed as possible from past failures—Žižek encourages a politics based precisely on the repetition of past failure. But, these failures are not to be understood in terms of actions taken that turned out to be unsuccessful. Rather, these "failures" constitute potential actions that we failed to undertake. As Žižek puts it in terms of his call to "repeat Lenin," "to repeat Lenin does not mean a return to Lenin . . . to repeat Lenin is not to repeat what Lenin did, but what he failed to do, his missed opportunities."[6]

This political deployment of repetition depends upon conceiving of the political sphere as fundamentally non-totalizable, not just in the past, but also in the present and the future. A Žižekian notion of utopia, therefore, does not involve striving for completion, but rather the repetition of a constitutive lack or failure. And again, following Lacan, Žižek underscores that such repetition of failure produces *jouissance*—painful enjoyment that lies "beyond the pleasure principle."

Adrian Johnston provides a useful elaboration of Žižek's position here. He credits Žižek with offering a novel distinction between drive and desire in terms of their relationship to repetition. Desire, for Žižek, can be thought of as a "teleology without repetition," while drive operates as "repetition without teleology." The purposelessness of *jouissance* carries with it the potential to introduce what cannot be made sensible within the established symbolic coordinates. The production of unintergrateable excess thus highlights the incompleteness of symbolic order and opens the door for the emergence of what is deemed "impossible" within the established symbolic coordinates. For Žižek, this engagement with hopelessness carries radical political potential, in large part because it requires the recognition that nothing within the existing set of possibilities can change the situation. Instead, it is this incompleteness that paves the way for the impossible to break through the established symbolic coordinates of the possible.

Žižek's critique of hope in *The Courage of Hopelessness* invokes the convergence of two ideological maneuvers: naturalizing of the contingent, and making the necessity appear exceptional. These two strategies operate in tandem: for example, when an ongoing crisis can be no longer be credibly dismissed as exceptional, it is recast as a "normal," even mundane, condition of everyday life.[7] Žižek illustrates this point by turning to the example of how the life-altering effects of ecological disasters such as China's 2016 smog "'airpocalypse'" became seamlessly routinized into "new procedure[s] that would somehow enable people to continue their daily life ... as if the catastrophic smog was just a new fact of life."[8] What is conveniently skipped over in the discreet folding of catastrophe into business-as-usual is the moment of living with recognition of the crisis's inexorable endurance. As Žižek puts it, "we have to go through this zero point of hopelessness."[9] For Žižek inhabiting such "hopelessness" works to derail the stabilizing influence of the pleasure principle. He argues that,

> We have to accept the threat as our fate .... So the solution is not to be very careful and avoid risky acts—in acting like this, we fully participate in the logic that leads to catastrophe .... [rather] once we embrace the courage that comes with hopelessness, we should embark on the long and difficult work of changing the coordinates of the entire situation.[10]

This call to act against the preservation of the established symbolic system aligns with the destructive logic of *jouissance*, which, I argue, for Žižek is the source of radical political possibility.

Žižek's orientation toward hopelessness offers us no reprieve. In calling on us "to accept the threat as our fate," he opposes attempts to look for ways mitigate its effects or delay its inevitable impact.[11] Drawing upon Alenka Zupančič's insights regarding the "relations between repetition and endings," Žižek highlights the importance of locating the ending within the present rather than in the future.[12] As Zupančič argues, holding out the possibility of an end-to-come (in her example, anticipating the end of smoking) enables us to sustain our present habits (I can keep smoking today if I know that I can end it tomorrow). It is "the *possibility* of ending it . . . . [that] allows us not to act . . . . How many people would start smoking if . . . the state . . . would pass a law stating that if you start smoking, you are not allowed to quit?"[13] Zupančič turns to Frank Ruda's critique of how this "possibility" creates a sense of freedom that works to constrain "actual freedom."[14] The location of an "End"—no matter how "definitive" or "irreversible"—"situated at some point in the *future*," thus, functions to preserve current practices and systems.[15] Following Ruda, actual freedom to change a given condition is only possible if we "act as if the end has already happened."[16]

For Žižek, as for Zupančič, the importance of seeing the crisis as what has already happened lies in the collapse of the space for pseudo-freedom, where we busy ourselves with empty actions that ensure that nothing will happen. It also interrupts the equally paralyzing investment in impending catastrophe as a deus ex machina that will "sweep all our troubles away and 'reset' the world."[17] Locating crisis in the present forces us to confront both the futility of trying to ward off disaster, and the recognition that we cannot wait for an external calamity to solve our problems.

Not only does Žižek's work caution about positing catastrophe in the future, rather than the present, he contends that a similar move must be made with regard to *jouissance* itself. "The trouble with *jouissance*," he argues, "is not that it is unattainable, that it always eludes our grasp, but rather that one can never get rid of it, that its stain forever drags along."[18] Žižek's insight challenges accounts which, in identifying *jouissance* as a key impediment to social change, tend to emphasize its elusiveness, rather than its tenacity. In particular, it challenges the commonly held idea that *jouissance* is an (imaginary) wholeness, which was sacrificed upon the subject's entrance into the world of language. For Žižek, however (as for Lacan), this sacrifice is only part of the story, and notably not the beginning of it. By framing subjective lack as an *effect* of this *loss* of *jouissance*, the inverse understanding is obscured: namely, that lack is the *cause* of both the subject's formation and the precipitating condition for the emergence of *jouissance* (as a retrospectively created sense of impossible fulfilment). The subject, in other words, does not simply come to be marked by lack as a result of entering into the symbolic; the subject enters into the symbolic because of lack. As Bruce Fink clearly puts it, lack is a necessary condition for entering into language: "if nourishment is never missing, if the desired warmth is never lacking, why would the child take the trouble to speak? ... Without lack, the subject can never come into being."[19]

An emphasis on lack as the *effect* of the sacrifice of *jouissance* sustains the illusion of the possibility of lack's fulfillment, whereas a focus on lack as the *cause* of *jouissance*, establishes lack as primary and constitutive. This recognition of lack's inherent status within the symbolic mars any claim to wholeness, and thus reframes the understanding of the relationship of *jouissance* to the political. We see this in the way that an emphasis on lack as fundamental to subjectivity and the symbolic helps disrupt a key premise of racist logic, highlighted in Žižek's work (and extended by other thinkers, such as Sheldon George and Derek Hook[20]): namely, that external obstacles (often embodied by an "other" are responsible for the loss of socio-cultural harmony. In such configurations as Hook proposes, "others" are perceived as both culprits who "stole" our *jouissance*, and as bearers of an unruly enjoyment of their own.[21] In this context Žižek stresses the importance of recognizing that the limit to our "full satisfaction" comes from within the subject itself: "the foreign body, the intruder, which disturbs the harmonious circuit ... run by the 'pleasure principle' is not something external to it, but strictly *inherent* to it."[22]

Jouissance, thus, not only gloms on to lack, but incessantly repeats it. As Moustafa Safouan underscores, since "there never was a primary satisfaction which is to be repeated," the drive must repeat this very failure.[23] This perspective enables a shift in focus from seeing *jouissance* as something that we once had, but lost, to its paradoxical inverse form: *jouissance* as something we never had, but cannot get rid of. Zupančič describes this dimension of *jouissance* as the "enjoyment [which] appears at the place of the nonexistent ('originally missing') signifier."[24] *Jouissance*, in this sense, persists as a surplus enjoyment—a perverse satisfaction generated by the drive's repetitious failure to fulfill our desire. In short, Žižek contributes a key insight, which carries with it significant political consequences. The repetition of the "failure to integrate some 'impossible' kernel of the Real [the "self-impediment"]," he contends, can activate the "impossible" which the symbolic has foreclosed.[25] Repetition, in this sense, is not only of the impossible, but it can create the impossible by unleashing its barred potential.

Present Hopelessness/Present Satisfaction

I now argue that Žižek's call for inhabiting hopelessness as a radical political strategy can be seen as a way to derail the ideologically conservative role that he claims is played by the small pleasures snatched from the unrelenting pressures of neoliberal productivity culture—pleasures which, Žižek argues, provide us with the necessary breathing room for enduring its continuation. As he puts it, workers are thrown "crumbs of enjoyment" and opportunities for "small transgressions [to] keep [them] satisfied, as ways to secure the smooth running of productivity.[26] Rather than designating these pleasures as interruptions to or breaks from ideology, Žižek contends they constitute ideology itself.

But this position should be refined in the light of Todd McGowan's apparently contrary argument that a recognition of our present satisfaction can derail the future-oriented, promise-driven logic of capitalism. Specifically, McGowan contends, "capitalism depends on a psychic investment in the promise of the future and that a sense of one's [present] satisfaction is incompatible with the continued survival of capitalism."[27] At first blush,

McGowan's advocacy for inhabiting the pleasures of the moment seems to fall into the trap about which Žižek warns: namely that providing enough relief and distance from mechanisms of control enables us to continue to bear their oppressive conditions. But on closer inspection, McGowan not only avoids this problem but also introduces a complication into Žižek's position. Rather than see present satisfactions as ameliorating loss, McGowan emphasizes how loss itself creates enjoyment. As he puts it, "There is no satisfaction without loss . . .. Even when we are right next to someone we love, we enjoy what is absent in the beloved, we enjoy what is absent, not what is present: that part of the beloved that we can't decipher."[28] Rather than formulate loss as a contingent impediment to our satisfaction, McGowan (and Žižek) insist that our satisfactions, subjectivity, and the social are rooted in constitutive loss. This position is foregrounded by Žižek's emphasis on the political implications of drive over desire. Although desire is both mobilized and sustained by loss, it nevertheless fuels the fantasy that our dissatisfaction is contingent and surmountable, rather than constitutive and intractable. In drive, by contrast, subjective loss is repeated (generating *jouissance*) rather than concealed.

On this basis, I suggest that rather than read Žižek's politics of hopelessness as an anti-pleasure position, we see it instead as hinging on a foundational Lacanian–Žižekian insight (also expounded by McGowan): namely, the necessary role that loss plays in our satisfaction. It is thus not pleasure, per se, that contributes to ideological complicity, but rather its function as a salve for loss. In sum, although McGowan underscores the importance of recognizing our present pleasures (satisfaction) and Žižek calls on us to inhabit our present suffering (hopelessness), this apparent conflict between them is resolved by pointing out that although the present pleasures ("crumbs of enjoyment") that Žižek discusses do play a conservative ideological role, they also take on a potentially radical political role by occupying a necessary relationship to loss. It is precisely in Žižek's politics of hopelessness that this radical potential can be realized through the opening of a space of repetition inaugurated by loss.

Potentiality, Otherwise, and Muñoz

Where does this leave us with respect to the question of the political role of hope? Is hope necessarily tethered to the logic of desire and the fantasmatic coordinates of the possible? Or can we locate a radical potential in hope as operating in terms of the drive? In addressing this question, we turn briefly to Muñoz's development of a politically transgressive view of hope. Although Muñoz does not articulate his position as one that harnesses *jouissance* and the drive for emancipatory politics, I suggest that his insights help to illuminate such a position. In particular, I propose that despite the apparent opposition between their positions, Žižek's call to inhabit present hopelessness and Muñoz's commitment to hope for the future point in a similar political direction—a direction that does not simply point forward or back, but opens up the possibility of what Muñoz calls the "otherwise," and what Žižek calls "potential."

This turn to Muñoz might seem like a leap for several reasons, not least of which is his indictment of the present (which he calls "a prison house") and the drive, in favor of futurity and desire—a stance which seems to place him starkly at odds with Žižek's position. Specifically, for Muñoz, by contrast with Žižek, the future can be described as "queerness"—"a structured and educated mode of desiring that allows us to see and feel beyond the quagmire of the present."[29] I suggest that, despite these tensions with Žižek, Muñoz's work offers productive companionship to Žižek's thinking. This is because Muñoz's concern with the present lies not its lack, but rather in its fullness. Specifically, for Muñoz, the problem with the "here and now" stems from its "totalizing rendering of reality."[30] It follows that the importance of desire for Muñoz lies not in its striving for completion, but rather in its potential to rupture entrenched present systems. As he puts it, "Some will say that all we have are the pleasures of this moment, but we must never settle for that minimal transport; we must dream and enact new and better pleasures, other ways of being in the world, and ultimately new worlds."[31]

Perhaps these "better pleasures" have more in common with the *jouissance* beyond the pleasure principle (if not at the level content, then at the level of function) than at first appears. Muñoz's previous monograph, *Disidentifications*, sets the scene for this interpretation by pointing to how surplus pleasures can play a key role in political transformation. This point emerges most clearly at the end of Muñoz's long introductory chapter when he returns to his opening example of "disidentification" (a strategy for "minoritarian" subjects to find a place of agency—and pleasure—within mainstream culture) in the performances of Marga Gomez. Gomez, in a 1992 performance, reminisces about her adolescent interaction with a television talk-show interview with "lady homosexuals," in which she finds both erotic charge and subjective validation in the homophobic imagery. Muñoz quotes from Gomez's performance: "'[I] sat next to my mother on the sofa. I made sure to put on that homophobic expression on my face. So my mother wouldn't think I was mesmerized by the lady homosexuals .... [They were] all disguised in raincoats, dark glasses, wigs. It was the wigs that made me want to be one.'"[32] Gomez's performance might be seen as challenging contemporary political orthodoxy by glamorizing "pre-Stonewall stereotypes." Muñoz complicates this interpretation, however, by contending that, via "disidentificatory desire," "the phobic object, through a campy over-the-top performance, is reconfigured as sexy and glamorous, and not as the pathetic and abject spectacle that it appears to be in the dominant eyes of heteronormative culture."[33] Gomez pushes the boundary even further when she recalls how the lesbians on the show chain-smoked throughout the episode—"'all the smoke curling up made *the life* seem more mysterious.'" She then laments the loss of *"the life,"* explaining "that's what they called it back then when you were one of us. You were in *the life*! It stood for *the hard and painful life* . . . . I wanted to be in *the life, too*. But I was too young . . . . By the time I was old enough, no one called it the life anymore. It sounded too isolating and politically incorrect. Now they say *the community* . . . . And in the community there is no smoking."[34]

Muñoz cautions against reading Gomez's "longing for a pre-Stonewall version of queer reality" as "self-hating" or as romanticizing suffering.[35] Rather, he contends, her work enacts a "look toward the past that critiques the present and helps envision the future."[36] The more politically correct move of rejecting the oppressive past and valorizing our present progress can be seen as risking cementing ego-pleasure and symbolic closure, which thwarts the potential for radical political change. As Muñoz stresses, Gomez's longings for "*the life*" function as a "critique of a sanitized and heteronormativized *community*."[37] The transition from "the life" to "the community" (with its erasure of surplus pleasures such as cigarette smoking and wig-wearing, and its emphasis on inclusion over transformation) strips gay life of its potential to disrupt established social arrangements.

Thus, in Lacanian terms, Gomez can be seen as calling not for a *return* to the oppressive past, but rather for the *repetition* of what Žižek would call the past's unrealized "potential." Whereas "return" aims to bring about the same, "repetition" (as a form of *jouissance*) unleashes the "virtuality" or "potential" of the past—what Muñoz calls the "otherwise." Thus, rather than work to bind us to present suffering or lead to the utter destruction of the current symbolic system, *jouissance* can move us beyond the fantasmatic circumscription of what is possible. By repeating fundamental lack, *jouissance* keeps potential open by thwarting attempts at symbolic closure.

In developing his account of queer utopia as built around the "not-yet-here," Muñoz draws explicitly upon insights developed by Ernst Bloch's *The Principle of Hope*. In particular, in following Bloch, Muñoz shares with Žižek the "critique of a totalizing and naturalizing idea of the present."[38] Muñoz even concedes that "radical negativity" can function as a "resource for a certain mode of queer utopianism."[39] But Muñoz, again in alignment with Bloch, but in disagreement with Žižek, emphasizes the necessary role that desire plays in bringing about the "not-yet." As Peter Thompson describes, "Hope, for Bloch, was the way in which our desire to fill in the gaps and to find something that is missing took shape."[40] Although lack is necessary to—indeed is the cause of—desire, this formulation positions lack as a contingent rather than a constitutive, enduring phenomenon.

Here, I suggest that Žižek provides a useful intervention into Muñoz's work, even as Muñoz's examples help to sharpen Žižek's position. To be specific, Žižek reads Lacan's well-known assertion that "desire defends against *jouissance*" by highlighting how desire perpetuates the fantasy of the possibility of completion, which *jouissance*—as the satisfaction produced by the drive's tracing of lack—makes impossible.[41] Žižek's indictment of Yannis Stavrakakis's "politics of *jouissance*" drills this point deeper and helps to further illuminate his difference from Muñoz. Stavrakakis, Žižek points out, "reduces the *objet a* to its role in fantasy ... which sustains desire."[42] As the "object cause of desire," Žižek highlights, the *objet a* functions as "an object which is originally lost," while in the case of *objet a* as "object of the drive, the 'object' *is directly the loss itself.*"[43] In sum, by staying within the realm of the logic of desire, Muñoz's account depends upon the "'impossible' quest for the lost object," whereas Žižek's commitment to drive involves the perpetual "enact[ment of] the 'loss' itself."[44] Žižek's work facilitates an approach to seeing hope and *jouissance* not as locking us into an impossible pursuit, but rather as bringing about the impossible itself.

These connections help illuminate a provocative claim that Žižek makes in his essay "Do We Still Live in a World?" regarding how repetition can carry transformative political potential. In particular, he addresses Giorgio Agamben's[45] contention that one should see the Holocaust as the "conclusive argument against ... the Nietzschean eternal return." Specifically, in opposition to Agamben, Žižek contends, that "one should will the repetition of the potential which was lost through the reality of the holocaust, the potential whose non-actualization opened up the space for the holocaust to occur."[46] Rather than aim to avoid past horror at all cost, Žižek reveals how a specific type of engagement with past suffering, in particular an engagement that embraces the failure of hope, is necessary to transform the coordinates of the possible. It is precisely in the possibility of such a transformation that Žižek's politics of hopelessness also becomes a politics of hope.

Notes

1   Geoffrey Boucher, "Revolutionary Hope in Dark Times: Žižek on Faith in the Future." *Religions 2020,* 11, 243.
2   Slavoj Žižek, *In Defense of Lost Causes* (London: Verso, 2009), 307.
3   Ibid., 307, 311.
4   Ibid., 311.
5   Jacques Lacan, *Seminar XI: The Four Fundamental Concepts of Psychoanalysis*, trans. Alan Sheridan (New York: W. W. Norton & Company, 1998), 50.
6   Žižek, *In Defense of Lost Causes*, 326.
7   Slavoj Žižek, *The Courage of Hopelessness: Chronicles of a Year of Acting Dangerously* (London: Allen Lane, 2017), 238.
8   Ibid., 237.
9   Ibid., 8.
10 Ibid., 239–40.
11 Ibid., 239.

12 Ibid., 7.
13 Alenka Zupančič, "The End of Ideology, the Ideology of the End," *South Atlantic Quarterly* 19, no. 4 (2020): 833–44, here: 835, 837 (italics original).
14 Ibid., 836.
15 Ibid., 842.
16 Ibid., 836.
17 Ibid., 843.
18 Žižek, "Desire to Drive."
19 Bruce Fink, *The Lacanian Subject: Between Language and Jouissance* (Princeton, NJ: Princeton University Press, 1995), 103.
20 George and Hook develop this compelling argument across much of their work. Some references to their respective elaborations include: Sheldon George, *Trauma and Race: A Lacanian Study of African American Racial Identity* (Waco, TX: Baylor University Press, 2016); and Derek Hook, "Racism and *Jouissance*: Evaluating the 'Racism as (the Theft of) Enjoyment' Hypothesis," *Psychoanalysis, Culture & Society* 23 (2018): 244–66.
21 Hook, "Racism and *jouissance*."
22 Žižek, *Enjoy*, 55.
23 Moustafa Safouan, "*Jouissance* and the Death Drive," *Literature and Psychology* 46, ½ (2000): 78–91, here: 86.
24 Alenka Zupančič, "Ontology and the Death Drive: Lacan and Deleuze." In *Subject Lessons: Hegel, Lacan, and the Future of Materialism*, eds. Russell Sbriglia and Slavoj Žižek (Evanston, IL: Northwestern University Press), 142–68, here: 155.
25 Žižek, *Enjoy*, 91.
26 Slavoj Žižek, "The Libidinal Economy of Singularity." Available online: https://thephilosophicalsalon.com/the-libidinal-economy-of-singularity/ (accessed January 3, 2022).
27 Todd McGowan. *Capitalism and Desire: The Psychic Cost of Free Markets* (New York: Columbia University Press, 2016), 244.
28 Ibid., 241–2.
29 José Esteban Muñoz, *Cruising Utopia: The Then and There of Queer Futurity* (New York: NYU Press, 2009), 1.
30 Ibid.
31 Ibid.
32 José Esteban Muñoz, *Disidentifications: Queers of Color and the Performance of Politics* (Minneapolis: University of Minnesota, 1999), 3.
33 Ibid.
34 Ibid., 34 (italics original).
35 Ibid.
36 Ibid.
37 Ibid.

38 Muñoz, *Cruising*, 12.
39 Ibid., 13.
40 Peter Thompson, "Introduction: The Privatization of Hope and the Crisis of Negation." In *The Privatization of Hope: Ernst Bloch and the Future of Utopia*, eds. Peter Thompson and Slavoj Žižek (Durham, NC: Duke University Press, 2013), 1–20, here: 3.
41 Jacques Lacan, *Écrits A selection*, trans. Alan Sheridan (London: Routledge, 2001), 246.
42 Slavoj Žižek, *In Defense of Lost Causes* (London: Verso, 2009), 327.
43 Ibid., 328 (italics original).
44 Ibid.
45 It is also from Agamben that Žižek takes the phrase "the courage of hopelessness."
46 Slavoj Žižek, "Do we still Live in a World?." Available online: https://www.lacan.com/zizrattlesnakeshake.html (accessed 20 November 2021).

Response to Friedlander

Slavoj Žižek

Since Friedlander's text is more a (very perspicuous) interpretation of my work than a critical reading, I would just like to note a couple of points where I would put a slightly different accent on the topic. I not only "insist that our satisfactions, subjectivity, and the social are rooted in constitutive loss," I also insist that this loss is the other side of an excess. Plus, I find problematic the distinction between "life" and "community" on which Friedlander relies: "The transition from 'the life' to 'the community,' (with its erasure of surplus pleasures such as cigarette smoking and wig-wearing, and its emphasis on inclusion over transformation) strips gay life of its potential to disrupt established social arrangements." Cigarette smoking and wig wearing are surplus pleasures which form the way of life of certain communities, so I think the opposition Friedlander talks about could be better characterized as the one between multiple communities with their ways of life and a modern more anonymous space of society. And does the permissiveness (to gay life, for example) also not strip it of its potential to disrupt established social arrangements, maybe even more than outright prohibition? Finally, I agree with Friedlander's resume of my basic stance:

> Rather than aim to avoid past horror at all cost, Žižek reveals how a specific type of engagement with past suffering, in particular, an engagement that embraces the failure of hope, is necessary to transform the coordinates of the possible. It is precisely in the possibility of such a transformation that Žižek's politics of hopelessness also becomes a politics of hope.

However, I would insist a little bit more on the how thoroughly hopelessness is to be assumed: hopelessness is for me not just a zero level of getting rid of false hopes which opens up the way for a more authentic hope; it is in some sense also something we cannot ever be sure that we will really succeed in leaving behind—every hope involves an irreducible risk, it walks on the edge of a catastrophe. I am ready to go here even a step further and proclaim the right to apathy as one of the basic human rights. Enough of stupid calls to end up with apathy about the pandemic, to resolve, decide what future we want and get to work. Why this enforced optimism? Apathy—the lack of pathos, a form of subjective destitution which makes us enjoy our disengagement—is one of the basic rights that should be unconditionally protected. Adrian Johnston provided an accurate description of today's geopolitical situation:

> This is a situation in which the world's societies and humanity as a whole are facing multiple acute crises (a global pandemic, environmental disasters, massive inequality, ballooning poverty, potentially devastating wars, etc.), yet seem unable to take the (admittedly radical or revolutionary) measures necessary to resolve these crises. We know things are broken. We know what needs fixing. We even sometimes have ideas about how to fix them. But, nevertheless, we keep doing nothing either to mend damage already done or to prevent further easily foreseeable damage.[1]

Where does this apathy come from? I deal with this in my new book *Heaven in Disorder*.[2] The main reason is, I think, that today's global capitalism generates apathy precisely because it demands from us permanent hyper-activity, constant engagement in its devastating dynamic—are we aware how thoroughly our lives have changed in the last decades? At the beginning of the pandemic, I wrote that the disease would deal a mortal blow to capitalism. I referred to the final scene of Tarantino's *Kill Bill: Volume 2* where Beatrix disables the evil Bill and strikes him with the "Five Point Palm Exploding Heart Technique," the combination of five strikes with one's fingertips to five different pressure points on the target's body—after the target walks away and has taken five steps, their heart explodes in their body and they fall to the ground. My point was that the coronavirus epidemic is a kind of "Five Point Palm Exploding Heart Technique" attack on the global capitalist system—a signal that we cannot go on the way we were up until now, that a radical change is needed. Many people laughed at me afterwards: capitalism not only contained the crisis but exploited it to strengthen itself ... I still think I was right: in the last years, global capitalism changed so radically that some (like Varoufakis) even no longer call the new emerging order capitalism but corporate neo-feudalism. Capital obviously tries to profit from emergencies like the Covid pandemic or the global warming, but it is totally wrong to conclude from this fact that capital invents such emergencies in order to open up a new field of its expansion. Bill Gates claimed that people "might have to take multiple doses of a potential COVID-19 vaccine to protect themselves from the disease" since "none of the vaccines at this point appear like they'll work with a single dose":

developing a safe and effective vaccine is an urgent need to combat the pandemic. We need to make billions of doses, we need to get them out to every part of the world, and we need all of this to happen as quickly as possible [. . .] The world will need to manufacture and distribute at least seven billion doses of the vaccine—or possibly 14 billion, if it is a multi-dose vaccine—to beat the pandemic.[3]

The Left's reaction should not be to disagree with him but to raise the obvious question: how comes that a lone billionaire assumes the role of a wise man who pronounces claims which should be the basic premise of global health politics? China detected the problem—keeping not just the economy but also healthcare under social control—and correctly presumed this cannot be solved by mere multiparty democracy (the liberals' favorite alternate history: if just China would have gone to the end and followed economic opening with full democracy) and kept the Party in control of social life, but I doubt this will work in the long term. Ultimately, we are thus reduced to a simple basic choice: community or collective, socialism or communism. Otto Weininger was right to claim that socialism is Aryan, while communism is Jewish: socialism counts on organic social unity while communism mobilizes a more radical egalitarian collectivism that disbands the existing social links. In the long term, only the latter can save us.

Notes

1. Adrian Johnston, "Capitalism's Implants: A Hegelian Theory of Failed Revolutions," *Crisis and Critique* 8, no. 2 (12/2021), 140. Available online: https://www.crisiscritique.org/volume_8-issue_2/CC_8.2_Adrian%20Johnston.pdf (accessed December 20, 2021).
2. See Slavoj Žižek, *Heaven in Disorder* (New York: OR Books, 2021).
3. Bill Gates, "What You Need to Know about the COVID-19 Vaccine," *GatesNotes*, April 30, 2020. Available online: https://www.gatesnotes.com/health/what-you-need-to-know-about-the-covid-19-vaccine (accessed December 20, 2021).

CHAPTER THIRTEEN

Žižek and the War in an Era of Generalized Foreclosure[1]

Duane Rousselle

Jean Baudrillard famously wrote three provocative essays in which he claimed that the Gulf War did not take place.[2] Most commentators understood this to mean that the media produced a spectacle detached from the actual ongoings of the war, such that the spectacle took on a reality of its own. For Baudrillard, it is not that there is some deeper truth hidden behind media portrayals of the war but rather that these portrayals—simulacra, as he called them—become exposed as the proper domain of truth itself: "the simulacrum is never that which conceals the truth—it is the truth which conceals that there is none. The simulacrum is true."[3] The events which unfolded on the ground during that war were therefore entirely occluded or eclipsed by media images and commentary. Baudrillard was amplifying the tragic dimension of the war by reminding us that there is also a cultural one, one that disconnects us, irrevocably, from the reality of horrific events. However, what if the ultimate thinker of simulacra also missed something important about the way war relates to the real? The real is lawless. It relates to a mode of *jouissance* outside of any scope of truth or meaningful fiction.

What is at stake in the current tragedy in Ukraine?[4] Today's wars occur without any *disconnection* from the real. Hence media, knowledge, information, culture, all offer us a return to that which was repressed within our own social and individual worlds, namely, our own inhumanity. It is for this reason that I quite like the phrase that now seems to have gone out of fashion: "echo chamber." It was used for quite some time to describe the way social media walls become insular communicative realities, completely detached from the realities of others (which does not at all mean that it is detached from the real). My conviction is that we are now in an era of foreclosure, such that traditional notions of political uprisings, civil wars, and revolutions (insofar as they operate within a shared social world, and precisely against the world within which they stage their revolt) seem increasingly impotent. In a time of total war—an era that I elsewhere refer to as "the era of singularities"—civil war and political revolutions are impossible. I therefore make a distinction between "civil war" and "general war," with the understanding that the latter runs very deep and occurs across all strata and scales (e.g., micro-, meso-, and macrological). The function of every *general* war is precisely to render impossible *civil* war.

General war, unlike civil wars or political uprisings, have one important feature: an incredulity toward meta-narratives. I borrow this expression from one who in some way seemed nonetheless to champion it, namely Jean-François Lyotard. There is no recourse anymore to marriage contracts, international treaties, or third-party negotiations. Hence, it does not partake in the same logic as that laid out by Immanuel Kant in his notes on *Perpetual Peace*[5] which claimed that war leads toward the establishment of trade agreements and contracts (symbolic social ties). What one increasingly confronts today is a heightened paranoia, collective paranoia, as we project our own inhumanity, thereby misperceiving it as a threat felt upon ourselves, onto others. We are often like the child on the playground, commented upon by Lacan in his earlier seminars: the child punches another child and then cries, explaining to the teacher that it was he himself who was punched. For this child, he is a prophet of his own pain. Indeed, we are all prophets today, prophets of the realities that we set out for ourselves. The other day I was reminded of a conversation that I had with my son when he was very young, which I reproduce below:

Duane Look, Soren, there is the library.

Soren Yes, I already know that.

Duane How did you already know that?

Soren You just told me.

This is perhaps how prophecies function. They are retroactive justifications for that which one anyway claims to have already known in advance. In such circumstances, of course, one is never wrong, one never fails. This is why I maintain that Slavoj Žižek's analysis of the Ukraine situation proceeds from the one position: that of a shared Oedipal world. He remains in some sense attached to a politics of "unknown knowns."

Recall his infamous portrayal of Donald Rumsfeld's justifications for the war in Iraq. Rumsfeld claimed that there are three types of knowledge concerning Iraq: (1) "known knowns," which are the things we know perfectly well (consciously) that we know (e.g., I know that this essay was written in haste, and I know very well that I know that); (2) "known unknowns," which concerns conscious knowledge of the limitations of our knowledge (e.g.,

I know that there are people currently writing essays in this cafe, and yet I do not know what they are writing; but, precisely, *I know* that *I do not know* what they are writing), and; (3) "unknown unknowns," the abyss of knowledge (e.g., the things we do not even know that we do not know). Rumsfeld reasoned the following: "we don't even know what we don't know about weapons of mass destruction." Yet, Slavoj claimed that what was missing was the field known as ideology, or, rather, unconscious knowledge: (4) "unknown knowns," which are the things I did not know that I know, or, in other words, the field of suppositions which implicitly or unknowingly determine the scope of my knowledge. But it is clear that Rumsfeld was not confronting some domain of ideology. Rather, he confronted what psychoanalysts refer to as "hole." My claim is that Slavoj is too optimistic since it is not clear that Rumsfeld had an unconscious (in the traditional Freudian sense of the term). In such cases it is not the "transferential unconscious," the unconscious of suppositions and ideological determinations that is at stake. Rather, when one cancels one's subscription to the unconscious we are better equipped to see the effects of the "real unconscious." Against the backdrop of a *hole*, a certain domain of unthinkable trauma, one has recourse only to certainties: "known knowns."

It was the "known knowns" that drove us to war in Iraq: Rumsfeld knew perfectly well, despite the missing evidence, that there were weapons of mass destruction in Iraq. It was precisely because there was no evidence that he saw the evidence everywhere and with absolute certainty. This is what happens in a political age defined by "generalized foreclosure." Remember that in Lacan's third seminar on psychosis he claimed that what is foreclosed in the symbolic reappears in the real. When castration has not been internalized, that is, when the space of lack itself goes missing—a space that would have offered the possibility for internal rebellions, political uprisings, and civil wars—it returns from without, in the real. In such circumstances, the outside, which consists of everything outside of oneself or outside of one's social group, becomes a threat: castration returns with a vengeance.

There were plenty of warning signs that this was occurring. For example, take the curious homology of Western "cancel culture" and Russian "foreign agent" laws. To be very clear: I am not suggesting that they are the same practices or that they exist within the same context. However, they do share a structural relation that should be delicately examined: in both cases, whether as "cancel culture" or "foreign agent status," is the goal not to extinguish the space of internal opposition in order to render consistent the inner world of the social group as well as its certainty of knowledge? Thus, the "splitting element" is rejected, spit out of the social bond, refused, and forced to publicly declare itself an enemy to the social group (e.g., the "people"). In the era of singularities, there can be no internal opposition.

Hence, today when we witness students and everyday citizens in Russia protesting against the horrible events occuring in Ukraine, we should be prepared to ask ourselves the following question: how does this oppositional group sustain itself amidst the general war? For example, Antonio Gramsci popularly offered a distinction: "war of position" and "war of maneuver." The former was described by Gramsci (at the time) as the only possible point of opposition within Western civilization. Its practice consisted of the formation and defense of oppositional or counter-hegemonic "blocs," cultures of opposition to the overarching hegemony. These consist of universities, media/radio and television programs, non-governmental organizations, social movements, and so on. However, are the Western sanctions against Russia during the most recent conflict not designed, whether willingly or unwillingly, precisely to destroy the "war of position" within Russia? The very spaces within which "civil wars" and "political uprisings" were made possible are now being uprooted by removing their funding, their access to vital resources required to stage their revolt. This is true especially of those institutions whose mere existence was a threat to the ruling orthodoxy, demonstrated most obviously by the fact that they were constantly under surveillance by Russian intelligence agencies. Indeed, I was forced to flee, during the war, from one such institution. In such cases, civil war is rendered impossible and Western sanctions perhaps ensure a state of perpetual war between the West and Russia (or worse, West and East).

The problem with the media is not that it is not free. Hence, Elon Musk's solution of "free speech absolutism" misses the point, noble as his argument may seem. There are those who claim that blocking RT (Russia Today) in the West, or, similarly, blocking Western media in retaliation within Russia, is a rejection of one of the pillars of an "open society," that is, of Western civilization (e.g., a rejection of "free speech"). This vision remains tethered to an Oedipal or classically Freudian worldview. There remains a belief in a "shared world" within which one might be capable of socializing and communicating with one another. It is in this sense, and only in this sense, that Aleksandr Dugin has a point *but for the wrong reason*. Indeed, at first appearance, there does seem to be two truths: a Russian truth and a Western truth. However, what is missed, crucially, is that there is no possible truth *within* the West or *Russia*. Their worlds—the very social bond which sustains them—has collapsed, and what we confront are rather singular modes of *jouissance*. We no longer live in a world where the category of truth makes any sense because the very space within which it can be articulated, even, in the Lacanian sense as a "half-saying," has collapsed.

My claim that the category of truth has largely been lost does not imply that I am advancing some sort of "postmodern relativism." For Lacan, particularly in his earlier period, truth exists as a concept within the coordinates of a shared symbolic world. For example, it is possible to claim that the category of truth locates revelations of the "symbolic" or "transferential" unconscious, or, in Marxian language: it locates a space of determinative "totality" obscured by the imaginary relations of capitalist commodities. Or, put into the language of the American sociologist C. Wright Mills: it concerns the explication of the "sociological imagination," which sees political and historical determinations hidden deep inside of the narratives we tell about our personal biographies. But singularities do not exist within that world.

They cannot see outside of themselves, even, especially, when they claim to be doing so. For the singularity, there is no world. Thus, I return to my oft-quoted example: when, many months ago, the American president Joe Biden looked into the eyes of Vladimir Putin and saw a killer, Putin responded that Biden was seeing his own soul reflected back at him. But we should be prepared to now add the following: when Putin looks into the eyes of his "Western partners" and sees those who continually expand NATO and infiltrate his country, is he not seeing his own imperialist ambitions reflected back at him?

The problem in the era of singularities is not that the war in Ukraine "did not take place" and that it is too detached from a "real" which never existed anyway. Rather, what the recent crisis demonstrates is precisely the inverse: it is too real. This is why the theory of simulacra will not get us any further in understanding what is most at stake today. The war is already here, and we are in the midst of it. None of us are untouched by it. Our worlds have collapsed, and this is demonstrated, most obviously, in our inability to communicate with one another: in the projection of transphobia and racism onto those who are perhaps more inclined toward our dispositions than we might have first believed (e.g., the recent transphobic accusations against Jacques-Alain Miller, and so on).

In any case, some political commentators among the Left have claimed that there is a Western double-standard in its handling of Ukrainian refugees (e.g., support for white refugees but not for those of color, and so on). This position, though it is no doubt true, nonetheless neglects to mention a few important points: first, it is largely simulacra, since many Ukrainians have yet to see concrete results from Western governments; second, the current crisis, unlike many other crises around the world today, may actually lead us toward World War III. This makes the current crisis much more difficult to articulate in terms of Western double standards (e.g., "we help white Ukrainians but not . . ."). While this claim is no doubt true, it fails to recognize that if we do not continue to do so then we risk a rapid escalation of the situation.

We are now living in an era that cannot articulate its own insularity. It is not that we lack the very language to articulate our unfreedom, but rather that we lack the very language to articulate the immense cruelty of freedom. Freedom is only possible precisely from within the prison-house of language; that is, from within the confines of a shared world or civilization. But today we struggle to relate to one another, and civilization seems to no longer exist as a possible space of refuge. For example, my Russian students have frequently explained to me that they are at war with their family members, at risk of being kicked out from their homes, precisely over their narrative about what is happening in Ukraine. The fragility of the social bond *as such* is at stake. This, precisely, is the problem with the clinical structure that psychoanalysts name psychosis: it is not, as some psychologists maintain, that in psychosis one suffers from delusions "detached from reality." Rather, the problem with psychosis, obviously, is that there is "too much" reality

It seems to me that we often begin today with a conviction. It is an unshakable conviction, a statement of certainty. It is clear that these convictions are never statements of doubt. It is the other who threatens our convictions. But this is not how things used to function in our societies: we used to doubt our intellectual and political positions, and we presumed that there was an Other out there who had the certainties that we lacked. We should not be nostalgic for a lost time, but we should be prepared to admit that a transition has most definitely occurred: we have lost the Other, and we have assumed the position of the one who supposes knowledge. When we assume the position of the one who knows, the world itself collapses: the threat is no longer contained *within* but hits us everywhere from *without*. This, I maintain, is the source of the great wars that are occurring in all aspects of our lives today.

We should absolutely reject this road of political discourse which insists that to be a good "leftist," or to be recognized as a member of a social community known as "Left," one must adopt a commonsensical point of view by "taking sides" or explicitly declaring allegiances. For example, look at the words of Slavoj Žižek. (I should preface this by stating the obvious: among all thinkers today, I continue to truly admire his bold thinking.) He recently took aim at "leftists" (though he insisted that he certainly wouldn't recognize them as leftists) for "blaming the West for the fact that US President Joe Biden was right about Putin's intentions." Is this not precisely what we are up against today, namely the fact that we are *always correct about the other's intentions* (even, and especially, before we have any proof of the fact)? "Have no fear," they might claim, "the proof is coming in the future!" Perhaps Putin would offer a similar rebuttal: "See, I told you that the West has been aligned with Ukraine, transforming it into a de facto NATO state." If we are against this war, it seems to me that we must be prepared to examine it as an exemplary case of war in a time of generalized foreclosure.

Notes

1. The editors thank the *European Journal of Psychoanalysis* for permission to reprint the article which was published on March 15, 2022 under the title "Psychoanalysis in Exile: Ramblings without a World." http://www.journal-psychoanalysis.eu/psychoanalysis-in-exile-ramblings-without-a-world-d-rousselle/ (accessed May 15, 2022).
2. Jean Baudrillard, *The Gulf War Did Not Take Place* (Sydney: Power Publications, 2012).
3. Jean Baudrillard, *Selected Writings* (Cambridge: Polity, 1988).
4. At the time of writing, March 20, 2022.
5. Immanuel Kant, "Perpetual Peace: A Philosophical Sketch, 1795," Mount Holyoke College, March 21, 2022. Available online: https://www.mtholyoke.edu/acad/intrel/kant/kant1.htm (accessed March 22, 2022).

Response to Rousselle

Slavoj Žižek

What makes Duane Rousselle's critical intervention into the debate on the war in Ukraine[1] so captivating is that he does much more than analyze the Russian aggression on Ukraine as "an exemplary case of war in a time of generalized foreclosure" (in contrast to my analysis of the Ukraine war which remains within the coordinates of a "shared Oedipal world." His critique is grounded in the general premise that

> we are now in an era of foreclosure, such that traditional notions of political uprisings, civil wars, and revolutions (insofar as they operate within a shared social world, and precisely against the world within which they stage their revolt) seem increasingly impotent. In a time of total war—an era that I elsewhere refer to as "the era of singularities"—civil war and political revolutions are impossible.

I think Rousselle relies here too much on Jacques-Alain Miller's idea of today's global capitalist order as the order of generalized foreclosure of the symbolic Law: "The real is lawless. It relates to a mode of *jouissance* outside of any scope of truth or meaningful fiction." (I find it ironic that Miller, after decades of downplaying anti-Oedipal critiques of Lacan as superficial, suddenly went to the other extreme and declared that we live in an era of post-Oedipal Real.) Rousselle exemplifies this notion of "generalized foreclosure" through a critique of my interpretation of the category of "unknown knowns" missing in Donald Rumsfeld's justification of the attack on Iraq: unknown knowns are

> the things I did not know that I know, or, in other words, the field of suppositions which implicitly or unknowingly determine the scope of my knowledge. But it is clear that Rumsfeld was not confronting some domain of ideology. Rather, he confronted what psychoanalysts refer to

as "hole." It was the "known knowns" that drove us to war in Iraq: Rumsfeld knew perfectly well, despite the missing evidence, that there were weapons of mass destruction in Iraq. It was precisely because there was no evidence that he saw the evidence everywhere and with absolute certainty. This is what happens in a political age defined by "generalized foreclosure."

My reading is exactly the opposite one: the US not only were not sure if Saddam had the WMD or not, they *positively knew he did* not *have them*—which is why they risked the ground offensive on Iraq. (If the US were to take seriously their own claims that Iraq had the WMD which can be immediately unleashed, they probably would not launch a ground assault, fearing too many casualties on their side, but would stick to air bombing.) So the mechanism at work here was not that of a psychotic foreclosure (in which the lack itself is lacking, so that *objet a* whose exclusion from reality is constitutive of reality falls directly into reality): the non-existing "Iraqi weapons of mass destruction" fitted perfectly the status of the Hitchcockian MacGuffin. (Incidentally, one of the most famous Hitchcockian MacGuffins *is* a potential weapon of mass destruction—the bottles with "radioactive diamonds" in *Notorious*!) Iraqi WMD were an elusive entity, never empirically specified—when, some years ago, the UN inspectors were searching for them in Iraq, they were expected to be hidden in the most disparate and improbable places, from the (rather logical place of) desert to the (slightly irrational) cellars of the presidential palaces (so that, when the palace is bombed, they may poison Saddam and his entire entourage?), allegedly present in large quantities, yet magically moved around all the time by the hands of workers, and the more all-present and all-powerful in their threat, the more they are destroyed, as if the distraction of the greater part of them magically heightens the destructive power of the remainder? As such, they by definition cannot ever be found, and are therefore all the more dangerous. In the Ukrainian war, the MacGuffin are "secret bio-weapon labs" funded and organized in Ukraine by the US, developing poisonous stuff that transmits human sicknesses.[2] They are evoked as the reason why Russia does not just plan to occupy the south-western area of Ukraine where there is a strong Russian minority but plans to seize all of Ukraine—to destroy these labs. But, again, I claim Russia positively knows there are no such "secret bio-weapon labs" in Ukraine full of dangerous poisons: if such labs were there, Russia would act in a different way, with much greater urgency: it would directly attack these labs or try to occupy them with elite parachute units.

To avoid a fatal misunderstanding: this does not mean that there are no bio-weapons being developed in secret labs—all big countries have them, of course, and our media are right in treating these Russian accusations as a dark hint or threat that they themselves may use bio-weapons. The Ukrainian war can take many further turns for the worse, not just the recourse to nuclear weapons: use of bio-weapons, use of gasses which hinder the functioning of our brains, full digital attack on the cyberspace of the enemy, etc.; however, we are still far from a generalized foreclosure which breaks down a shared symbolic space.

The proof that we are far from it is that that the autonomy of the symbolic order (which opens up the space for metaphoric substitutions in which a universal can stand for a particular) is still operative. Recall a video that went viral on social media mid-March 2022 showing a woman being arrested by the Russian police for holding up a small piece of paper that reads "two words" ("два слова" in Russian) which, of course, referred to the forbidden slogan "no to war" ("нет войне" in Russian). At its extreme, absence (void) itself can be "determinate," i.e., it can refer to a specific content—Russian police also arrested demonstrators who protested with blank signs: a video that received millions of views shows a woman holding a blank sign among a group of people before police officers approach her and escort her away from the crowd.³ This substitution worked because everybody knew at that point what is prohibited in Russia: to publicly reject the war against Ukraine.

I remember from the 1970s another case of similar censorship in communist Czechoslovakia. When Martina Navratilova (at that time the world's top female tennis player who emigrated to the West and became a non-person even for the Czech sports media) reached the semi-finals in a big international championship, a Czech sports daily reported on it with the title "The four semi-finalists known," followed by *only three* names—Navratilova was simply ignored, although the title implied four players. Weird as it was, this censorship was not psychotic since the very open inconsistency of the title pointed toward the excluded fourth name which was thus "present in the mode of absence" (to use the structuralist jargon).

All these (and other similar) phenomena cannot be accounted for in the terms of Lacan's first definition of psychosis ("what is foreclosed in the symbolic reappears in the real"). In a psychotic universe, there is no space for internal rebellions, political uprisings, and civil wars: the excluded "returns from without, in the real. In such circumstances, the outside, which consists of everything outside of oneself or outside of one's social group, becomes a threat: castration returns with a vengeance." Along these lines, Rousselle emphasizes the "curious homology of Western 'cancel culture' and Russian 'foreign agent' laws": each in its own way works as a desperate measure to fortify a social bond by excluding from it (what is perceived as) a threatening element. The MeToo strict control of language and body is a desperate attempt to control and regulate our speech and bodily movements up to minor details (a gesture that I involuntarily make with my hand, how I look at a person next to me)—the target is here the inconsistent chaos of our language games invested by sexuality and power relations. Such a controlling procedure can be found even where one wouldn't expect it. In January 2022, the Royal Opera House in London announced that it is

> consulting with Ita O'Brien—an intimacy coordinator who ensures actors feel comfortable during such scenes—for Katie Mitchell's new production

of *Theodora*, opening on Monday.... "There's consent each and every day. You might agree one day that you're very happy to kiss lip to lip, and then you develop a cold sore, so it's not suitable any more. So you explore what the moment is about, different ways to tell the same story," she said.[4]

While one should support the fight against any form of harassment, there are some details in this announcement that make me "feel uncomfortable." First, why, again, the (implicit) reduction to women as victims of harassment here? Second, while, obviously, there are scenes in which playing a victim of rape or violence may make the actor as a person traumatized, how could one enact on screen or stage a brutal scene without feeling uncomfortable? Third, the example mentioned ("You might agree one day that you're very happy to kiss lip to lip, and then you develop a cold sore, so it's not suitable anymore") is ridiculously obvious and has nothing to do with harassment—it throws a strange light on the entire argument by putting a cold sore in the same series with, say, touching a breast of an actress. Fourth, the very term "intimacy coordinator" sounds (and *is*) ominous: at the end of this road lurks the idea that (why not?) even when a couple is intimate alone but not sure about how to interact, they should hire an intimacy coordinator. Is not, in a way, such "intimacy coordination" even worse than the Russian "foreign agent" law which excludes from public media and official state or cultural activities people who "systematically distribute materials to an indefinite circle of persons, while receiving foreign funds" (the Pussy Riot member Nadezhda Tolokonnikova is the latest addition to the list of over one hundred).[5] Ominous as it sounds, the "foreign agent" law excludes you from institutional public life but doesn't imply any legal measures against you (I am, of course, aware that de facto many other ominous things happen to you, from secret police observation to being prosecuted for false "corruption" charges)—there is no psychotic foreclosure at work here, you just don't exist for the institutional big Other.

So Rousselle is right to emphasize, apropos "the curious homology of Western 'cancel culture' and Russian 'foreign agent' laws," that they are *not* "the same practices" and that they don't "exist within the same context." The first big difference is obvious: the Russian exclusion is the exclusion of a subgroup of enemies from the public space; in the politically correct cancelling, there is no clear delimitation, no clear criteria, rules are changing constantly, *everybody* is under suspicion and can be all of a sudden "cancelled," excluded from social space, a small gesture he or she made can be proclaimed "racist" or "sexist" (it almost happened to me: when, in Slovenia, a couple of years ago, I gave an interview together with my wife apropos her first novel, I said that, while she was writing it, I often made and brought her fresh tea—for this, I barely missed being proclaimed the male chauvinist of the year). The structure remains here that of the university discourse, but the weight of the terms changes: the agent is the knowledge enabling the prosecutor to detect problematic statements or gestures; the object is *objet a*, surplus enjoyment embodied in the problematic entity, the product is a subject all the time under suspicion and plagued by guilt, and the "truth" beneath knowledge is the anonymous Master, the one who (often in a very arbitrary way) decides when an act that deserves to be cancelled is committed. So one could say that the difference is the one between masculine and feminine versions of Lacan's formulas of sexuation: in Russia, the excluded/cancelled is the exception which sustains the universal unity of the people ("all Russians support the special operation in Ukraine, with the exception of foreign agents"), while in the Western cancel culture not all are cancelled but there is no exception (everybody is under suspicion). However, Rousselle nonetheless argues that in both cases, whether in "cancel culture" or in "foreign agent status," the goal is "to extinguish the space of internal opposition in order to render consistent the inner world of the social group as well as its certainty of knowledge. Thus, the 'splitting element' is rejected, spit out of the social bond, refused, and forced to publicly declare itself an enemy to the social group (e.g., the 'people')."

The reason I don't endorse such an interpretation is that, if we accept it, we should say that Stalinism was incomparably more "psychotic": it is only in Stalinism that the excluded enemy is "forced to publicly declare itself an enemy to the social group (e.g., the 'people')"—recall the public confessions in Stalinist trials where the accused admitted their guilt and demanded the death penalty for themselves, while in Putin's Russia, opposition, marginalized and under threat as it is, still exists and there are still some media who oppose the regime. Putin's Russia is still far from full "totalitarian" closure. In Russia, there are still traces of "the formation and defense of oppositional or counter-hegemonic 'blocs,' cultures of opposition to the overarching hegemony" which "consist of universities, media/radio and television programs, non-governmental organizations, social movements, and so on." Just think of the figure of Navalny who is able to appeal to people to protest against the war from the prison—can one even imagine something like this to happen in Stalinism? For this reason, I don't think

> there is no possible truth *within* the West or *Russia*. Their worlds—the very social bond which sustains them—has collapsed, and what we confront are rather singular modes of *jouissance*. We no longer live in a world where the category of truth makes any sense because the very space within which it can be articulated, even, in the Lacanian sense as a "half-saying," has collapsed.

I think, on the contrary, that the dimension of truth is still operative in the present situation—the question is what occupies the place of truth. We are overflown by knowledge which (to refer to Lacan's formula of the university discourse) acts as the agent of today's predominant cynical discourse; the object of this knowledge is *objet a*, which are (as we have seen in the case of the US attacking Iraq and Russia attacking Ukraine) WMD; the "product" of this discourse is the agent presumed to manipulate WMD (the drug-addicted neo-Nazi Ukrainian leadership), and at the place of truth is the Master whose paranoia concocted the object (WMD), Putin and his circle.

We have to draw here what may appear as a naïve distinction, the distinction between the paranoiac knowledge about the fantasized object (WMD) and the factual knowledge about what is going on in Ukraine (and around it). The status of the two knowledges is different: while the paranoiac knowledge is a fake, it succeeds to mobilize people into a war, while the factual knowledge, although literally true (adequate to facts), fails to mobilize us. What makes our situation so debilitating is that we know how things are but are unable to act upon this knowledge. Adam McKay's *Don't Look Up* (2021) tells the story of a comet heading directly toward earth, and of two scientists who struggle to convince the rest of the world that it's not a hoax (the government and a population refuse to believe in the existence of the comet). This ultimate apocalypse (life on earth will end in six months and everybody knows it even if this knowledge is disavowed) is presented as a political satire—more precisely, as a satire beneath which utter darkness lurks all the time (for example, the president is concerned about how this news will affect midterm elections). This choice of satire is correct: when we are dealing with true catastrophe, we are beyond tragedy, and only a comedy can do the job through its very inadequacy to the actual situation—remember that the best films on concentration camps are comedies.

No wonder some critics were displeased by the light tone of the movie, claiming that it trivializes the ultimate apocalypse. What really bothers these critics is the exact opposite: the trivialization that permeates not only the establishment but even the protesters. The president (played by Meryl Streep) is obviously modelled on Hillary Clinton, so her resistance to take the threat to life on earth seriously does not come from a rightist populist position. And even the protesters who, later in the film, chant "Look up!", imploring us to take the approaching comet seriously, are not proposing any effective measures, they are just performing a big spectacle with pop star singers, chanting obvious slogans. So the film is not yet another cheap attack on rightist populists; it targets the two predominant reactions to today's threats like global warming, by the liberal establishment and by the ecological protesters.

It is not enough to tell the truth; one has to tell it in a way that mobilizes people to act on it, not to indulge in self-righteous satisfaction. "Truth" (the urgent need for global cooperation, etc.) is repelled by publicly embracing the need for green action, for collaboration to fight pandemic, as it happened in the Glasgow conference full of declarative blahblah but with very little precise obligations. More precisely, the lesson of *Don't Look Up!* is that conspiracy theorists (about the pandemic or global warming) in a way *give body to the "unconscious" of the "rational" liberal establishment itself*.[6] The truth is exactly the opposite of the conspiracy-theory claim that the forces of establishment don't really believe in the danger of a forthcoming catastrophe and manipulate this danger as a conspiracy to control people: the forces of establishment know reality but they intimately don't believe in it—they are the true deniers. The lesson of Boris Johnson's garden parties at the time of strict lockdown tells a lot here: although he knew well the reality of Covid (he almost died of it), his activity (like partying) demonstrates that he didn't really believe in it, that he perceived himself (and the circle around himself) as somehow exempted from it. When, in the movie, the president asks, worried, "But will the comet hitting the earth prevent the Super Bowl?", she perfectly renders this stance: as if the end of life on Earth doesn't render this question meaningless. That's why the true target of our critique should not be the outright deniers (of the pandemic, of global warming) but the false "rationalism" of the establishment itself—and, again, the mechanism at work here is not a direct psychotic foreclosure but a form of fetishism, a fetishist disavowal in which knowledge itself can work as a fetish.

None of the two forms of knowledge, the mobilizing fake and the factual truth, involves a psychotic foreclosure. Back to Rousselle—this is why I think the psychotic-paranoiac communication in which I only get back from the other my own foreclosed content projected onto the other is not sufficient—here is Rousselle's description of such communication:

> when, many months ago, the American president Joe Biden looked into the eyes of Vladimir Putin and saw a killer, Putin responded that Biden was seeing his own soul reflected back at him. But we should be prepared to now add the following: when Putin looks into the eyes of his "Western partners" and sees those who continually expand NATO and infiltrate his country, is he not seeing his own imperialist ambitions reflected back at him?

I think that this formula of paranoiac projection ignores the properly symbolic mechanism of a redoubled lie, of lying in the guise of truth, which was at work in the predominant Western perception of Putin's words—our mistake was not to take Putin's threats literally enough—we thought he didn't really mean it but was just playing a game of strategic manipulations. The supreme irony is that, bearing in mind that now (end of March 2022) Russians are targeting Lviv, one cannot but recall the famous Jewish joke quoted by Freud, "Why are you telling me you are going to Lviv when you are really going to Lviv?" where a lie assumes the form of factual truth: the two friends established an implicit code that, when you go to Lviv, you say you are going to Cracow and vice versa, and within this space, telling the literal truth means lying. When Putin announced military intervention, we didn't take Putin's declaration that he wants to pacify and denazify all of Ukraine literally enough, so the reproach of the disappointed "deep" strategists to Putin is now: "Why were you telling me you are going to occupy Lviv when you really want to occupy Lviv?"

The war in Ukraine is thus, I think, not a clash of psychotic singularities each of which just projects onto the other its own foreclosed content; it is also not just a clash between superpowers over the control of disputed spheres of influence. It remains a genuine "metaphysical" conflict, a conflict of two global visions of what humanity is, liberal and conservative. Each side is intimately related to the other; it needs its other to sustain itself. So, again, the clash is not, I think, a clash of psychotic singularities—it fits perfectly Lacan's formula of (symbolic) communication in which I get from the other my own message in its inverted and true form (note the term "true"). The US got from its Iraq intervention the truth about its intervention: Iraq is now more than ever under the influence of Iran, more Islamic fundamentalist than under Saddam, with a much lower position of women in public life. And the same goes for Russia: it invaded Ukraine claiming that there is no separate Ukrainian nation, that they are parts of the same large ethnic and cultural group, and—at this moment, at least—the result is that today the Ukrainian identity is stronger than ever, and that more of them really hate Russians and don't want to have anything to do with them.

Rousselle's counter-argument here[7] is that the social structure of "generalized foreclosure" does not preclude that in the domain of more special and localized socialized exchanges the Oedipual structure of the link grounded in symbolic castration is largely not still operative: in our daily interactions, we are not all singularities, islands of *jouissance*, with no shared symbolic pact sustaining us. Hegel himself was aware of this gap: in one of the most famous passages in his *Phenomenology*, the dialectic of master and servant, he imagines the confrontation of the two self-consciousnesses engaged in the struggle to life and death; each side is ready to go to the end in risking its life, but if they both persist to the end, there is no winner—one dies, the other survives but without another to recognize it. The whole history of freedom and recognition—in short, the whole of history, the whole of human culture—can take place only with an original compromise: in the eye-to-eye confrontation, one side (the "future servant") "averts its eyes," is not ready to go to the end. But as Hegel knew very well, there is no such compromise-resolution in the relations between the states: the co-existence of sovereign nation-states implies the necessity of war. Each state disciplines/educates its own members and guarantees civic peace among them in the guise of state power, but the relationship between different states is permanently under the shadow of potential war, with each epoch of peace nothing more than a temporary armistice. As Hegel conceptualized it, the entire ethic of a state culminates in the highest act of heroism, the readiness to sacrifice one's life for one's nation-state, which means that the wild barbarian relations between states serve as the foundation of the ethical life within a state. Is today's North Korea with its ruthless pursuit of nuclear weapons and rockets to hit distant targets not the ultimate example of this logic of unconditional nation-state sovereignty?

So we have a struggle to death between the states and the mutual recognition within each state; today, however, there are (interconnected) changes on all levels. At the lowest level of family life, the paternal authority is shifting from the symbolic Law ("Name-of-the-Father") to superego; the international relations are shifting from relations between sovereign states to a couple of superpowers controlling their spheres of influence; and the nation-states themselves are gradually transforming themselves into neo-tribal communities held together by a specific and exclusive way of life.

The ultimate problem with Rousselle's analysis is that it is self-defeating—it leaves us in a dead end: if it is true, if we already live in a universe of generalized foreclosure, then there is no way out, and our very awareness of it plays no role; the game is over if we know it or not. But I think that knowledge matters, that knowing something always affects this thing, somehow changes its status. In this case, it is the very act of knowing that the game is over which effectively makes the game over—it is as if we have to know that the game is over since, if we were not to know it, we might have actually change something, so the game will not be over.

Notes

1 See Douane Rousselle, "Psychoanalysis in Exile: Ramblings without a World *European Journal of Psychoanalysis* (journal-psychoanalysis.eu), March 15, 2022. (Non-attributed quotes are from this source.) Available online: http://www.journal-psychoanalysis.eu/psychoanalysis-in-exile-ramblings-without-a-world-d-rousselle/ (accessed March 25, 2022).

2 "2022 Ukraine, Russia and Us—Russia Claims US Implementing 'Secret Bio-Weapon Project' in Ukraine to Transmit Human Diseases," *SEGATE*—English Version (promoseagate.com), March 22, 2022. Available online: https://en.promoseagate.com/2022-ukraine-russia-and-us-russia-claims-us-implementing-secret-bio-weapon-project-in-ukraine-to-transmit-human-diseases/ (accessed March 25, 2022).

3 "Viral Protests: Russians Continue to Denounce War, Risking Imprisonment," *Deutsche Welle* (DW), March 16, 2022, Europe | News and current affairs from around the continent. Available online: https://www.dw.com/en/viral-protests-russians-continue-to-denounce-war-risking-imprisonment/a-61143188 (accessed March 25, 2022).

4 Nadia Khomami, "Royal Opera House Hires Intimacy Coordinator for Sex Scenes." *Guardian*, January 29, 2022. Available online: https://www.theguardian.com/culture/2022/jan/29/royal-opera-house-hires-intimacy-coordinator-ita-obrien-handel-theodora-sex-scenes (accessed March 25, 2022).

5 "Russia labels Pussy Riot members, satirist 'foreign agents'," *France24* (france24.com), December 30, 2021. Available online: https://www.france24.com/en/live-news/20211230-russia-labels-pussy-riot-members-satirist-foreign-agents (accessed March 25, 2022).

6 See Alenka Zupančič, "Teorija zarote brez zarote," *Mladina*, Ljubljana, January 28, 2022, 54–6. Available online: https://www.mladina.si/213709/teorija-zarote-brez-zarote/ (accessed March 25, 2022).

7 Made in personal communication with me.

CHAPTER FOURTEEN

Harpo's Grin

Rethinking Lacan's Unthinkable "Thing"[1]

Richard Boothby

One of the stranger threads in the unfolding arc of Lacan's career concerns his notion of *das Ding*. As part of his seventh seminar and in connection with a brief passage from Freud's "Project for a Scientific Psychology," Lacan put forward the unknown "Thing" in the Other as an absolutely key concept.[2] As Freud had posed it, *das Ding* named the enigmatic remainder in the infant's cognition of the mother. The primal experience of something unknown in the maternal Other, he argued, later provides the template for all of the infant's explorations of objects. Lacan takes up this idea but also significantly builds upon it, linking the Thing more expressly with the core formation of the unconscious. *Das Ding*, he said, "is a primordial function which is located at the level of the initial establishment of the gravitation of the unconscious *Vorstellungen*."[3] It's hard to overstate the importance Lacan attached to this novel piece of theorizing. "At the heart of man's destiny," he said, "is the *Ding* [...] the *causa pathomenon*, the cause of the most fundamental human passion."[4] "It is around *das Ding* that the whole adaptive development revolves, a development that is so specific to man insofar as the symbolic process reveals itself to be inextricably woven into it."[5]

Surprisingly, however, despite so conspicuously emphasizing the weightiness of his breakthrough, Lacan seems almost immediately to step away from his own idea. *Das Ding* all but disappears from the second half of the *Ethics* seminar, and it shows up only rarely in subsequent years.[6]

Perhaps more than anyone, Slavoj Žižek has kept up discussion of *das Ding*, granting it a significance nearly on a par with that of Lacan's concept of the *objet petit a*. The two arguably form the twin lodestars of Žižek's thought: the monstrous and the anamorphotic.[7] It is, for example, the monstrousness potentially inhabiting every other human being that grounds Žižek's critique of Levinas's ethics of the face. "In a properly dialectical paradox," Žižek points out, "what Levinas (with all his celebration of Otherness) fails to take into account is not some underlying Sameness of all humans but the radical 'inhuman' Otherness itself."[8] Žižek then goes on to wonder whether the primary function of the symbolic law is to keep the Other-Thing at a safe distance. "What if the ultimate function of the Law," he asks, "is not to [. . .] retain our proximity to the neighbor, but, on the contrary, to keep the neighbor at a proper distance, to serve as a kind of protective wall against the monstrosity of the neighbor?"[9]

The question remains as to why Lacan himself appears to take some distance from *das Ding* after his initial, strikingly enthusiastic embrace. Actually, he doesn't completely leave it behind. Things would be easier if he had abandoned it altogether, ideally telling us why he dropped it. But that's not the case. A year after introducing it, Lacan returns to it in a brief passage of the seminar on *Transference*. In the lectures on *Ethics*, Lacan theorized that sublimation is achieved when "the object is elevated to the dignity of the Thing."[10] He then adds in the *Transference* seminar that the function of the beautiful is essentially defensive. He therefore speaks of "beauty rising up such as it is projected at the extreme limit in order to stop us from going any further toward the heart of the Thing."[11] Two years further on, in the seminar on *Anxiety*, Lacan refers once again to the Thing, this time associating it with the primal source of anxiety. "Not only is [anxiety] not without object," he says, "but it very likely designates the most, as it were, profound object, the ultimate object, the Thing."[12] These two references are obviously important, touching as they do on two of the most central concerns of psychoanalytic theory—sublimation and anxiety. Yet both points are confined to single sentences. No where else in either seminar is *das Ding* mentioned. In subsequent years, it appears only a handful of times. How to explain this relative silence?

While this question is not often explicitly raised among commentators, an answer to it appears to be available just about everywhere in the literature. For most scholars of Lacan, his most valuable contribution to psychoanalysis— he said so himself—was his concept of the *objet a*. It is tempting to suppose that *das Ding* merely gets eclipsed by its more frequently discussed successor. The obvious question then becomes how exactly we are to interpret the relation between the two. Might we conceive *das Ding* and *objet a* as somehow internally connected with one another? If so, how?

Žižek appears to be on the verge of posing this question in his "Self-interview" attached as a postscript to his *Metastases of Enjoyment*. "How does the *objet petit a* differ from the primordial Thing?" he asks.

Perhaps the best way to distinguish them is via a reference to the philosophical distinction between ontological and ontic levels. The status of the Thing is purely ontic, it stands for an irreducible excess of the ontic that eludes *Lichtung*, the ontological clearance within which entities appear: the Thing is the paradox of an ontic X in so far as it is not yet an "innerworldly" entity, appearing within the transcendental-ontological horizon. In contrast, the status of the *a* is purely ontological—a frame that determines the status of positive entities.[13]

On this reading, the Thing is an unknown, unseen entity that somehow refuses to enter the clearing of phenomenal disclosure that Heidegger called *die Lichtung*. The *objet a*, by contrast, wholly transcends the ontic plane. It is "purely ontological." This formulation makes a certain amount of sense. Both Freud and Lacan treat *das Ding* as a local, situated upsurge of strangeness. It is essential that Freud locates it in the field of the most familiar object—the mother.[14] In this sense, the Thing can readily be said to participate in ontic particularity. The Thing is a horizon of something unknown that arises from the encounter with something otherwise recognizable. At the same time, attributing to the *objet a* a purely ontological status seems appropriate in so far as the *objet a*, at first glance a definite object or feature thereof, somehow immediately evacuates itself, throwing the observing subject into a state vertiginous uncertainty that may alternately stimulate anxiety or desire. Such would be the case in the apparently formless anamorphotic stain in the foreground of Holbein's "Ambassadors," which calls out to be viewed from the side. From that oblique angle, the mysterious blot shows itself to be a skull. Even when the blurry stain is revealed to be a grinning skull, however, the viewer is thrown into an abyssal confusion, a kind of destabilization of the subject's own location and self-understanding. A parallel point would seem to be at stake in Lacan's definition of anxiety as arising from the unanswered question of the subject's acceptability to the desire of the other. As Lacan puts it, "anxiety is bound to the fact that I don't know which object *a* I am for the desire of the Other."[15] Trying imagine oneself from the point of view of the unknowable Other is to be plunged into a kind of vertigo.

In what follows I would like to argue an interpretation diametrically opposed to Žižek's. The *objet a* is the ontic element, though to be sure an element that immediately opens out onto an ontological horizon. *Das Ding*, on the other hand, is purely ontological. It is, in fact, the originary opening of the human relation to the ontological as such. It is to be identified precisely with the dimension of "the ontological clearance within which entities appear." The key point, however, is that there is an intimate relationship between the two. *Objet a* and *das Ding* form an essential couplet. The *objet a* is a kind of incongruous but vanishing trace, a strange detail, that sparks a vague awareness of a yawning void.

While Lacan leaves us precious little help to clarify the relation between the *objet a* and the Thing, there is at least one brief text that suggests a confirmation of their intimate relationship with one another. In the sixteenth seminar of 1968–9, "From an Other to the other," Lacan links the two, playfully but very suggestively quipping that the *objet a* "is what tickles *das Ding* from the inside."[16] This text suggests that, far from being independent of one another, the Thing and the *objet a* are rather two sides of a fundamental dynamic. The *objet a* and *Ding* mark an unstable junction between an object and a void. They appear to be linked very specifically at the site of the intersection between the ontic and the ontological.

In clarifying the relation between these two key Lacanian concepts, it is vital to remember that Lacan introduces *das Ding* before he arrives at his notion of the *objet a* and that he at first characterizes *das Ding* in terms he will later use to describe *objet a*. Where the *objet* becomes the "object-cause of desire," for example, Lacan first describes *das Ding* as "the cause of the most fundamental human passion." Moreover, when Lacan first puts forward his notion of *das Ding*, he links it with what will later constitute the prime characteristic of *objet a*, that of being an ancillary detail in the field of perception that somehow makes all the difference. "The Thing," he says, "is something that presents and isolates itself as the *strange feature* around which the whole movement of the *Vorstellung* turns."[17] If *das Ding* is initially tied to such an odd but eye-catching element, however, the more important point is the way that it immediately opens upon something invisible that is connected with the unknown desire of the Other. The way Freud originally poses this pivot from something seen to something unseen intriguingly anticipates Lacan's categories of the imaginary and the real. Freud notes how the child divides the figure of the *Nebenmensch*, the "neighbor" or fellow human being, between what can be recognized as similarities to its own body—precisely the sort of mirror recognition that Lacan associates with the imaginary—as opposed to a locus of something "new and non-comparable" that indicates a zone of something unknown.[18] It is this unrepresentable excess that Freud calls *das Ding*. That excess is the unknown desire of the Other. No wonder Lacan found Freud's formulation here to be of such singular promise. Lacan's crucial intervention in the history of psychoanalytic theory shifted the emphasis from Freud's preoccupation with the paternal threat of castration to a focus on the mystery of the Other's desire.

The role of a "strange feature" pivoting toward the unseen and unknown is well illustrated in Freud's discussion of the case of a young woman, Emma, which he presents only a few pages after introducing his notion of *das Ding*.[19] Emma's terror of entering shops alone was triggered, Freud discovers, by an experience in which two shop assistants appeared to laugh at her clothes. But that triggering event took its traumatic power from a scene in her childhood in which an obscenely leering older shopkeeper had grabbed at her genitals. The prime feature that Emma remembered was the strange and disturbing smile on his face. It was that feature that short-circuited the two scenes and set up the retroactive trauma. What was called up by the dreadful smile, however, was the way in which it pointed disturbingly to something abyssal and threatening in the unknown desire of the Other. The smile was a harbinger of *das Ding*.

The example of the shopkeeper's unnerving grin signals some unknown intention on the part of the Other, thereby repeating the shift from the imaginary to the real. The same shift characterizes the most elementary instantiations of the *objet a*, which Lacan early on identifies with Freud's famous "part objects."[20] Lacan proposes that the most primordial indications of the Thing in the Other are embodied in the breast, the feces, and the penis. Such part objects mark the boundary between the known and the unknown. In effect, the infant seizes on one or another appendage of the body as a means of getting a handle on what remains in the Other mysterious and ungraspable, the ever-elusive unknown that the subject will attempt to refind. As Lacan puts it,

> lack is radical, radical in the very constitution of subjectivity such as it appears to us on the path of analytic experience. I should like to set it out in the following formula—as soon as it becomes known, as soon as something comes to knowledge, something is lost and the surest way of approaching this lost something is to conceive of it as a bodily fragment.[21]

If encounter with *das Ding* is announced in the function of bodily part objects and later by other, often more trivial features or anomalies, Lacan's primary emphasis is unquestionably on the way such object-details call to mind a lack, emptiness, or void. "The question of *das Ding*," he says, "is still attached to whatever is open, lacking, or gaping at the center of our desire."[22] It is this opening upon a void that links the Thing to the function of the signifier. *Das Ding*, Lacan says, "is the very correlative of the law of speech in its most primitive point of origin."[23] "The Thing only presents itself to the extent that it becomes word."[24] And finally: "The fashioning of the signifier and the introduction of a gap or a hole in the real is identical."[25]

This abyssal dimension of the signifier underlies one of Lacan's most fundamental claims, namely that what most characterizes the unique function of language for the human being is less a matter of its capacity to denote one or another particular entity than its power to call up a margin of indeterminant expectation. It is that open horizon of possible-but-as-yet-unspecified meaning that ensures that I can always ask about something spoken to me by another: "Yes, I heard what he just said, but what did he really mean by telling me that?" In fact, by attending only to the way the signifier calls up a definite signified, focusing narrowly on its ostensible meaning, we risk losing sight of the way in which the signifier rolls along in front of itself a kind of sliding void, the space of potential meaning. It is this aspect of the signifier that supports a continually renewed anticipation of significance.

> The signifier, by its very nature, always anticipates meaning by deploying its dimensions in some sense before it. As is seen at the level of the sentence when the latter is interrupted before the significant term: "I'll never . . .,"

> "The fact remains . . .," "Still perhaps . . .," Such sentences nevertheless make sense, and that sense is all the more oppressive in that it is content to make us wait for it.[26]

The concept of *das Ding* points to the radicalizing dimension of our relation to the signifier. Every entrance into language doesn't merely project one or another specific anticipation but also potentially opens a zone of radically empty expectancy. It is at this point that Lacan's conception of the speaking being intersects with the Heideggerian notion of Dasein "held out into the nothing." By its very nature, the signifier always projects forward some potential for opening a wholly unspecified domain.

The interpretation I'm trying to articulate here allows us to locate the dynamic between *objet a* and *das Ding* at the heart of Lacan's crucial departure from Freud, that of rejecting Freud's formulation of the Oedipus Complex, replacing the *non du père*, the No of the father who bars the child's access to the mother, with the openness of signification, the *nom du père*, the Name of the father. For Lacan, the child is not torn away from the mother under threat of castration. On the contrary, Lacan insists, "it's not true that the child is weaned. He weans himself. He detaches himself from the breast."[27] For Lacan, the problem is less the desire of the child that is interdicted by the threatening figure of the father than it is the desire of the mother, in as much as her desire is encountered as a vaguely ominous unknown. It is that inaccessible core of the mother's desire that Lacan names "*das Ding*."

> *Das Ding* is the element that is initially isolated by the subject in his experience of the *Nebenmensch* as being by its very nature alien, *Fremde*. [. . .] *Das Ding* has to be posited as exterior, as the prehistoric Other that is impossible to forget—the Other whose primacy of position Freud affirms in the form of something *entfremdet*, something strange to me.[28]

It is in the light of this perspective that we can make sense of Lacan's unsettling comparison of the mother to the specter of a giant praying mantis.[29] Elsewhere, Lacan invokes a similar metaphor, likening the mother to a crocodile and the phallic signifier to a stick with which to keep its jaws from snapping shut.[30] Lacan's thesis of *das Ding* thus intersects with what is arguably his most important addition to psychoanalytic theory, his concept of "the paternal metaphor." In the paternal metaphor, the "Name of the Father" is substituted for the unknown Desire of the Mother. The upshot is that the subject's insertion into the web of the signifier is what mediates the relation to the maternal Thing.[31] Or, as Žižek puts it: "the ultimate function of the Law [is] to serve as a kind of protective wall against the monstrosity of the neighbor." The crucial proviso, however, is that the Thing that is guarded against by the Law can also under the right conditions be "sampled," either by the play of signifiers or by the unexpected upsurge of the *objet a*.

On the basis of these considerations, the *objet a* and *das Ding* can readily appear to take their places in a two-fold dynamic in which the *objet a* is identified with the "odd feature," a peripheral but strangely insistent object or aspect of an object, which then immediately dissolves into an indefinite and mysterious impingement of the unthinkable Real, the vacuity of *das Ding*. This slippage from object to oblivion, the unfolding movement that warrants Žižek's association of *objet a* with an ontological dimension, is what Lacan later calls "*la chute de l'objet*," the fall or collapse of the object. The appearance of the *objet a* almost immediately gives way to a yawning emptiness of something unknown, the abyss of the Thing. We might even read this dynamic into Lacan's matheme of the fantasy: $ <> a. The lozenge-shaped poinçoin between the subject and the *objet a* could be taken to mark the void of the Thing, the opening that establishes the "frame" of the fantasy that Lacan so emphasizes in the seminar on Anxiety.[32]

The ontic-ontological dynamic that we pose here between the *objet a* and *das Ding* is readily discernible in Guy de Maupassant's short story "Le Horla," to which Lacan makes passing reference in *Encore*.[33] Returning to his solitary room, the narrator notices that the glass by his bedside is only half full and, with a chill of terror, becomes convinced that some unseen, alien being has been in his room and drunk the water. Tormented by his obsession with the malign intent of this invisible Other, he finally sets his apartment building on fire in an attempt to kill the intruder. As he watches the fire engulf the entire structure, he's horrified by the screams of the occupants on the upper floor, whom he had neglected to warn. But that horror, however unnerving, is immediately displaced by an even more terrifying and abyssal realization: the Horla has *not died*. It remains, as the title of the story suggests, what is simply "out there," *hors là*. The only way to free himself from the alien intrusion of the Horla, the narrator realizes in a moment of blood-curdling certainty, is to kill himself.

In de Maupassant's story, a trivial objective anomaly—the half-full glass on the bedside table—triggers an oppressive and traumatic sense of something unknown, a mysterious Other whose intentions remain completely obscure. The story thus presents an objective trigger, to be associated with the *objet a*, that calls up the threatening enigma of the supposed Other, the uncognized void of the Other-Thing. Such a view, linking the *objet a* to the objective pole of a psychical dynamic in which the something specific and concrete serves to open a door upon an uncanny and terrifying void, would be the very opposite of Žižek's suggestion that the *objet a* is essentially ontological and *das Ding* is something ontic. On the contrary, things now appear the other way round. The *objet a* is the obstinate objective clue that opens the subject to the abyssal Thing.

In the compass of Maupassant's story, the unknown and unnerving Thing is what remains wholly "out there"—*hors là*. What Lacan crucially adds is the way that the unimaginable excess in the real "out there" implicates an unthinkable excess in the subject itself. It is this ontological reversion that

Lacan calls the dynamic of the "extimate." The Thing in the Other is ultimately inseparable from the "Thing" in oneself. Lacan thus reveals the way in which Freud's concept of *das Ding* is finally to be linked with his much later concept of *das Es*. The "Thing" is the herald, located in the Other, of the "It" in oneself.[34] In this way, Lacan's theory of *das Ding* reveals the human being as ineluctably haunted, forever susceptible to being discomfited by something undefinable in the world outside itself, only because there is something unknown and deeply unsettling inside itself.

On the hypothesis at which we have arrived, *das Ding*, far from being an entity excluded from the Heideggerian *Lichtung*, as Žižek suggests, is identifiable with a radical opening or extension of the *Lichtung* itself. As Lacan said of it, *das Ding* is comparable to the *ex nihilo* of creation.[35] It is precisely the dizzying indeterminacy of the Thing that makes it anxiety producing. It is everything and Nothing, Nothing and everything. What makes it potentially monstrous is precisely its absolute and abyssal openness.

This conclusion, while providing a satisfying integration, leaves us with a number of odd tangles. We might first wonder if the very proximity of *das Ding* to Heidegger is what drives Lacan to step away from it. Lacan's highly charged adoption of the Freudian *Ding* occurred not long after the period of his greatest interest in the Heideggerian treatment of the Thing, for which Heidegger's favorite example was the earthen vase, a skin of clay wrapped around an empty void.[36] Fashioning or using even the crudest jug requires some baseline awareness of the pure potentiality of emptiness.

A prime danger of modeling the Lacanian Thing on Heidegger's vase is the way that it may incline us toward reifying or over-substantializing what is involved. The issue concerns the baseline ontology of psychoanalysis for Lacan. The key point is that the Thing is not a *thing* at all. As Lacan says of it, "the Thing is also the Non-Thing."[37] *Das Ding* has no objective existence whatsoever. If it is not an object, nor is it any sort of prehistorical perceptual givenness. It is rather a locus of pure lack, a zone of something unknown. To use the term from Lacan's own lexicon most appropriate for the purpose, *das Ding* is something purely *supposed* by the subject.[38]

But there is another fundamental problem for Lacan with linking his own conception of *das Ding* too closely with Heidegger. The key point for Lacan is, at the outset anyway, what remains unknown *in and about the Other*. The difference in perspective is clearest in relation to the way that Lacan's conception of anxiety differs from that of Heidegger. In Heidegger's theory, anxiety arises when Dasein comes face to face with its own pure potentiality. Anxiety is the dizziness of Dasein's raw exposure—at once and in its totality—to the lighting of Being. Dasein trembles in anxiety before the sheer openness of the clearing of disclosure that Dasein itself is.

The elegance of Heidegger's definition derives from the way that it neatly certifies Dasein's wholeness from out of its own being. Because anxiety, itself a global and all-encompassing state-of-mind, is grounded in nothing but Dasein's encounter with itself, the essential mineness of Dasein, the *Jemeinigkeit* of existential identity that Heidegger so stresses from the outset, comes to function as its own guarantee. It is for this reason, as Heidegger puts it, that "anxiety individualizes Dasein and thus discloses it as *'solus ipse'*."[39]

From a Lacanian point of view, the very compactness and elegance of Heidegger's conception is the problem. Where the Heideggerian account roots anxiety in a loop of existential self-reference, the way in which Dasein poses a challenge to itself, anxiety for Lacan is emphatically eccentric. "Anxiety," he insists, "resides in the subject's fundamental relationship [. .] with the desire of the Other."[40] According to Lacan, anxiety is triggered by the subject's primordial alienation in the Other, the fact that the path by which the subject comes to itself necessarily begins outside itself. If Heidegger locates anxiety in Dasein's uncanny self-encounter, Lacan finds it precisely in the subject's lack of itself, its being in the Other. The problem is not unnerving intimacy but unavoidable extimacy. The Lacanian subject is emphatically *not whole*. The upshot of Lacan's notion of extimacy is that of pointing to the primordial dislocation of the subject, which is condemned to come to itself only in and through the Other external to itself.[41]

Is this, then, why Lacan took some distance from his notion of *das Ding*? Was he leery of being too closely associated with Heidegger's account of anxiety and its supposition of Dasein as *'solus ipse'*? Perhaps, but that would also be somewhat strange, for the simple reason that Lacan's own treatment of *das Ding*, the prime point of which was to insist on the subject as finding itself outside itself, the subject as essentially *extimate*, should be recognized as marking what most distinguishes him from Heidegger.[42] So long as we emphasize that the Thing is primally encountered *in the Other*, we cannot accept the self-referential character of anxiety as Heidegger poses it.

I'm curious to know how Žižek would respond to this sketch of a structured dynamic between the *objet a* and *das Ding*. It's hard not to suspect that he would regard it as an attempt to spin too neat a theoretical synthesis, indulging a hunger for integration that runs against the grain of his own penchant for waging a sort of intellectual guerilla warfare. Žižek's signature move is to utilize one or another theoretical distinction to stage a dazzling analysis of one or another film scene, artwork, short story, or political phenomenon. Once that analysis is sketched, he generally tends to leave it as a passing vignette. The result is an intellectual style that delights in loose-endedness. Žižek prefers to leave his rapid-fire mini-studies on a ragged edge of incompletion.

But can the integration I've put forward here be so easily dismissed? In the relation between *objet a* and *das Ding* as I've tried to adumbrate it, an ineluctable and radical loose-endedness is itself what is at stake. *Das Ding* is the ultimate "loose end." If my account here integrates the *objet petit a* with the Lacanian Thing, the upshot is to leave everything hanging on a ragged edge—the edge of an abyss. The conclusion to be drawn, we might say, is that integrating the Lacanian *objet a* with his notion of *das Ding* as I've tried to articulate it here paradoxically offers a coherent theoretical account that points toward the impossibility of any ultimate theoretical coherence.

Notes

1. Lacan: "Is there anything that poses a question which is more present, more pressing, more absorbing, more disruptive, more nauseating, more calculated to thrust everything that takes place before us into the abyss or void than that face of Harpo Marx, that face with its smile which leaves us unclear as to whether it signifies the most extreme perversity or complete simplicity?" Jacques Lacan, *The Seminar of Jacques Lacan, Book VII: The Ethics of Psychoanalysis 1959–60*, ed. Jacques-Alain Miller, trans. Dennis Porter (New York: W. W. Norton & Co., 1986), 55.
2. Sigmund Freud, *The Standard Edition of the Complete Psychological Words of Sigmund Freud*, ed. and trans. by James Strachey et. al. (London: Hogarth Press and the Institute of Psycho-analysis, 1955), Vol. 1, 331.
3. Lacan, *The Ethics of Psychoanalysis*, 62.
4. Ibid., 97
5. Ibid., 57
6. Todd McGowan has convincingly argued that *das Ding*, while not explicitly mentioned in the second half of the *Ethics* seminar, is nevertheless indispensable to Lacan's discussion insofar as it is discernible in Antigone herself, both in her absolute devotion to Polynieces that leads her to break the law (taking him as embodying for her the sublime Thing), and later becoming in herself the unfathomable Thing (as she deliberately chooses death over capitulation to Creon's edict). See his forthcoming essay "Ethics amid Commodities: *Das Ding* and the Origin of Value."
7. The thematic of *das Ding* is unmistakeably discernible in one of Žižek's favorite quotes from Hegel: "The human being is this Night, this empty nothing which contains everything in its simplicity – a wealth of infinitely many representations, images, none of which occur to it directly, and none of which are not present. This [is] the Night, the interior of [human] nature, existing here – pure Self – [and] in phantasmagoric representations it is night everywhere: here a bloody head suddenly shoots up and there another white shape, only to disappear as suddenly. We see this Night when we look a human being in the eye, looking into a Night which turns terrifying." G. W. F. Hegel, "The Philosophy of Spirit," Jena Lectures 1805–6. "Part I: Spirit according to its Concept," https://www.marxists.org/reference/archive/hegel/works/jl/ch01a.htm
8. Slavoj Žižek, "Neighbors and Other Monsters: A Plea for Ethical Violence." In Slavoj Žižek, Eric Santner, and Kenneth Reinhard, *The Neighbor: Three Inquiries in Political Theology* (Chicago: University of Chicago Press, 2005), 160.
9. Ibid., 163.
10. Lacan, *The Ethics of Psychoanalysis*, 112.
11. Jacques Lacan, *The Seminar of Jacques Lacan, Book VIII, Transference*, ed. Jacques-Alain Miller, trans. Bruce Fink (Cambridge: Polity Press, 2015), 309.
12. Jacques Lacan, *The Seminar of Jacques Lacan, Book X, Anxiety*, ed. Jacques-Alain Miller, trans. A. R. Price (Cambridge: Polity Press, 2014), 311. To my knowledge, this is the only instance, emphatic though it is, in which Lacan

makes a specific reference to *das Ding* in the *Anxiety* seminar, though it can clearly be taken to be implicit throughout.

13 Slavoj Žižek, *The Metastases of Enjoyment: Six Essays on Woman and Causality* (London: Verso, 1994), 181.

14 It is in this sense that the relation between the mother and the unknown Thing parallels the relation Freud later charts between the *Heimlich* and the *Unheimlich*. The strange and unsettling is capable of rising up in the very heart of what is familiar.

15 Lacan, *Anxiety*, 325

16 Jacques Lacan, *Seminar XVI: From an Other to the other*, translated for private use from the unpublished French transcript of the seminar by Cormac Gallagher, Session of 3/12/69. In this reference, Lacan cites *das Ding* explicitly. There are a number of other sites, however, where Lacan evokes the contours of the Thing without expressly naming it. A good example is to be found in his thirteenth Seminar, in which Lacan provides a commentary on Velásquez's masterpiece "Las Meninas," a comment that is quite intentionally meant as a rejoinder to Foucault's famous analysis in *The Order of Things*. Lacan observes that the giant unseen canvas in the foreground of Velásquez's painting (the canvas being worked upon by a figure generally taken to be a representation of Velásquez himself) implicitly poses the anxiety-producing question of *das Ding*: "*You do not see me from where I am looking at you.*" See Jacques Lacan, *Seminar XIII: The Object of Psychoanalysis*, translated for private use from the unpublished French transcript of the seminar by Cormac Gallagher, Session of 5/25/66.

17 Lacan, *The Ethics of Psychoanalysis*, 57 (my emphasis).

18 Freud, *Standard Edition*, I: 331.

19 Freud, *Standard Edition*, I: 352–6. While Freud does not expressly link the case of Emma with *das Ding*, Lacan certainly does. See Lacan, *The Ethics of Psychoanalysis*, 73–4.

20 This identification is especially prominent in the seminar on *Anxiety*.

21 Lacan, *Anxiety*, 134.

22 Lacan, *The Ethics of Psychoanalysis*, 84.

23 Ibid., 83.

24 Ibid., 55.

25 "Now if you consider the vase from the point of view I first proposed, as an object made to represent the existence of the emptiness at the center of the real that is called the Thing, this emptiness as represented in the representation presents itself as a nihil, as nothing. And that is why the potter, just like you to whom I am speaking, creates the vase with his hand around this emptiness, creates it, just like the mythical creator, ex nihilo, starting with a hole. [. . .] The fashioning of the signifier and the introduction of a gap or a hole in the real is identical" (Lacan, *The Ethics of Psychoanalysis*, 121).

26 Jacques Lacan, "The Instance of the Letter in the Unconscious." In *Écrits*, trans. Bruck Fink, in collaboration with Héloïse Fink and Russell Grigg (New York: W. W. Norton & Co., 2006), 419.

27 Lacan, *Anxiety*, 327. And elsewhere: "It's not longing for the maternal breast that provokes anxiety, but its imminence" (ibid., 53). "The most decisive moment in the anxiety at issue, the anxiety of weaning, is not so much when the breast falls short of the subject's need, it's rather that the infant yields the breast to which he is appended as a portion of himself" (ibid., 313).

28 Lacan, *The Ethics of Psychoanalysis*, 52, 71.

29 See Lacan, *Anxiety*, 22.

30 Jacques Lacan, *The Seminar of Jacques Lacan, Book XVII, The Other Side of Psychoanalysis*, ed. Jacques-Alain Miller, trans. Russell Grigg (New York: W.W. Norton & Co., 1991), 112.

31 Lacan thus remarks that "what we find in the incest law is located as such at the level of the unconscious in relation to *das Ding*" (Lacan, *The Ethics of Psychoanalysis*, 68).

32 Actually, if we follow this logic, it would be even more appropriate to rewrite the formula with the subject on one side and the Other-Thing on the other side, linked by the *objet a*: $ a <>. To traverse the fantasy is to achieve the double realization that both the Other and the subject itself are inhabited, indeed constituted, by a void.

33 Jacques Lacan, *The Seminar of Jacques Lacan, Book XX: Encore: On Feminine Sexuality, The Limits of Love and Knowledge, 1972–73*, ed. Jacques-Alain Miller, trans. Bruce Fink (New York: W.W. Norton & Co., 1998), 85. The Maupassant text can be found at http://www.eastoftheweb.com/short-stories/UBooks/Horl.shtml. Lacan doesn't explicitly cite *das Ding* in reference to the Maupassant story, but fifteen pages later he does make one of his rare mentions of the Other-Thing in connection with the problem of jealousy. Cf. Lacan, *Encore*, 100.

34 Cf. "The *Es* is not sufficiently emphasized by the way it is presented in the texts of the second topic. It is to remind us of the primordial and primary character of this intuition in our experience at the level of ethics that this year I am calling a certain zone of reference "the Thing" (Lacan, *The Ethics of Psychoanalysis*, 137).

35 "The notion of creation *ex nihilo* is coextensive with the exact situation of the Thing as such" (Lacan, *The Ethics of Psychoanalysis*, 121).

36 Martin Heidegger, "The Thing." In *Poetry, Language, Thought* (New York: Harper & Row, 1971), 165–86.

37 Lacan, *The Ethics of Psychoanalysis*, 136.

38 Such "supposition" is of course to be related to Lacan's multiple references to "the subject supposed to know." But while Lacan usually draws on that formula to name the subject's relation to the psychoanalyst, we constantly suppose the knowledge of others, and suppose also our knowledge of them, but do so precisely in order to cover over *das Ding*, as what we *don't* know about the Other.

39 Martin Heidegger, *Being and Time*, trans. John MacQuarrie and Edward Robinson (New York: Harper & Row, 1962), 233.

40 Lacan, *Anxiety*, 27.

41 It is along these lines that we should read Lacan's insistence, precisely in rebuttal of Heidegger's position, that anxiety "is not without an object." Lacan's point, however, is that the object involved is the *objet a*, and one of the prime values of the interpretation I am offering here is that the *objet a* is merely the point of entrée into the void of *das Ding*.

42 Heidegger himself arguably broke with the *solus ipse* posture of his analysis in *Being and Time*, criticizing the position taken in his early work for being overly caught up in subjectivistic assumptions. The emphasis on *Ereignis* in his later work can intriguingly be read as implying something very like what Lacan called *extimacy*.

Response to Boothby

Slavoj Žižek

It is quite appropriate for Boothby's text to conclude this volume since it focuses on what I see as the basic philosophical (or post- or anti-philosophical) dimension of Lacan's thinking. Boothby opposes my claim that *das Ding* is ontic while *objet a* is ontological, turning it around:

> The *objet a* is the ontic element, though to be sure an element that immediately opens out onto an ontological horizon. *Das Ding*, on the other hand, is purely ontological. It is, in fact, the originary opening of the human relation to the ontological as such. It is to be identified precisely with the dimension of "the ontological clearance within which entities appear." *Objet a* and *das Ding* form an essential couplet. The *objet a* is a kind of incongruous but vanishing trace, a strange detail, that sparks a vague awareness of a yawning void.

There is something obvious in these lines: is not "ontic" in the sense of a "little bit of the real" a moment of our reality in which the abyss of the Void resonates—so why do I claim the opposite? Why is for me *a* ontological and the Thing ontic? We should always bear in mind that, for Lacan, *a* is not the object of desire but its object-cause, that what makes me desire an (ontic) object. It is the name of a void (specifically colored void, true) which structures our approach to reality: as Lacan himself put it, (what we experience as) reality emerges by the subtraction of objet a from it—is there a more concise definition of the ontological dimension? So what about the Thing—is it not simply the Void itself, the empty frame of ontological disclosure? Here things get more complex: there is what one could call a trans-ontological dimension in the Thing, and Lacan himself points toward this dimension of the Thing in the very passage quoted by Boothby:

> *Das Ding* is the element that is initially isolated by the subject in his experience of the Nebenmensch as being by its very nature alien, Fremde. [. . .] *Das Ding* has to be posited as exterior, as the prehistoric Other that is impossible to forget—the Other whose primacy of position Freud affirms in the form of something *entfremdet*, something strange to me.[1]

Note the weird term "prehistoric Other" Lacan uses here—insofar as, from Heidegger's standpoint, history is the history of transcendental-ontological disclosures of Being, "prehistoric Other" can only refer to a trace of something that was there before entities were disclosed to us in an ontological horizon—here is Heidegger's own ambiguous formulation of this obscure point: "I often ask myself—this has for a long time been a fundamental question for me—what nature would be without man—must it not resonate through him in order to attain its ownmost potency."[2] Without man as Da-Sein, the site (the being-there) of the disclosure of being, which means without the disclosure of Being, without the ontological dimension.

This is why I disagree with Boothby when he writes:

> The key point is that the Thing is not a thing at all. As Lacan says of it, "the Thing is also the Non-Thing." *Das Ding* has no objective existence whatsoever. If it is not an object, nor is it any sort of prehistorical perceptual givenness. It is rather a locus of pure lack, a zone of something unknown. To use the term from Lacan's own lexicon most appropriate for the purpose, *das Ding* is something purely supposed by the subject.

I consider this (clear) line of thought a little bit too simple. The Thing is, of course, not just another ontic object, part of (what we experience as) external reality, it is not some sort of "prehistorical perceptual givenness"; i.e., it is never given, but it is "prehistoric" in the sense of a trace of something that is originally hidden (*verborgen*) in any historic disclosure of Being. So, again, although Heidegger is the ultimate transcendental philosopher (in the sense of the event of Disclosure of Being as the transcendental-ontological opening), there are mysterious passages where he ventures into the pre-transcendental domain. In the elaboration of this notion of an untruth /lethe/ older than the very dimension of truth, Heidegger emphasizes how man's "stepping into the essential unfolding of truth" is a "transformation of the being of man in the sense of a derangement"—*Ver-rückung*, going mad of his position among beings.[3] The "derangement" to which Heidegger refers is, of course, not a psychological or clinical category of madness: it signals a much more radical, properly ontological reversal/aberration, when, in its very foundation, the universe itself is in a way "out of joint," thrown off its rails. What is crucial here is to remember that Heidegger wrote these lines in the years of his intensive reading of Schelling's *Treatise on Human Freedom*, a text which discerns the origin of Evil precisely in a kind of ontological madness, in the "derangement" of man's position among beings (his self-centeredness), as a necessary intermediate step ("vanishing mediator") in the passage from "prehuman nature" to our symbolic universe: "man, in his very essence, is a catastrophe—a reversal that turns him away from the genuine essence. Man is the only catastrophe in the midst of beings."[4]

So, the Thing is not just "a locus of pure lack" but also a locus of pure excess, of something that is neither ontic reality nor ontological horizon within which this reality appears, the excess over the entire ontological-ontic domain. To put it in somewhat simplified way, it is what the ontic was before it became properly ontic (i.e., brought to light within an ontological horizon). And, incidentally, in order to avoid the danger of subjectivism which tends to reduce everything to something supposed by the subject, one should go to the end here and posit that subject itself is ultimately something supposed—there are not only subjects supposed to ... (know, believe, enjoy ...), subject as such is a supposition, it is never directly given as a positive fact but is supposed as the bearer of experiences. To quote Kant, "through this I, or He, or It (the thing), which thinks [*Ich, oder Er, oder Es (das Ding) welches denket*], nothing further is represented than a transcendental subject of thoughts = x, e which is recognized only through the thoughts that are its predicates, and about which, in abstraction, we can never have even the least concept."[5] Is there a better formulation of the status of subject itself as a supposition? In short, what if the ultimate Thing is not the reality-in-itself, "independent of us," pursued by sciences, but the subject itself.

Notes

1 Jacques Lacan, *The Seminar of Jacques Lacan, Book VII: The Ethics of Psychoanalysis 1959–60*, ed. Jacques-Alain Miller (New York: Norton, 1986) 52, 71.

2 *Martin Heidegger—Elisabeth Blochmann. Briefwechsel 1918–1969*, ed. Joachim W. Storck (Marbach: Deutsches Literatur-Archiv, 1990), Letter from October 11, 1931, 44 (own translation).

3 Martin Heidegger, *Beiträge zur Philosophie*, in *Gesamtausgabe* (Frankfurt: Vittorio Klostermann, 1975), Vol. 65, 338.

4 Martin Heidegger, "Hölderlin's Hymne 'Der Ister'," in *Gesamtausgabe* Vol. 53 (Frankfurt: Vittorio Klostermann, 1984), 94.

5 Immanuel Kant, *Critique of Pure Reason*, in *The Cambridge Edition of the Works of Immanuel Kant* (Cambridge: Cambridge University Press, 1998), 414 (A346/ B404). Available online: https://cpb-us-w2.wpmucdn.com/u.osu.edu/dist/5/25851/files/2017/09/kant-first-critique-cambridge-1m89prv.pdf (accessed 20 December 2021).

INDEX

abortion 134, 152, 156 n.25
act 4, 15, 19, 21, 60–1, 69–70, 94,
    98–9, 101, 105, 107 n.19,
    110 n.43, 112–14, 119, 126,
    130–1, 131 n.2, 132 n.8, 134,
    179, 193–4, 200, 216, 222–3,
    230, 237, 244–9, 256 n.55,
    256–7 n.56, 257 n.58, 257–
    8 n.60, 260–3, 265, 267–71,
    273, 282, 285, 288–90, 311–12
Adorno, Theodor 5, 99, 233, 242,
    251 n.20
Agamben, Giorgio
Allison, Henry 106 n.8
Althusser, Louis 10, 19, 23 n.19,
    143–52, 155 nn.5–6
antagonism 14–17, 21, 24 n.27, 36,
    103, 104, 106–7 n.15, 136, 147,
    149–53, 156 n.20, 162, 196,
    218, 227, 231, 238, 262, 269
Antigone, see Sophocles
antinomy
anti-Semitism 8, 75, 159, 195–6, 231
"Archais Torso of Apollo, The" see
    Rilke, Rainer Maria
Arendt, Hannah 126–7, 132–3 n.15,
    241, 244, 252 n.22
Aristotle 9, 35, 75, 92
Assange, Julian 176

Badiou, Alain 13, 76, 79, 83 n.7, 91,
    110 n.43, 122–3, 131 n.3,
    131 n.7, 173, 187, 199, 217,
    256 n.53
Barad, Karen 74, 78
Beckett, Samuel 9, 23 n.17
Benjamin, Walter 57, 125–6, 191
Bernstein, Eduard 120, 131 n.2
Big Other, see Lacan, Jacques

Birds, The, see Hitchcock Alfred
Black Lives Matter 125, 135
Bloch, Ernst
Bloom, Harold 73
Bohr, Niels 78, 80–1, 85–6, 170
Bolick, Shawna 136
Bolsonaro, Jair 139
Borges, Jorge Luis 77
Boucher, Geoff 3
Bowman, Paul 3
Brandom, Robert 19, 22 n.12, 57–63,
    71 n.1, 96, 105 n.5, 105 n.7
Breazeale, Daniel 31
Brecht, Bertolt 212
    The Decision 122–3
Bubner, Rüdiger 111 n.56
Buddhism (Western) 11, 91
Bush, George W. 132 n.8
Butler, Judith 20, 22 n.10, 179,
    181 n.1, 196, 218–19, 226–8
Butler, Rex 3–4

Caesar, Julius 76
capitalism 11–12, 16–19, 21, 55, 57,
    90, 94, 99, 101–2, 105 nn.3–4,
    107–8 n.25, 110–11 n.51, 114,
    119–21, 124–7, 132 n.8, 140–4,
    149, 151, 153–4, 155 n.2,
    155 n.5, 159, 167, 185, 195
    198–203, 210–11, 220–3, 227–8,
    249, 262, 266–7, 277–8,
    279 n.6, 281–2, 291, 299, 304,
    307
Carnap, Rudolf 1
Carpenter, John
    They Live 154
castration (symbolic) 14
Chesterton, Gilbert K. 3, 159
Chiesa, Lorenzo 158

Christianity 13–14, 16, 77, 91, 100, 104, 121, 159, 190, 193, 220, 223
 fundamentalism 8, 14
Churchill, Winston 12
Coetzee, J. M.
 Disgrace 102–3
Communism 12–14
Conrad, Joseph 73
Covid-19 pandemic 135, 140, 153, 159–60, 263, 299–300, 313
Critchley, Simon 77

Daly, Glyn 75
Darwinism 91
De Bont, Jan
 Speed 121
death drive 9, 90, 115, 121, 123, 222, 233
Decision, The, see Brecht, Bertolt
DeLanda, Manuel 80
Deleuze, Gilles 5, 7, 90, 94
democracy 12–13, 23 n.23, 52, 102, 130, 135, 141, 158, 181, 186, 208, 210, 300
Dennett, Daniel 2
Derrida, Jacques 2, 4–7, 10, 20, 240, 250 n.16
 differance 61
 hospitality 183–203, 208
 Pharmakon 75
Descartes, René 5, 81
Devenney, Mark 4
dialectics 8, 15, 18, 20, 27–30, 34–7, 44, 54, 56–64, 67–9, 75–80, 85, 94, 99–104, 146–50, 172, 176–7, 189, 200, 209–11, 216, 221, 232–3, 238–9, 247, 256–7 n.56, 266, 314, 318
Dickey, Laurence 111 n.55
Disgrace, see Coetzee, J. M.
Divine violence 126
Dolar, Mladen 167, 218, 222

Einstein, Albert 79–80
Eliot, T. S. 77
Engels, Friedrich 140, 143, 209–10, 228
enjoyment 7–11, 10–11, 16, 23 n.20, 55, 142, 158, 167–70, 180, 203, 213, 220, 222, 232, 243, 246, 270, 272, 283, 288, 291–2, 311
Esposito, Roberto
Eurocentrism
evil 13, 23 n.15, 186, 188, 241, 244, 252 n.22, 253 n.35, 256 n.53, 261–2, 331

Fanon, Frantz 189
fantasy 9–12, 20, 78, 103, 142, 148, 165, 175, 186, 199, 201, 244–9, 255 n.44, 269–71, 274–8, 292, 294–5, 323, 328 n.32
Faulkner, William 73
Feldner, Heiko 3–4
Fichte, Johann Gottlieb 36, 91–7, 106 n.11, 107 n.19, 110 n.41, 148–9, 221
Fight Club, see Fincher, David
Fincher, David
 Fight Club 19, 124, 130
Finkelde, Dominik 3, 165
Fitzgerald, F. Scott 73
Ford, John
 The Man Who Shot Liberty Valence 106 n.8
Foster, Michael Beresford 110 n.49
Foucault, Michel 4–5, 7, 10, 78, 91, 258–9 n.66, 327 n.16
freedom 8, 16–17, 34, 53–4, 62, 76, 86, 89, 99, 101, 110 n.41, 113–15, 121–2, 148, 152, 159, 183, 185, 196, 222, 226, 243, 245, 260–1, 269–270, 278, 290, 305, 314
Frege, Gottlob 1, 94, 112
French Revolution 70, 76–7, 209–10
Freud, Sigmund 1, 4, 8–9, 33, 73, 78, 87, 90–1, 106 n.9, 106–7 n.15, 108 n.28, 144–8, 152, 155 n.10, 155–6 n.14, 166, 174, 218, 220, 223, 226–8, 231–3, 247–249, 258 n.61, 262, 274, 288, 303–4, 313, 317, 319–24, 327 n.14, 331
Fukuyama, Francis 115, 199

gender 100, 179, 218
German idealism 1, 9, 17–18, 28–9, 41, 44, 57, 94, 148, 171, 215

Gilbert, Jeremy 22 n.10
Gilets Jaunes 125
Glucksmann, André 131 n.7
Glynos, Jason 3
God 13–14, 30, 33–4, 42, 62, 84 n.23, 90–1, 159, 212, 223
Gonzales, Christian Alejandro 127
Gramsci Antonio
Gray, John 119, 131 n.1
Green, Christopher 145
gulag 128, 132–3 n.15

Habermas, Jürgen 2, 13, 62, 64, 68–9, 105 n.5
Haitian Revolution 185, 209–11, 227
Hall, Granville Stanley 145
Hamza, Agon 3–4
Handmaid's Tale, The (television series) 159
Harvey, David 110–11 n.51
Hegel, G. W. F. 1–9, 17–20, 55–64, 67–9, 71 n.1, 89–105, 105 nn.3–7, 106 n.12, 106–7 n.15, 107 n.16, 107 n.20, 108 n.29, 110 n.43, 110 n.46, 110 nn.48–9, 110–11 n.51, 112–15, 147–51, 171, 173, 209–11, 219, 221, 230–3, 238, 256 n.55, 262, 314, 326 n.7
  absolute knowing 8, 15, 28, 39, 42, 59–60, 74–5, 78, 89–90, 92, 148, 159, 211, 216
  beautiful soul 60–1, 69, 77–8, 98, 200
  Encyclopedia 35, 108 n.29
  end of history 89
  History of Philosophy 30, 53
  master and servant 314
  nature philosophy 28–44, 52–3
  Phenomenology of Spirit 29, 39–40, 58, 76, 90, 92, 95–6, 107 n.31, 109 n.31, 173, 314
  Philosophy of Nature 108 n.29
  Philosophy of Religion 13–14
  Philosophy of Right 23–4 n.24, 76, 89–90, 100–1, 115, 124, 130
  retroactivity 18, 54, 61, 68, 70, 74–81, 85–6, 98, 113, 149, 151, 153, 175, 210, 216, 219–22, 227, 231, 239, 288, 302, 320

Science of Logic 35–6, 76, 109 n.31
  subjectivity 79–82
Heidegger, Martin 1–2, 6, 56, 79, 86, 91, 107 n.31, 109 n.31, 195, 247, 256 n.55, 319, 322, 324–5, 329 nn.41–2, 331
Heisenberg, Werner 78, 80
Hemingway, Ernest 73
Henrich, Dieter 96, 106 n.8, 109 n.35, 110 n.43
Herder, J. G. 39
Heydrich, Reinhard 8, 128
Hitchcock, Alfred 7, 238
  Birds, The 17
  MacGuffin 308
  Vertigo 103–4, 208–9
Hitler, Adolf 128, 159
Hobbes, Thomas 100–1
Holbein, Hans
  The Ambassadors
Hölderlin, Friedrich 104, 256 n.55
Holocaust 13, 23, 62, 90, 295
Horkheimer, Max 242, 251 n.20
hospitality, *see* Derrida, Jacques
Howard, Ron
  Ransom 121
Hume, David 62, 80–1, 86
Husserl, Edmund 79–80, 94, 112

ideology 1, 4, 7, 17, 19–20, 23 n.15, 65 n.10, 68, 75, 91, 104, 119–22, 139–54, 155 nn.5–6, 156 n.17, 157–60, 163–77, 177 n.14, 179–80, 186–87, 191–5, 202, 221, 228, 238, 243–5, 248, 254–5 n.43, 278, 289, 291–2, 303, 307
  obscene underside 10–11, 23 n.22, 139, 168, 229–30, 238, 241
identity 15–17, 32, 53, 86, 93, 99, 104, 120, 157, 161, 163–5, 169–73, 177 n.14, 180, 183, 189, 192–3, 198, 201, 217, 219–20, 223, 227–31, 314, 325
  politics 12, 179
imaginary, *see* Lacan, Jacques
Inwagen, Peter van 80

James, Henry 73
Jefferson, Thomas 135
Johnston, Adrian 85, 289, 299
Joplin, Janis 122
Judaism
jouissance, see Lacan, Jacques

Kafka, Franz 77
Kant, Immanuel 2, 5, 10, 18, 20, 29, 36, 43, 56–9, 62–3, 66 n.31, 67–9, 73–8, 81–2, 85–6, 89, 91–6, 106 n.8, 107 n.16, 109 nn.34–6, 112–13, 148–9, 173, 183, 217–21, 226, 230, 237–49, 250 n.9, 251 nn.19–21, 252 n.26, 254 n.37, 254 n.41, 255 nn.44–5, 260–3, 302, 332
Kapuscinski, Ryszard 161
Kellogg, Paul 133 n.18
Key, Sarah 3
Kierkegaard, Søren 3, 18, 57, 74, 78, 90, 168, 170–1, 221, 261
Kirsch, Adam 119, 131 n.1

LaCapra, Dominick
Lacan, Jacques 1–10, 30, 39, 41, 55–7, 73–4, 82, 89–92, 95–102, 108 n.28, 144–53, 159, 163–76, 220–3, 258 n.61
  alienation 120, 248
  anxiety 328 n.27
  Big Other 10, 13–14, 18–19, 77–8, 94, 97–9, 102–3, 114, 132 n.8, 148–51, 157–8, 161, 174, 179, 229, 247, 257 n.58, 262, 265, 282–4, 310
  Borromean knot 198, 241
  ethics of desire 256 n.53, 265–79, 281–5
  four discourses 53, 237
  gaze 147
  imaginary 7, 147, 163, 171, 188–9, 233, 239, 265, 273–6, 283, 290, 304, 320–1
  jouissance 7, 9–10, 20–1, 158, 202, 218, 232–3, 242–4, 266–79, 281–3, 287–95, 301, 304, 307, 311, 314
  "Kant with Sade" 20, 237–49, 252 n.23, 252 n.26, 252–3 n.27, 253 n.35, 253–4 n.36, 254 n.37, 254 n.41, 260–3
  Moebius strip 15, 52, 54 n.1
  objet a 15–16, 21–2, 79, 103, 216, 232, 242, 269, 270, 274–8, 281, 295, 308, 311, 318–25, 329 n.41, 330–2
  psychosis 302–4, 309
  real 2, 7–8, 10–12, 15, 18, 21, 24 n.24, 35–43, 52–3, 147, 151, 159–60, 180, 186–9, 198, 202, 208, 215–16, 218–20, 228, 231–3, 260, 265, 270, 272–6, 284, 291, 301, 303, 305, 307, 309, 320–3, 327 n.25, 330
  Seminar VII 240, 246, 250 n.15, 253 n.30, 256 n.54, 257–8 n.60, 271, 273, 317–18, 326 n.1, 326 n.6, 327 n.25
  Seminar VIII 317–18
  Seminar XI 164–5, 251 n.19
  Seminar XIII 327 n.16
  Seminar XVI 320, 327 n.16
  Seminar XX 158
  sexuation 16, 156 n.20, 217–18, 226–8, 231, 311
  sublimation 230, 268–70, 274–5
  symbolic order 7–10, 16–17, 52, 61, 64, 73, 78, 87, 89, 103, 108 n.28, 113–14, 120, 124, 147–8, 150–1, 153, 171, 179, 185, 187–9, 193–5, 198, 209, 215–16, 220–4, 227–8, 231–3, 245, 247–9, 257 n.58, 265–6, 273, 278, 282, 284, 289–91, 294, 302–4, 307, 309, 311, 313–14, 317–18, 332
  Thing [*das Ding*] 21–2, 188–9, 198, 228, 230, 265–79, 281–5, 317–25, 326 n.6, 326 n.7, 326–7 n.12, 327 n.16, 327 n.19, 327 n.25, 328 n.31, 328 nn.33–5, 328 n.38, 329 nn.41–2, 330–2
  traversing the fantasy 103, 249, 265, 328 n.32
Laclau, Ernesto 23 n.23, 61, 64, 169
Laibach (band) 19–20, 64, 163, 167–5, 178 n.19, 180–1

Larsson, Stieg 114
Laruelle, François 79
Latour, Bruno 79
Lebrun, Gerard 109 n.36
Lefort, Claude 135
Leibniz, Gottfried 42
Lenin, V. I. 33, 59, 115, 127, 131 n.1, 133 n.18, 134, 209–10, 263, 288
Levi, Primo
Lévi-Strauss, Claude 150–1
Levinas, Emmanuel 13, 20, 91, 183–92, 197, 208, 318
Linera, Álvaro García 159, 161
love 11–12, 20, 77, 99, 103–4, 152–3, 174, 184, 186, 188–90, 194–8, 202, 208, 220, 275–6, 283, 292
Lubitsch, Ernst
 Ninotchka 85–6
Lukács, Georg 107 n.20, 142, 155 n.3
Lyotard, Jean-François

McDowell, John 19, 57–8, 63
McGowan, Todd 64, 267, 279 nn.6–7, 291–2, 326 n.6
McTeigue, James
 V For Vendetta 125
Maher, Bill 132 n.8
Malabou, Catherine 109 n.36
Mankell, Henning 114, 157
Man Who Shot Liberty Valence, The, see Ford, John
Mao, see Zedong, Mao
Marchart, Olivier 4
Marcuse, Herbert
Marx, Harpo 21, 326 n.1
Marx, Karl 2–9, 12, 18, 23–4 n.24, 55–7, 74–8, 106–7 n.15, 114–15, 124, 209–11, 221–4, 225 n.26, 227–8
 class struggle 151–2
 commodity fetishism 142–3, 217, 222
 ideology 140–50
Marxism 1, 6, 12, 18, 24 n.27, 120, 125, 127, 161, 176, 199, 215, 231, 263, 304
 false consciousness 65 n.10
 reification 142–3
 state 159, 162

Master-Signifier
materialism 1, 13, 17, 23–4 n.24, 27–36, 41, 44, 58, 67, 89, 94–5, 100, 124, 149, 159, 196–7, 221, 243, 253 n.32
Maupassant, Guy de
Mbembe, Achille 186–7
Meillassoux, Quentin 76, 79, 84 n.23
Melville, Herman 73
Mensheviks
MeToo 135, 309
Miller, Jacques-Alain 6, 20, 221, 237–40, 250 n.15, 252–3 n.27, 255 n.21, 305, 307
Milner, Jean Claude
Moebius strip, see Lacan, Jacques
Muselmann
Myers, Tom 3

Nail, Thomas 83 n.6
Name-of-the-Father
Nazism 2, 62, 69, 90, 127–9, 132 n.8, 132–3 n.15, 167–8, 195
negation
Newton, Isaac 35, 37, 79–80
Nietzsche, Friedrich 18, 57, 63–4, 90, 97, 108–9 n.30, 242, 251 n.20, 295
Ninotchka, see Lubitsch, Ernst

object oriented ontology 80, 85, 87
objet a, see Lacan, Jacques
Occupy Wall Street 6, 12, 77, 125, 176
October Revolution 77, 115, 209–10
ontology 2–3, 17–18, 20, 31–43, 54, 56–64, 74–81, 85–7, 91–5, 99, 110 n.41, 112–13, 175, 183, 186, 194–5, 198, 216–21, 247, 262, 266, 319–20, 323–4, 330–2
Orbán, Viktor 19
Other, see Big Other

Palestine
 Palestinian intifada
 Palestinians
 Palestinian question
Parallax
Parker, Ian 3
phallus

phenomena
Pippin, Robert 57–64, 71 n.1
Plato 4, 16–17, 31, 35, 75, 91, 93, 273, 275
Pussy Riot (musical group) 176, 310
Putin, Vladimir 139, 305–6, 311–13

quantum physics 17–18, 27–44, 53–4, 74, 78, 85, 87, 91, 159, 221, 263

Rachmaninov, Sergei 74
racism
Ramses II 79
Ransom, see Howard, Ron
Rasmussen, Eric Dean 23 n.16
Raud, Rein 83 n.6
real, see Lacan, Jacques
Rée, Jonathan 127
retroactivity, see Hegel, G. W. F.
Rilke, Rainer Maria
  "The Archais Torso of Apollo" 174
Rödl, Sebastian 93
Rorty, Richard 22 n.12, 65 n.10, 105 n.5
Ruda, Frank 101, 290

Sade, Marquis de
Schelling, Friedrich W. J. 17–18, 28–44, 53–4, 90–2, 97, 99, 221, 331
Schiller, Friedrich 104
Schmitt, Carl 18, 57
Schoenberg, Arnold 74
Schuster, Aaron
Scruton, Roger 127
Sellars, Wilfrid 60, 63
sexual difference, see Lacan, Jacques
Sharpe, Matthew 3
Singer, Bryan
  The Usual Suspects 121–2
Sisyphus 140
Smith, Zadie 105 n.3
Sophocles
  Antigone 257–8 n.60
Speed, see De Bont, Jan
Spinoza, Baruch 18, 29–31, 34–5, 38–40, 43–4, 45 n.5, 53, 85
Stalin, Joseph 54 n.1, 76, 90, 115, 126–30, 131 n.1, 132 n.13, 132 n.15, 133 n.18, 178 n.19, 311
Stamp, Richard 3
Steinberg, Stefan 127
Stewart, Jon 171
Structuralism 7, 76, 146–7, 150, 165, 218, 309
sublimation, see Lacan, Jacques
substance
superego 55, 145–6, 148, 155 n.9, 168, 223, 283, 314
symbolic order, see Lacan, Jacques

Tahrir Square 125
Taylor, Charles 110 n.48
They Live, see Carpenter, John
Thing [*das Ding*], see Lacan, Jacques
Thunberg, Greta 2
Tilliette, Xavier 31
Tito, Josip Broz 6
tolerance
totalitarianism 127, 123–33 n.15, 167, 169–71, 180–1, 247, 311
Trump, Donald 19, 56, 135–6, 139, 162, 178 n.19, 222
truth 2–3, 10, 58–63, 68, 78–9, 103–4, 151, 199, 232, 241–2, 245, 258–9 n.66, 263, 271, 274–5, 301, 304, 307, 311–14, 331
Twain, Mark 73

uncanny
unconscious
universality 14–17, 20, 33, 59–60, 78, 99, 127, 168, 175, 185, 188–9, 195–6, 199–202, 208–11, 217–19, 226–8, 241, 243, 247–8, 255 n.44, 257 n.58, 258–9 n.60, 261, 309, 311
Usual Suspects, The, see Singer, Bryan

V for Vendetta, see McTeigue, James
Vertigo, see Hitchcock, Alfred
Vighi, Fabio 3–4

Wagner, Richard
Whitehead, Alfred North 81–2
Wittgenstein, Ludwig 18, 57, 105 n.5
Wolff, Christian 42

Yancy, George 186–7
Young, Niki 83 n.10

Zedong, Mao 15, 24 n.29, 131 n.1, 167, 209
Zhuang Zi 19–20, 163–9, 172–4
Zionism 8, 23 n.8, 191–6
Zitelmann, Rainer 136
Žižek, Slavoj (works)
  Absolute Recoil 112, 248, 253 n.35, 254 n.41, 257–8 n.60
  Courage of Hopelessness 287, 289
  Did Somebody Say Totalitarianism? 23 n.15, 253 n.35
  Disparities 252–3 n.27, 253 n.30
  Enjoy Your Symptom! 252–3 n.27, 253 n.30
  For They Know Not What They Do 252–3 n.27
  Fragile Absolute 13, 121, 257–8 n.60
  Hegel in a Wired Brain 29
  In Defense of Lost Causes 132 n.8, 253 n.35, 257 n.58
  Incontinence of the Void 34
  Indivisible Remainder 29–30, 238, 242
  Less Than Nothing 7, 18, 65 n.8, 73–82, 89, 105 nn.3–4, 106 n.12, 110–11 n.51, 112–15 257–8 n.60, 257–8 n.60
  Looking Awry 6–7, 243
  Metastases of Enjoyment 23 n.22, 246, 254 n.41
  Most Sublime Hysteric, The 252–3 n.27, 253 n.30
  Pain of Difference, The (in Slovene), 6
  Parallax View 7, 92, 108 n.28, 121, 151, 256 n.54, 253 n.35
  Plague of Fantasies 23 n.22
  Sex and the Failed Absolute 29, 34–7, 41–3, 156 n.20, 252 n.25, 252–3 n.27
  Sublime Object of Ideology 5–6, 10, 12, 75, 172, 217, 238, 240, 246, 252–3 n.27, 274, 253 n.30
  Tarrying with the Negative 7, 92
  Ticklish Subject 7, 132 n.13, 257 n.58
  Trouble in Paradise 128
  Universal Exception, The 254 n.41
  Violence 126
Zupančič, Alenka 87 n.1, 180, 217–18, 256 n.53, 272, 289–91

CPSIA information can be obtained
at www.ICGtesting.com
Printed in the USA
LVHW021058120523
746841LV00003B/83